Frontispiece:
Typical postcards of the period

"Emmanuel College, Cambridge" by Jotter.
Boots Cash Chemists "Pelham Series".

"When Pa Fell Off the Steps This Morning
Whilst Hanging the Mistletoe..." by
Lawson Wood. Valentine. P.U. 1908.

The Coronation of George V. J.S. Fry & Sons
Ltd. Published by A. Vivian Mansell.

THE DICTIONARY OF
PICTURE
POSTCARDS
IN BRITAIN

1894~1939

A.W. Coysh

Antique Collectors' Club

First published 1984
© 1984 A.W. Coysh
Reprinted in laminated paper boards 1996

World copyright reserved

ISBN 1 85149 231 3

British Library Cataloguing-in-Publication Data
A catalogue record for this book is available from the British Library

By the same author

The Antique Buyer's Dictionary of Names
Blue and White Transfer Ware, 1780-1840
Blue-printed Earthenware, 1800-1840
British Art Pottery, 1870-1940
Collecting Bookmarkers
Historic English Inns
The Dictionary of Blue and White Printed Pottery, 1780-1800 (with Dr. R.K. Henrywood)

The endpapers show a selection of envelopes in which postcards – usually in sets of six or twelve – were sold.

Printed in England on Consort Royal Satin paper from Donside Mills, Aberdeen, by the Antique Collectors' Club, Woodbridge, Suffolk IP12 1DS

Contents

Colour Plates

Abbreviations and Conventions

Abbreviations

b.	born.
c.	*circa*. An approximate date.
C.I.	Channel Islands.
d.	died.
Exh.	This abbreviation, followed by the initials of a gallery and a number, indicates the number of works that an artist exhibited at that gallery.
facsim.	facsimile. Used to indicate the postcard is a reproduction of a painting.
fl.	*floruit* — flourished. Used here to indicate the period when a firm, artist or designer was actively involved in the production of picture postcards.
Ill.	Illustrated in/illustration. This is followed by a book reference and the number of the illustration or the page on which it appears.
I.N.	Individually numbered.
I.O.M.	Isle of Man.
I.O.W.	Isle of Wight.
P.P.	Photographic portrait.
pre-	Before. When followed by a date this indicates the earliest postmark noted on the work of a publisher or artist.
P.U.	Postally used.
(q.v.).	*quod vide* — which see.
Ref:	Precedes the title of a book/article which provides useful background information on the subject of the entry.
R.P.	Real photograph.
U.B.	Undivided back.
W.W.I./II.	World War I/II.

Book References

Book or periodical references which occur frequently are given by stating only the name of the author/publication and the number of the illustration or page. Books referred to in this way are:

Byatt	Byatt, A., *Picture Postcards and their Publishers*.
Cope	Cope, D. and P., *Illustrators of Postcards from the Nursery*.
D. & M.	Duval, W., and Monahan V., *Collecting Postcards, 1894-1914*.
Fletcher/Brooks, I	Fletcher, T.A., and Brooks, A.D., *British Exhibitions and their Postcards, Part I 1900-1914*.
Fletcher/Brooks II	Fletcher, T.A., and Brooks A.D., *British and Foreign Exhibitions and their Postcards, Part II 1915-1979*.
Hill	Hill, C.W., *Edwardian Entertainments: A Picture Postcard View*.
Holt	Holt, T. and ʼʼ., *Till the Boys Come Home: Picture Postcards of the First World War*.
Monahan	Monahan, V., *Collecting Postcards, 1914-1930*.
Picton	*Picton's Priced Postcard Catalogue and Handbook*.
P.P.A.	*Picture Postcard Annual*.
P.P.M.	*Picture Postcard Monthly* (27 Walton Drive, Keyworth, Nottinghamshire).
R.O.P.L.	Alsop, J., *Railway Official Postcard Lists*.
S.G.P.C.	*Stanley Gibbons Postcard Catalogue*.

Galleries, Societies and Honours

C.B.E.	Commander of the British Empire.
D.B.E.	Dame Commander of the British Empire.
D.C.L.	Doctor of Civil Law.
F.A.S.	Fine Art Society.
F.L.S.	Fellow of the Linnean Society.
F.R.G.S.	Fellow of the Royal Geographical Society.
F.R.P.S.	Fellow of the Royal Photographic Society.
F.R.S.A.	Fellow of the Royal Society of Arts.
F.R.S.E.	Fellow of the Royal Society of Arts, Edinburgh.
F.Z.S.	Fellow of the Zoological Society.
LL.D.	Doctor of Laws.
N.E.A.	New English Art Club.
N.S.A.	Nottingham Society of Artists.
O.B.E.	Order of the British Empire.
R.A.	Royal Academy.
R.B.A	Royal Society of British Artists.
R.B.S.A.	Royal Birmingham Society of Artists.
R.C.A.	Royal Cambrian Academy.
R.E.	Royal Society of Painters and Engravers.
R.H.A.	Royal Hibernian Academy, Dublin.
R.I.	Royal Institute of Painters in Water Colours.
R.M.S.	Royal Miniature Society.
R.O.I.	Royal Institute of Oil Painters.
R.S.A.	Royal Scottish Academy.
R.S.W.	Royal Scottish Society of Painters in Water Colours.
R.W.A.	Royal West of England Academy.
R.W.S.	Royal Society of Painters in Water Colours.
S.G.A.	Society of Graphic Artists.
S.W.A.	Society of Women Artists.

Dates

When a single date is shown (i.e. 1904) this indicates the date a firm started to publish postcards. However in many cases this is not known, and an approximate date, e.g. "pre-1904" is sometimes used to indicate the earliest date noted on a postmarked card (in which case it is reasonable to suppose that the firm started postcard work at least a year previously).

Entries with no dates mean no information is available as to dating a firm, personality, etc.

Acknowledgements

Information for this dictionary has been gathered from many sources, mainly from the postcards themselves, but I am grateful to all previous writers on the subject, particularly to Anthony Byatt whose book on *Picture Postcards and their Publishers* entailed much painstaking research and will long remain the standard work on the history of the subject.

It has not been possible to trace all those who may still hold the copyright of some cards; if I have transgressed I offer sincere apologies. The following publishers have been kind enough to allow me to reproduce their work: Bamforth & Co., Cadbury Ltd., Clare, Son & Co., Judges of Hastings, The Medici Society, J. Salmon Ltd., Simpsons-in-the-Strand, Raphael Tuck and Valentine of Dundee.

Many people have allowed me to study their private collections and have provided me with useful information. For their generous help I should like to thank John Braddock, Lord Brightman, Dr. Peter Carter, David Dury, Jean Eastwood, the Rev. Ian Gardner, Cliff Gazely, Timothy Harding, Ian T. Henderson, Sybil Henley, Dr. R.K. Henrywood, Wendy Holloway, Simon Olding, Pat and Reg Simmonds, Rheidoles Smart, Stream Antiques, Styles of Hungerford, Derek Tempero, Tish Thompson, Ena Wells and many postcard dealers who have suffered my presence for long periods while I have studied the cards in their possession.

I owe a special debt of gratitude to my wife who prepared the final manuscript and to Cherry Lewis of the Antique Collectors' Club for seeing the book through the press.

The Rise and Decline of the Picture Postcard

This dictionary is an attempt to gather together relevant facts about the artists, photographers, printers and publishers who were responsible for the vast output of picture postcards sold in Britain between 1894 and the start of World War II.

The first picture postcard appeared in Britain less than one hundred years ago. Plain postcards with a stamp printed on them were first sold by the Post Office in the United Kingdom on 1 October, 1870. The address only was allowed on the stamp side. On 1 September, 1894 private cards could be sent through the post using an adhesive halfpenny stamp. In this year George Stewart & Co. of Edinburgh published postcards with views and other firms soon followed. In 1895 a change in postcard size was introduced. The new cards, known as court cards, measured 4¾ x 3½ins. There was little room on the card for a picture, since space had to be left for the sender to write a message. In 1899 the size limit was increased, and most cards became uniform in size with those used abroad, i.e. 5½ x 3½ins. The address restriction, however, remained until 1902 when the divided back was introduced, one half for the message, the other half for the address. This made it possible for publishers to use the whole of one side for a picture. The public welcomed these attractive missives and not only used them extensively as a new and cheap form of communication but also collected them — nearly every family had a postcard album in which to store its cards.

The number of postcard publishers increased rapidly. Firms that had already been producing Christmas cards found little difficulty in turning their attention to this new field. These included Birn Bros., Davidson Bros., Max Ettlinger & Co., C.W. Faulkner, S. Hildesheimer & Co., W. Mack, Misch & Stock, Raphael Tuck and Valentine. Other publishers followed and many photographers left their studios and started to photograph local landscapes. These were retailed direct or through tobacconists, stationers and post offices. Certain retailers also regarded themselves as publishers and this was sometimes stated on cards supplied by such firms as Frith and Valentine; other suppliers were specific and printed the origin on the cards, e.g. "Produced by A. Camburn for A. Church, Stationer, Langton, Kent". Cards were mainly sold in envelopes in sets of six or twelve.

Collectors began to specialise and soon every possible subject was covered — actors and actresses, aeroplanes, cycling, diabolo, exhibitions, fairs, horses, industry, locomotives, military uniforms, paddle steamers, piers, railways, shipping, theatres, windmills and zoological gardens. There were views of every city, town and village in the country. Floods of comic cards came from specialist publishers. The demand for designs was enormous. Artists and cartoonists were commissioned to paint landscapes and humorous subjects. Existing pictures were used from journals such as *Punch* and *The Bystander,* as well as from books, while pictures in public galleries were reproduced. The volume of this outpouring may be gathered from the figures issued by the Post Office. Over 860 million cards passed through the post in the year 1908-9 and the traffic was still expanding.

German, French and Italian firms had their agents in Britain who imported cards by such artists as Raphael Kirchner, Alphonse Mucha and Achille Mauzan. Hence the title chosen for this dictionary —"Picture Postcards in Britain" rather than "British Picture Postcards". Cards were issued throughout World War I with patriotic and human sentiment playing a large part.

On 3 June, 1918 the postage rate for a postcard doubled. This fact, together with the spread of the private telephone and greater mobility provided by the motor, led to a decline in demand and standards of production, though some high quality art deco cards were popular in the 'twenties.

It is not easy to date a postcard. Postally-used cards give a clue if the date is legible on the postmark, but it must be remembered that this only indicates that the card was published before this date, often some years earlier. Subject matter helps — the period of the costumes, the motor cars in use. The dates when the publisher is known to have been in business can be another indication. It is hoped that this dictionary may provide collectors with useful clues.

A

A.B. Co.
Arcadia Bazaar Co. (q.v.).

Abbey Studios
Publishers, Tewkesbury, Gloucestershire. Local sepia views.

Abbeys
Views of Britain's old abbeys, mainly in ruins since the suppression of the monasteries in the years 1536-9, were included in the output of most publishers of topographical cards. The Great Northern Railway, for example, published a set of "Famous Abbeys".

The following may be found on postcards and make an attractive collection:

Bolton Abbey, Yorkshire.
Buildwas Abbey, Shropshire.
Byland Abbey, Yorkshire.
Chepstow Abbey, Monmouthshire.
Crowland Abbey, Lincolnshire.
Dryburgh Abbey, Berwickshire.
Dunstable Priory, Bedfordshire.
Fountains Abbey, Yorkshire.
Furness Abbey, Lancashire.
Glastonbury Abbey, Somerset.
Hexham Abbey, Northumberland.
Jedburgh Abbey, Roxburghshire.
Kelso Abbey, Roxburghshire.
Kirkham Abbey, Yorkshire.
Llanthony Abbey, Monmouthshire.
Malmesbury Abbey, Wiltshire.
Mount Grace Priory, Yorkshire.
Muckross Abbey, Kerry.
Netley Abbey, Hampshire.
Rievaulx Abbey, Yorkshire.
Selby Abbey, Yorkshire.
Tintern Abbey, Monmouthshire.
Tynemouth Priory, Northumberland.
Valle Crucis Abbey, Denbighshire.
Walsingham Abbey, Norfolk.
Whitby Abbey, Yorkshire.

Ref: Beard, G.W. and Billington, A.R., *English Abbeys*, 1949.

Abeille, Jack   fl. c.1898-1916
French art deco artist who contributed to many humorous journals. His imported glamour postcards are highly valued. Designed some military cards during W.W.I.

Abery, Percy Benzie
Photographer/publisher, West End Studios, Builth Wells, Radnorshire. Local R.P.s.

Abraham & Sons
Publishers, Devonport. Naval action scenes during W.W.I. Ill. Holt 319.

Abraham, Ashley
Photographer, Lake Rd., Keswick, Cumberland.
  See: George Perry Abraham (Ltd.).

Abraham, George Dixon   1872-1965
Painter of moonlight views for G.P. Abraham based on photographs by his brother Ashley Abraham. These were reproduced, c.1909, as black and white postcards but later, c.1912, with hand colouring. Sepia views can also be found. There are about 40 scenes which depict the Lake District, e.g. "Skiddaw and Derwentwater".
  Ref: Rowley, B., 'The "Moonlight Paintings" of G.D. Abraham', P.P.M., May 1981, pp. 8-9, gives a check list of these views.

Abraham, George Perry (Ltd.)   c.1907 (Ltd. 1917)
Photographer/publisher, Lake Rd., Keswick, Cumberland. This business was established by George Perry Abraham, F.R.P.S., in 1865. Subsequently his two sons, Ashley and George Dixon, joined the firm which was engaged in the postcard trade by 1907.
  Ashley Abraham was a photographer; George Dixon Abraham an artist. The firm published several books on rock climbing, illustrated with Ashley's photographs, and many views of climbers on high lakeland peaks were issued as postcards. The output, which soon reached over 2,000 R.Ps., included a series of a shepherd on horseback. Painted moonlight scenes by George Dixon Abraham appeared in several

Abbeys. *"Fountains Abbey, Ripon". A Cistercian building completed in the 13th century. Fine Art card by Shurey's Publications, printed by Delittle, Fenwick & Co. of York.*

forms. Early cards can be distinguished from later issues which include Ltd. after the firm's name.

Ref: Rowley,B., p.12, in P.P.M., May 1983, gives a useful check list of Abraham's 'Early Coloured Cards'.

Abraham, John
Advertisers of men's clothing, 3 Shooters Hill, Cowes, I.O.W.
See: Colour Plate 1.

A.C.
Initials of the artist Alfred Crowquill (q.v.).

A.C. & Co.
Publisher of tinted views with captions in red, e.g. "The *Formidable* in her last days".

A. & C.B.
A. & C. Black Ltd. (q.v.).

Accidents
Most accidents were photographed by local firms able to get a photographer to the scene quickly while rescue and salvage work was in progress.
See: Mine Disasters; Motor Accidents; Railway Disasters.

Ackroyd, W.M.
Animal painter.

Adams and Co.   pre-1908
Publisher, 44 Bristol St., Birmingham. Trademark "Adeo". R.P. views of Birmingham.

Adams, Frank   fl. c.1903-1935
Artist who exhibited many landscapes at Walker's Gallery, London. He designed a set of cards for William Collins & Sons under the title "Parodies on book names".

Adams, J. Talbot   fl. 1880-1911
Landscape artist who painted a Tuck series on Haslemere. Exh. R.A. 3. He lived in Surrey.

Adams, Marcus
Court photographer.

Adan, Emile Louis   b. 1839
Paris artist. Facsims. by Hildesheimer.

Addison, William Grylls   fl. 1880-1903
Landscape artist. Exh. R.A. 7.

Ade, S. Harrison
Pen and ink artist who designed for Hook & Co.'s "Sanbride Series" (q.v.).

Adkins Tobacco
Poster-type advertising cards using an original design by Tom Browne.

Admitt & Naunton   pre-1908
Publishers, Shrewsbury, Shropshire.

Advance Publishing Co.   pre-1908
Photographer/publisher, Bridlington, Yorkshire.

Advertising Cards
Many commercial firms, and some private organisations, published postcards to promote their products or their services. These are entered in this dictionary under their individual names or the products advertised, whichever appears most prominently on the cards. Sometimes the whole of the reverse side of advertising cards is filled with promotional material. These are really postcard-size trade cards but since they are

Ainsley, Anne. *"Easter Greetings". Regent Publishing Co.*

collected they have been included. A few cards were reproductions of well-known advertising posters. Tuck produced a number of these under the title "Celebrated Posters".
See: Colour Plate 1; Order Form Postcards.

Advice Cards
Some advertising cards were sent by firms to advise customers when they might expect a representative to call or a delivery to be made. They are sometimes called Correspondence Cards.

A.E.
Archibald English (q.v.).

A.E.B.
A.E. Banks, publisher, Hove, Sussex.

A. & E.C.
A. & E. Coppock, publisher, Blackpool, Lancashire (q.v.).

A.E.H.
Alfred E. Hilton (q.v.).

A.E.K.
A.E. Kennedy (q.v.).

Aerial Post
The first United Kingdom aerial post in 1911 was marked by the issue of postcards designed by Warwick William Lendon and a number of firms used them to advertise their wares.
Ref: Byatt pp. 355-6.

Aerofilms Ltd.   pre-1921
Photographers who supplied views to other companies, e.g. W.H. Smith for their "Kingsway" Real Photo Series.

A.F.B.
Publisher of a "Westminster School Series".

Agazarion, J.M.L. (Mrs.)   fl. c.1900-1938
Landscape painter who contributed a set on "Constantinople" to Tuck's "Wide Wide World" Series, 7724.

Agricultural Shows
Photographs are often taken of prize stock, e.g. Clydesdale Stallion at Glasgow Show, 1929.

A. & H.
Art & Humour Publishing Co. Ltd. (q.v.).

A.H.J.
Judd, A.H., & Co. (q.v.).

Ainsley, Anne
Animal painter who designed greetings cards for the Regent Publishing Co.

Aircraft
Local photographers sometimes issued cards of aeroplanes seen in their districts but most aircraft cards were by well-known publishers including:
(i)   Avis Publishing Co., Birmingham, "Advance Series".
(ii)   Barton, Harvey & Sons, planes at Bournemouth Aviation Meeting, 1910.
(iii) Edward Cook & Co., the "Lightning Series of Flying Machine Postcards".
(iv)   A.M. Davis, "British Commercial Aircraft".
(v)   W.E. Mack, sepia "Satin" Series of R.P.s including such planes as the "Gamecock", a standard machine of the R.A.F. constructed at Cheltenham by the Gloster Aircraft Co.
(vi)   Photochrom, "Aeroplanes of the Allies"; facsims. of paintings by Algernon Black.
(vii) Science Museum.
(viii) Tuck, "Famous Aeroplanes and Airships".
(ix)   J. Welch & Sons, planes at the Bournemouth Aviation Meeting, 1910.
See: Aviation Meetings, Aviators.
Refs: Graham-White, C., *Aircraft in the Great War,* 1915; *The Guinness Book of Air Facts and Figures,* 1970.

Airships
The first airships appeared in France in the 1880s and by the time picture postcards were in common use they were attracting general attention. The first zeppelin flew in 1900 and between 1910 and 1914 they were used for passenger travel. Over 34,000 passengers were carried without fatality. During W.W.I. zeppelins were used for bombing raids on London and the east coast. In 1919 the British R34 crossed the Atlantic from Scotland to New York and back.

After the war airships were used by the Americans for passenger transport, and Britain used the R100 and R101. The R101 was totally destroyed by fire in 1930 on a flight to India with the loss of 48 lives. There were other disasters to airships and several countries, including Britain, abandoned their use though the Graf Zeppelin continued to carry passengers until 1938.

Airships were also used for military purposes and it is the military ships which are most frequently seen on cards. Most of these are photographs by W. May (q.v.) of Aldershot, e.g. the "Delta", 1915. Ill: Monahan, 11.
Other publishers of airship cards include:
(i)   Gale & Polden, e.g. the airship "Gamma".

Aircraft. *"The Gloster Gamecock". W.E. Mack. Sepia "Satin" Series. P.U. 1928.*

(ii) Photochrom, a Celesque Series of airship cards.
Refs: Collier, B., *The Airship: A History,* 1974; Ege, L., *Balloons and Airships, 1783-1973,* 1973; Jackson, R., *Airships in Peace and War,* 1971.

"Ajax Series"
Publisher unknown. R.P.s of Oldham, Lancashire, with embossed borders.

Ajelli, G., & Co. Ltd.   fl. 1919-c.1922
Publisher, 13 Grays Inn Rd., London, W.C.1. Trademark "A.G. Co.", held by a girl, the whole within an inverted triangle. Sometimes the letters G.A. & Co. are used. The tradename for their cards was "Olio" and these consisted of views printed in France to simulate oil paintings.

Akerman, I.M.
Publisher, Keston, Kent. R.P. views.

A.L.
Aristophot Co. Ltd., London (q.v.).

"Albany Series"   pre-1904
Publisher unknown. Coloured views with titles in red on a plain white band. Many Scottish views. Serial nos. to 1886.

"Albertine"
Artist's signature found on some glamour cards.

Albery & Son
Publishers, Horsham, Sussex.

Alden & Co. Ltd.
Publisher, Bocardo Press, Oxford. Trademark a coat of arms with three crowns. A "Garden Series" after paintings by J.A. Shuffrey, and a Matthison Series of college views.

Aldershot Tattoo
Views by Gale & Polden.

Alderton, J., & Co.   fl. 1903-1905
Publisher, 2 Pond Place, Fulham Rd., London, S.W. A short-lived firm which published a series of humorous sporting cards by Finch Mason under the title "Sporting Notions".

Aldin, Cecil Charles Windsor   **1870-1935**

Sporting and humorous illustrator. Studied animal painting and, as a Master of Foxhounds, had opportunities to research his material at first hand. He contributed to magazines and some of this material found its way on to postcards, e.g. from *London Opinion*. Aldin cards were published by Lawrence & Jellicoe, Savory, Valentine and Voisey. His work also appears in Tuck's "Celebrated Posters" Series.

Alexander, Edgar (Ltd.)   **pre-1908**

Publisher, 71 Southampton Row, London, W.C. Trademark "E.A." in monogram within a circle. Alexander had been involved in the postcard trade before he established his own firm which became a limited company in 1908. Issued R.P. greetings cards (printed in France) and cards for the Franco-British Exhibition of 1908.

Alexander, E.R., & Sons

Publisher, Leyton, London.

Alexander, George   **1859-1918**

Actor-manager. Closely associated with Henry Irving at the Lyceum Theatre, London, in the 1880s. Manager St. James's Theatre, 1891-1919. Knighted 1911. P.P.s by Beagles and Millar & Lang.

Alexander, Janet   **d.1961**

Actress. P.P. by Rotary. First stage appearance in 1898.

Allan, Andrew   **fl. 1888-1940**

Scottish artist. Exhibited frequently at the Glasgow Institute of the Fine Arts and the R.S.A. Painted view of Edinburgh for a Millar & Lang series.

Allan, Maud

Classical dancer. First appeared in London Palace Theatre in 1908. P.P. as "Salome" by Rotary.

Allan, T. & G.   **pre-1914**

Publisher, Newcastle upon Tyne, Northumberland. "Atlas Series" of patriotic cards, ill. Holt 153. Printed card for North East Coast Exhibition of 1929.

Allen & Sons

Publisher, Blackpool. R.P. local views.

Allen, David, & Sons Ltd. (& Co.)   **pre-1903**

Printer/publisher, Fleet St., London, E.C., with works at Harrow, to 1918, and Belfast. This firm catered for advertisers, printing chromotypes for the paper *Answers,* and for various commercial enterprises. It specialised in poster work for theatres and hotels. Many of the theatre posters were reproduced on postcards which could be distributed locally to individuals. First class artists were used including L. Barribal, John Hassall, E.P. Kinsella and Lance Thackeray.

    Ref: A list of poster cards is given by Byatt p. 339.

Allen, S.J.

Landscape painter.

Allen, William Herbert   **fl. c.1888-1933**

Landscape artist who lived at Farnham, Surrey. Exh. R.A. 15. He travelled in Europe and painted a set of "Continental Towns" for Tuck, 7299.

Allenson, W.R.

Bookseller/publisher, 1-2 Ivy Lane, Paternoster Row, London, E.C. Specialised in producing sets of cards of the old buildings of London.

Alexander, George. *Millar & Lang. "National Series".*

Alliance Ltd.   **1902**

Publishers, 115 Newgate St., London, E.C. A firm formed to produce bas-relief cards, a type invented by Freeman Augustus Taber of San Francisco. See Byatt p. 279. The Alliance output included:

(i) P.P.s of actors and actresses.

(ii) R.P.s of horses and jockeys.

(iii) Views of the River Thames.

    The firm was closely associated with A.G. Scopes & Co. which shared the patent for a process registered in 1908.

Allsops Beers

Advertising cards.

Allworth Bros.

Photographer/publisher, Tonbridge, Kent. Army groups. Ill. Holt 102.

Alpha Hosiery and Underwear

Advertisers, 52-6 Broad St., Reading, Berkshire. Cards show a Scottish shepherd with his sheep.

Alpha (Alphalsa) Publishing Co. (Ltd.)   **1916**

Publisher, 2, 4, 10 and 12 Scrutton St., London, E.C. This firm continued the output of Alfred Stiebel & Co. (q.v.) using its original tradename. Within a very short time it became the Alphalsa Publishing Co. In the early 1920s a limited company was formed using the name Alpha Publishing Co. Ltd. The output of the original company continued but silk cards were

Alphabet Cards. *"B". Rotary Photographic Series. P.U. 1904.*

added, woven in Coventry or in France.

The range of cards included:
(i) Birthday cards, "Elegant" Series.
(ii) Comic cards, "Modern Humour".
(iii) Novelty cards (q.v.) with moving parts and appliqué cards.
(iv) Glamour cards, e.g. "American Girl" set imported from New York.

See: Colour Plates 5 and 22.

Alphabet Cards
These were published in sets of 26 and may well have been used to teach children their letters.

Aluminium "Cards"
Some firms printed designs on thin postcard-size sheets of aluminium, one North Country firm using black and white views under the tradename "Alumino". However, these are hardly true postcards since they could only be sent through the post in an envelope.

See also under Novelty Cards.

Alys, M.
Painter of child subjects.

Alzarian, S.A.
Artist who contributed a set on "Village Life in Armenia" to the Tuck "Wide Wide World" Series.

Amami Shampoo
Advertisement cards.

Ambler, C.   **fl. c.1910-1914**
Animal painter who lived at Buckhurst Hill, Essex. Exh. R.A. 2.

A.M.H.
South Shields publisher of a "Meldon Series" (q.v.).

Amsden, Olney, & Sons Ltd.
Publisher, 9-11 Falcon St., London, E.C. A wholesale trading firm which published a few cards designed by Ernest Klempner (q.v.).

Anacker, O., Ltd.   **pre-1916**
Publisher, Soho Square, London, W. Deckle-edged cards in a "Fleur-de-lys" Series.

Ancient House Press
Printers/publishers, Ipswich, Suffolk. Issued facsims. of paintings of the Ancient House, presumably with publicity in mind.

Ancient Order of Foresters
Publisher of cards concerning the Order which was established in 1834 and is one of the largest friendly societies.

Anders, O.
Painter of animals and children. Contributed a set titled "The Good Old Days" to E.W. Savory's "Clifton Series".

Anderson, Anne   **fl. c.1917-1937**
Painter of children in the "Dutch" style for E.W. Savory. Ill. Byatt 271.

Anderson, Martin   **1852-1932**
Born in Scotland, he trained as an artist and contributed sketches to Scottish magazines. In 1888 he moved to London and adopted the pseudonym Cynicus. Working as a political and social cartoonist he published several satirical books from 57 Drury Lane, e.g. *The Satires of Cynicus*. In 1902 he moved his Cynicus Publishing Company to Tayport, Fife, and continued to publish his own work, mainly postcard designs. His cards for the seaside resort market are usually packed with comic figures.

See: Cynicus Publishing Co.

Anderson, V.C.
American artist who painted child subjects for Reinthal & Newman, and Wildt & Kray.

Andersons   **pre-1935**
Publisher, The Arcade, Princes St., Edinburgh. Local R.P.s.

Andrews, Eddie J. (Miss)   **fl. 1897-1902**
Landscape artist. Exh. R.A. 1. Painted a set on "Caithness" for Tuck.

Angell, Maude   **fl. c.1902-1924**
Flower painter. Exh. R.A. 18. Facsims. in McKenzie & Co.'s "Artistic Series", pre-1903.

Animals, Domestic
See: Cats; Dogs; Donkeys; Horses.

Animals, Wild
Several publishers produced coloured cards of wild animals in their natural surroundings, e.g. J. Salmon of Sevenoaks.
Illustration overleaf.
See: Zoological Gardens.

Annan, T.R., & Sons Ltd.   **1901**
Photographer/publisher, Woodland Rd., Glasgow. The main

Animals, Wild. *"Bison". J. Salmon.*

This Picture illustrates a dramatic incident in the Powerful New Story entitled: "PUT YOURSELF IN HER PLACE," starting in "ANSWERS," July 4.

Answers. *"Move — and I Fire". A dramatic incident trailing a new story in this periodical. Chromotype by David Allen & Sons.*

postcard output consisted of photographic reproductions of paintings exhibited at the Glasgow International Exhibition of 1901, the Scottish Exhibition of 1911 and the Empire Exhibition, Glasgow, 1938.

Answers   **pre-1904**
A periodical which advertised forthcoming stories on cards produced by David Allen & Sons (q.v.).

Antarctic Exploration
   See: South Polar Expedition.

Anthony
Publisher, Killarney, Ireland. R.P.s of West Ireland.

Anthony, Hilda   **b. 1886**
Actress whose favourite part was Carlotta in *The Morals of Marcus*. P.P. in Tuck's "Celebrities of the Stage".

A.O.S.
   See: A.S.O.

A.P. Co.
Artistic Publishing Co.

A.P. Co. (B)
Avis Publishing Co., Birmingham.

Aplin & Barrett   **c.1909**
Publisher of advertising cards. The "St. Ivel" set of 12 "Beautiful Houses near Yeovil" advertised the firm's dairy products on the reverse side of each card. Examples include Abbey Farm and Newton House.

Apollinaris
Table water advertisements supplied by Tuck.

Appleby, B.
Designer of comic cards.

A.R. & Co. Ltd.
Andrew Reid & Co. Ltd. (q.v.).

Arbuthnot, Malcolm
Photographer for Rotary.

"Arcade Real Photo Series"
Davidson Bros. cards; facsims. of oil paintings by Professor Van Hier (q.v.).

Arcades
Arcades were pedestrian precincts consisting of a wide pathway between double rows of shops and usually covered in with a glass roof. They included the Burlington Arcade, London; the Midland Arcade, Birmingham, ill. Hill 64, and the Bristol Arcade.

Arcadia Bazaar Co.
Publisher, 32 High St., Ramsgate, Kent. Trademark "A.B. Co." within a horseshoe. R.P. views sometimes printed within a frame.

"Arcadia" Series
   See: Davidson Bros.

"Arcadian" Series
   See: J.J. Samuels Ltd.

Archer, H.   **pre-1911**
Publisher, 51 Dickson Rd., Blackpool. Local R.P. views.

Architecture
Some cards depict a single building and these are of particular interest to students of architecture.
   Many architectural cards are based on photographs but several artists specialised in this field, e.g. Charles Flower

Architecture. *"Four Courts, Dublin"*. *Built between 1786 and 1796 with a 450ft. frontage and a large Corinthian portico. Chas. L. Reis & Co., Dublin.*

Architecture. *"Entrance to St. Bartholomew's Hospital" by Charles E. Flower. R. Tuck & Sons. "Oilette" "Old London Gateways". P.U. 1916.*

Architecture. *"Marble Arch, London"*. *Designed by John Nash in 1828 as a gateway to Buckingham Palace. Moved to present position in 1851. Photochrom Celesque Series.*

Architecture. *"New Street, Leicester" by T.D. Newham. H. & A. Bennett.*

Aris, Ernest. *"Having a Real Holiday". R. Tuck & Sons.*
"Glosso Oilette" in "Seaside Humour" set.

(q.v.) who painted sets of buildings for Tuck, including "Old
London Gateways", four sets; "The Tower of London";
"Westminster Abbey", etc.

Arctic Exploration
Some cards depict the ships in which such men as F.A. Cook
and R.E. Parry explored the Arctic. They usually have inset
portraits of the explorers.

Argall, E.C.
Publisher, Truro. Cornish coloured views.

Aris, Ernest Alfred   fl. 1904-1920
Watercolour artist who trained at Bradford College of Art.
Exh. R.A. He worked as a teacher from 1909 to 1912 but spent
most of his life as a commercial artist. He designed comic postcards for a Tuck "Glosso Oilette" set of "Seaside Humour"
and several humorous cards for the Bradford Pictorial Post
Card Company.

Aristophot Co. Ltd.   fl. 1905-1910
Publisher, 11 Southampton Row, London, W.C., for the
short period of 1908-10. Before 1908 Edgar Alexander acted as
a retail agent; after 1910 Misch & Co. marketed their cards
which may have been remainders. Trademark "AL" within a
circle and "ARISTOPHOT" on a ribbon beneath. Output
included:
(i) Greetings cards including a "Lifebuoy" Series, e.g. ill.
    Byatt 11.
(ii) R.P.s of actresses and royalty.
(iii) Flags of the Empire.
(iv) Cards for the Franco-British Exhibition of 1908, e.g. ill.
    Byatt 16.

Armitage, Alfred   fl. 1890s
Animal and flower painter who lived at Ripley in Yorkshire.

Armitage, William   fl. c.1891-1939
Versatile painter closely associated with the Nottingham
Society of Artists of which he was Vice-President from

1908-17. Exh. R.A. 5. He painted "A Tribute to our
Colonies" for a Boots "Patriotic Series".

Army Camps
Many cards, mainly photographic, depict army camps in many
parts of the country. They were presumably produced for
soldiers to send to their relatives and friends. The following
have been noted:
   Aldershot Camping Ground, Hampshire.
   Belton Park Camp, near Grantham, Lincolnshire.
   Berwick on Tweed Territorial Camp, Northumberland.
   Bordon Camp, near Farnham, Hampshire.
   Bovington Camp, Dorset.
   Caton Camp, Lancashire.
   Coddington Camp, Cheshire (Sherwood Rangers Yeo-
      manry).
   Conway Camp, North Wales, camp on Conway Marsh.
   Crowborough Camp, Sussex.
   Eastbourne, Surrey Brigade Camp, Sussex.
   Frensham Camp, Surrey.
   Hassocks Camp, Sussex, 1911.
   Horton Army Camp.
   Lowther Park Camp, Westmorland.
   Lydd Camp, Kent "where siege and field artillery and mus-
      ketry practice are carried on", Cassell's *Gazetteer,* 1896.
   Norwood Park Camp, 1918, Southwell, Nottinghamshire.
   Park House Camps, Salisbury Plain.
   Shorncliffe Camp, near Folkestone, Kent.
   Tidworth O.T.C. Camp, Wiltshire, 1913.
Correspondence leaving these camps usually carries a camp
cancellation on the stamp. These are of particular interest to
postmark collectors.

Army & Navy Stores   pre-1907
Publisher, Stonehouse, Plymouth, Devon. R.P.s of South
Devon, e.g. the Eddystone Lighthouse.

Arnold   pre-1907
Publisher, High St., Fordingbridge, Hampshire. Local views.

Arnott, F.J.   pre-1908
Photographer/publisher, Lymington, Hampshire. Local views
including wreck of H.M.S. *Gladiator* off Yarmouth, I.O.W.
in 1908.

A.R.Q.
A.R. Quinton (q.v.).

Art in Commerce Co. Ltd.
   See: Hancock & Corfield Ltd.

Art Deco
A decorative style of the 1920s, which emerged after W.W.I. It
was a reaction after the hardships and deprivations of the war
years associated with a new gaiety and a loosening of conven-
tional standards. The Exposition des Arts Décoratifs held in
Paris in 1925 gave the style its name, though some art deco
design was anticipated in the art nouveau period. The style
flourished particularly in France and Italy and is exemplified
in the work of some of their poster artists; the Vienna Workshop under Joseph Hoffman also used this geometric
"modern" style. The designs of some art deco artists such as
Adolfo Busi, Carlo Chiostri, and Tito Corbella appear on
postcards which were imported into Britain between the wars.
However, the term art deco is often used loosely in postcard
catalogues to cover a variety of styles of the 1920s and 1930s.
   See: Colour Plate 2.

"Brilliant Shinio Liauid Metal Polish".

John Abraham's "Gent's and Boys' Summer Clothing",
Cowes, Isle of Wight.

"Simpson's-in-the-Strand. The Famous Old
English Eating House. The gentleman who asked
the carver whether the meat was English or
Foreign". Cartoon by H.M. Bateman.

Art Galleries. *"Art Galleries, Glasgow" by C.E. Flower. Erected in 1901 in Kelvingrove Park. R. Tuck & Sons. "Oilette". P.U. 1921.*

Art Galleries. *"Art Galleries, Glasgow". Interior view. W. Ritchie & Sons. "Reliable Series". P.U. 1903.*

Art Galleries

Interior views of art galleries are not common. Those that can be found usually reveal how very different tastes and interests of the Victorians and Edwardians were from those of today. The view of the main hall of the Gallery at Glasgow with its marble statuary is in striking contrast to the smaller showcases and coffee bar which are now to be found in the hall.

Art & Humour Publishing Co. Ltd.   **fl. 1915-1926**
27 Chancery Lane, London, W.C. Trademark two ovals, one with a statue (Art), the other with a jester (Humour), linked by the words "Art and Humour". Output included some coloured views and many sets of comic cards, e.g. Bathing Charmers, Brilliant, Burlesque, By the Sea, Charmer, Civil Life, Comedy, Food Budget, Footer, Jocular, Now Smile, Seaside, Topole, Topping. A number of these were designed by Fred Spurgin.

The firm also imported cards by European artists, e.g. S. Bompard, for sale in Britain.

See: Colour Plate 23.

Art Nouveau
This style, first established in the 1880s, was characterised in form by sinuous curves based on those of a plant, its stem and its flower. Its finest development in painting is found in the work of the French poster artists. Some of their posters were reproduced on postcards.

Art Publishing Co.   **c.1903**
Publisher, 48 King St., Glasgow. Trademark an artist's palette with three brushes. Coloured views of areas as far apart as Scotland and Devon. Output included views of steamships and a number of comic cards.

Art Ray Co.   **1911**
Publisher, 115 Fleet St., London. Trademark "ART RAY" within a sunburst circle. Artistic photographs and drawings of London scenes.

Art Reproductions
The reproductions of existing paintings, in public galleries or in private ownership, as postcard facsims. These were popular with a number of publishers.

"Artist Series"
See: J.W. Ruddock & Sons.

Artistic Photographic Co. Ltd.   **pre-1906**
Publisher, 90-2 Oxford St., London, W., and later at 63 Baker St., W. This firm sold large reproductions of well-known paintings, e.g. Lord Leighton's "Wedded", and used postcards to advertise them.

"Artistic Series"   **pre-1929**
A title used by W. McKenzie & Co. for a set of "Bevelled Pictorial Cards".

"Artistique" Series
A series by the Inter-Art Co.
See: International Art Co.

Arundale, Sybil   **1882-1965**
Music hall actress who played in *The Toreador* in 1901. P.P.s by Dainty Novels and by R. Dunn & Co.

Arundel Art Publishing Co.   **fl. 1930s**
Publisher, Arundel, Sussex. Sepia views of Arundel Castle.

A.S.
Initials of an artist who painted battleships for Gale & Polden and zeppelins for Coleby•Clarke.

Asche, Oscar   **1871-1936**
Actor noted for his role in the Oriental fantasy with music, *Chu Chin Chow*, produced in 1916. It ran for five years. P.P. by Rotophot with his wife, Lily Brayton (q.v.).

Ash, Maisie   **1888-1923**
Actress featured in the Tuck "Framed Gem" Series and Woolstone's Milton "Glossette" cards.

Ashdown, Horace
Photographer/publisher, Tenterden, Kent. Local R.P. views.

Asher, Joseph, & Co.   **pre-1906**
Publisher, 14 Cheapside, London, E.C. and later, c.1908, at 22 Paternoster Rd., and 3-4 Ivy Lane. Trademark "J.A. & Co."

as a monogram within a circle or a shield. The output consisted of comic cards by Will Adams and Donald McGill. Series names include "Kismet" and "Selwell".

Joseph Asher and his associates were German citizens and, in 1914, with the outbreak of war, they were interned as enemy aliens and the firm closed down, though their stock was still on sale.

See: Colour Plate 18.

Ashton, Teddy   **c.1909**
Publisher and newspaper editor, 47 Osborne Rd., Blackpool, Lancashire. This was the trading name of Charles Allen Clarke (q.v.) who was an artist. His first designs were issued by E.R. Green & Co. before he started to publish his own work which reflected the characters and dialect of the area around Blackpool.

Ashton, William, & Sons Ltd.   **c.1904**
Publisher, Grosvenor Works, Southport Lancashire. Issued a "Grosvenor Series" of coloured views of Lancashire, the Lake District and North Wales, and a "Sepia Plate-marked" Series. Serial nos. to 2,500.

Ashwell, C.C.
Landscape artist whose work was used by L. Wilding & Son Ltd. Ill. Byatt 341.

Ashwell, Lena, O.B.E.   **1872-1957**
Actress-manager. First stage appearance 1891. In 1915 she organised several companies to entertain the troops in France and by the time the armistice was signed in 1918 there were 26

Association Cards. *"Plas Newydd, Llangollen"*. *Photochrom Co. Ltd.*

companies with 600 artists in France. P.P. by Gottschalk, Dreyfus & Davis.

Ref: *Myself a Player,* autobiography, 1936.

Ashworth, J., & Sons   **pre-1914**
Photographer/publisher, Scarborough, Yorkshire. Issued cards of the damage done by enemy bombardment on 16 December, 1914. Ill. Holt 481.

A.S.O.
Alfred Savage, Oxford. These letters are above a coat of arms, in order (left to right) A.O.S.

Asquith, Rt. Hon. H.H., M.P.   **1852-1928**
Statesman, Prime Minister 1908-16. P.P. by Rotary. Ill. Hill p. 10.

Association Cards
Association items, as they are known in the world of antiques, do not seem to have been recognised as such by many postcard collectors. An example is given here which concerns "The Ladies of Llangollen". These ladies were the Rt. Hon. Lady Eleanor Butler, daughter of the Marquess of Ormonde, and Miss Sarah Ponsonby, daughter of Viscount Duncannon. Following some years of unhappiness in society, and one attempted escape when they ran away together, they were given a small allowance, and in May 1778 left Ireland and set up home together in a cottage in North Wales at Llangollen where they lived from 1780 to 1831. They were noted for their eccentricity but came to know many of the leading personalities of the day, especially authors and poets, including Wordsworth and Scott. They soon started to transform their cottage adding oriel windows with richly carved canopies below, all in the Gothic style. They named it Plas Newydd.

Postcards can be found to illustrate the story. Two publishers issued reproductions of an earlier print of the two ladies based on an original sketch by Lady Leighton; Frith's was printed in sepia, the Pictorial Stationery Co. used colour, "Autochrom". They show slight variations. Photochrom published a view of Plas Newydd. This card shows the house c.1906 when it was owned by Mr. G.H. Robertson, a Liverpool cotton broker. In 1932 the house was acquired by the

Association Cards. *"The Ladies of Llangollen"*. *Frith's Series.*

Attwell, Mabel Lucie. *"Us!"* *"Valentine's 'Attwell' Series"*. 1925.

Llangollen Town Council, now the Glyndwr District Council. The portraits and views of the house may be regarded as association cards.

Ref: The story is told in full in Elizabeth Mavor's *The Ladies of Llangollen*, 1971.

Asti, Angelo   **1847-1903**
Portrait painter born in Paris. He made a career there painting beautiful women and exhibited at the Salon. Postcard facsims. of his work were published by Ettlinger, H.J. Smith, and Tuck.

Astronomy
Not a subject that lends itself to postcard treatment but cards have been noted recording three stages of the eclipse of the sun on 30 August, 1905.

Asylums
Examples have been recorded, e.g. Cane Hill Asylum, Surrey, and Surrey County Asylum, Netherne.

Athletics
Some cards depict sports grounds where important events took place, such as the Olympic Games which were revived in Athens in 1896 as a result of the enthusiasm of Baron Pierre de Coubertin. These were held in Britain in 1908.

However, the most interesting photographs are those of individual athletes, posed or in action, e.g. the photo-portrait of E.D. Mountain, half-mile champion of Britain in 1922. Ill. Monahan 36.

Atkinson, George   **fl. 1909-1916**
Landscape artist who studied at the Royal College of Art and became Headmaster of the Metropolitan School of Art, Dublin. Exh. R.A. 41. His views of Cork were used on postcards to mark the Cork Exhibition of 1902.

Atkinson, James
Printer/publisher, 6 King St., Ulverston, Lancashire. "Atkinson Series" of Lake District R.P. views.

Atkinson & Pollitt
Publisher, Kendal, Westmorland. Local black and white views.

"Atlas Series"
See: T. & G. Allan.

Attwell, Mabel Lucie   **1879-1962**
Artist who studied at the Regent Street Art School and at Heatherleys. In 1908 married Harold Earnshaw, an illustrator. She wrote stories and verse for children and illustrated children's books herself. She lived in London and in 1924 was elected to the S.W.A.

Her postcard work for Valentine extended over a long period and remained popular long after she ceased to contribute new designs. Her cards were reprinted again and again.

Her work falls into three categories:
(i) Early cards from 1911 to 1920 can be recognised by their description as "Valentine Series", from 1914 by the slightly brown wartime card on which they were printed.
(ii) The 1920s' cards can usually be recognised by their subject matter, e.g. crystal sets with earphones or prevailing fashions and hairstyles. Here is a typical caption:
Perplexities her mind beset
Dread fears with hopes are mingled
Whether to keep those tresses long
Or, have the d...d lot shingled.
These 1920s' cards are labelled "Valentine's 'Attwell' Series".
(iii) The 1930s' cards bear the Valentine two-globe trademark. By about 1935 the cards bore the statement "All Genuine Attwell Postcards have the Artist's Signature". The statement is followed by a specimen signature .
See: Colour Plate 9.

Augarde, Adrienne   **d. 1913**
Actress and vocalist who played with Mabel Green in the French operetta *The Little Michas*. P.P.s by Aristophot, Ralph Dunn & Co., Misch & Co., Rotary, and Rotophot.

Augener Ltd.   **pre-1913**
Publisher, 63 Conduit St., London, W.1. Issued several sets of cards designed by H. Willebeek Le Mair, e.g. "English and Dutch Rhymes", "Little Songs of Long Ago", etc.

Ault, Norman
Artist whose work was used by Charles Voisey.

Austen   **pre-1906**
Publisher, Ludlow, Shropshire. Local views with a Ludlow coat of arms.

Austen, Alex   **fl. c.1906-1914**
Landscape artist who painted sets for the Regal Art Publishing Co., e.g. "Beautiful Bedfordshire", "Charming Cambridgeshire", "Picturesque Hampshire", "Picturesque Oxfordshire" and "Picturesque Surrey".

Austerlitz, E.
Designer of comic cards.

Austin, J.H.
Photographer/publisher, 23a Bristol St., Birmingham. He also supplied photographs to Adams & Co. of 44 Bristol St.

Austin, Winifred
Dublin artist. Exh. Royal Hibernian Academy 1902. Noted for her bird studies published by Mansell.

"Autochrom (Colour Photo) Series"   **pre-1905**
Title of a series by the Pictorial Stationery Co. Ltd.

Autographed Cards

Some photo-portraits, especially those of actors, actresses and film stars are autographed. Most of these are facsimile autographs printed on the photograph but a few are true autographs written by hand. They are readily distinguished. Very occasionally cards turn up with autographs of famous people on the address side signing the message. These have a special interest and value.

Auty Ltd.   **1899**
Publisher, Tynemouth. Local photographic vignettes.

Auty, Charles   **fl. 1881-1919**
Watercolour painter. Exh. R.A. 1. Lived at Port Erin, I.O.M.

Aveline, F.
Artist who worked at Bolton Studios, South Kensington, London. Exh. R.A. 1, 1905. Painted beautiful ladies for J. Henderson & Sons.

Aveling, Stephen
Landscape painter of Rochester, Kent. "Picturesque Castles" for Tuck, 7591.

Avenue Press Ltd., Avenue Publishing Co.   **fl. 1906-1914**
These firms as printers and publishers were established at 6 and 8 Bouverie St., London, E.C., and later moved to 60 Avenue Chambers, W.C. Two main series were published under the titles "The Avenue Series" and "Paternoster Series". These included a number of comic cards. A set titled "London Nooks and Corners" by S.T.C. Weeks was produced for the Underground and London Electric Railway.
    Ref: Check list in R.O.P.L., No. 16, p. 15.

Averill, Joyce
Artist who designed cards for V. Mansell & Co.

Avery, E.C.
Designer of comic cards.

Avery's Bros.
Photographer/publisher, Brighton, Sussex. R.P.s of local views.

Avery's Library and Post Office
Publisher, Butlin's Skegness Holiday Camp. R.P.s of camp personalities, e.g. Joe Velich, the Chef.

Aviation Meetings
Events recorded on postcards:
1908 Competition for Archdeacon Deutch prize, Farman's aeroplane the winner.
1909 First Aviation Meeting at Doncaster, a multi-view card showing planes in flight.
1909 Blackpool Aviation Meeting.
1910 Wolverhampton Meeting.
1910 International Aviation Meeting at Bournemouth, a six day event.
        The following aircraft with their pilots (in brackets) appear on postcards:
            Bleriot Monoplane (Drexel; Morane; Radley).
            Cody Biplane (Cody).
            Demoiselle (Andermans).
            Farman Biplane (Christiaens; Cockburn; Dickson; Gibbs; Graham-White; Loraine and Rawlinson).
            Hanriot Biplane (Wagner).
            Howard Wright Avis Monoplane (Boyle).
            Humber-Bleriot Monoplane (Barnes).
            Short S26 (Colmore).

Augarde, Adrienne. *"Miss Adrienne Augarde"*. Actress. P.P. in Rotary Photographic Series. P.U. 1906.

            Short S27 (Grace).
            Short-Wright Biplane (Ogilvie, Rollo).
            Sommer Biplane (Gibbs).
        The publishers who issued at least 16 cards reflecting the meeting were Harvey Barton & Sons.
        Other cards were produced by J.T. Harris and J. Welch & Sons.
        Ref: Lonworth-Dames, Conway, 'Bournemouth Aviation Meeting', P.P.M., May 1981.
1910 Scottish Aviation Meeting, Lanarkshire.
1911 Coronation flights.
1912 *Daily Mail* Circuit of Britain and Waterplane Tour.
1924 Aviation Meeting in Germany.
1929 Schneider Trophy.
1934 England Australia Air Race.

Aviators
Postcards are to be found with identifiable pilots, some with inset portraits. The following have been noted:
    Bleriot, Louis, 1872-1936, a French pioneer of the monoplane which he started to fly in 1907. He was the first to fly the English Channel in 1909. Tuck Educational Series, no. 9 "Aviation".
    Cody, Samuel Franklin, 1862-1913, an American who became a naturalised British citizen and made the first official powered aircraft flight in England at Farnborough in 1908. Avis Publishing Co. no. 103. A postcard

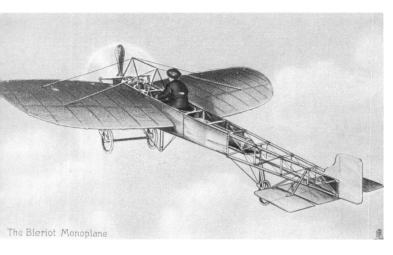

The Bleriot Monoplane

CODY FLYING WITH PASSENGER.

COPYRIGHT. ILLUSTRATED BUREAU.

Time simply Flies at BRIGHTON.

14 bis

SANTOS DUMONT'S AEROPLANE.

by W. May shows his funeral at the Military Cemetery at Aldershot. It was also covered by John Drew, R.H. Mills, and Gale & Polden.

Delagrange, Leon, 1873-1910, a French pioneer who, with E. Voisin, made a powered biplane flight in 1907.

Drexel, A.J., cards show him flying on the Aviation Ground at Lanark. Ill. Hill p. 34.

Dumont, Alberto Santos, 1873-1932, flew the first powered aeroplane in Europe in 1906. Tuck "Airships", 9495.

Farman, Henri, 1874-1958, French pioneer who learned to fly in 1907 and won many honours. In 1909 he built the aircraft which bore his name and did much to popularise flying in Europe.

Graham-White, Claude, 1879-1959, aviator and aeronautical engineer. The first Englishman granted a certificate of efficiency. He established an aviation school at Pau, France, and a school of flying at Hendon. Wrote several books including *Aircraft in the Great War,* 1915.

Pegoud, Adolphe, 1889-1915, French aviator known for aerobatic flying and the first aviator to loop the loop.

Rolls, Hon. C.S., 1877-1910, first aviator to fly the Channel from England to France. Crashed and was killed at Bournemouth Meeting of 1910.

Sopwith, Sir Thomas, 1888-1963, won the Baron de Forest prize in 1910 for a flight from England to the Continent.

Wright, Wilbur, 1867-1912, and Orville, 1871-1948, American brothers who designed and built the world's first powered aircraft capable of sustained and controlled flights.

Avis Publishing Co. c.1906

Publisher, Birmingham. Tradename "Advance Series". Output consisted mainly of black and white and coloured views of the Midlands and North of England.

A.W.W.

A.W. Wardell of Brighton (q.v.).

A.Y.

A.W. Yallop of Yarmouth.

Aylward, H.A.

Photographer, Alton, Hampshire.

Aylwin, Jean 1885-1964

Actress. Played Minna in *The Girls of Gottenberg* in 1907. P.P. by Philco.

Aviators. *Top left, "The Bleriot Monoplane". First man to fly from France to England. 25 July, 1909. R. Tuck & Sons. Educational Series, 9.*

Centre, "Cody Flying with Passenger". Avis Publishing Co., Birmingham. "Advance Series".

Left, "M. Santos Dumont's Aeroplane". Experiments with this plane were successfully carried out on 12 November, 1906. R. Tuck & Sons. "Oilette" "Airships". P.U.1913.

B
W. Bramley of Leeds (q.v.).

B. & Co.
Bamforth & Co. (q.v.).

Babies
Postcard photographs of babies have always been popular, some humorous, others merely appealing. They were produced by many publishers. Rotary issued a series.

Badges
See: Regimental Badges.

Bailes, G.
Publisher, 24 Silver St., Durham. Local sepia views supplied by Frith.

Bailey, F., & Son
Publisher, Dursley, Gloucestershire. Local sepia views.

Bailey, W. & E.
Publisher, Monksilver, Taunton, Somerset. Sepia views of the county.

Baird
Photographer/publisher, Belfast.

Baird, Dorothea   **1873-1933**
Actress. P.P.s by Misch & Co. ("Stage Beauties"), Rotary, and in Tuck's "Bookmarker" Series IV (with H.B. Irving).

Baird, H.   **pre-1922**
Publisher, Main St., Dailly, Ayrshire. Local coloured views.

Bairnsfather, Bruce   **1888-1959**
Illustrator and cartoonist. Born in India, son of an army officer. Joined the British army in 1911 and served in France in W.W.I. until 1916. He contributed humorous sketches of life in the trenches to *Bystander* and *Tatler*. He was wounded at Ypres but this did not stop him from producing cartoons. He is best remembered for the cockney character Old Bill. Many of the cartoons were published as postcards by the *Bystander*. They also appear in his book *Bullets and Billets*, Grant Richards, 1916, which describes his experiences in France. Eight sets of sepia postcards titled "Fragments from France" were issued. They include:

Set 1:
    Keeping his hand in.
    There goes our blinkin' parapet again.
    Better 'ole.
    Things that matter.
    Fatalist.
    Obvious.
Set 2:
    Coiffure in the trenches.
    The eternal question.

    The innocent abroad.
    No possible doubt whatever.
    That evening star-shell.
    The thirst for reprisals.
Set 3:
    Directing the way at the front.
    Our democratic army.
    The tactless Teuton.
    That sword.
    They've evidently seen me.
    Where did that one go to?
Set 4:
    A.D. nineteen fifty.
    Gott straffe this barbed wire.
    A Maxim Maxim.
    "The Push" — in three chapters.
    Vacant situation.
Set 5:
    Dear —, At present we are staying at a farm.
    The ideal and the real.
    In and Out I.
    In and Out II.
    — these — rations.
    Watch me make a fire-bucket of 'is 'elmet.
Set 6:
    Adaptable armies.
    That 16 inch sensation.
    Same old moan.
    What it really feels like.

continued

Babies. *"A Knight of the Bath"*. *R. Tuck & Sons.* *"Silverette"*. *P.U. 1905.*

Keeping His Hand In.

Private Smith, the company bomber, formerly "Shinio," the popular juggler, frequently causes considerable anxiety to his platoon.

Bairnsfather, Bruce. *"Keeping His Hand In"*. *A* Bystander cartoon. *"Fragments from France" Series*.

Dream.
Night-time patrol.
Set 7:
The conscientious exhilarator.
My dreams for years to come.
The historical touch.
Springtime in Flanders.
The dud shell — or the fuse top collector.
When one would like to start an offensive of one's own.
Set 8:
Happy memories of the zoo.
Trouble with one of the souvenirs.
The nest.

Baker, A.K.
Publisher, 15a Bridge St., Taunton, Somerset. Local views.

Baker, Bernard Granville   fl. 1911-1930
Painter of military subjects who worked in London and Suffolk. He served in the army as a colonel and contributed to series by Tuck.

Baker, Ewart
An artist who designed moonlight scenes for Barton, Harvey & Son.

Baker, J., & Son
Publisher. R.P.s of musical comedy stars.

Baker, Minnie
Actress who played in *The New Aladdin* c.1906. P.P. by Beagles.

Baker, Richard St. Barbé   b.1887
A tree expert who provided pictures of trees for cards by the Ruskin Studio Art Press Ltd. He was a keen preservationist.

Baldwyn, Charles   fl. 1887-1905
Bird painter for Worcester Porcelain Co. Exh. R.A. 14. He also designed postcards.

Balestrieri, Lionello   b. 1874
Italian portrait artist born in Sienna who became a favourite pupil of Morelli in Naples. He went to Paris in 1897, exhibiting at the Salon and then travelled to various countries in Europe and to America. He designed glamour postcards.

Balfour, Rt. Hon. A.J.   1848-1930
Philosopher and statesman. Prime Minister 1902-5. P.P. by Philco.

Ball, Frederick Henry
Landscape artist who painted a "Lorna Doone" set for Frith.

Ball, Salisbury
Publisher, Sheffield. Advertising cards for local firms, e.g. J.B. Eaton of the Fargate, Sheffield.

Ball, Wilfred Williams, R.E., R.B.A.   1853-1917
Landscape and marine painter. Exh. R.A. 58, mainly etchings. From about 1881 to 1886 he designed Christmas cards for Hildesheimer & Co. including miniature sketch-book cards with facsim. watercolours. Until 1898 he lived in Putney when he moved to Godalming and then to Lymington. He then started to design cards of rural scenes for Salmon. He was a great traveller in Europe and also journeyed to Egypt and the Sudan; he died of heatstroke in Khartoum.
    See: Colour Plate 7.

Ballet
Occasional cards reflecting ballet may be found including portraits of ballet stars, e.g. Karsavina (q.v.).

Balloons
Balloon cards usually depict a special event such as *The Daily Mail* balloon ascents of 1907, or the Shrewsbury Flower Show of 1908. Ill. Hill p. 34. Photographs of army observatory

Ball, Wilfred Williams. *"The River, Lymington"*. *J. Salmon*.

Ballroom Dancing. *"The Palace Ballroom, Douglas, I.O.M."*
Photochrom Celesque Series.

balloons used for reconnaissance during W.W.I. are fairly
common. The most valuable card shows a balloon marked
"Life-Boat Saturday" which ascended on 29 August, 1903.
Correspondents who took a stamped card to the Life-Boat
Fund Office in Manchester by 28 August had it delivered by
"Balloon Post". A single "Life-Boat Saturday" card sold in
1983 for £1,675.

Ref: Ege, L., *Balloons & Airships, 1783-1973,* 1974.

Ballroom Dancing
Relatively few cards reflect the keen interest the Edwardians
took in ballroom dancing. Some cards advertising hotels show
the guests dancing. The most colourful examples are probably
of the Belle Vue Ballroom at the Zoological Gardens,
Manchester, the Palace Ballroom at Douglas, Isle of Man, and
the Empress Ballroom at Blackpool.

Bamber, George A.
Designer of comic cards.

Bamforth & Co. (Ltd.)   **1902 (Ltd. 1910)**
Publisher, Holmfirth, Yorkshire, London, and New York.
Trademark "B. Co." within a circle separating the words
"POST CARD" the whole with decorative art nouveau motifs.
Some cards merely use "B. & Co. Ltd." within a triangle. This
firm was founded by a photographer, James Bamforth, who
started to produce slides for magic lanterns in the 1870s,
including some with illustrated songs, entering the postcard
field in 1902 with this experience to draw on. The firm became
noted for:
(i) Song and Hymn Cards. At first these used the negatives
     from the illustrated songs used on lantern slides but soon
     branched out in a big way to illustrate the popular songs
     of the day. Local people, not all of them actors, were
     photographed in appropriate settings and three or four
     cards would be sold as a set, according to the number of
     verses in the song. Hymns were treated in the same way.
     These song and hymn cards were numbered consecutively
     from 4500 to at least 5119. A brief selection of song and
     hymn cards with their serial numbers gives the flavour of

the series. All are in sets of three unless otherwise
indicated.
4501 Love's old sweet song.
4512 Rock of Ages.
4570 When the harvest moon is shining.
4620 Annie Laurie.
4658 Eileen Alannah (4).
4673 Would you care?
4704 Thora (4).
4739 Tosti's "Good-bye".
4761 Nearer my God to Thee.
4778 Just before the battle, Mother.
4786 The rosary.
4830 The lost chord (4).
4857 Queen of the Earth.
4872 Till the boys come home.
4890 I hear you calling me.
4905 When the war is over, Mother dear.
4955 If you were the only girl in the world.
4971 Some night, some waltz, some girl.
4999 Don't go down the mine, Daddy (4).
5023 When the bells of peace are ringing.
5068 Where the black-eyed Susan's grow.
5115 Let the rest of the world go by.
See: Colour Plate 3.
Refs: Pearsall, R., *Victorian Popular Music,* 1973; Walsh,
C., *Mud, Songs and Blighty: A Scrapbook of the First
World War,* 1973.
(ii) Comic Cards. Large numbers of comic cards were issued
     in a "Comic Series", "Holiday Series", "Seaside
     Comic", "Witty Series" and a "Witty Comic Series",
     mainly designed by artists who worked full time for
     Bamforth. The main output came after the firm became a
     limited company in 1910. Douglas Tempest was with the
     firm from 1911 until after W.W.II. and was responsible
     for most of the early comic cards, including a "Tempest
     Kiddy" Series. Ill. Monahan 134.
See: Colour Plate 23.
(iii) Patriotic Cards. Anti-Kaiser cartoons in black and white
     published soon after the outbreak of war in 1914, and

Ballroom Dancing. *"Empress Ballroom, Winter Gardens,
Blackpool". "Advance Series". Avis Publishing Co.*

Bamforth & Co. *The company's trademark. Note art nouveau style.*

other W.W.I. cards in a "Patriotic Series".
(iv) Greetings Cards. These included the "Message Series" and "Song Greeting Series".
(v) "Real Photographs". These often bear a different trademark, i.e. "B. & Co. Ltd." within a triangle.
   Ref: A Scherer-Silman Bamforth Postcard Catalogue, 1981, is available from Bertram H. Silman, 3500 Pineland Drive, Birmingham, Alabama, U.S.A.

Banana Bread and Flour Co.
Poster-type advertising cards.

Bands
Brass bands were very popular in Edwardian times, often playing at holiday resorts during the summer. The card of "Besses o' th' Barn Band" for example, has "Sandown Pier, May 6, 1906" written on the back. One of the best known seaside bands was established by Harry Mogg (1860-1929). He was a postman and an expert clarinettist. Mogg's Military Prize Band played near the Old Pier at Weston-Super-Mare from 1887 to 1953, retaining the name long after Mogg's death. Postcards may be seen in Woodspring Museum, Weston-Super-Mare. Bands played for special events. The local band at Tingewick, Buckinghamshire, celebrated the Liberal victory of 1912. The Wingate's Temperance Band

Bands. *"Besses o'th' Barn Band". Martin Prestwich. Sandown, Isle of Wight, 1906.*

Bandstands. *"Clacton-on-Sea: The Band Pavilion". Photochrom Sepiatone Series.*

played to become World Champions at the Crystal Palace in 1931.

Bandstands
In Edwardian times almost every large town or city had a bandstand in its public park or, in the case of seaside resorts, on the esplanade or near the pier. An example in the Wellington Gardens at Great Yarmouth is ill. Hill p. 58.

Baness, Mrs. Mary   **fl.c.1904-1914**
Landscape artist whose work was used in facsims. by J.W. Ruddock of Lincoln.

Bankhead, Tallulah   **1903-1968**
Film star. P.P. by *Picturegoer*.

Banknote Cards
These were produced by some countries, e.g. Sweden, together with coin cards.

Banks, A.E.
Publisher, Hove, Sussex.

Banks, J.J.   **1902**
Publisher, Cheltenham. U.B. cards with local black and white views, e.g. Cheltenham Ladies' College.

Banky, Vilma
Film star. P.P. by *Picturegoer*.

Bannerman, Alexander Islay
An Edinburgh artist who designed several Boer War postcards for George Stewart & Co.

Bannister, A.F.D.   **pre-1930**
Marine artist who painted sailing ships for Salmon.

Baptist Missionary Society
Publishers, Furnival St., London, E.C.

Barber, C.W.   **fl. 1908-1914**
London artist who painted children and glamorous young ladies using such titles as "Coming Out", "The Flirt" and "Danger". Exh. R.A. 5. Designed for the Carlton Publishing Co.

"At the window"
by Tito Corbella, Italy. P.U. 1930.

"Serenade" by Tito Corbella, Italy. P.U. 1932.

"The Cigarette". Birthday card by C.E. Shand. P.U. 1929.

Barons Art Pottery. *"Wheelman, Barons Art Pottery, Barnstaple". Advertising card printed by Senior & Co., Bristol. P.U. 1919.*

Barbier, René
American artist who designed patriotic glamour cards. Ill. Monahan 94.

Barclay, Mrs. Hubert
Watercolour painter who spent many years in Canada, the Middle East, India and Japan. She exhibited at the Brook Street Art Gallery in 1923. In 1921 she painted a postcard of the tomb of the unknown warrior in Westminster Abbey for the Mothers' Union.

Bard, Wilkie   **1874-1944**
Music hall and pantomime artist who appeared in a Royal Command Performance in 1912. P.P. as "Mother Goose". W.H. Smith & Son.

Barham, Sybil
Artist who lived in the Priest's House, Bromsgrove, and exhibited in Birmingham in 1910. She designed children's postcards for Faulkner, e.g. "Peter Pan", "In Poppy Land".

Barker, C.
Photographer/publisher, Windsor. R.P.s of Windsor Great Park.

Barker, Cicely Mary   **1895-1973**
Painter of children's cards with fairies, and children from Shakespeare's plays for Faulkner and Salmon.
    Ref: Cope p. 5 and ill. 34.

Barkham, S.
Artist who designed children's cards.

Barlow, G.H.   **pre-1904**
Publisher, 74 Knowsley St., Bolton, Lancashire.

Barlow, John Noble, R.B.A., R.O.I.   **1861-1917**
A Manchester born artist who settled in St. Ives, Cornwall. Exh. R.A. 28. He designed postcards for Savory, using the pseudonym Jan Stroom.

Barnard, Frederick, R.B.A., R.O.I.   **1846-1896**
Humorous artist who contributed to *Punch* from 1863. Exh. R.A. 6. Illustrated the Dickens' *Household Edition,* published between 1871 and 1879. His drawings for Cassell's Art Postcards are dated 1884 so they must have been derived from pre-picture postcard sources. Three sets, titled "Character Sketches from Dickens", were published on and after 1904.

Barnardo's Homes, Dr.
Publisher, Stepney Causeway, London, E.1. Postcards of hospital wards, nursery scenes and Barnardo himself were issued to give publicity to the cause. Their charter states that no destitute child is ever refused admission.

Barnes, A.E.
Painter of animals.

Barnum & Bailey
Advertisers of circus performances on U.B. cards.
    See: Circus.

Barons Art Pottery   **fl. 1899-1939**
Cards showing pots being thrown were obviously intended as publicity for the pottery. They were printed by Senior & Co. of Bristol.

Barracks
A number of cards depict army barracks, sometimes with troops on parade. Valentine, for example, published a photograph of the Hyderabad Barracks, Colchester, showing troops in training.

Barratt, George W.
Painter of "Life's Comedy" Series published by James Henderson.

Barratt, Reginald   **1861-1917**
Landscape painter in watercolour. Exh. R.A. 28. Travelled widely in Europe and the Middle East and designed sets on Egypt and Venice for the Medici Society.

Barraud, Allan F.   **fl. c.1880-1908**
Landscape painter. Exh. R.A. 40. Painted a set titled "In the Country" for Tuck.

Barracks. *"Hyderabad Barracks, Colchester". Valentine.*

Barribal, L. *"Loving Wishes for your Birthday"*. Inter-Art *"Artistique"* Series.

Barrett, Howard   **pre-1910**
Publisher, Southwell, Nottinghamshire. His view cards state "Three times patronised by His Majesty King Edward VII".

Barrett, T.L.
Publisher/draper, Peterborough. Black and white local views supplied by Tuck.

Barrett, Wilson   **b. 1900**
Actor-manager. First appearance on London stage 1921. Spent four years in Edinburgh and Glasgow from 1933 to 1936. Became manager King's Theatre, Hammersmith, 1939. P.P. by A. & G. Taylor.

Barribal, L.   **fl. c.1911-1931**
Versatile figure painter who designed advertising cards, theatre posters and cards of bathing beauties, children and glamorous ladies for J. Henderson & Sons, the Inter-Art "Artistique" and "Comique" Series, and for Valentine.
   Ref: Many of his Inter-Art designs were listed in S.G.P.C., 1983, p. 39.

Barry Railway Co.
This company operated docks at Barry Docks, Glamorgan. Their ships sailed under the subsidiary Barry & Bristol Channel Steamship Co. from 1905 to 1910. Three ships, *Gwalia, Devonia* and *Westonia,* appear on cards published by W.H. Smith.

Barrymore, Ethel   **1879-1959**
American actress who appeared several times on the London stage between 1879 and 1904. Her film career began in 1914. P.P. by *Film Weekly.*

Barrymore, John   **1882-1942**
American actor who started a film career in 1912. P.P. in scene with Greta Garbo by *Film Weekly.*

Barthel, Paul
Artist who contributed to Tuck "Oilettes" in 1904.

Bartholomew, J., & Co.
Engravers of an ambitious series of postcard maps for John Walker & Co. Ltd. (q.v.).

Bartle, L. Frank   **pre-1913**
Publisher, Central Library, Penmaenmawr, Carnarvonshire. Black and white and sepia local views.

Bartlett, Arthur E.   **fl. 1890-1916**
Architect. Studied at R.A. Schools and exh. R.A. 9. Designed humorous cards.

Barton, Dora   **d. 1966**
Actress. First appearance London stage 1892. P.P. in "Yes and No" Series.

Barton, Frank M.
Painter who contributed 12 views of express trains to J.W. Bland's "Commercial Series".

Barribal, L. *"Trusty Comrades"*. Inter-Art *"Artistique"* Series.

Colour Plate 3: Bamforth song cards

WOULD YOU CARE? (1).

Lift your eyes to mine, my darling,
    Let me see the lovelight there,
For you know I love you dearly,
    And to me there's none so fair;
Yet at times I often wonder,
    Would you care, if I'd dare
Tell you that my love had vanished—
    Tell me, sweetheart, would you care?

WORDS BY ARRANGEMENT WITH B. FELDMAN & CO.
Bamforth (Copyright)

WOULD YOU CARE? (2).

Would you care if I should leave you?
    Would you care if we should part?
Would you care if someone told you
    That another won my heart?
Would you care if you had found me
    Closely held in someone's arms?
Would your heart ache just a little—
    Tell me, darling, would you care?

WORDS BY ARRANGEMENT WITH B. FELDMAN & CO.

WOULD YOU CARE? (3).

Just suppose I should forsake you;
    Break my vows—leave you alone;
Just suppose I should reject you,
    Take another for my own;
Just suppose that duty call'd me,
    Would you cry if I'd die
And my eyes were closed for ever—
    Tell me, sweetheart, would you care?

WORDS BY ARRANGEMENT WITH B. FELDMAN & CO.
Bamforth (Copyright)

A set of cards illustrating three verses from the song "Would You Care?".

Barton, Harvey, & Son Ltd.   **1905**

Publisher, St. Michael's Hill, Bristol. Trademark a view of the Clifton Suspension Bridge, though this does not appear on all cards. The output was mainly of photographic views tinted in their own workshop. The views covered a large area including the south west of England, Wales and the Midlands. The firm was the first to photograph the caves at Wookey Hole, near Wells, Somerset. Multi-view cards and facsims. of moonlight scenes by Andrew Beer were also published. In 1907 the firm covered the Lady Godiva Procession in Coventry, and in 1910 the Bournemouth Aviation Meeting and issued some glossy sepia cards, nos. 58-73.

Ref: A check list is given in P.P.M., May 1981, p. 7.

Barton, M.

Publisher, Gloucester. Sepia views of Cotswolds. Cards with narrow frames.

Basch, Arpad   **fl.c. 1900-1914**

Hungarian painter who studied in Budapest in the 1870s, later moved to Munich and then to Paris. He contributed to many illustrated journals. His postcards, which include a set of "International Girls" and a "Town Portraits" Series, are very highly valued.

Bas-Relief Cards

See: P. Scopes & Co. Ltd.

Bass & Co.

Brewers, Burton upon Trent. Cards of their yards, private railway engines, etc.

Bassano

Photographer, London. Supplied photographs for Philco, portraits of stage celebrities for Tuck's "Bookmarker" Series, and scenes from London plays for Wrench.

Batchelder Bros.

Photographer/publisher, Croydon, Surrey. Local photographic views.

Bateman, Henry Mayo   **1887-1970**

Designed advertising card for Simpson's in the Strand in the 1930s.

See: Colour Plate 1.

Ref: Anderson, A., *The Man Who Was Bateman*, 1982.

Bateman, Jessie   **1877-1940**

Actress. First appeared in ballet at age of 10 and later toured in Frank Benson's Shakespeare Company. First film appearance in 1933. P.P. by Misch & Co., 1909.

Bates, Marjorie Christine   **1883-1962**

Painter who exhibited at the R.A. and Nottingham Art Gallery. She lived at The Grange, Welford, Nottinghamshire. Town sketches and characters from Shakespeare for the British Art Co.

Bathing Beauties

Rotary published photographs of beauties discreetly attired in bathing costumes but British cards are far less daring than cards published in France, Germany and Italy. Large numbers were, however, imported from the Continent.

Ref: Barker, Ronnie, *Book of Bathing Beauties*, 1974.

Bathing Machines

In Edwardian times every sandy beach had its row of bathing machines on wheels. These were drawn by horses to the edge

Bathing Machines. *"Marine Parade and Dover Castle"* with bathing machines along the shoreline. Gale & Polden Ltd. *"The Wellington Series"*. Note the winches for controlling the positions of the machines.

of the water and bathers would undress and dress in them. Sometimes they were then drawn up the beach by winches.

Battleships

These are seen in the cards of a number of publishers, usually under such titles as "Our Navy", "The Empire's Navy", "Britain Prepared" or "Our Ironclads". They include His Majesty's Ships:

	Africa.	T	*Erin.*
	Agamemnon.		*Exmouth.*
T	*Agincourt.*		*Formidable.*
	Ajax.		*Glory.*
	Albemarle.		*Goliath.*
	Albion.	T	*Hannibal (also Birn Bros.).*
T	*Audacious.*		*Hercules.*
	Barfleur.		*Hibernia.*
	Barham.		*Hindustan.*
T	*Bellerophon.*		*Howe.*
T	*Benbow.*	T	*Illustrious.*
T	*Blenheim.*		*Implacable.*
	Britannia.		*Indefatigable.*
	Bulwark.	T	*Iron Duke.*
	Caesar.		*Irresistible.*
T	*Camperdown.*		*Jupiter.*
	Canada.		*King Edward VII.*
	Canopus.	T	*King George V.*
	Centurion.		*London.*
T	*Collingwood.*	T	*Lord Nelson.*
T	*Colossus.*	T	*Magnificent.*
	Commonwealth.	T	*Majestic.*
T	*Conqueror.*		*Malaya.*
	Cornwallis.		*Marlborough.*
T	*Devastation.*		*Mars.*
	Dominion.	T	*Monarch.*
T	*Dreadnought.*		*Montagu.*
T	*Duncan,* ill. D. & M. 51.		*Nelson.*
T	*Emperor of India.*	T	*Neptune.*
	Empress of India.	T	*New Zealand.*

continued

Battleships. *"H.M.S. New Zealand". R. Tuck & Sons.* *"Oilette". P.U. 1919.*

Battleships. *"H.M.S. Russell". R. Tuck & Sons. "Oilette".* *"Our Navy" Series II.*

	Ocean.	T	*St. George.*
T	*Orion.*	T	*St. Vincent.*
T	*Powerful.*	T	*Superb.*
	Prince George.		*Swiftsure.*
T	*Queen Elizabeth*	T	*Temeraire.*
	(also Gale and Polden).	T	*Thunderer.*
	Repulse.		*Triumph.*
T	*Resolution.*		*Valiant.*
	Revenge.	T	*Vanguard.*
	Rodney.		*Vengeance.*
	Royal Oak.	T	*Victory.*
T	*Royal Sovereign.*	T	*Warspite.*
T	*Russell.*		*Zealandia.*

T indicates that the ship appears in a Tuck Series.
See: Colour Plate 4; Cruisers; Destroyers; Naval Postcards.
Ref: Pears, R., *British Battleships, 1892-1957*, 1957, facsim. ed. 1979.

Bauermeister, F. 1899
Publisher/bookseller, Glasgow. Output included:
(i)   Vignette views of Scotland, e.g. Glasgow University.
(ii) Comic cards.
(iii) Romantic cards.
(iv) Cards for the Glasgow Exhibition, 1901.

Baumer, Lewis C.E. 1870-1963
His humorous drawings were reproduced in Tuck's "Good Jokes from Punch".

"Bay Series" pre-1927
Views of the Isle of Wight.

"Bayfields Series"
A title noted on coloured views of Lowestoft.

B.B.
Birn Bros. (q.v.).

B.B./C.
Batchelder Bros., Croydon, Surrey (q.v.).

B. & D.
Blum & Degen (q.v.).

Beach Scenes
These abound on postcards and give a fascinating glimpse of Edwardian holidays when families sat on beaches in full everyday clothing, hats and all, and bathers were hidden in huts or the sea. Comic artists exploited the "naughty" aspects of beach behaviour.

Beagles, J., & Co. (Ltd.) 1903 (Ltd. 1908)
Printer/publisher, 9 and 10 Little Britain, London, E.C. Trademark "Beagles Post Cards" printed around a globe and the word "Best" in script across the globe and "Best in the World" beneath. This firm specialised in "Real Photographs". Some Taber Bas-Relief Cards were used. Output included:
(i)   "Phototint Series" of coloured views, sometimes with an inset portrait. Westminster Abbey, for example, has a portrait of Dean Robinson.
(ii) Greetings cards with R.P.s of flowers and a narrow embossed border of trailing ivy or forget-me-nots. These include leap year cards.
(iii) Portraits of celebrities including churchmen, politicians, scientists and sportsmen.
(iv) Portraits of royalty and military leaders.
(v)   Portraits of stage celebrities including scenes from plays.
(vi) "Famous Cinema Stars".
(vii) "Famous Boxers".
(viii) "Zoo Favourites".

(ix) Events, e.g. Victory march of allied troops in London, 19 July, 1919.
(x) Humorous compilations of photographs.
(xi) "Matrimonial Cats", a Louis Wain series.
See: Colour Plate 5.

Beale, J.E.   pre-1929
Publisher, Bournemouth, Hampshire. Cards have been noted marked only with the firm's rubber stamp.

Beale, Sarah Sophia   fl. 1880-1909
Marine artist. Exh. R.A. 3. Painted a set on "Venetian Lagoons" for Tuck's "Wide Wide World" Series, 7747.

Bealing & Hickson
Publisher, Southampton, Hampshire. Local views.

Bears
See: Teddy Bears.

Bebb, Minnie Rosa   b. 1857
Animal painter who worked in Bristol.

Becker, C.J.
Military and sporting artist of Philadelphia, U.S.A. Designed some German regimental cards for F. Hartmann.

Bedwell
Publisher, Bedford. Local views.

Bee, John William   b. 1883
Landscape painter who lived in Sheffield.

Beecham's Pills
Advertising cards designed by Tom Browne.

Beechings Ltd.   1895
Publisher/bookseller, 174 The Strand, London. Started publishing in the days of the court card. Ill. Staff p. 88. Later published photographic views of London.

Beer, Andrew
Painter of landscapes and moonlight scenes for Harvey Barton & Son of Bristol.

Beirne, F.O.
Military artist who designed U.B. cards of regimental uniforms for Blum & Degen which were published in 1901, e.g. "Argyll & Sutherland Highlanders".

Beken
Publisher, Cowes, I.O.W. Yachting photographs, including Sir Thomas Lipton's *Shamrock*.

Belcher, George Frederick Arthur, R.A.   1875-1947
Illustrator and poster artist noted particularly for his charcoal drawings. Contributed to *Punch, Tatler* and *Vanity Fair*. His work appears in the Tuck "Celebrated Posters" Series.

Belgian Soldiers' Fund
A souvenir card dated 1916 was published by Joseph Clarkson of Manchester in connection with the appeal for this fund. Ill. Monahan 2.

Belinbau, Adolf
Italian artist who painted landscapes used by E.W. Savory.

Bell, Hilda
Landscape artist.

Bell, S.J.
Publisher of an "S.J. Bell's Series" of black and white views of Hampshire villages.

Bell's Photo Co. Ltd.   pre-1906
Publisher, Willesden, Middlesex until 1906, then at Westcliff-on-Sea, Essex. Local sepia photographic views.

Bemrose & Sons Ltd.
Printer/publisher. Issued the official cards for the Festival of Empire Exhibition at the Crystal Palace in 1911.

Bender, Paul
Landscape artist.

Bendix, Julius   pre-1909
Publisher, London, E.C. The "Charterhouse Series" of greetings cards printed in Saxony.

Bennett, Frank   pre-1916
Publisher, Sutton Coldfield, Warwickshire. Local black and white views.

Bennett, Godwin
Landscape artist.

Bennett, H.A.
Publisher, Leicester. Local coloured views chromotyped in England.

Bennett, Ian
Photographer, Burton upon Trent. Supplied Rotary, including a photograph of Edward VII. Ill. Hill frontispiece.

Benson, Lady   1860-1946
Actress. Stage name Constance Featherstonehaugh. Joined the Benson Company and married her manager in 1886, thereafter playing leading parts with him all over the country. P.P.s as Mrs. F.R. Benson in Millar & Lang's "National Series" and by Tuck.
Illustration overleaf.

Benson, Sir Francis Robert (Frank)   1858-1939
Actor-manager. Appeared in Irving's *Romeo and Juliet* in 1882. Organised a Shakespeare Festival at Stratford-upon-Avon for 33 years from 1886. Knighted 1916. P.P.s by Beagles (as Caliban) and in Millar & Lang's "National Series".
Illustration overleaf.

Benton, W.   pre-1913
Photographer/publisher, Newcastle upon Tyne and 138 George St., Glasgow. He covered a wide area and even made photographic records of the pit disaster at Senghenydd in South Wales, 1913, and the flood at Louth in 1920.

Beraud, N.
French military and sporting artist. Painted oilette sets — "Infanterie de Ligne" for Tuck, 984/7.

Beringer, Esmé   1875-1972
Actress. First stage appearance 1888, the start of a long career. P.P. in Tuck's "Bookmarker" Series IV.

Berkeley, Edith   fl. 1880-1897
Landscape painter. Exh. R.A. 13. Lived for some time in London and later in Surrey.

Berkeley, Stanley   1855-1909
Animal and sporting painter. Exh. R.A. 23. Designed early cards for Hildesheimer.

Berry, W.H.   1870-1951
Actor and comedian. First appearance at Empire, Leicester Square, London, in 1905. P.P. by Rotary.

Benson, Lady. *"Mrs. F.R. Benson". Actress. Tinted P.P. by Millar & Lang.*

Benson, Sir Francis Robert. *"Mr. F.R. Benson". Actor-manager. Tinted P.P. by Millar & Lang.*

Berry, William
Publisher, Bradford, Yorkshire. Ill. D. & M. 159.

Berry's Boot Polishes
Advertising cards dated 1907, e.g. "The Pacemaker".

Berthon, Paul   **1848-1909**
Swiss painter and illustrator, pupil of Eugene Grasset. Cards in the art nouveau style are highly valued.

Bertiglia, A.   **fl. c.1900-1918**
Italian art deco artist who painted scenes in Venice, e.g. a boy and girl cuddling in a gondola. During W.W.I. he designed anti-Kaiser cartoons.

B.F.G.
Monogram of Bernard Finnegan Gribble, marine painter (q.v.).

Bianchi   **fl. 1920s**
Italian artist who designed glamour cards, ill. Monahan 122, and painted some motoring and steeplechasing scenes. His work was published in Milan and imported into Britain.

Bicycles
  See: Cycling.

Biddles Ltd.
Publisher, High St., Guildford, Surrey. Facsims. of local views painted by A. Nelson Mapple.

Bideford, Westward Ho and Appledore Railway
Issued one set of North Devon views with a white border.
  Ref: Check list in ·R.O.P.L., No. 18, p. 4.

Biggar, J.L.
W.W.I. artist who painted romantic scenes for E.T.W. Dennis & Sons "Dainty" Series and patriotic cards for T. & G. Allan's "Atlas" Series, and for Brown & Calder, ill. Holt 428.

Biggs & Co.   **1898**
Printer/publisher. A firm which issued a few poor quality cards over a short period.

Billiards
A subject for many comic cards by such publishers aᶜ Inter-Art and A.V.N. Jones & Co.

Billing, M.
Artist who painted fruit, flowers and still life. Facsims. of her work were used by Hildesheimer, Nister and Tuck.

Bilton, W.A.
Publisher, Picture Post Card Emporium, York. Photographic views. Acted as agent for W. Bramley of Leeds.

Binder, Tony
Designer of Tuck's "Sights in Egypt".

Biograph Studio
107 Regent St., London, W. Sepia portraits of music hall stars.

Bioscopes
Bioscopes, chromographs and electrographs were all devices for showing moving pictures. Apart from special buildings in London, and later in the provinces, which were equipped for the purpose, the devices were used to attract the crowds on fairgrounds.

Biquard, Armand   **fl. c.1894-1905**
Artist who lived near Regent's Park, London. Exh. R.A. 1,
1904. He designed at least two Boer War postcards for the
Picture Postcard Co.

Birch, J.
Publisher, Southampton, Hampshire. Sepia views of shipping.

Birch, Nora Annie   **fl. 1920-1930**
Artist who painted children behaving as adults. Designed cards
for William Ritchie & Sons of Edinburgh, including a "Nora
Birch Series".

Bird, Alfred, & Sons Ltd.
Advertisers of custard powder. Issued four U.B. cards to mark
the Coronation of Edward VII in 1902. They were designed by
William H. Caffyn. Ill. Byatt col. pl. IIIP.

Bird, Harrington   **fl. c.1870-1904**
Painter of animals and sporting scenes. He was, for a time,
Director of Art to the Board School Commission, Quebec,
Canada. Designed cards for F.C. Southwood (q.v.).

Birds
(i)   W.E. Byers & Co., a series of birds on their nests. Ill.
       Byatt, col. pl. IC.
(ii)   M. Ettlinger, a series on "Favourite Birds", designed and
       printed in Germany.
(iii) The Natural History Museum in London issued a con-
       siderable number of bird cards in the 1920s. Some are
       photographs of museum specimens; others were painted
       by bird artists — J.C. Dollman (q.v.) and H. Gronvald
       (q.v.). The series included:
       Birds: British (2 sets of 10).
       British Birds: Summer Visitors (3 sets of 5).
       British Birds: Winter Visitors (1 set of 5).
       British Birds: Residents (2 sets of 5).
       British Sea Birds (2 sets of 5).
       British Game Birds (2 sets of 5).
       Birds: General (3 sets of 10, 2 of 5).
       Eggs of British Birds (4 sets of 5).
       Pigeons, Ducks and Fowls (1 set of 5).
       Some additional cards were issued separately, making 128
       in all.
          Ref: Collins, Philip, 'British Museum (Natural History)
       Bird Postcards', P.P.M., November 1982, p. 24.
(iv)   Ruskin Studio Art Press, birds illustrated by Roland
       Green, F.Z.S. Ill. Byatt 254.
(v)   Tuck's Educational Series of cards included sets of
       "Birds".
       See: Canary & Cage Bird Life; Capern's Bird Food.

Bird's Custard
Poster type advertising cards.

Birmingham Novelty Co.
Publishers of comic cards.

Birn Bros. (Ltd.)   **c.1903 (Ltd. 1915)**
Publisher, 67-70 Bunhill Row, London, E.C., and New York.
Trademark "B.B." sometimes in script form. Their range included:
(i)   "London Series", views printed in Bavaria. These,
       oddly enough, include a view of Edinburgh framed in
       tartan.
(ii)   "Excelsior Series", photo-portraits of royalty.
(iii) Photo-portraits of actresses.

Birds. *"Favourite Birds: Chaffinch". M. Ettlinger & Co.,
"The Royal Series".*

Birds. *Barn Owl by George Rankin. Facsim. by J. Salmon.*

Birds. *"The Common Pheasant" by George Rankin. "Oil-facsim" by A. & C. Black Ltd. "British Game Birds". P.U. 1934.*

(iv) Battleships printed in colour.
(v) Steeplechasing, coloured scenes.
(vi) W.W.I. patriotic cards including portraits of wartime leaders, e.g. Field Marshall Lord Kitchener (q.v.).
(vii) Regimental cards, embossed. Ill. Monahan 65.
(viii) Heraldic cards, embossed.
(ix) Comic cards, e.g. "The Kissing Club's Season Ticket".
(x) "Stile Series", romantic views by a stile. A man has his arms round a woman and the caption reads:
"Owing to extreme pressure I find it impossible to write more now."
(xi) Greetings cards and valentines, many are embossed and have a framed view.
(xii) Railway express trains, often with greetings. Set of six.
(xiii) Fiscal Series, comic Chamberlain cards.
(xiv) "Trafalgar Series", centenary postcards.

Birthday Cards
See: Greetings Cards.

Bishop & Sons
Advertisers of their business as furniture removers of High St., Pimlico, London, S.W. Photographs of their traction-engine vans.

Bisson, F.V.
Artist who contributed a set titled "Types of Beauty" to Tuck's "Glosso Connoisseur" Series.

B.K.W.I.
Initials of a publisher who used facsims. of Ludwig Koch's horse-racing pictures and published portraits of musicians.

Black, A. & C., Ltd.
Publisher, 4-7 Soho Square, London, W.1. This firm produced a series of *Beautiful Books* each illustrated by water-colour reproductions by such artists as Wilfred Ball, Heaton Cooper and H.B. Wimbush. Some of these illustrations were printed as postcards by the publishers; others by arrangement were used on postcards by Tuck.
Ref: A check list of Black's postcards is given in Byatt pp. 340-1.

Black, Algernon
Painter of aeroplanes and airships for Photochrom, e.g. "Aeroplanes of the Allies".

Black, Montague Birrell   **b. 1889**
Poster artist who painted ocean liners for the White Star Line for reproduction on postcards. He lived in Liverpool.

Black, W. Milne
Glasgow landscape artist who exhibited from 1908 to 1912. He also designed some comic postcards.

Blackall, W.G.
Painted two sets of cards of Cambridge for A. & C. Black.

"Blacket's Series"   **pre-1906**
Views of Newbury, Berkshire.

Blacksmiths
Photographic cards by Wildt & Kray depict the work of the blacksmith. Titles include "The Old Smithy", "Taking off the Old Shoe" and "Nailing on the Shoe". T.L. Fuller published a fine card of a blacksmith on Salisbury Plain.

Blacksmith's Shop Co.
Publisher, Gretna Green. A company formed to exploit the interest in runaway marriages. Cards show the bridge over the river which forms the boundary between England and Scotland and the famous Smithy.

Birds. *"The Swans, Weymouth". Blum & Degen "Kromo" Series.*

Blacksmiths. *"The Smithy at Figheldean, Salisbury Plain"*. Photo by T. Fuller, Amesbury.

Blackwell, E.   **1903**
Publisher, The Post Office, Northampton. A "Rowland Hill Penny Post Series" was published, the proceeds of which were given to the Rowland Hill Benevolent Fund.

Blair, Andrew   **fl. c.1882-1910**
Dunfermline landscape artist who exhibited from 1883 to 1885, mainly at the Royal Scottish Academy. He painted "Edinburgh" and "Scottish Lochs" for Tuck, retitled "Scotch Lochs" when reprinted.

Blair, John   **fl. 1880-1920**
Edinburgh artist. Exh. R.S.A. 83. Painted such scenes as the Tolbooth, Edinburgh, which was used in facsim. by Tuck in the "Edinburgh" set.

Blake, A.W.   **pre-1909**
Naval and military photographer/publisher, Eastney, Portsmouth.

Blake & Edgar
Publishers of a "Picturesque Bedfordshire Series".

Blake, J.H.
Publisher, Putney, London, S.W. Issued an "Idler's Own Series of Local Views" in black and white.

Blampied, Clifford George   **b. 1875**
Channel Islands painter born in St. Helier, Jersey. He was noted for his Alpine landscapes which he exhibited at the Alpine Club Gallery and London Salon. Facsims. of his Channel Island views were published by J. Salmon.

Bland, J.W.   **1909**
Publisher, 122 Commercial Rd., London, E. Trademark a winged Mercury holding scroll with "Commercial Series" title. A wide range of subjects included coloured scenes of country life, views in tourist country, coastal scenes, animals, children and railways.

"Blighty"
The name used by troops during W.W.I. for the home country. It is a corruption of the Hindustani "belati". It appears on cards showing troops bound for Britain embarking in France.

Blind, Rudolf   **fl. 1854-1888**
An artist whose work was used in facsims. by Langsdorff & Co.

"Bliss Series"
Black and white and tinted views of Yarmouth by an unknown publisher.

Bloomfields
Publisher, Woking, Surrey. A "Photo Series".

Bloor, E.J.
Publisher, Castleford, Yorkshire. Trademark an owl sitting in the forked branch of a tree. Cards with tinsel decoration.

Blue Cross Fund
Publisher, 58 Victoria St., London, S.W.1. This organisation was registered under the War Charities Act of 1916 and sold cards to raise money. The cards included a coloured view of a wounded or dying horse tended by a soldier. The picture was reproduced by permission of *The Sphere*.

"Bluebird"
The famous car in which Sir Malcolm Campbell (q.v.) established the world land speed record in 1928 was issued on a card by Pratt.
    See: Pratt's Ethyl Petrol.

"Bluette" Series
A humorous series by W.E. Mack published in the 1930s. It included silhouettes.

Blum & Degen (Ltd.)   **1895 (Ltd. 1909)**
Publisher, Paternoster Row, and from 1905 at 108 City Rd., London, E.C. Trademark from 1905 a shield enclosing a rose spray and a sword on a shield with a shaded ground, the whole surmounted by a crown. The stamp rectangle sometimes has the firm's initials "B. & D." with "Pictorial Postcard Pioneers". The firm claimed to have published the first coloured postcards with views of London in 1895. Their range

Blampied, Clifford George *"Natural Arch, Port du Moulin, Sark"*. J. Salmon.

included:
(i) Early views of London vignetted and printed on matt card.
(ii) Views of many towns and cities in the provinces. These are printed on a pale blue card and are vignetted. They are identified by printing, usually in red.
Ref: Full details with a list of over 300 such views are given in Byatt p. 341.
(iii) "Kromo" or "Chromo" Series of tinted views and staged tinted photographs were issued under these titles.
(iv) Marine series on the Fleet, yachting and life at sea.
(v) Famous Musicians and Eminent Writers.
(vi) Humorous cards by Cynicus, George R. Sims and others.
(vii) Boer War cards with portraits of generals.
(viii) "Our Royal Family" and cards for the Coronation of Edward VII.
(ix) "Racing Stud" Series of photographs.
(x) Animal cards, e.g. "Our Pets".
(xi) Regimental uniforms.

By 1906 serial numbers had exceeded 20,000 and the firm's stock amounted to several million cards.

Blythe, Coralie   **1880-1928**
Actress. P.P. by Tuck shows her playing diabolo. Ill. Hill p. 32.

B.M. & Co.
B. Marks & Co. (q.v.).

Boarding Houses
Since seaside resorts were major markets for picture postcards it is not surprising to find that seaside boarding houses feature largely on comic cards. The subject of many of the cards is the bedside hunt for fleas!

Boat Racing
Boat races occasionally feature on postcards, particularly the Oxford and Cambridge event. They usually show the teams in their boats or posed in a group. A number of boat race photographs were taken by Morse of Putney and Mrs. Albert

Boarding Houses. *"The Boarding House Beauty"*. *"Valentine's Boarding House Series"*. P.U. 1911.

Boarding Houses. *"Just Room for Another, Sir!"* Delittle, Fenwick & Co.'s *"Defco Series"*. P.U. 1906.

Broom (q.v.) issued a card in 1910 showing the Oxford crew preparing for the race.

Bodger, J.W.
Publisher, Peterborough and Hunstanton. Black and white views.

Boer War
Few publishers were in business early enough to reflect the Boer War on postcards. Blum & Degen issued a set in 1900 with portraits of Baden Powell, Buller, French, Kitchener, Roberts and White. Tuck printed a card in the same year in their Empire Series captioned "Paardeberg, Feb. 27th 1900. Ladysmith, Feb. 28th 1900. 120 days siege", followed later by a card with Lord Kitchener seated with the Boer leaders, Botha, Delarey and De Wet, captioned "I had rather have such men my friends than enemies — Shakespeare". W. & B.K. Johnston issued a "Peace with Honour" series in 1902. The Picture Postcard Co. issued a series by artists such as R. Caton Woodville.
See: R. Tuck & Sons Ltd.
Ref: Conan Doyle, A., *The Great Boer War,* 1900.

Boer War Memorials
South African War Memorials are to be found at Alloa, Hawick (unveiled by Lord Roberts in 1903), and at Shrewsbury.

Boileau, Philip   **1864-1917**
North American painter who was born in Quebec and died in New York. Noted for his glamour cards published by Reinthal & Newman (ill. D. & M. 59) which were imported by Charles Hauff & Co. Also worked for some British publishers including Tuck.

Bolas, S.B., & Co.   **pre-1905**
Publisher, 68 Oxford St., London. Black and white views of London.

Bolland, T.   **pre-1905**
Publisher/photographer, St. Leonards-on-Sea, Sussex. Local views.

Boer War Memorials. *"South African War Memorial, Alloa"*. Valentine.

Boer War Memorials. *"South African War Memorial, Shrewsbury"*. R.M. & S., Shrewsbury. Princess Series.

Bollington, A.C.
Cinema organist of Paramount Cinema, Tottenham Court Rd., London. P.P. by Regent Portraits Ltd.

Bolton, Gambier, F. & S.
Planned two "Silverette" sets of "Animal Studies" for Tuck.

Bolton, John N.
Warwick landscape artist who covered the Warwick Pageant of 1906 for the Water Colour Post Card Co. and the Dover Pageant of 1908 for W.H. Smith & Sons.

Bolton, Thomas Samuel   **1879-1943**
Photographer/publisher, Fore Hall, Ely. Cambridgeshire views and local events. His cards usually bear his name "T. Bolton" or the initials "T.B.".
   Ref: Rouse, M., 'T.B., All Kinds of Photographic Work', P.P.M., April 1983, p. 10.

Bompard, Luigi   **1873-1953**
Italian artist who designed glamour cards.

Bompard, S.
Artist who designed glamour cards in the 1920s which were printed in Italy, and exported and distributed in Britain by the Art & Humour Publishing Co. Ltd. (q.v.) (ill. D. & M. 64).

Bond, Acton   **1861-1941**
Actor noted particularly for his performance as the Comte de Fauchet in *The Only Way*. Sepia P.P. by London Stereoscopic Co.

Bond, E.H.
Publisher, Beaconsfield. Cards supplied by Radermacher, Aldous & Co.

Bond, F.W.   **pre-1934**
Photographer for the Zoological Society of London.

Bone, Sir Muirhead   **1876-1953**
Glasgow painter and etcher. Exh. R.A. 17. Etched postcards for the Glasgow Exhibition of 1901. Became an official war and Admiralty artist in W.W.II.

Bonzo
The mischievous puppy invented by G.E. Studdy (q.v.).

Book Advertisements
Some publishers issued cards advertising new publications, often using an illustration from the book.

Booklet Postcards
From about 1903 postcards were sometimes issued in booklets from which individual cards could be detached. Such cards may be recognised by the serrated left-hand edge.

Bookmarker Cards
Long narrow cards (5¼ × 1¾ins.) intended for use as bookmarkers were introduced c.1903 by Beagles, Giesen Bros. (called — Panel Cards), Rotary and Tuck. Tuck issued 16 packets, each with 12 cards. Most carried a full or three-quarter length portrait of an actor or actress but set 13 was called "Our Pets", 14 and 15 "Rough Seas" and 16 "Land

Bookmarker Cards. *"Forbes Robertson"*. Actor. Rotary
Photo Series.

and Sea''. For Post Office purposes they were all described as
"Book Post" cards.

Boon's Cocoa
Give-away advertising view cards.

Boot Blacks
Men and small boys often set up a small footrest on the pave-
ments of towns and cities and offered to shine the shoes of
passers-by for a penny or so. The boot blacks, as they were
called, are occasionally seen in street scenes. A card by A. & G.
Taylor shows one opposite the Bank of England.

Booth, "General"   1829-1912
Portraits of "General Booth" published before 1912 show
William Booth who organised the Salvation Army in 1878 and
became the first "General". He was succeeded by his son,
William Bramwell Booth (1856-1929). P.P. by Rotary.

Boots Cash Chemists Ltd.   pre-1899
Publisher/printer, Nottingham. Tradename "Pelham Series".
After the beginning of W.W.I. a large "B" is found on their
cards, and post W.W.I. cards bear the full name in script.
Output included:
(i)   Views phototyped in Berlin.
(ii)   R.P. series of sepia views supplied by Valentine.

(iii)   Coloured views in which the colouring is brash; one can
        soon recognise these cards as typically "Boots" even
        from a distance.
(iv)   Animal Series.
(v)   "Famous Pictures", reproductions of contemporary
        paintings.
(vi)   "Nation's Pictures", framed reproductions of gallery
        paintings.
(vii)   Patriotic cards.
(viii) "Regimental Colours".
        See: Frontispiece.

Borden, Maria
Ballet dancer. Card of her dancing in *L'Amour*.

Borelli, Zoe
Polish artist who painted girls in their traditional costumes.

Boriss, Margret
Designer of cards featuring children.

Borrow, William H.   fl. c.1880-1904
Landscape and marine watercolour artist who lived in
Hastings. Exh. R.A. 14. Painted Sussex scenes for the Water
Colour Post Card Co., e.g., "Bodiam Castle", "Brighton
from Black Rock" and "The Pavilion, Brighton". His work
was also used by Raphael Tuck in a "Country Life" set.

Bothams, Walter   fl. c.1882-1914
Landscape artist and figure painter. Exh. R.A. 19. Coloured
cards in Tuck's "Country Life" set are described as after
black and white drawings by Bothams.

Bothams, William   fl. c.1896-1904
Landscape artist who lived at Churchfield, Salisbury, Wiltshire.

Bottaro, E.
Artist who painted glamour cards.

Bottomley, George
Artist who painted glamour cards.

Bouchier, Arthur   1863-1927
Actor-manager who played Old Bill in *The Better 'Ole*. P.P.s
by Beagles as Shylock and in "Dainty Novels" Series.

Boucicault, Nina   1867-1950
Stage and film actress. First appeared London stage, Strand
Theatre, 1892. P.P. by Rotary (midget postcard).

Boughton, F.
Publisher, St. George's Rd., Brighton. Local views supplied
by Valentine.

Boughton, R., & Sons Ltd.   pre-1904
Publisher, Thetford, Norfolk. "Britannia Series" of views.

Boulanger, Maurice
French designer of cards featuring cats and kittens. His work
was used by Tuck.

Bourillon
Military artist. Painted a set of six glamour cards of girls using
allied flags as scarves.

Bourne, A.W.
Publisher, 32 Babingley Drive, Leicester. Local views.

Bourne, Cardinal Francis Alphonsus   1861-1935
Became a priest in 1884, a Bishop in 1897, Archbishop of

THE APPROACH TO BOURNVILLE WORKS.

"Bournville Series". *"The Approach to Bournville Works"
by Fred Taylor. Cadbury.*

Westminster from 1903-35 and Cardinal in 1911. P.P. by
Beagles.

"Bournville Series"
Facsims. of paintings of Cadbury's Bournville Estate by
Frederick Taylor.

Boutet, Henry   1851-1921
Paris artist who painted models, bathing beauties and partially
clad women, e.g., "La femme au corset". His cards were
distributed in Britain by Southwood.

Bovril
Advertising cards using reproductions of well-known paintings
and posters.

Bow, Clara   1905-1965
American film actress. Has been described as an "expressive-
eyed, cupid-bow-mouthed flapper". P.P. by *Picturegoer.*

Bowden Bros.
Firm which held the copyright of an Edward VII Coronation
card.

Bowden, Doris W.   1900-1943
Designer of two series of children's postcards for Faulkner
published in 1922.
   Ref: Cope p. 6, ill. p. 35.

Bowden, E.B.
Landscape artist whose work was used by J. Salmon. Exh.
S.W.A. 1919.

Bowers, Albert Edward
Landscape painter who exhibited from 1880 to 1893, mainly at
the Royal Society for British Artists. His work was used in
Tuck's "Gem Scenery" sets.

Bowers, Stephen   fl. c.1880-1895
Landscape painter who lived at Kew. Facsims. of his work
appear in Misch & Stock's Nature Miniatures: "Views of Scotland".

Bowley, May   fl. c.1895-1908
Artist who painted scenes with children and fledgling birds.

Exh. R.A. 3. Bird facsims. by Salmon and Valentine. Also
scenes from the Oxford Pageant of 1907 for Tuck.

Boxer Rebellion
The Boxers were members of a Chinese secret society which
opposed foreign influence. They murdered foreigners and
besieged foreign legations. In 1900 Americans, Japanese and
Europeans intervened and suppressed them. Photographs and
coloured cartoons of the hostilities may be found on postcards.

Boxing
Major boxing events were sometimes photographed for repro-
duction on postcards. The sensational fight between Joe
Beckett and the French boxer Georges Carpentier for the
Championship of Europe on 4 December, 1919, is an example.
Joe Beckett was knocked out soon after the fight started. Lily-
white Ltd. of Halifax had the sole postcard rights for this
event. Beagles published a "Famous Boxers" Series and
"Health & Strength" issued sepia portraits of boxers. The
Beagles Series included P.P.s of Corbett, Doyle, Harvey,
Hood, Lewis, Peterson, Schmeling, Sullivan, Tunney, Wells
and Willard.

Boy Scouts
Groups have been recorded on postcards, e.g. The Birmingham Boy Scouts Pipers with President and Instructor.

Boyack, O.
Publisher, The Arcade, Sunderland. Local views supplied by
Valentine.

"Health & Strength" Series.

Tommy Burns. Champion of the World.

Boxing. *"Tommy Burns. Champion of the World". "Health
& Strength" Series.*

Boyd, W.J.   pre-1909
Designer of comic cards. Railway situations.

Boyne, Tom
Landscape artist who painted Yorkshire views for J.W. Ruddock & Sons.

B.P.C. Co.
Bradford Post Card Co.

B. & R.
Brown & Rawcliffe Ltd. (q.v.).

Bradbury & Co.
Advertisers of cycles, Oldham. This firm issued a "Famous Poster Series of Pictorial Post Cards", many of them comic cards.

Bradfield, Louis W.   1866-1919
Actor and vocalist. P.P. by Rotary.

Bradford Pictorial Post Card Company
Publishers, Thornton Rd., Bradford. Comic cards designed by E.A. Aris (q.v.).

Bradley, Llewellyn
Publisher, Petersfield, Hampshire. Photographic views.

Bradley, William   fl. 1880-1889
Painter in oils of scenes in the Scottish Highlands. Exh. R.A. 4. The Ellanbee "Oilosimile" Series included his "Highland Monarch".

Bradshaw, Percy V.
Painter of comic cards for Misch & Co., "Excentricity"; H. Moss & Co., "Musical Terms Up-to-Date"; Wrench, "Historical Toasts"; many for Tuck, e.g. "General Election", "Market Reports" and "A Telephone Tragedy". Often signed "P.V.B.".

Bragg, E.A., & Co.   pre-1905
Publisher, Illogan, Redruth, Cornwall, and later at Llanhydrock House, Claremont Rd., Falmouth. Photographic views of Cornwall and a "Titanic In Memoriam" card.

Braithwaite
Publisher, Headley Heath, Surrey. "Photo Series".

Bramley, W.
Publisher, Electric Printing Works, Cross Gates, Leeds, Yorkshire. Trademark "B" within a laurel wreath. R.P. cards of Yorkshire.

Brampton, Lily
Actress. P.P. by Birn Bros.

Brampton's
Advertiser of cycle accessories — chains, pedals, saddles, etc. Their cards have a wide border on which the name of the agent is printed.

Bratby
Designer of Tuck "Butterflies on the Wing" set.

Braun, W.
Painter who designed glamour cards.

Brayton, Lily   1876-1953
Actress. First appearance in London with Frank Benson's company in 1900 playing Alice in *Henry V*. Married to Oscar Asche (q.v.). P.P.s by Dunn, Philco, Rotary, Rotophot (with Oscar Asche), and Vertigan.

Breach, T.W.   pre-1907
Publisher, Richmond, Surrey. R.P. views, e.g. Queen's Cottage, Kew.

Breanski De
See: Alfred De Breanski.

Breininger, Ambrose
Designer of comic cards for Inter-Art. Ill. Byatt 134.

Breitkoff & Härtel
Music publisher, 54 Great Marlborough St., London, W. This firm issued cards with a musical theme, including portraits of composers, singers and instrumentalists, as well as scenes from operas.

Brenchley, F.
Photographer/publisher, Chilham Lees, Kent. R.P. views.

Brennan, Eva
Artist whose work was used by Valentine.

Brett, Molly   fl. from c.1928
Designer of a "Fairy Folk" Series for Faulkner and many sets for Salmon and Valentine.
   Ref: Cope p. 7 and ill. p. 36.

Breweries
Postcard views of breweries were usually taken by local photographers, often as advertisements for the owners. The following have been noted:
   Guinness Brewery, Dublin, Eire.
   Hardy's Brewery, Kimberley, Nottinghamshire.
   Ind Coope Brewery, Burton upon Trent, Staffordshire.
   Marston, Thompson & Son, Burton upon Trent, Staffordshire.
   Mitchell & Butlers Ltd., Birmingham, Warwickshire.
   Robert & Wilson's Brewery, Ivinghoe, Buckinghamshire.
   Royal Wells Brewery, Malvern, Worcestershire.
   Smith's Brewery, Tadcaster, Yorkshire.

Bridgeman, Arthur W.   fl. pre-1907
Landscape painter. Facsims. of his work in Tuck sets, including "Picturesque Counties", "Clovelly" and "The Avon Valley, Ringwood".

Bridges and Viaducts
Collections of architectural and historic interest include the old stone bridges of rural areas, and major engineering feats such as Telford's bridge over the Menai Straits, and Brunel's Clifton Suspension Bridge. Railway and canal viaducts are included in this field and there are even "disaster" cards, e.g. the collapse of the viaduct at Penistone, Yorkshire on 2 February, 1916, which was photographed by Gothard, and a Valentine card of the "Fallen Girders, Old Tay Bridge".

Briggs, Barbara   fl. c.1910-1922
Artist who lived in Wakefield, Yorkshire, and exhibited at the Walker Art Gallery, Liverpool. She painted "Our Dogs" Series for Humphrey Milford.

Briggs, W.G., & Co. Ltd.
Printer/publisher of coloured views. Supplied cards to the Southern Railway.

Brighton Camera Exchange
Photographer/publisher, 26 Market St., Brighton, Sussex. R.P. views. Cards bear the initials "D.M. & W.".

Bridges. *"Conway Castle" Bridge. E.T.W. Dennis & Sons. P.U. 1919.*

Bridges. *" 'Flying Scotsman' Crossing the Royal Border Bridge, Berwick-on-Tweed". Valentine. 1934.*

Bridges. *"Menai Suspension Bridge". Publisher unknown.*

Bridges. *"The Tower Bridge". R. Tuck & Sons. London.*

Bridges. *"Pont-y-pant, Wales". Shurey's Publications.*

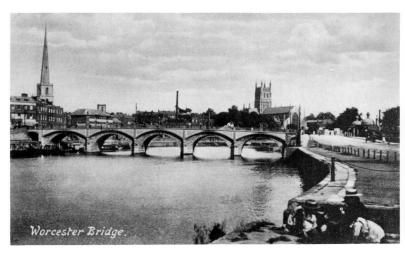

Bridges. *"Worcester Bridge". Thomas Newbury, Worcester.*

British Empire Exhibition. *"Interior, Palace of Engineering".*
Fleetway Press. P.U. 1924.

Brisley, Ethel C   **fl. 1908-1940**
Portrait painter. Exh. R.A. 40. Designed children's cards and
W.W.I. patriotic card for Mansell.

Brisley, Nina Kennard   **fl. c.1919-1922**
Illustrator and writer of children's books. Exh. R.A. 3.
Designed cards for Mansell.

Bristol Printing & Publishing Co.
Publishers of "Ye Olde English Inns". Cards with oval
frames.

Britannia Pictorial Postcard Co. Ltd.   **fl. c.1904-1907**
Publisher, 45 Union St., Glasgow. Published a wide range of
cards including series which dealt with symbolism, e.g. "The
Key to Dreams", "The Language of Flowers" and "The
Lover's Secret Signs".

"Britannia Series"
See: R. Boughton & Sons Ltd.; Hardings.

British Antarctic Expedition
See: South Polar Expedition.

British Art Co.   **pre-1914**
Publisher, London, E.C. The "Britart Series" of comic cards.
Town sketches and Shakespearian characters by M.C. Bates
(q.v.).

British Empire Exhibition, Wembley, 1924
The Fleetway Press was the sole concessionaire for the official
postcards of this major Exhibition, though many individual
exhibitors gave away photographic cards by the official
photographer, Campbell-Gray. At least 12 other publishers
issued exhibition cards, including Beagles, Philco, Photochrom, Tuck, and Wildt & Kray. E.T.W. Dennis & Sons
produced 30 views of the Isle of Man and various colonial
governments also had cards printed. Special postage stamps
were issued for the occasion.
    Ref: A comprehensive list of all cards is given in
Fletcher/Brooks II.

"British Mirror Series"   **1905**
A trademark used by Knight Bros. for glossy tinted views. It
shows a hand mirror with the words "Hold a Mirror up to
Nature" on a ribbon below. The views were printed in Saxony.

British Museum (Natural History Museum)
Publisher.
    See: Birds.

British Photogram Co.   **pre-1912**
Publisher, High St., Exeter, Devon. Trademark an owl and an
open book with the words "A Photogram 'tis Wisdom". The
main series published by this firm deals with regimental
badges.

British Photographic Publishing Co.   **fl. 1894-1900**
Publisher, 2 Museum Terrace and later 36 Lower Hastings St.,
Leicester. Early cards with views of Leicester.

British Photoprint Co. Ltd.   **1897**
Printer/publisher, 17 Farringdon St., London. Firm which
issued "court" size cards of British cities and of views along
the River Thames.

British Showcard & Poster Co.   **fl. 1901-1904**
Publisher, 37 Snow Hill, London, E.C. Their cards reflected
life at the Zoological Gardens, some sporting subjects (including comics) and literary subjects, e.g. "Titles of Shakespeare's
Plays".

"British Wild Flowers"
Two series by A. & C. Black based on paintings by C.A. Hall.

Brittain & Wright   **pre-1905**
Publisher, Stockton on Tees, Durham. A "Phoenix Series" of
coloured views of the North of England, followed by a
"Phoenix Photo Series".
    Ref: Suggitt, S. 'The Postcards of Brittain and Wright',
P.P.M., March 1982, p. 40.

Broadcasting
See: Wireless.

Broadrick, Jack
Designer of comic cards, some dated 1907.
    See: Dialect Cards.

Brock, Charles Edmund, R.I.   **1870-1938**
Cambridge artist who shared a studio with his brother, H.M.
Brock. Illustrated many books and contributed to *The
Graphic, The Quiver, Good Words* and *Punch*. Some cards,
based on his black and white drawings for *Punch*, were
coloured and reproduced by Tuck.

Brodie, M.S.   **pre-1922**
Publisher, 62 High St., Folkestone, Kent.

"Broma Cocoa"
Advertising cards with views of cocoa plantations.

Broman, Mela
Maiden name of Mela Koehler (q.v.).

Brook, Clive   **1891-1974**
Film actor. Card by *Film Weekly* with scene from *Shanghai
Express* with Marlene Dietrich, and P.P. by *Picturegoer*.

Brookes
Publisher, Pontypridd, Glamorgan. Sepia scenes of local
collieries, some with miners working underground.

Brooklands
Brooklands motor circuit was constructed at Weybridge,
Surrey in 1906-7 and became the track on which world records

were established. After 1939 it was no longer in use for this purpose. Postcards of the circuit are hard to find but tinted cards of "Brooklands Favourites" were published by Valentine, each with a car and a driver's portrait inset, e.g. "Gordon Watney and his Mercedes".

Brooks, Warwick
Photographer/publisher. Manchester views.

Broom, Mrs. Albert   c.1902
Publisher, Fulham, London. Photographs taken at Chelsea Barracks and at the Royal Mews were the first to be issued. Thereafter her postcards reflected local events, e.g. the Oxford University Boat Race crew of 1910. Ill. Byatt 45.

Broomfield, S.W.   pre-1905
Publisher, King St., Weymouth, Dorset. Local collotype views.

Brown
Photographer/publisher, Savoy Studios, Blackpool. Local views.

Brown & Calder   pre-1903
Publisher, London. "Savoy" Series of birthday cards.

Brown, Dorothy
Landscape artist who painted for Salmon.

Brown, Francis
Contributed wartime caricatures of the Kaiser to A.M. Davis's "Nothing to laugh at" Series.

Brown, Graham
Actor. P.P. by Beagles.

Brown, James, & Son   1909
Publisher, 52-6 Darnley St., Glasgow. Official publishers to the Boy Scout Movement.

Brown, Maynard   fl. c.1883-1904
Figure and historical painter. Exh. R.A. 6. Known for his glamour cards and for poster advertisements for Schweppes Table Waters, e.g. "The Lady of the Waterfall".

Brown, Paul John
Newcastle artist who designed comic cards for the Technical Art Co. of that city.

Brown & Rawcliffe Ltd.   pre-1904
Publisher, Exchange Works, Pall Mall, Liverpool. This firm seems to have had a special interest in civic heraldry and Scottish tartans. Most of the views occupy only part of the picture side, the remainder having a coloured coat of arms relating to the view. Views include a "B. & R. Camera" and a "Manx Camera" Series, which cover most of Britain. A few views were facsims. of watercolours. Some humorous cards complete the range.

Brown, Samuel John Milton   fl.c. 1900-1937
Marine painter who lived in Liverpool and often exhibited at the Walker Art Gallery. Moved to North Wales in the 1930s. Two sets of his paintings were reproduced as postcards by the *Liverpool Daily Post and Mercury.*
Ref: Check list Byatt pp.356-7.

Brown & Woodley   pre-1904
Publisher, White Rock, Hastings, Sussex.

Browne, Gordon Frederick, R.I.   1858-1932
Illustrator. Designed a set of four humorous cards for John Walker & Co. depicting the game of Ping-Pong (q.v.) which was very popular between 1899 and 1904.

Browne, John Stewart
Poster artist whose work was reproduced on postcards by David Allen. These advertised theatrical productions, e.g. *Old Heidelberg* and *Quo Vadis.*

Browne, Thomas Arthur, R.I., R.B.A.   1872-1910
Tom Browne was apprenticed to a firm of lithographic printers in Nottingham from 1884 to 1891. In 1895 he moved to London contributing black and white sketches to British and American periodicals. He created the characters Wearie Willie and Tired Tim. In 1897 he founded the colour printing firm of Tom Browne & Co. in Nottingham and started to make drawings for *Punch.* In 1904 and 1905 he published *Tom Browne's Comic Annual.* Exh. R.A. 9.

He designed many advertisements including 18 for *The Weekly Telegraph,* a number for J.S. Fry (q.v.) which were later issued as postcards, and publicity cards for plays issued by Miles & Co., e.g. *The Arcadians* (four cards).

Browne's comic postcards were mainly published by Davidson Bros., though a series of "Proverbial Parodies" was published by William Collins, "Celebrities in the Days of Their Youth" by Hartmann and some humorous street scenes by Valentine. Tom Browne appears to have had a personal stake in Davidson Bros. for he commissioned other artists to do work for them. Browne's early cards were captioned by the artist, e.g. "Pa has his bumps felt", 2566, on the face of the card. Later cards have the caption printed on both sides.

A series revives the characters of Mr. and Mrs. Caudle who first appeared in a series of contributions to *Punch* by Douglas Jerrold in the 1840s under the title "Mrs. Caudle's Curtain Lectures". Some of Browne's black and white drawings for *Punch* were coloured and used in Tuck's "Good Jokes from Punch" Series.

Browne's titles for Davidson included:
2504 "Cricket phrases illustrated".
2515 "Soldier and a man".
2534 "Hi! Look out mate".
2548 "When Father carves the goose".
2570 "Mr. Caudle, unable to stand".
2575 "Sea side comforts", set title.
2578 "Have the rest", billiards.
2580 "Changing seats/trying to save him/cheerful".
2582 "Honeymoon", set title.
2583 "Can't you come in the proper way?".
2588 "Johnny's Pa learns to play saxhorn".
2591 "Awfully sorry".
2598 "Man falls off cliff".
2600 "Out of the deep".
2604 "Twins have the measles".
2607 "It will bring good luck".
2642 "Joys of the ocean", set title.
8003 "Is that all you've brought home?".
8021 "Beware of the man traps".
8026 "Taking a mean advantage".
8036 "This is ripping".
8039 "The only mount left".
8062 "Tommy Atkins".
9073 "The Milk Seller".
See: Colour Plate 6.
Ref: An appreciation of the artist is given in Johnson, A.E., *Tom Browne, R.I.,* A. & C. Black's Pen and Pencil Series, 1909.

Building Construction. *"University Tower, Bristol" under construction. It was completed in 1925. Photo by Garratt.*

Brumwell, C.E.
Publisher, 10 Broad St., Hereford. Local sepia views supplied by Frith.

Brundage, Frances   **1854-1937**
Versatile American artist who illustrated Nora Chesson's *Tales from Tennyson*. Tuck, who published the book c.1900, used the illustrations on postcards.

Brunelleschi, Umberto   **1879-1949**
Italian art deco artist who studied in Florence, moved to Paris, c.1900, and contributed colour plates to *The Illustrated London News* in 1913. His cards depict exotic dancers, lightly draped, in settings with plants and butterflies. They are highly valued.

Brunskell & Son
Photographer/publisher, Windermere, Westmorland. Local R.P. views.

Brusher Mills
See: Harry Mills.

Bryan, W.
Publisher, Burgess Hill, Sussex. "Real Photo Series".

Bryant & May
Cards advertising matches.

Buchanan, Fred   **1879-1941**
London draughtsman who made humorous drawings for *The Graphic, Fun, London Opinion* and *John Bull*. He designed comic postcards for Woolstone Bros., ill. Byatt 350, and for Tuck, "Unsolicited Testimonial", 3012.

Buchanan, James, & Co. Ltd.
Advertisers of whisky. "Dealers under Royal Warrant".

Buchanan, P.A., & Co.
Publisher, Chiswick, London, W. Black and white views printed in Berlin.

Buchel, Charles A.   **1872-1950**
Portrait painter. Exh. R.A. 20. Designed theatre posters which

were reproduced as postcards by David Allen, e.g. *Quality Street*. He had a studio in Hampstead, London.

Buckland, Arthur Herbert, R.B.A.   **fl. 1895-1925**
Landscape painter whose work was used by E.W. Savory. Exh. R.A. 19.

Buckton, R.H.
Artist who designed a set titled "Good Dog" for the Medici Society.

Budd, Obadiah
Designer of a composite set of four cards published by Charles Voisey under the title "Elongated Dachshund".

"Buffalo Bill"   **1846-1917**
William Frederick Cody, better known as Buffalo Bill, served in the American Civil War. He was later given a contract to supply railway workers in the prairie lands with fresh buffalo meat. Hence his nickname. He finally organised his cowboys into a Wild West Show which he brought to Britain. It was advertised on a postcard in which he appears on a prancing horse with the British and American flags in the background. Buffalo Bill's Indians appear on a Valentine card. Ill. Hill p. 30.

Building Construction
Few cards show 20th century buildings under construction. The rare examples are of particular interest. A Bristol photographer by the name of Garratt recorded the construction of George Oatley's tower at the University of Bristol encased in scaffolding. The building was completed in 1925.

Bull, Rene   **fl. 1892-1928**
Versatile artist and illustrator who covered many military campaigns and served in W.W.I. in the R.N.V.R. and the R.F.C. He also designed strip cartoons. His work as a postcard artist however was in the field of humour. Publishers: Davidson, e.g. "Banking Expressions" and "Illustrated Limericks"; Faulkner; Landeker & Brown; Charles Voisey.

Bunneys Ltd.   **pre-1906**
Publishers/stationers, Llandudno and Liverpool. Glossy coloured views printed in Saxony.

Burchnall, C.T.
Publisher/stationer, Midhurst, Sussex. Sepia views.

Burgen & Co.
Publisher, Bristol. Framed local views.

Burger, R.
Landscape artist.

Burgess & Co.   **pre-1912**
Publisher, Bristol. "Bee" Series of black and white facsims.

Burgess & Son
Publisher/stationer, 5 Market Place, Abingdon, Berkshire. Local views.

Burgess, Arthur James Wetherall, R.I., R.O.I.   **1879-1956**
Marine painter. Studied in Sydney, New South Wales and in 1918 became naval artist for the Commonwealth of Australia. Art Editor of the *Naval and Shipping Annual*. Exh. R.A. 53. Burgess's paintings of ships were published as postcard facsims. by Cammell Laird of Birkenhead, e.g. S.S. *Oropesa*.

Burgess, R. Briant   **pre-1914**
Publisher, Bognor Regis, Sussex. Local black and white views.

Burkart & Co.
Publisher of coloured views and of a series of hotel cards designed by "Jotter".

Burke, Billie   **1885-1970**
Actress. First appeared on London stage 1903. Debut as a star in New York, 1908. Started film career 1916. P.P.s by Beagles, Davidson, Philco, Pictorial Post Card Co., and Rotary.

Burleigh Ltd.
Publisher, Bristol. W.W.I. cards with regimental badges.

"Burlesque Series"
See: Eustace Watkins.

Burnand, Victor Wyatt, R.B.A., R.M.S.   **1868-1940**
Illustrator and landscape artist. Born at Poole, Dorset; lived at Guildford from 1912. Was for a time a master at the Royal College of Art. Postcard facsims. of his work were published by A.G. Curtis, High St., Guildford.

Burnham, Ernest J.
Publisher, The Library, Seaton, Devon. Local coloured views.

Burnistan, H.
Publisher, Leeds, Yorkshire.

Burns & Son
Publishers of Welsh views.

Burns, Robert   **1759-1796**
Cards associated with the poet Burns include his portrait, views of inns, and sculptured figures of characters in his poems.

"Burns Studio Series"
Views of the Robert Burns country in Scotland by William Ritchie & Sons Ltd. (q.v.).

Burns, Tommy   **b. 1881**
Champion heavyweight boxer of the world 1906. P.P. by "Health & Strength".

Burrell, Elsie
Portrait painter. Watercolour portrait of Gladys Cooper for Henry Stone of Banbury.

Burrow, Edward J., & Co.
"Publishers, Artists & Printers", Cheltenham, Gloucestershire. Several series were produced:
(i)   "Burrow's Royal Series", general views of Gloucestershire and Herefordshire; photos by R.E. Davies.
(ii) "British Colour Series", general views.
(iii) Fine quality sepia views of places as far afield as Essex, e.g. Leyton Parish Church in 1932, in 1832 and in 1732, the last two obviously from old prints.

Burrow, J.F.   **pre-1909**
Publisher, Ely, Cambridgeshire. Local sepia views.

Burt, A.H., & Co.   **pre-1905**
Publisher, Wanstead, Essex. Glossy black and white local views and coloured views.

Burton, Dudley L.
Designer of a card for Thridgold & Co., titled "Father Will Agree".

Burton, Sir Frederick William, R.H.A.   **1816-1900**
Irish landscape painter who was Director of the National Gallery of Ireland from 1874 to 1894. Facsims. of his work are

Burns, Robert. *"Stone Figures of Tam o' Shanter, Souter Johnnie"*, *characters in a Robert Burns poem, with the "Landlord and Landlady of Tam o' Shanter Inn, Ayr".* Photo by A.D. Henderson.

"Burns Studio Series". *"The House in which Burns Died, Dumfries".* William Ritchie & Sons.

signed "F.W. Burton". These were used by Salmon some years after Burton's death.

Bury, W.   **pre-1922**
Publisher, Rochdale, Lancashire. Photographic views.

Bush, E.T.
Photographer/publisher, Cardiff. Local R.P. views.

Bushby, Thomas   **fl. 1898-1914**
Landscape artist of Victoria Lodge, Currock, Carlisle. Exh. R.A. 4. Designed watercolour views for E.T.W. Dennis.

Busi, Adolfo
Italian art deco artist who designed postcards in the 1920s, usually with children. A card entitled "Surprise" shows a half-clad girl hiding behind a mirror.
See: Colour Plate 10.

I'M KEEPING AS MUCH IN THE AIR AS POSSIBLE.

Butcher, Arthur. *"I'm Keeping as Much in the Air as Possible"*. Inter-Art Co. *"Artistique"* Series.

Busk, William   **fl. c.1890-1908**
Dorset artist. Exh. R.A. 3. Painted a set on the county for Tuck, 7700.

Bustin, F.
Publisher, Bristol. Black and white pictures of concert parties.

Butcher, Arthur   **fl. c.1910-1925**
Versatile figure painter who designed for the Inter-Art "Artistique", "Comic", "Song", and "Ten-Nine-Eight" Series. A popular series shows wounded soldiers with nurses in W.W.I. He also designed Christmas cards for E. Mack and a "Song Series" for an unknown publisher which carries a French translation below the caption on each card. A few glamour cards may also be found, painted in the art deco style.

Bute, E.S.
Designer of Japanese studies for William Lyon.

Butler, Charles Ernest   **b. 1864**
Landscape painter. Exh. R.A. 22. Designed cards for the Indian Tea Association which were published by A.V. Mansell.

Butt, Clara   **1873-1936**
Contralto. Popular concert singer who travelled in Europe. D.B.E. 1920. P.P., with her baby, in Rotary Book Post Series.

Butt Studio
Bourton-on-the-Water, Gloucestershire. Local photographic views.

Butterflies
Two "Aquarette" sets by Tuck bear the title "Butterflies and Moths". The paintings were by R.J. Wealthy. Cadbury also published a "Butterflies" Series.

"Butywave Shampoo"
Advertising cards with film stars who were alleged to have used the shampoo.

Buxton, Dudley   **fl. c.1910-1920**
Cartoonist who contributed sporting drawings to *Punch* in 1904 and later turned to designing comic cards for Inter-Art, A.V.N. Jones, and Charles Voisey. These included comic children, comic drunks, and patriotic W.W.I. cards. Ill. Holt 397.

Buzzard, Percy James
Watercolour artist who painted views of Oxford for Robert Peel.

B. & W.
Brown & Woodley (q.v.).

Byers, W.E., & Co.   **fl. c.1904-1908**
Publisher, 42 Moorfields, London, E.C. Their cards were grouped in a "Favourite" Series and included sets on birds, ill. Byatt, col. pl. IC, and London views combined with coats of arms. There were also P.P.s of actresses.

"Bystander"
The periodical which published Bruce Bairnsfather's "Fragments from France" wartime cartoons and reprinted them in sepia as postcards.

Butterflies. *"Butterflies and Moths"* by R.J. Wealthy. R. Tuck & Sons. *"Aquarette"* Series II. P.U. 1920.

Cachet
Handstamp on a card made by someone other than the Post Office, e.g. "Land's End", "John o'Groats", "Summit of Snowdon" or "Cruise of the Northern Bell".

Cadbury's
Advertisements by this firm give publicity to its paternal attitude to staff. It sponsored a "Bournville Series" of scenes of their model estate painted by Frederick Taylor. The firm also supplied postcard size trade cards of butterflies to education authorities.

Caffyn, William Henry
Designer of advertising cards for Bird's Custard.

Caine, T.
Publisher, Post Office, Southsea, Hampshire.

Cairnie
Chemist/publisher, Thurso, Caithness. A "John o'Groats Series" including views of trains snowed up on the local railway line.

Caldecott, Randolph, R.I.   **1846-1886**
Watercolourist and noted illustrator of children's books first published by G. Routledge & Sons and later republished by F. Warne & Co. Ltd. Warne published some of the pictures in 1914 as sets of postcards. The Caldecott picture books from which these were taken were:
The House that Jack Built, 1878.
John Gilpin, 1878.
Elegy on the Death of a Mad Dog, 1879.
The Babes in the Wood, 1879.
Three Jovial Huntsmen, 1880.
Sing a Song of Sixpence, 1880.
The Queen of Hearts, 1881.
The Farmer's Boy, 1881.
The Milkmaid, 1882.
Hey-diddle-diddle the Cat and the Fiddle, and Baby Bunting, one volume, 1882.
The Fox Jumps over the Parson's Gate, 1883.
A Frog he would a-wooing go, 1883.
Come Lasses and Lads, 1884.
A Farmer went Trotting upon his Grey Mare, and Ride a Cock Horse to Banbury Cross, one volume, 1884.
There were 48 cards in all which were reprinted in 1933. An example is ill. Byatt p. 335.

Caldwell, Marianne
Actress. P.P. by Rotary, with Marie Studholme in *The School Girl*.

Caledonia Post Card Co.   **pre-1938**
Publisher. Issued cards for the Empire Exhibition, Glasgow, 1938.

Caledonia Railway
Many cards were issued in association with the Caledonian Railway including a set of engines, two of trains in motion, and 40 sets of Scottish views, some in Millar & Lang's "National Series" and others by Valentine. One set bears the name of M. Wane of Edinburgh. In addition there were a number of cards with views in tartans and some poster reproductions. Hartmann also issued a series of views.
    Ref: Complete list of all cards is given in R.O.P.L., No. 15.

"Caledonia Series"   **pre-1906**
The tradename used by J.A. McCulloch of Edinburgh (q.v.).

Caledonian Steamers
Seven steamers served ports on the Firth of Clyde:
Duchess of Fife.
Duchess of Hamilton.
Duchess of Montrose.
Duchess of Rothesay.
Ivanhoe.
Marchioness of Breadalbane.
Marchioness of Lorne.
A series of 30 by William Ritchie & Sons includes cards of these vessels and of the waterways they plied.
    Ref: Full list in R.O.P.L., No. 15, p. 29.

Calendar Cards
A few publishers issued sets of 12 cards, one for each month of the year and E. Hamel & Co. of Nottingham produced cards for each month with the days numbered.

Call, W.A.
Photographer/publisher, The County Studio, Monmouth. The "Cambria" Series of R.P. views.

Callander & Oban Railway
Most of the territory served by this railway is illustrated in the sets issued by the Caledonian Railway. One booklet of cards, however, produced by McCorquodale, covers the line between Glasgow and Oban on which an Observation Car was used.
    Ref: R.O.P.L., No. 15, p. 30.

Calvert, F.C., & Co.   **c.1900**
Advertising cards for their "Carbolic Prickly Heat and Bath Soap". U.B.

Cambrian Railways Co.   **1905**
Ten views were issued by this company c.1905. In addition, its territory was covered by at least 28 cards in the Photochrom "Celesque" Series and over 50 by Valentine.
    Ref: Views are listed in R.O.P.L., No. 5, pp. 4-8.

Cambridge Picture Post Card Co.   **1904**
Publisher, 3 Market Hill, Cambridge. The firm was owned by Harry Allan Moden, a cartoonist who shared the design work with another cartoonist, Frank Keene. Many cards deal with

REAL PHOTOGRAPH POST CARD
THE WELLS SERIES
Name & Address Only

Camburn, Harold. *Trademark "The 'Wells' Series"*.

Cambridge University life, reflecting personalities with wit and humour. There are also more serious cards of college rowing crews.

Cambridge, S. pre-1906
Publisher, Cambridge's Library, Hove, Sussex. Trademark fleur-de-lis. Facsims. of paintings by W.E. Croxford (q.v.) and Warren Williams (q.v.) of Sussex villages and downland, and some P.P.s of cricketers.

Camburn, Harold 1877-1956
Photographer/publisher, Grove Hill Rd., Tunbridge Wells, Kent. Trademark a well with "The 'Wells' Series" printed on the tiled roof. R.P.s mainly of the south-east of England though he covered the railway disaster at Shrewsbury in 1907. He supplied other publishers with his photographs which were of high quality.

Cameron, Alexander fl. 1921-1930
Scottish artist whose painting of Islay was used in facsim. by Salmon.

Cameron, Archie fl. pre-1916
Painter of comic cards for Hutson Bros.
  See: Colour Plate 14.

Camp Coffee
Advertising cards by R. Paterson & Co., Glasgow. Fine military facsims. with the slogan "First and Best". Some Paterson cards were designed by Henry Payne (q.v.).

Campbell, John F.
Artist who painted pictures of the winning of the Victoria Cross which were used in facsims. by W. & A.K. Johnstone.

Canals. *"Canal, Exeter". "Arcade Real Photo Series"*.

Campbell, Sir Malcolm 1884-1949
Racing motorist who frequently held the world motor speed record. He is seen in an inset on a card issued in 1928 showing his *Bluebird* Napier car, used to advertise Pratt products. Ill. Monahan 34.

Campbell, Mrs. Patrick 1865-1940
Actress who made her London debut in 1890. Was a great success as Paula in *The Second Mrs. Tanqueray,* 1893. P.P.s by Rotary and Shurey.

Campbell, Reginald John 1876-1956
Minister of the City Temple from 1903 to 1915 who expressed his controversial views in a book *The New Theology.* P.P. by Rotary. Ill. Hill p. 12.

Campbell-Bannerman, The Rt. Hon. Sir H. 1836-1908
Leader of the Liberal Party in election victory of 1906. P.P. by Rotary. Ill. Hill p. 10.

Campbell-Grey
Photographer/publisher who issued a series of sepia R.P.s for the British Empire Exhibition at Wembley, 1924-5.

Campbell's Soup
Advertising cards, including designs by Grace Wiederseim.

Campbeltown & Machrihanish Light Railway
Issued a single poster-type card with three versions depending on train times.
  Ref: R.O.P.L., No. 12, p. 3.

Canals
Views of canals are not common, particularly those which show horse-drawn barges and locks in close-up.
  There is a Canal Card Collectors' Circle which encourages the study of inland waterways.
  Refs: Edwards, L.A., *Inland Waterways of Great Britain and Ireland,* 1962; Gladwin, D.D., *A Pictorial History of Canals,* 1977; McKnight, H., *Waterways Postcards 1900-1930,* 1983.

Canary & Cage Bird Life
Publisher, 9 Arundel St., Strand, London. This journal gave away cards of postcard size with a coloured picture of a bird on one side and "Aids to Amateurs" printed on the other with no space for an address. They were, therefore, trade cards. However, they were also published as ordinary cards at 1½d. each or 7d. for a packet of six.
  See: "Feathered World".

Cannon, Walter fl. c.1908-1913
Seascape artist who painted shipping scenes which were used by Salmon.

"Cantab Series"
Views of Cambridge colleges, published by J.P. Gray of Cambridge.

Cantrell & Cochrane
Advertiser, Dublin and Belfast. Cards to promote the sales of ginger ale, e.g. a coloured card with a lady winning a yacht race titled "An Easy First".

Cape, F., & Co. pre-1904
Publisher, Oxford. Facsims. of local scenes after Leslie Pavièr.

Capern's Bird Foods
Advertising cards with bird studies, e.g. budgerigar, blackbird, canary, linnet, etc. Nine complete sets, each of six cards, were

Canary & Cage Bird Life. *"Canary-Bullfinch"*. *Postcard-size trade card.*

issued, together with one or two odd cards.

Ref: For check list see Collins, P., 'The Capern Mystery', P.P.M., July 1983.

Car Accidents
Not commonly recorded on postcards. Those that do turn up are the result of enterprise by a local photographer.

Carbonora Co.
Photographer/publisher, Wild St., Liverpool, Lancashire. Noted for their extensive coverage of the Liverpool Strike of 1911, when the Government sent in troops and two men were killed. The full story is told in a magnificent series of 80 real photographs.
Ref: Check list by J. Brindle, P.P.A. 1982, pp. 80-1.

"Carbofoto"
See: Photochrom Co. Ltd.

Carey, John
Artist who designed comic cards for W. Lawrence of Dublin.

Carlin, Charles A.   **fl. 1923-1931**
Designer of cards for Photochrom.

Carline, George F., R.B.A.   **1855-1920**
Landscape artist who lived in Lincoln until 1887 when he moved to London. In 1899 he moved to Derbyshire and in 1903 to Oxford, returning to London during W.W.I. Was very interested in flowers and gardens. Exh. R.A. 10. Postcard views of "Sunny Newquay" appear to have been commissioned by the Headland Hotel.

Carlisle, Wilson   **1847-1942**
Founder of the Church Army. P.P. by Church Army.

Carlton Publishing Co.   **pre-1913**
London, E.C. Published vignette photographs of children, hunting scenes and many greetings and glamour cards imported from France and Germany, ill. D. & M. 67.

Carnation Milk
Advertisement cards.

Carnell, Albert E.   **fl. c.1918-1926**
Artist who painted children, often as adults. His cards usually

show a small fair-haired girl in strap shoes and a ribbon in her hair, with a boy in long trousers, both with chubby red cheeked faces and blue eyes. Carnell designed cards for:
(i)   E.J. Hey & Co. under the pseudonym of Ludgate, which is derived from the address of this publisher in Ludgate Hill and may have been used by more than one artist. The pseudonym Clearwell was also used.
(ii) Photochrom "Celesque" Series signed "A.E. Carnell".
(iii) Valentine, signed "Albert Carnell".
Byatt, p. 130, likens the style of the "Ludgate" cards to that of T. Gilson.
See: Colour Plate 8.

Carnivals
These were often preceded by a procession of floats which were photographed so that postcard prints could be made available locally, e.g. Weymouth Carnival, Dorset.

Carpenter, L.G.   **pre-1909**
Publisher, Ramsgate, Kent. Coloured local views.

Carr, Charles J.   **pre-1906**
Publisher/stationer, Great Yarmouth. Local coloured views.

Carr, Percy Colin   **fl. c.1906-1908**
Artist who published his own cards and designed an advertising card for "Jasmine Self-Raising Flour".

Carrere, F. Cuillon
Paris artist who painted glamour subjects. He exhibited at the London Salon in 1913.

Carroll, M., & Co.
Publisher, High St., Roehampton, London, S.W.

Carruthers, W.   **fl. 1930s**
Watercolour artist who painted landscapes in Devon, Edinburgh and Stratford-upon-Avon. They were used in facsims. by Salmon.
See: Colour Plate 7.

Carson, Sir Edward   **1854-1935**
Leader of the Irish Unionist campaign against the Parliament Act. P.P. by Baird of Belfast.

Carter, A.J.
Publisher, 17 Terminus Rd., Eastbourne. Cards supplied by E. Mack.

Carter, D. Broadfoot
Illustrator who studied at Glasgow School of Art and in Paris. Designed cards for William Lyon of Glasgow.

Carter, Nell   **1894-1965**
Actress. First appeared in musical comedy at the Aldwych Theatre, London, 1905. P.P. by Foulsham & Banfield.

Carter, Reginald Arthur Lay   **1886-1950**
Artist who contributed humorous black and white illustrations to various periodicals and designed postcards signed "Reg Carter". He lived at Southwold in Suffolk and designed sets of his own cards under the title "The Sorrows of Southwold" which were printed by the Southwold Press. Designed comic cards for many publishers including the Bradford Post Card Co., Dennis, Ettlinger, Mack, Millar & Lang, Ritchie, Salmon, Stiebel, Tuck, Valentine, Verdier and Wildt & Kray.
Illustration overleaf.

Carter, Sydney   **1874-1945**
Landscape artist. Exh. R.A. 10. Lived in Essex but moved to

Scarborough in 1919. Designed write-away and comic cards for Hildesheimer.

Carter-Paterson
Cards advertising this firm of carriers.

Carter's Little Liver Pills
Poster-type advertisements.

Cassell & Co. Ltd.   pre-1903
Publisher, La Belle Sauvage, London, E.C. Primarily book publishers but some cards were produced as "Cassell's Art Postcards" and "Cassell's Saturday Journal Portraits". They included sepia reproductions of drawings by Frederick Barnard (q.v.) depicting characters from Dickens and some coloured reproductions of well-known paintings, e.g. C.R. Leslie's "Uncle Toby and the Widow Woman". Two sets of drawings of "The Tower of London" and a set to mark "The Nelson Centenary" were also produced.

Cassells, C.I.
Publisher, Liverpool. Issued a "Renfrew Series".

Casserley, H.C.
Photographer/publisher. R.P.s of locomotives and railway stations.

Cassiers, Henri   b. 1858
Belgian landscape and marine artist. Lived in Brussels but exhibited from time to time at the Fine Art Society in London. He designed cards sold by P.G. Huardell, F.C. Southwood,

Castelli, V. *"Bonne Fête". The title has been rubber-stamped. P.U. 1932.*

and Henry Moss & Co., made sketches for cards at the Glasgow Exhibition of 1901, and painted views of ships for the Red Star Line.

Casswell Ltd.
Belfast. Produced hotel cards, e.g. Slieve Castle Hotel, Newcastle, Co. Down.

Castelli, V.   fl. c.1920-1932
Italian artist who painted pictures of children and dogs. Post-cards of his work were published in Italy.

Castle, Mrs. Vernon
Film actress. P.P. by Pathe Frères.

Castles
Postcards were published of most British castles, including, for example:

Arundel.	Inveraray.
Beaumaris.	Lowther.
Bodiam.	Pendennis.
Carnarvon.	Penrhyn.
Carlingford.	Rockingham.
Conway.	Scarborough.
Culzean.	Stirling.
Donnington.	Tonbridge.
Harlech.	Tiverton.
Hertford.	Windsor.

Refs: Sorrell, A., *British Castles,* 1973; *Historic Houses, Castles & Gardens,* annual; A.A. and Welsh Tourist Board, *Welsh Castles,* 1982.

Carter, Reginald. *"I'm Coming Home by Rail from Bournemouth". E. Mack. P.U. 1920.*

Windsor Castle from the Home Parc.

3462 B.

SCARBOROUGH CASTLE

Castles. *"Windsor Castle from the Home Parc"* [sic]. *U.B. card printed in Hamburg for the Pictorial Stationery Co. "Peacock Brand"*.

Castles. *"Scarborough Castle". Thomas Taylor & Son, Scarborough. "Queen Series"*.

Newbury. Donnington Castle

THE KEEP, ARUNDEL CASTLE

Castles. *"The Keep, Arundel Castle". Arundel Art Publishing Co. P.U. 1935*.

Castles. *"Newbury. Donnington Castle". Photochrom*.

Castrol Motor Oil
A series of advertising cards was issued in 1938 of car drivers and T.T. riders, e.g. Malcolm Campbell (in *Bluebird*), George Eyston and Jimmy Guthrie.

Catford, J.S.
Photographer who supplied views to a number of publishers in the South of England. Provided a photograph of the "ghost" at Hampton Court.
See: Ghosts.

Cathedrals
Many individual photographs of cathedrals were taken in most cathedral cities. Wells Cathedral, by Dawkes & Partridge, is a good example. There were, however, several publishers who issued sets:
(i)   London Stereoscopic Co. "Cathedrals of England".
(ii) R.P. Phillimore's "Historical Series" includes a number of cathedrals.

Cats. *"Mischief"*. Giesen Bros. Rotophot. P.U. 1904.

Cathedrals. *"The Cathedral, Exeter"*. Great Western Railway Series 5.

Cathedrals. *"Truro Cathedral"*. Frith's Series.

(iii) Tuck published six "Oilette" sets by Charles Flower.
(iv) Charles Voisey published 24 sets of cathedral views, the most comprehensive collection of the period.

Cats
Cat cards abound. Many photographs of individual cats were published and several firms issued cat series, they include:
(i)   Boots Cash Chemists, R.P.s of cats and kittens.
(ii)   Ettlinger, paintings of kittens, T. Sperlich.
(iii) Faulkner, "Cat Musicians".
(iv)   Giesen Bros.
(v)   Tuck, sets include "Catland", "Cats and Kittens", "In Kittendom".
(vi)   Valentine, XL Series, photographs.
(vii) Welch "Caught by the Camera" Series.
Cats often appear on greetings cards.
See: Wain, Louis.
Ref: Silvester, S. and Hobbs, A., 'A Guide to Cat Post-cards', *The Cat Fancier,* 1983.

Cattieri, V.
Italian artist who painted Italian scenes for Tuck's "Wide Wide World" Series.

Cattley, P.R.
Designer of comic cards, featuring army life, for Photochrom.

Cavell, Edith   **1865-1915**
Nurse Cavell was arrested by the Germans on 5 August, 1915, and charged with harbouring refugees. On 12 October she was shot. On 15 May, 1919, her body was buried in Norwich Cathedral and in 1920 a memorial to her was erected in St. Martin's Place, London. Edith Cavell remembrance cards sometimes include her portrait.

Cavendish, Lady Rachel
P.P. by Beagles.

Caves
The entrances to caves may be seen on many topographical cards. Interior views are less common. The most comprehensive series was produced by Frith. At least 60 sepia cards reflect

Cavell, Edith. *"Nurse Cavell's Memorial, London"*. Publisher unknown. R.P. P.U. 1929.

the underground wonders of Cox's Cave, Cheddar, Somerset. Chapman & Son of Dawlish produced an R.P. series of Gough's Cave, Cheddar pre-1927, when it was described as "electrically illuminated". Kent's Cavern, Torquay, also appears on R.P. cards.

C.-C.
G.M.H. Coleby-Clarke (q.v.).

"Cecily Series"
Views published by Dennis Moss of Cirencester.

"Celesque"   **c.1911-1918**
A type of coloured topographical card by Photochrom issued over a period covering W.W.I. Some cards carry the words "Passed for publication by the Press Censor".

Central London Railway
Cards of this underground system were produced by:
(i)   Photochrom, "Celesque" London views.
(ii) Giesen Bros., trains and stations.
(iii) Hartmann, scenes at stations.
(iv) Wrench, scenes at stations.
   Ref: Detailed lists in R.O.P.L., No. 16, pp. 4-6.

Cerebos Table Salt
Chromolithograph advertising cards depicting tropical and arctic scenes with the sub-title "Used in all parts of the World".

№ 22 Cox's Cave, Cheddar.

Caves. *"Cox's Cave, Cheddar. Visited by H.M. King Edward VII. 600 Caves Visited by M. Martel, Paris. Cox's Admired the Most". "Cox's Series" by Frith. P.U. 1908.*

C.E.S.
Initials used by the artist C.E. Shand (q.v.).

Chairman "Cigarette" Series
Twenty-four postcard-size cigarette cards on "Old English Pottery & Porcelain".
   See: R.J. Lea Ltd.

Chalker
Designer of comic postcards.

Chamberlain, Sir Austen   **1863-1937**
Statesman, Chancellor of the Exchequer 1903-6 and 1919-21. Foreign Secretary 1924-9. P.P. by Rapid Photo Printing Co.

Chamberlain, Joseph   **1836-1914**
Statesman. After a distinguished political career he resigned from his Government post because he failed to persuade his

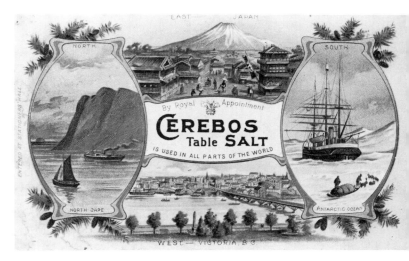

Cerebos Table Salt. *Advertising card.*

Char-à-banc Tours. *The departure for a tour. Photographer and location unknown.*

Char-à-banc Tours. *"Motor Drive, Showing Both Piers, Brighton". Valentine's "Valesque" Series. P.U. 1928.*

colleagues to support his programme for tariff reform. From 1903 to 1906 he carried out an intensive campaign for imperial preference. This brought him before the public eye and the cartoonists had a heyday. Many cartoons appeared on postcards. Ill. D. & M. 112.

Champion's Vinegar
Advertising cards, e.g. a lady holding a bottle of vinegar.

Chandler, S.A., & Co.   fl. c.1910-1926
Photographer/publisher. R.P.s of Devon scenes.

Chaplin, Charles Spencer   1889-1977
Film star Charlie Chaplin started his career in music halls. Made his first film for the Keystone Co. in 1914 and subsequently became one of the founders of the United Artist Corporation. P.P.s by Essanay and Rotary.

Chaplin, Stanley T.   fl. 1920-1939
Black and white artist who designed cards under the title "A Cornish Litany" dealing with the supernatural.

Chapman & Son   pre-1919
Photographer/publisher, Dawlish, Devon. R.P.s of Devon, Somerset and Berkshire. Serial nos. over 16,000.

Chapman, E.
Publisher, Salcombe, Devon. Local views.

Chapman & Hall
Publisher, 11 Henrietta St., London. Issued a set of cards reproducing the designs on the covers of the monthly paperback instalments of the novels of Charles Dickens.

Char-à-banc Tours
In the days when relatively few people owned a motor car the char-à-banc tour was extremely popular. The char-à-banc would seat 20 to 30 people and a day or evening excursion of 50 or 60 miles opened up new vistas. They were open cars but had folding hoods which could be raised.

Most char-à-banc cards are privately printed photographs for the use of passengers. Cards often show rows of parked char-à-bancs on the seafronts of holiday resorts.

Chard, Dorothy
Actress. P.P. by Rotary.

Charlet, Jane A.   fl. 1923-1932
Belgian artist who painted glamour cards.

Charlton, J.G.
Photographer/publisher, 14 Mercury Lane, Canterbury. Local views, some hand-coloured.

"Charterhouse Series"
See: Julius Bendix.

Chase, Pauline   1885-1962
Actress. First London stage appearance 1901. In 1904 played in Barrie's *Pantaloon* and gave two performances before the King and Queen at Windsor. Played *Peter Pan* several times. P.P.s by Aristophot, Beagles, Rotary, and Vertigen.

POST CARD.

Inland ½d.
STAMP
Foreign 1d.

THE ADDRESS ONLY TO BE WRITTEN HERE.

CHARLES FROHMAN
PRESENTS

PETER PAN or The Boy Who Wouldn't Grow Up

By J. M. BARRIE

PAULINE CHASE
AS
PETER PAN.

King's Theatre, Hammersmith
Special Attraction for one week only.
Commencing Monday, 23rd Mar., 1914.
Matinees, Wednesday, Thursday & Saturday.

Chase, Pauline. *Typical advertising card for a theatre production. Reverse side shows the statue of Peter Pan in Kensington Gardens.*

Chatterton, F.J.S.
Designer of a set on Prize Poultry for Tuck.

Chaucer Postcard Publishing Co.
129 Railton Rd., Herne Hill, London, S.E.

Cheesewright, Ethel S.   **fl. 1896-1913**
Miniaturist. Designed cards for Robert Peel of Oxford.

Cheetham, R.A.
Photographer/publisher, Station Rd., Woburn Sands, Buckinghamshire. R.P. local views.

Chelsea Pensioners
Views of Chelsea Hospital and the pensioners were published by Stengel & Co.

Chéret, Jules   **1836-1932**
French art nouveau artist who designed a series called "Seasons of the Year".

Cheshire Lines Railway   **fl. 1907-1919**
Issued a single set of 12 cards with views of Liverpool, Southport and Cheshire.

Chess
The game of chess is seldom featured on postcards. A few, however, deal with it in a humorous vein, e.g. Bamforth's "Chessnuts".

Chevalier, Maurice   **1888-1972**
Stage and film star. P.P. by *Picturegoer*.

Cheviot, Lilian   **fl. 1894-1902**
Animal painter whose work was used by Wildt & Kray.

C. & H.G.
C. & H. Gurnsey (q.v.).

Chidley, A.
Painter of regimental scenes for Gale & Polden, and warships for the Ruskin Studio Art Press.

Childeric, A.
Publisher, Leicester. Facsims. of painting of the Leicester area in a "Wyvern" Series.

Chiostri, Carlo   **fl. 1920s**
Art deco artist whose work includes small children. Cards were published by Ballerini & Fratini of Florence, Italy, and imported into Britain. They are highly valued.
    See: Colour Plate 10.

C.H.N.C.
C.H. Nadin, Chesterfiled (q.v.).

"Christchurch Series"
    See: W.S. Cowell.

Christian Novels Publishing Co.   **pre-1908**
Give-away cards which bear the following wording: "This beautiful series of Fine Art Post Cards is supplied free exclusively by Christian Novels Publishing Co. for pure reading matter 'Christian Novels' is the World's Best." This wording is almost the same as that on give-away cards by Shurey's Publications (q.v.).The cards were printed by Delittle, Fenwick & Co., York.

Christiansen, Hans   **b. 1866**
Art nouveau artist who studied in Munich and Paris. His work is highly valued.

Chelsea Pensioners. *"Recreation Room, Chelsea Hospital"*. O.F. (Stengel & Co., Ltd.). P.U. 1919.

Christie, A.   **pre-1926**
Publisher, Oyne, Aberdeenshire. Local views.

Christie, George Fyffe   **fl. c.1900-1920**
Artist who designed cards for several publishers including William Lyon of Glasgow, Misch & Co., Photochrom, William Ritchie's "Reliable" cards for the Scottish Exhibition of 1901, and Wrench. His cards have a Scottish flavour.

Christmas Cards
    See: Greetings Cards.

Christy, F. Earl   **1883-1961**
American artist who specialised in glamour. His cards were published by Reinthal & Newman.

Chrom-Art Publishing
London, W.C.1. P.P.s of royalty.

Chromo
A misleading abbreviation sometimes used by postcard dealers which could be interpreted in several ways, i.e. colour-printing of chromographs or of chromolithographs.

Chromograph
Colour reproduction using a gelatine copying apparatus in which aniline dye is used for ink.

Chromolithograph
Colour printing from a lithographic limestone of which the finest quality stone is found in Bavaria; it is not surprising, therefore, that some of the foremost colour printers operated in Germany or Austria. Many British publishers sent their printing work abroad before W.W.I., including Faulkner, Tuck, and Stewart & Woolf.

Chronicle Co. Ltd.
Publisher, Scott Lane, Doncaster. Issued over 500 cards including election propaganda.

Church Army
Publisher. R.P.s of choirs and personalities.

Church, B.W.
Artist who designed aviation cards for Salmon.

Churches. *"Interior, Ramsbury Church"*. *Tomkins & Barrett, Swindon. P.U. 1923.*

Church Family Newspaper
Publisher of cards advertising the paper using R.P.s of churches and churchmen by Mayall & Co.

Church Lads' Brigade
R.P.s of activities, e.g. a camp at Felixstowe.

Churches
There is a postcard view of almost every church in Britain and the very fact that this category is so common may well have discouraged collectors. Some do, however, collect examples from their own area or from a single county. There are collectors of Suffolk churches, for example, a county well endowed with fine examples.

Churchill, E.   **pre-1912**
Publisher, Pier View, Swanage, Dorset. Local R.P. views.

Churchill, Rt. Hon. Winston S.   **1874-1965**
Portrait when he was First Lord of the Admiralty in 1914. R.P. by Valentine. Ill. Holt 79.

C.I.C.L.
C.I. Cassells, Liverpool (q.v.).

Cinema
The first performance of projected moving pictures or cinematograph to be given before a paying audience was in Paris in 1895. The following year performances were given in London at the Empire Theatre, Leicester Square, and at the Alhambra. A cinema called "Hale's Tours of the World" was at 165 Oxford St., London, from 1906 to 1912. It was fitted out like a railway coach and showed a film called "Scenes from Many Lands". Similar cinemas opened in Leeds and Manchester. They were advertised on postcards.
   Ref: Mellow, G., 'Hale's Tours of the World', P.P.M., January 1983, p. 4.

Cinema Organists
In the mid-1920s special organs were installed in the larger cinemas which employed a full-time organist. Compton and Wurlitzer were the names of the organs familiar to cinemagoers. The organists, some of whom broadcast on radio, became popular figures. A few appear on commercial postcards, others had postcard-size photographs taken which could be signed and sent to their fans. Well-known names include Al Bollington, H. Robinson Cleaver, Reginald Dixon, Quentin Maclean, Sandy McPherson, Reginald New and G.T. Pattman.

Circus
The circus was first made popular as a form of entertainment when Lord George Sanger (1825-1911) travelled all over Europe with his show. Postcards were sometimes used to advertise circus shows and occasionally pictures were taken by local photographers of the circus site and of circus stars. The Barnum and Bailey Circus, Fossett's Grand Circus and the Sanger Circus may all be found on cards, usually depicting performing animals.
   See: Buffalo Bill.

City Post Card Co.   **fl. 1916-1927**
Publisher, London, E. Coloured views. Comic cards by George Piper and romantic wartime cards.
   See: D. Eisner.

Clacton Graphic Co. Ltd.   **pre-1915**
Publisher, Clacton-on-Sea, Essex. Some cards supplied by Tuck.

Clapsaddle, Ellen E.   **1865-1934**
American artist particularly noted for child subjects.

Cinema. *"The New Egyptian Hall, 170 Piccadilly"* and the adjacent *"Cinematograph Tea Rooms"*. *Printed by Alf Cooke Ltd.*

Clarkson, R. *"A Bit of Old Scarborough, Parkin Lane"*. *Facsim. by E.T.W. Dennis in the "Dainty Series"*.

Clark, Bennett
Photographer/publisher. Local views, e.g. Boscobel House.

Clark, Christopher   1875-1942
Designer of cards for F.C. Southwood.

Clark, E.J. & H.
Publisher, East Finchley, Middlesex. Local R.P. views.

Clark, Ingram, & Co.
Publisher, Ilfracombe, Devon. Local views.

Clark, S.
Landscape artist noted for winter scenes. Facsims. by Faulkner.

Clarke, Charles Allen   fl. c.1907-1914
Publisher and artist. 47 Osborne Rd., Blackpool. Used the pseudonym of Teddy Ashton. His cards, some of which were published by E.R. Green & Co., deal with the marriage problems of Sammy and Sally. His cards under the Ashton imprint deal in a humorous style with his holiday town. He also published the work of other comic artists.

Clarke, J., & Son
Publisher, Guildford, Surrey. "Simile Carbon Series" of local views.

Clarke, Joseph Clayton   fl. 1882-1900
Illustrator and caricaturist who used the pseudonym Kyd. He is best known for his illustrations of Dickens' works. These were followed by:

(i)   Three sets of Dickens characters by Faulkner, nos. 497-9.
(ii) Dickens' Series by Tuck, U.B. cards chromographed in Bavaria.
(iii) "Studies from Life by Charles Dickens" by Welch & Sons.
(iv) Dickens character cards by E. Wrench Ltd.
    In addition Kyd designed a series for Hildesheimer, "Heads — and the Tales They Tell"; and for the Pictorial Stationery Co., "People Who Ought to be Kidnapped".

Clarke, Scotson
Artist who designed a set titled "Dainty Damsels" for McCaw, Stevenson & Orr.

Clarke & Sherwell Ltd.
Firm which produced cards for the Royal Botanic Gardens, Kew, London, in the 1930s.

Clarkson, G.T.
Artist who painted scenes for Tuck's "In the Air" Series during W.W.I.

Clarkson, Joseph
Publisher, Manchester. Issued a card in 1916 in aid of the Belgian Soldiers' Fund.

Clarkson, Robert   fl. 1880-1914
Yorkshire landscape painter. Exh. R.A. 4. Contributed views of Scarborough to E.T.W. Dennis's "Dainty Series".

Clay Cross Company
A coal mining company which won a gold medal for its coal in 1908 and marked the award by publishing a set of 25 cards showing their miners at work.

Claymore Whisky
This firm used a Harry Payne card by Tuck to advertise its whisky.

Clayton, H.
Publisher, Monmouth. Local views.

Clayton, Henry
Clerkenwell artist who designed transparencies for the Marks firms.

Clayton, J. Hughes   fl. 1891-1929
Liverpool artist who exhibited frequently at the Walker Art Gallery. Designed cards for Lever Bros. Ltd. under the general title "Pictorial Post Cards of Port Sunlight."

Clayton & Shuttleworth
    See: Traction Engines.

Clearwell
The pseudonym of a postcard designer who painted comic pictures of children.
    See: Albert Carnell.

Clee, W.
Publisher, 150 High St., Cheltenham, Gloucestershire. Local black and white views.

Clegg, John
Manchester artist who designed cards for the Continental Post Card Co.

Clement & Sons
Publisher, Aldershot, Hampshire. R.P. views.

Clifford, Camille
Actress noted for her part in *The Catch of the Season,* 1904, in

Climbing. *Portrait of a climber by an unknown photographer.*

which she sang "Why do they call me a Gibson girl?" P.P.s by Beagles; Odol, advertisement; Philco; Rapid Printing; Rotary, ill. Hill p. 25; Rotoprint.

Clift & Ryland
Publisher, Stow-on-the-Wold. Local sepia views.

Climbing
Photographic cards sometimes show climbers in action, resting with their equipment or standing proudly on summits. Few carry the name of a publisher. An exception is G.P. Abraham.
Ref: Byatt p. 25 and ill. 7.

Clinch, A.
Stationer, Langton, Kent. Cards supplied by H. Camburn.

Clocks
Clocks are often visible in street scenes but are usually so small that they have little impact. Larger clocks, especially those in clock towers, are exceptions. Floral clocks attract a good deal of attention in summer.
See: Town Halls.

Cloke, Rene   **fl. 1930s**
Painter of birds, fairies and children for Faulkner, the Medici Society, Salmon, and Valentine.

Clough
Publisher, Skipton, Yorkshire.

Cluff, Lucy Elizabeth
Dublin artist who designed patriotic cards for the "Shamrock Series" by the Irish Pictorial Card Co.

Clyde Shipping Co. Ltd.
Advertising cards.

C.M. & Co.
C. Modena & Co. (q.v.).

C.M.B.
Cicely Mary Barker (q.v.).

Coaching
Horse-drawn coaches were still operating on British roads when the first picture postcards were published and a few photographic cards show them, usually outside an inn. However, there was a market for nostalgic cards depicting the real coaching days of the 19th century. Several series were published by:
(i) Faulkner, facsims. after Alan Wright and Vernon Stoke.
(ii) Tuck, Oilette cards including "Coaching", two sets after

Clocks. *"Jubilee Clock, Weymouth". Millar & Lang's "National Series". P.U. 1908.*

Clocks. *"Floral Clock, West Princes Street Gardens, Edinburgh". Durie, Brown & Co., Edinburgh.*

Gilbert White: "Coaching Days" and "Coaching Scenes".

Coal Mining
See: Collieries; Mine Disasters.

Coates, A.
Landscape artist.

Coates, H.
Photographer/publisher, Wisbech, Cambridgeshire. R.P. views.

Cobbe, H. Bernard   fl. c.1895-1918
Animal painter who lived in London and designed Oilette sets for Tuck including "Among the Bunnies", "When Cats are Kittens" and "When Dogs are Puppies."

Cock, Stanley
Cartoonist. Designer of comic cards.

Cody, William Frederick
See: Buffalo Bill.

Coe Collotype Co.
Printer/publisher, Bradford, Yorkshire. Humorous cards including a set on the names of the Continents.

Coffin, Charles Hayden   1862-1935
Actor and vocalist, best known for his song "Queen of My Heart". P.P.s by Rotary and Tuck.

Coffin, Ernest
Photographer who worked for the Fleetway Press at the British Empire Exhibition, Wembley, in 1924.

Coin Cards
A number of countries produced cards with illustrations of their coinage accompanied by a table giving exchange rates. Some are embossed. Max Heimbrecht was a noted German publisher of coin cards.

Colborne, Lawrence
Artist who designed comic cards, especially wartime propaganda cards ridiculing the enemy. Publishers Mack, and Salmon.

Cole, Edwin
Landscape painter whose views of Shropshire and the Welsh Border were used by L. Wilding of Shrewsbury.

Coleby-Clarke, G.M.H.   1916
Publisher, 53 Poland St., London, W. W.W.I. subjects — tanks, zeppelins, etc.

Coleman, William Stephen   1829-1904
Landscape and figure painter. At one time Director of Minton's London Art Pottery and Studio. Designed a set for Tuck titled "Sweet Childhood".

Coley, Hilda May   fl. 1920s
Flower painter who was born in Bristol and studied at the Liverpool School of Art. She designed two sets of cards for the Medici Society — "The Herb Garden" nos. 1 and 2.

Collecting
The collecting of picture postcards started in the 19th century and spread rapidly between 1900 and 1914. The International Association of Postcard Collectors met in Berlin in 1898 and the following year similar meetings with exhibitions were held in Geneva, Nice and Venice. Collecting was naturally encouraged by publishers and Edwardian albums often contain

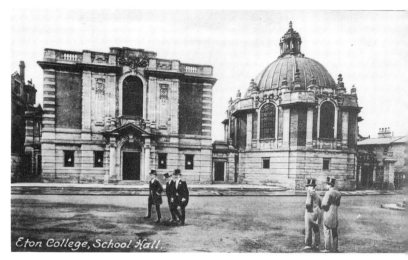

Colleges. *"Eton College, School Hall". Frith's Series.*

Colleges. *"Technical College, Colchester". Valentine's Series. P.U. c.1920.*

more unused cards than cards that have passed through the post. Raphael Tuck & Sons included a paragraph on their printed packets which referred to "Two Thousand collectors in every part of the World whose names appear in Tuck's *Postcard Exchange Register*", a document offered "post free on application".

Collectors' Clubs
Today few towns or cities are without a Postcard Collectors' Club. Other clubs exist to do specialist research, the members linked often only by post. These include:
The Canal Card Collectors' Circle.
The Exhibition Study Group.
The Fairground Postcard Society.
Judges Study Group.
Louis Levy Collectors' Society.
Pier Postcard Collectors' Circle.
A.R. Quinton Society.   *continued*

Collieries. *"Ludlows Colliery, Radstock"*. *Regal Art Publishing Co.*

Collieries. *"Ripping Top"*. *Western Mail. " Colliery Series".* *P.U. 1909.*

Royalty Postcard Collectors' Club.
Tuck Collectors' Circle.
Inevitably the officers of these clubs are liable to change from time to time. Details are frequently published in P.P.M.

Collectors' Publishing Co. Ltd., The   fl. c.1902-1907
Publisher and retail trader, 101 Fleet St., London. A firm which published a few Boer War cards but existed mainly to sell sets of postcards direct to collectors. They were closely associated with the magazine *The Picture Postcard*.

Colleen Shampoo and Soap
Advertising cards with vignettes of glamorous young ladies.

Colleges
Public schools, technical colleges and university colleges are commonly found on cards. The example of Eton College is of more interest for the styles of dress than the buildings.
Illustrations previous page.
See: Cambridge Picture Post Card Co.; Oxford Colleges.

Collier, Constance   1878-1955
Actress. After a successful career in London and New York she started a film career in 1915. Published her reminiscences under the title *Harlequinade,* 1929. P.P.s by Philco, Rapid Photo Printing Co., and Tuck "Bookmarker" Series.

Collieries
A "Colliery Series" published by the Western Mail Ltd., Cardiff, shows miners at work. The cards were designed by an artist who signed with the initials "J.M.S." Apart from this series, views of individual mines exist, including:
 Barrow, near Barnsley, Yorkshire.
 Celynen, Newbridge, Monmouthshire.
 Cwm, Merthyr Tydfil, Glamorgan.
 Cwmamman, Carmarthenshire.
 Cwmpennar, Mountain Ash, Glamorgan.
 Cwmtillery, Abertillery, Monmouthshire.
 Ferndale, Glamorgan.
 Fitzwilliam, Hemsworth, Yorkshire.
 Hamstead, Great Barr, Staffordshire.
 Hemsworth, Yorkshire.
 Houghton Main, Yorkshire.
 Llanover, Monmouthshire.
 Llwynypia, Glamorgan.
 Maypole, Abram, nr. Wigan, Lancashire.
 Midsomer Norton, Somerset.
 Old Colliery, Abercarn, Monmouthshire.
 P.D. Colliery, Bargoed, Glamorgan.
 Prince of Wales, Abercarn, Monmouthshire.
 Princess Royal, Forest of Dean, Gloucestershire.
 Radstock, Somerset.
 Tillery Collieries, Pen-y-Bont, Monmouthshire.
 Senghenydd, Glamorgan.
 Silkstone, Hoyland, Yorkshire.
 Silverdale Collieries, Staffordshire.
 Vivian's, Abertillery, Monmouthshire.
 West Stanley, Durham.
 Wharncliffe, Yorkshire.
 Whitehaven, Cumberland.

Collins, G.T.
Designer of glamour cards for Regal Art Publishing Co.

Collins, William, Sons & Co.   1903
Publisher, Herriot Hill, Glasgow. Cards were grouped in a "Herriot Series" and some first class artists were used such as Tom Browne and Louis Wain.
Ref: Byatt lists 14 sets, p.58.

Collister, D.
Photographer/publisher, Waverley Terrace, Broadway, Douglas, I.O.M. R.P. views. Series numbers exceed 500. Photographs supplied to Valentine.

Collotype
A print made from a plate coated with a sensitised gelatine emulsion. It is exposed to light in contact with a photographic negative and hardens in proportion to the transparency of the negative. The ink is accepted in proportion to the hardening so that fine detail is retained.

Colls, Harry   fl. 1882-1903
Landscape and marine painter. Exh. R.A. 4. Designed some early views for Faulkner.

Colman, Ronald   1891-1958
British actor who went to America in 1920 and became a Hollywood film star.

Colombo, E. *Child on horseback.*

Colman's Mustard/Starch
Advertising cards. Series of coloured views of abbeys and a "Postmen of the British Empire" Series. Poster reproduced in Tuck's "Celebrated Posters" Series.

Colombo, E.
Italian artist who painted small children with horses and glamorous ladies with dogs.
    See: Colour Plate 15.

Combas, Ghisbert   **1869-1941**
Art nouveau artist born at Anvers. His work is highly valued.

Combridge's Library
Publisher, Hove, Sussex. "Sunny Sussex" Series of coloured local views.

Comicus
Pseudonym used by Harry Parlett (q.v.).
    See: Colour Plate 12.

Comicus. *"I've Seen Her in White..."* Publisher unknown. P.U. 1916.

Comparisons. *"Hereford, Old House"*. Frith's Series. P.U. 1907.

Comparisons. *"Old House, Hereford"*. Publisher unknown.

"Commercial Series"
    See: J.W. Bland.

Commercial Vehicles
    See: Heavy Goods Vehicles.

Comparisons
It is interesting to compare the work of photographers. The two views of the Old House, Hereford, must have been taken, c.1905, from very nearly the same standpoint.

Composite Sets
Some sets of cards were printed like a jigsaw puzzle so that the purchaser had to fit them together before a complete picture was revealed.

Compton, Fay   **1894-1978**
Actress. First stage appearance in 1911 at the Apollo Theatre in The Follies which ran for two years. She started a film career in 1917. P.P. by Rotary.

Concert Halls. *"Albert Hall, London". View by an unknown publisher.*

Concert Halls
Concerts attracted many music lovers in Edwardian times, anxious to hear Melba and Patti sing and Kubelik and Kreisler play. The Albert Hall, London, which had been built in 1871, was the main rendezvous in London but most cities had a large hall which could be used for the purpose, e.g. The Free Trade Hall, Manchester, built in 1856, and the Colston Hall, Bristol, built in 1868. Most of these halls are to be found on postcards.

Concert Parties
The theatres and music halls which provided a main source of entertainment in late Victorian and Edwardian times existed only in towns large enough to support them. Small towns and villages had to depend on touring companies and concert parties. J.B. Priestley wrote about the experiences of such a group in *The Good Companions*, 1929. Such groups were sometimes photographed and postcards made available either

Concert Parties. *"Gilbert Rogers Jovial Jesters. Season 1909". Publisher unknown.*

for publicity or as mementoes of an occasion. The "Gilbert Rogers Jovial Jesters" card, taken in 1909, is a good example.
Ref: Other concert parties on cards are described by Michael Rouse in P.P.M., May 1983, p. 18.

"Constable's Country"
Wildt & Kray facsim. series of "Jotter" paintings. Photochrom also issued a "Phototype" Series of sepia prints with this title.

Constance, D., Ltd.
Publisher, 4A Ivy Lane, Paternoster Row, London, E.C. A company formed to use many of the earlier designs of Donald McGill under the title of "New Donald McGill Comics".

Continental Post Card Co.
Publisher, 33 Oxford St., Manchester. A firm which issued hundreds of comic cards which were printed in Shipley, Yorkshire.

Continental Tyres
Advertising cards.

Cook, A.
Photographer/publisher, St. Mary Bourne, Hampshire. Local views phototyped in Berlin.

Cook, C.K.
Designer of comic cards for Valentine.

Cook, Edward, & Co.
Publisher, Bow, London, E. Issued a "Lightning Series of Flying Machine Postcards".

Cooke, Alf, Ltd.
Printer of postcards; premises in Leeds and London.

Cooksey, S.J.
Stationer/publisher, Cinderford, Gloucestershire. Panoramic cards of local Forest of Dean views.

Coop, Hubert, R.B.A.   fl. c.1895-1925
Landscape and coastal painter. Exh. R.A. 19. Facsims. of his work were used by Photochrom.

Cooper, Alfred Heaton   1864-1929
Landscape watercolour artist. Exh. R.A. 15. Lived for many years at Ambleside in the Lake District. His book illustrations for the A. & C. Black books on *The English Lakes* and *The Norfolk Broads* were reproduced as postcards.

Cooper, Arthur Neville   b. 1850
Vicar of Filey, Yorkshire, from 1880 to 1935, and known as "The Walking Parson". Crossing the Channel, he walked to Rome and other European cities. He appears on postcards with his famous walking stick.
Ref: Clarkson, S., 'Man of Mileage', P.P.M., December 1981, p. 22.

Cooper, D.
Photographer/publisher, Markland Hill, Bolton, Lancashire. Local R.P. views.

Cooper, F.C.   pre-1910
Photographer/publisher, Eastbourne, Sussex. Local R.P. views.

Cooper, G.A.   pre-1909
Photographer/publisher, Maidstone, Kent. Local R.P. views in a "Cooper's Series" and a "Kent Series" which had a prancing horse on a shield as a trademark with the word "Invicta" beneath.

"Constable's Country". "Bridge and Cottage, Flatford". One of a Photochrom "Phototype" Series.

Cooper, Gary   **1901-1961**
American actor who became a film star with the first all-talkie — *The Virginians*, 1929.

Cooper, Gladys   **1888-1971**
Actress who appears on more postcards than any other stage personality. Her much-photographed aunt, Marie Studholme, took Gladys under her wing to the studios and she soon became the "most photographed child in London". She appeared on the stage in Colchester in 1905 as Bluebell in *Bluebell in Fairyland*, and the following year played in London. She made her first film — the first of 45 — in 1914. Gladys Cooper was regarded as a great beauty and her portraits appear on every kind of postcard — the straight portrait, in scenes from plays and films, on all types of greetings card, and with all kinds of props from dogs to garden rakes. At least 16 different publishers used her photographs including Aristophot, Beagles (13 different poses), J.W. Bland, Corona, Faulkner, Haydock, Hildesheimer, Lilywhite, Philco, Rotary (over 24 different poses), Savory, Stage Photo Co., Schwerdtfeger, Valentine, and Wildt & Kray.
  Gladys Cooper published her autobiography in 1931.

Cooper, M.B.
Artist who designed children's cards in the 1920s.

Cooper, Montague
Photographer/publisher, Taunton, Burnham, Lynton and Wellington. Views of North Devon and Somerset, sometimes tinted.

Cooper, Phyllis   **b. 1895**
London artist who specialised in child subjects. She designed a card for an Ovaltine advertisement and Christmas cards for Tuck's Happy Land Series, 2250.
  See: Colour Plate 11.

Cooper, Reginald
Sporting artist for F.C. Southwood. Each card has an amusing "coat of arms" appropriate to the sport.

Cooperative Press Ltd.
Printers, Newcastle upon Tyne. Printed postcards for Bamforth and other publishers.

Cooperative Wholesale Society
Advertising cards. The Society which was established in 1863 has its headquarters in Manchester. The address given on most advertising cards is Silvertown, an industrial suburb of southeast London. However, with a countrywide organisation a number of centres were advertised, e.g. the C.W.S. London Tea Department, etc. The cards were printed at Reddish, near Stockport, Lancashire.

Copping, Harold   **1863-1932**
Illustrator and traveller. Exh. R.A. 18. His work was used in facsims. by the Religious Tract Society. They include biblical scenes and scenes from *The Pilgrim's Progress*. He also painted a Tuck "Oilette" set of "Dickens' Characters", 3407.
  Illustrations overleaf.

Coppock, A. & E.   **pre-1911**
Publisher, Blackpool. Trademark a coat of arms with the word "Progress" on a ribbon below. Comic cards with captions in Lancashire dialect.

Coracles
The skiffs with their light wooden frames covered with hides and made waterproof with pitch were used by fishermen on several rivers in Wales, notably the Towy. They appear on postcard views.

Cooperative Wholesale Society. "C.W.S. Pelaw Liquid Metal Polish — Marvellous!!!" C.W.S. advertising card.

The Hope of the World
By Harold Copping

Copping, Harold. *"The Hope of the World"*. London Missionary Society.

Corbella, Tito. *Glamour card in the art deco style. P.U. 1932.*

Corbella, Tito   **b. 1885**
Prolific art deco artist who painted glamorous ladies. His post-cards, designed in the late 1920s and early 1930s were printed and published in Italy. He also painted an Edith Cavell set. His cards were imported into Britain in considerable quantities.
   See: Colour Plate 2.

Corbett, A.
Photographer, 2 Orchard St., London, W. R.P.s of actresses.

Corbyn, J.J.
Publisher, 68-9 York St., London, W.1. Souvenir postcard marking the Nelson Centenary.

Cordingley, George Richard   **fl. c. 1890-1904**
Landscape artist. Exh. R.A. 2. Specialised in coastal scenes. His "Tug bringing in the fishing boats" was included in Tuck's "Oilette Connoisseur" Series and he contributed a "Wide Wide World" set on "Boulogne".

Corke, C. Essenhigh, F.R.P.S.
Artist and photographer, 39 London Rd., Sevenoaks. His photographs were used to illustrate books on ornithology and on the Sevenoaks district in Kent, including the house at Knole, one of the largest private houses in England. Also a watercolour artist, the first to paint views which were used in facsims. by the local publisher, Salmon, c.1903.

Corkett, F.T., & Co.
Publisher, Leicester. One of the first publishers of picture postcards.

Copping, Harold. *"Mr. Pickwick Addresses the Club"*. *Raphael Tuck & Sons. "Oilette" Dickens' Characters.*

Corona Publishing Co. *"Coronation Series". Trademark of the Corona Publishing Co. with the address of their London premises.*

Corona Publishing Co.   **pre-1906**
Publisher, 44 Abingdon St., Blackpool, and 260 High Holborn, London, W.C. Trademark "Coronation Series" within a circle surmounted by a crown. Output included:
(i) General views.
(ii) Greetings cards.
(iii) Several named series, e.g. "Regal", "Rose".
(iv) R.P.s of stage celebrities.
(v) Anti-suffragette cards.
(vi) Comic cards.

Corris Railway
This small Welsh line ran from the Dovey Valley through Llwyngwern and Escairgeiliog to Corris serving the scenic district embracing Tal-y-llyn Lake and Cader Idris. Four series of photographic views have been recorded — a Corris Railway Series and others by George of Machynlleth, a local firm, George & Son of Brecon, and Renaud of Chorlton-cum-Hardy.
 Ref: R.O.P.L., No. 5, p. 9 gives detailed list.

Cortez, Ricardo   **b. 1899**
American leading man groomed to be a Latin lover in films of the 1920s. P.P. by *Picturegoer.*

Cosburn, George J.   **pre-1912**
Publisher, Caxton Printing Works, Market Place, Newbury, Berkshire. Local black and white views.

Cosser, Whitfield & Co.
Publisher, Salisbury and Devizes. R.P.s of Hampshire and Wiltshire.

Cossins, Thomas
Artist who designed postcards for the York Pageant of 1909.

Costard, S.H.
Publisher, 5 Colomberie, Jersey, C.I. Sepia island views.

Costello, Maurice
Film actor. P.P. by Vitagraph Films.

Costume
Many postcards, including street scenes, reflect the costumes of the period. "Hove Lawns from Brighton Parade" is a good example. This type of card is worth studying with a magnifying glass.

Cotswold Publishing Co. Ltd.   **fl. 1909-1919**
Britannia Mills, Wotton-under-Edge, Gloucestershire. Sepia views. This firm printed many postcards for Frith.

Couch, A.J.
Watercolour artist who painted cards for E.T.W. Dennis.

Coupon Photo Co.
Publisher, Caludon Rd., Coventry. Local R.P. views.

Court Size Postcards
When the General Post Office gave the go-ahead for private companies to print postcards they had to be of a particular size. The court shape postcards, as they were called, were 4¾ by 3½ ins. and a message could only be written on the picture side. Much ingenuity was required to tailor a picture or pictures to no more than two-thirds of the space available, the rest being left for a written message. The court size limit was raised in November 1899 when the oblong size of 5½ by 3½ ins. was allowed.
 Illustration overleaf.

Courtneidge, Dame Cicely, D.B.E.   **1893-1980**
Actress with an outstanding career in musical comedy, in partnership with her husband, Jack Hulbert. P.P. by Rotary.

Costume. *"Weston-super-Mare, Madeira Cove". A Photo-chrom "Celesque" Series seaside view.*

Costume. *"Hove Lawns from Brighton Parade". Valentine.*

69

POST CARD.

Court Size Postcards. *Advertising card by James Donnely of 3, 5 & 7 Henshaw St., Oldham. "Wholesale and Retail Pork Butcher, Lard Refiner, etc."*

Courtney, Kathleen
Actress who played in Aladdin. P.P. by Rotary.

Cowell, W.S., Ltd.   **pre-1907**
Publisher, The Corner Shop, Ipswich, and The Corner Shop, Felixstowe. Trademark "Christchurch" or "Christchurch Pictorial Post Cards". Output included:
(i) Local views, including sepia views and a "Naturette" Series of coloured views.
(ii) "Fac-simile" Series. Reproductions of watercolours of Suffolk by R. Gallon.
(iii) "Parsons Norman" Series of East Anglian landscapes.

Cowham, Hilda   **fl. 1911-1930**
Watercolour painter and illustrator. Exh. R.A. 3. She was the first woman to draw for *Punch*. Designed postcards with small boys for Inter-Art and Valentine.

Cowper, William   **1731-1800**
Poet who settled in Olney, Buckinghamshire. Several cards show the home he occupied from 1767-86, now The Cowper and Newton Museum.

Cox, Crowther J.
Publisher, 12 The Crofts, Rotherham. "Ivanhoe Series" of coloured views.

"Cox's Series"
An extensive series of at least 60 cards of sepia pictures of the interior of Cox's Cave, Cheddar, Somerset, published by Frith. No. 17 is a good example, showing "The Marble Curtain" stalactite formation, carrying the following statement below the caption: "Visited by the late King Edward VII. 600 caves visited by M. Martel, Paris. Cox's admired the most."
See: Caves.

Coyne, Joseph   **b. 1867**
Actor. P.P. by Rotary as Prince Danilo in *The Merry Widow*.

Cozens, C.
Photographer/publisher, Portsmouth. Topical naval scenes.

C.P.
Charles Pinchbeck (q.v.).

C.P.C.
Initials of a firm which published photographic portraits and patriotic cards in Leicester during W.W.I.

C.P.C.C.M.
Continental Post Card Co., Manchester (q.v.).

C.P.C., London
City Postcard Co., London (q.v.).

C.P.P.C.
Cerio Photo-Printing Co.

Crail, Reginald George
Watercolour artist known for a single card which he designed for *The Daily News* in 1909. Lloyd George's budget had been rejected by the House of Lords which precipitated a General Election. The political postcard shows John Bull urging voters to "Buy the Daily News and vote for the Budget".

Cramer, Rie
Dutch artist who was an illustrator of children's books and a designer of theatrical costumes. Designed postcards with children.

Crawford, Alice   **b.1882**
Actress. P.P. by Philco.

Crawford, Joan
Film star. P.P. by *Picturegoer*.
   Ref: Walker, A., *Stardom: The Hollywood Phenomenon*, 1970, Chapter 16.

Crawford's Cream Crackers
Poster-type advertising cards.

Cribb, Stephen   **pre-1908**
Photographer/publisher, Southsea, Hampshire. Local R.P.s especially of shipping in a "Spithead Series". Supplied photographs for Singer's "Our Ironclads" Series.

Crichton, Madge   **b.1881**
Actress. P.P. in motor car by Gottschalk, Dreyfus & Davis, and in studio by Beagles, Philco, Rapid Photo Co., and Woolstone ("Melton Photolette").

Cricket
Postcards reflecting cricket fall into three categories:
(i) Views of players in the field, e.g. George Hirst and Wilfred Rhodes.
(ii) Group photographs of teams, usually test or county teams, but village and school teams are also to be found.
(iii) Portraits of individual players such as W.G. Grace, Lord Hawke, G.H. Hirst, G.L. Jessop, W. Rhodes, T. Richardson, H. Sutcliffe, J.T. Tyldesley, all test match players.
   Refs: Altham, H.S., *A History of Cricket from the Beginning to the First World War,* 1962; Golesworthy, M., *The Encyclopaedia of Cricket,* 1962, fifth ed. 1974.

"Cries of London"
Series by Rotophot, e.g. "Knives, Scissors and Razors to Grind", and by Giesen Bros.

Crisp, H.B.   **pre-1906**
Stationer/publisher, Saxmundham, Suffolk. Local black and white views.

Croft, Anne   **fl. 1930s**
Watercolour painter of Cornish scenes used by Vivian Mansell.

Cricket. *"Cricket Team, St. Mary's Schools, North Hyde"*. P.U. 1905.

G. L. Jessop, Gloucester

Cricket. *"G.L. Jessop, Gloucester"* [Cricket Club]. P.P. by E. Hawkins & Co. Published by Valentine.

Crofton Publishing Co.   **pre-1907**
Brockley, London. "Crofton Series" of coloured views.

Crofts, Ernest, R.A.   **1847-1911**
Painter of battle scenes. Exh. R.A. 40. His work was used on postcards by Langsdorff & Co.

Crombie, Charles Edward
Designer of a "Crombie Series" of comic cards for Valentine which included golfing studies.

Crosland
Publisher, Arnside, Westmorland. Local R.P. views.

Cross, J.   **fl.1898-1939**
Grantham artist who designed a "Diabolo Series" for Tuck, 9566.

Cross, Norman
Designer of railway posters reproduced by E.T.W. Dennis and Andrew Reid.

Crosse, J.R.
Photographer/publisher, Whitchurch, Shropshire. Covered the Shrewsbury railway disaster of 1907.

Cross's Library
Publisher, Folkestone. Local views printed in Germany.

Crossword Puzzles
These became popular in the 1920s. The hobby is caricatured as a national pastime in Millar & Lang's "National Series".

Crow, E.   **pre-1930**
Publisher, Canterbury, Kent. Local views.

Crown Jewels
Postcards by Gale & Polden.

Crown Motor Spirit
Poster-style advertising cards. Seven cards have been recorded with the following captions:
   "Hail Spirit! Well met!"
   "Insist on Crown..."
   "No! Don't send any other."
   "Obtainable everywhere."

   "The spirit of the past...
   "A Tower of strength."
   "Use more air..."

Crown Publishing Co.   **c.1908**
A firm which presents a problem. It clearly started in St. Albans in late Edwardian times with an address at 23 St. Catherine St. Comic cards were published in a "Crown Series" of which some were signed Karaktus. No further cards appear to have been published from St. Albans after about 1911. However, a card obviously published in 1936 showing an artist's impression of H.M. The King in his Coronation Robes bears the words: "Issued by the Crown Publishing Co., 3 Pleydell Court, Fleet St., E.C.4." with the name "Burleigh Ltd., Engravers and Printers, Bristol" on the reverse side.
   Illustration overleaf.

Crowquill, Alfred
Designer of six sets of "Dickens Character Sketches" for Stewart & Woolf.

Croxford, William Edward   **fl. 1871-1906**
Sometimes called W. Croxford Edwards. Landscape and marine painter who worked in Sussex and later in Cornwall. Exh. R.A. 5. Sussex scenes were used by Salmon and he painted sets on Brighton and Eastbourne for S. Cambridge of Hove, though these may have been printed and supplied by Salmon.

Crown Publishing Co. *Comic card in their "Crown Series".*
P.U. 1911.

Cruisers and Battle Cruisers
Postcards of cruisers and battle cruisers include His Majesty's
Ships:

Aboukin, torpedoed.	*Inflexible.*
Arethusa, damaged	*Invincible.*
at Heligoland.	*Jamaica.*
Aurora.	*Kent.*
T *Australia,* battle cruiser	*Lion.*
from Australian navy.	*Liverpool.*
Bellona, attached to 1st	*Marne.*
Battle Squadron.	*New Zealand,* broken
Blonde, attached to 3rd	up 1922.
Battle Squadron.	*Norfolk.*
Boadicea, attached to 2nd	*Nubian.*
Battle Squadron.	*Oak.*
Bristol.	*Otranto.*
Cardiff.	*Powerful.*
Carnarvon.	*Princess Mary.*
Cressy, torpedoed.	T *Queen Mary.*
Diamond.	*Renown.*
Falmouth.	*Repulse.*
Fearless.	*Sapphire.*
Glasgow.	*Sappho.*
Good Hope.	*Sheffield.*
Hampshire.	*Southampton.*
Hawke, torpedoed.	*Terrible.*
Hogue, torpedoed.	T *Tiger.*
Hood, laid down 1916.	*Topaze.*
Indefatigable.	*Warrior.*
Indomitable.	*Yarmouth.*

T indicates that the ship features in Tuck's "Our Navy"
Series.

Crystal Palace
The Crystal Palace was the main feature of the Great
Exhibition of 1851. It was re-erected at Sydenham and re-
opened by Queen Victoria in 1854 for popular entertainment.
In 1936 the building was destroyed by fire, except for the two
towers which were pulled down during W.W.II lest they
should provide landmarks for enemy planes attacking
London.

Postcards showing the building with its two towers are
common; others showing the interior are not easy to find.
Photochrom published several sepia cards showing the Crystal
Palace War Museum and Great Victory Exhibition.

"Crystoleum"
Name adopted by Valentine for glossy coloured photographic
cards with a grey white-beaded frame.

Cubitt, Edith Alice (Mrs. Andrews)   **fl. 1900-1940**
Garden and flower painter. Exh. R.A. 11. Designed cards for
Faulkner.

Cubley, Henry Hadfield   **fl. c.1884-1904**
Landscape painter. Exh. R.A. 3. Painted a great deal in
Scotland and Wales. Contributed Tuck "Oilette" sets on
Buxton, Chester, Picturesque Derbyshire and Staffordshire.

Cumbo, V.B.   **pre-1902**
Gibraltar publisher whose black and white views appear
frequently in Britain sent, no doubt, by liner passengers to the
East when making the Rock a port of call.

Cumming, Neville
Watercolour marine artist who designed a series "Bulwark of
the Empire" depicting 12 flagships of the Royal Navy.

Cummings, H.
Publisher, Weymouth. Local views.

Cunningham, J.
Publisher, Brora, Sutherland. Cards supplied from the "R.A.
Series" of tinted views.

Curran
Publisher, Crow St., Dublin. Coloured and sepia views.

Current Event Postcards
  See: Henry Stead.

Curtis, A.G.
Publisher, Guildford, Surrey.

Curwood, J.W.
Photographer/publisher, Bromley, Kent. Local R.P. views.

Cut-Outs
  See: Novelty Cards.

Crystal Palace. *"Crystal Palace. From Italian Terrace".*
Photochrom "Sepiatone" Series.

Colour Plate 4: Battleship cards

"H.M.S. Hannibal*". Birn Bros.*

"H.M.S. Queen Elizabeth*". Gale & Polden.*

"H.M.S. Dreadnought*". R. Tuck and Sons. "Our Ironclads".*

C.V.
Charles Voisey (q.v.).

C.W. & Co.
Charles Worcester & Co. (q.v.).

Cycling
A great boom in cycling followed the introduction of the pneumatic tyre. Many cycle companies were floated in the 1890s and the cycle soon became a popular means of transport and a major source of pleasure.

References to bicycles are often found in the written messages on postcards: "Arrived safely at Oakwood Hill. *Very country*. 3 miles from the station and three miles to nearest chapel. Feel rather lonely after London. I wish I hadn't sold my bicycle", 1906.

Messages on cards also describe the hazards: "Arrived home about 8 o'clock fairly dusted by motors", 1906. "Arrived home safe at 3.30. Delayed three hours at Reading. Free wheel broke — cost me 5/−", 1909.

Cycles were used not only for private purposes but also by the army. Tuck produced an "Oilette" set of the "Volunteer Cycle Corps", 9120. Many R.P.s show cycling which reached its greatest popularity between 1900 and 1914, though the interest continued after W.W.I. Cards depicting cycling personalities are not uncommon, e.g. C.B. Kingsbury, an Olympic Gold Medallist in 1908.

Many comic cards relate to cycling. A W.E. Mack "Bluette" card shows a silhouette of a cat followed by five

Cycling. *"Ted, Winner of the Evershed Cup for the one mile Club Championship in 1929, 1930 and 1931". Photo by Marriott's Photo Stores, Hastings.*

emaciated kittens. The caption reads:
"This is the cat that ate the carbide
And has a-set-o'-lean kittens."
Ref: Wilkinson-Latham, R., *Cycles in Colour,* 1978.

Cynicus (Art) Publishing Co.   **fl. 1902-1916**
Tayport, Fife, Scotland. Cynicus was the pseudonym of Martin Anderson, 1854-1932, a Glasgow cartoonist who settled in London and produced satirical books from a studio in Drury Lane in the 1880s. By 1898 he had started to design court size postcards for Blum & Degen. He soon decided to publish his own and set up the Cynicus Publishing Co. at Tayport where he produced Christmas cards and U.B. vignette cards in 1902. Many of his comic cards, which are often packed with people, were designed for the seaside resort market and were often overprinted with the name of the town where they were to be sold. A favourite theme was "The Last Train to . . . . ." which made it possible to print in the name of the resort to which the cards were sent.

Despite a vast output the firm seems to have overreached itself and it failed in 1911. However, this did not deter Anderson. He had cousins in Leeds who helped him to establish the Cynicus Art Publishing Co. in 1914. However, the eve of W.W.I. was not the time to succeed in a new business and he soon moved to a studio in Edinburgh but no more than half a dozen cards were issued from it.

See: Colour Plate 12.

Ref: A valuable study of 'Cynicus, the Man: The Postcards of Martin Anderson' appeared in P.P.A. 1983, pp. 8, 10-14, 93-5. It gives a detailed check list of Cynicus cards.

Cycling. *Lady cyclist. Note the back wheel protection against long skirts.*

Daily Mail

Publisher, Associated Newspapers, London. During W.W.I. the *Daily Mail* published a series of "Official War Photographs". These were Crown Copyright scenes passed by the Censor. It was also possible to buy a special album in which to keep them. Some official photographs were supplied by the Sport & General Press Agency Ltd., others were "Official War Photographs" published in *Daily Mail* "Battle Pictures". The majority are listed below:

Series I (coloured)
1. Wounded Tommy to the photographer: "I'm not a German".
2. Highlanders pipe themselves back from the trenches.
3. Church service before battle.
4. British heavy gun in action.
5. Helping an ambulance through the mud.
6. Sir D. Haig introducing Sir Pentab Singh to Gen. Joffre.
7. Army chaplain tending British graves.
8. Thirsty German prisoners in their barbed wire cage.

Series II (coloured)
9. Ypres after two years of war.
10. R.A.M.C. picking up wounded in a captured village.
11. A "fag" after a fight.
12. Tommy's look-out in a captured German trench at Ovillers.
13. British mine exploding at Beaumont Hamel.
14. Crawling to the German trenches under fire.
15. British machine gunners wearing gas helmets.
16. A gallant rescue under fire.

Series III (coloured)
17. Tommy finds shell holes comfortable to sleep in.
18. After the first cavalry charge 1916.
19. Firing a heavy Howitzer in France.
20. Tommy at home in German dugouts.
21. Black Watch Pipers playing to the captors of Longueval.
22. Gordons bringing in a wounded German.
23. The burial of two British soldiers on the battlefield.
24. The hero: saving a wounded comrade under fire.

Series IV (sepia)
25. Decorating a Canadian in the field of battle.
26. London Scottish going to their trenches.
27. Happy Tommies wearing Hun helmets.
28. Loyal North Lancs. Regiment cheering when ordered to the trenches.
29. As III 20.

Series V (sepia)
33. The Worcesters going into action.
35. The burial of two British soldiers on the battlefield.
36. A British heavy gun in action.
37. Highlanders pipe themselves back from the trenches.
39. British Infantry practising an attack.
40. Australians parading for the trenches.

Series VI (sepia)
41. Church service before battle.
42. The Wiltshires cheering during the great advance.
43. "The Glorious First of July, 1916" — Our first prisoners.
44. Wounded Tommy to the photographer — "I'm not a German", as I1.
45. Helping an ambulance through the mud, as I 5.
46. The Fighting Fifth (Northumberland Fusiliers) after the Battle of St. Elvi.
47. As II 9.
48. Taking in prisoners during the Great Advance.

Series VII (black and white)
49. As I 6.
50. As IV 25.
51. Star shell bursting near the British lines.
52. As I 7.
53. As VI 46.
54. As II 12.
55. As IV 26.
56. As VI 43.

Series VIII (black and white)
57. As VI 44.
58. As III 21.
59. As III 23.
60. As II 11.
61. As VI 42.
62. As II 15.
63. As IV 29.
64. A big mine exploding.

Series IX (black and white)
65. As V 37.
66. Bringing in the wounded: an early morning scene.
67. As IV 28.
68. As VII 49.
69. Night scene on the British front, 1st July, 1916.
70. As V 39.
71. Back to Blighty, boarding the leave boat.
73. As IV 27.

Series X (black and white)
74. As I 3.
75. As V 36.
76. As V 33.
77. As III 17.
78. As III 18.
79. As III 19.
80. As V 40.

Series XI (coloured)
81. The King at the Front — The Smile of Victory.
82. The King at the Front — King George and King Albert enjoying an amusing episode.
83. The King at the Front — A talk to Peasants.
84. The King at the Front — The King meets a Hospital Matron.

continued

85. The King at the Front — Attending Church Service in the Field.
86. The King at the Front — At the Grave of a Fallen Hero.
87. The King at the Front — Outside a captured German Dug Out.
88. The King at the Front — A Greeting from the Troops.

Series XII
89-96   As XI but in sepia.

Series XIII (coloured)
97. One of our monster guns.
98. A present for the Kaiser.
99. A British Chaplain writing home for Tommy.
100. The King inspecting R.N.A.S. Officers.
101. East Yorks. going into the trenches.
102. Queen of the Belgians as photographer.
103. A captured dug-out near La Boiselle.
104. A London Heavy Battery in action.

Series XIV (coloured)
105. Anti-aircraft gunners spotting a Hun plane.
106. A British labour battalion at work.
107. An advanced Field Ambulance.
108. King George greets wounded officers.
109. Captured German guns.
110. An Indian Hotchkiss gun at work.
111. A wiring party going up to the trenches.
112. Clearing the way through Contalmaison.

Series XV (coloured)
113. Hot work by Australian gunners.
114. The Black Watch return to Camp.
115. Loading a trench mortar.
116. Keeping a sharp lookout.
117. Australian heavy gun at work.
118. Wounded waiting for the field ambulances.
119. King George in a gun pit.
120. Observation balloon ascending.

Series XVI, XVII and XVIII repeat in sepia the coloured scenes in Series XIII, XIV and XV.

Daily News   **pre-1930**
Publisher of "The Daily News Wallet Guide Series" of sepia views.

Dainton, Marie   **1882-1938**
Actress and mimic. P.P. Tuck "Bookmarker" Series V.

"Dainty Novels Series"   **pre-1906**
Give-away cards in the form of black and white views supplied by Frith.

"Dainty Series"   **1901**
The trademark of E.T.W. Dennis & Sons Ltd. of London and Scarborough.

Dalby-Smith   **pre-1910**
Photographer/publisher, St. Blazey, Cornwall. Local views and events including a fine R.P. of the St. Austell Carnival in 1910.

Dale, M.E.
Publisher, Yew Barrow Terraces, Grange-over-Sands, Lancashire. Coloured local views.

Dalglish, Elsa N.   **fl. 1904-1924**
Landscape artist who lived in the Cromwell Rd., London and travelled widely in Europe. Exh. at Beaux Art Gallery. Facsims. in sepia by the Artistic Photographic Co.

Dando, W.P.
Photographer who worked on a London Zoo series for Eyre & Spottiswoode.

"Dania Glossy Real Photograph"
See: Doncaster Rotophot Co. Ltd.

Daniell, Evangeline Mary   **1880-1902**
Art nouveau artist whose work was used by Tuck in a "Modern Art" Series.

Dannatt, Walter, F.L.S.   **1904**
A keen amateur entomologist who travelled widely collecting butterflies. He owned shops in Blackheath and published his own series of postcards under the title "Beautiful Butterflies from Nature."

Dare, Phyllis   **1890-1975**
Musical comedy actress who first appeared in a London production of *The Babes in the Wood* in 1899. There followed a long career on stage and in films. P.P.s by Beagles (including bas-relief), Birn Bros., Davidson, Misch & Co., Philco, Rapid Photo Printing Co., Rotary (ill. Hill p. 23), Rotophot and Valentine.

Dare, Phyllis and Zena
The sisters were photographed together by Aristophot, Davidson Bros., Foulsham & Banfield and Valentine.

Dare, Zena   **1887-1975**
Musical comedy actress. Often photographed with her younger sister Phyllis. P.P.s by Beagles, Millar & Lang, Novelty Post Card Co., Rapid Photo Co., Rotary (ill. Hill p. 23).

Darrell, Maudi   **1883-1910**
Gaiety Girl who died at the age of 27. P.P. by Philco.

"Dauber"
Pseudonym of a designer of comic cards for Watkins & Kracke Ltd. (q.v.).

Davey, George   **fl. c.1903-1914**
Designer of comic cards for James Henderson & Sons, Misch & Stock, and Valentine, e.g. ill. D. & M. 115.

David & Carter
Publisher, London. Model toy series, e.g. "Ocean Liners".

Davidson Bros.   **pre-1902**
Publisher, Marlborough House, Basterfield St., London, E.C. Trademark an artist's palette above a globe and with the name of the company "Davidson Bros. London" beneath. Output included:
(i)   Christmas postcards and greetings cards; the firm had been publishing ordinary Christmas cards for some years.
(ii)   Pictorial postcards; a "Photo-colour" Series.
(iii)   "Real Photographic Series"; this embraces all kinds of photographs including cats.
(iv)   Comic cards, a Davidson speciality using such artists as Tom Browne, John Hassall, Phil May, Will Owen, Louis Wain and Lawson Wood. Tom Browne had a close link with the firm.
(v)   Stage cards, e.g. "Footlight Favourites", "Stage Favourites" and "Stageland".
(vi)   "Celebrities at Home".
(vii)   "Moonlight Series" including "British Cathedrals" and "The Lakes of England".

(viii) Staged romantic scenes in a "Glazette Series" with such titles as "The Convenient Stile".
(ix) National Gallery reproductions.
(x) "Arcadia Series", facsims. of Van Hier paintings, e.g. "Autumn Tints". "Winter Days", etc.

See: Colour Plate 6.

Davies, Marion   fl. c.1914-1939
Film star. R.P. by *Picturegoer*.

Davies, R.E.
Photographer for "Burrow's Royal Series" of Gloucestershire and Herefordshire views.

Davies, W.   pre-1919
Publisher, 363 Chorley Old Rd., Bolton, Lancashire. North country views.

Davis, A.B., Ltd.   pre-1906
Publisher, Epping and Loughton, Essex. Sepia views on cream card, e.g. "The Hermit of Epping Forest".

Davis, A.M., & Co.   c.1913
Printer/publisher, 11 and 12 Finsbury Sq., London, E.C., and from the mid-1920s at 85 Worship St., London, E.C. Trademark "A.M. Davis & Co. Quality Cards" or "A Davis 'Message' Postcard" printed in a rectangle. The message cards differed from most greetings cards in that they were not tied to a particular anniversary or occasion. Entering the postcard business only a year before the outbreak of W.W.I. it was inevitable that the output should include many wartime sets. "Girls of the Allies" and "Khaki Kiddies" were painted by H.G.C. Marsh Lambert, and Kaiser cartoons by Francis Brown. War Bond Campaign cards were also issued.

Timeless series included children's cards, e.g. "Fairy Whispers" (Beryl Hay) and a number of animal cards, including Louis Wain cats in a "Prize Winners" Series.

Davis, Arthur A.
Painter of sporting subjects, e.g. Tuck's "Fox Hunting".

Davis, George   d.1918
See: Davis's Oxford Post Cards.

Davis, Henry William Banks, R.A.   1833-1914
Landscape and animal painter. Exh. R.A. 125. Spent most of his life in London but retired to Rhayader in Wales in 1910;

Davis, John. Trademark of the firm's "Victoria Series" named after the address of the premises at 24 Queen Victoria St., London, E.C.

he was a very popular artist, and his pictures which were greatly in demand fetched high prices. A number were reproduced as postcards.

Davis, John   c.1902
Publisher, 24 Queen Victoria St., London, E.C. Issued a "Victoria Series" of black and white and coloured views of the Southern counties, printed in Hamburg. Davis had for five years been associated with the Pictorial Stationery Co.

Davis's Oxford Post Cards   pre-1909
Publisher, 2 Cornmarket, Oxford, and later at 7 Turl St., Oxford. Trademark Jacobean Carfax Conduit building with "Davis's Oxford Post Cards" all within the stamp rectangle. Cards reproduced paintings "by permission of *The Graphic*" and the message space on the address side is taken up entirely with explanatory text. They were not, therefore, intended to

Davies, A.M., & Co. *Message postcard. P.U. 1918.*

"SOLVITUR AMBULANDO." The Proctor's Walk at a Conferring of Degrees in the Divinity School, Oxford
By Sydney P. Hall, M.V.O.   By permission of "The Graphic"

Davis's Oxford Post Cards. *"Solvitur Ambulando. The Proctor's Walk at a Conferring of Degrees in the Divinity School, Oxford".* Sydney P. Hall.

Dawson, Lucy. *"Close Friends"*. *Signed with her pseudonym Mac. Valentine's "Tailwagger" card, 1932.*

bear a message, but merely to be sent as souvenirs of Oxford. All cards by George Davis deal mainly with college life, including academic dress. Ill. Byatt col. pl. IV, p. 170.

Davy, W.S.　　　　　　　　　　　　**pre-1908**
Devon Brewery, Newark upon Trent, Nottinghamshire. Black and white pictorial advice cards (q.v.).

Dawkes & Partridge　　　　　　　　**pre-1937**
Publisher, Cathedral Studio, High St., Wells, Somerset. Black and white and sepia views of Wells, its cathedral and surrounding countryside.

Daws, Frederick Thomas　　　　　　**b. 1878**
Painter. Exh. R.A. 12. Designer of Spratt's "Champion Dog" Series.

Dawson, Lucy　　　　　　　　　　　**fl. 1930s**
Animal artist and illustrator who designed a "Tailwagger" Series of dog postcards for Valentine. She often used the pseudonym Mac.

Dawson, William, & Sons Ltd.　　　**pre-1909**
Publisher, Exeter. South Devon views.

Day, Marcus, & Co.　　　　　　　　**pre-1918**
Publisher. Views and birthday cards.

Day, Marjorie　　　　　　　　　　　**b.1899**
Actress. P.P. by Ralph & Co., Rapid Printing Photo Co.

D.B.
Initials of an artist who designed comic cards for W. Holmes of Glasgow, and for Salmon.

D.B.E.
Durie, Brown & Co., Edinburgh (q.v.).

D.C. Ltd.
D. Constance Ltd. (q.v.).

D.D. Fitz.
Dennis Dorian Fitzsimmons (q.v.).

De Blaas, Eugene　　　　　　　　　**fl. 1882-1907**
Italian figure painter. Exh. R.A. 11. Contributed to Hildesheimer's photogravure series.

De Breanski, Alfred Jr., A.R.C.A.　　　**1877-c.1945**
Landscape painter of mountain scenery following the style of his father with whom he is often confused. Exh. R.A. 24. Facsims. of his work were used by Faulkner and Salmon.

De Dion-Bouton Co. Ltd.
Advertiser of the 8 h.p. single-seater Tonneau. Ill. D. & M. 157.

De Reszke
Cigarette manufacturers Godfrey Phillips Ltd. published postcard portraits of film stars (e.g. Jessie Matthews), dogs (e.g. "Dachshunds"), and "Garden Studies". Their cards were about ⅜ in. shorter than the standard card since they were contained in the larger packets of De Reszke cigarettes.

Deacon, Dora　　　　　　　　　　　**fl. 1894-1939**
Painter of Tuck's "Sea Shells" oil facsims.

Dean, Dora　　　　　　　　　　　　**fl. 1920s**
London artist who contributed children's cards to a Kaygee "Kiddie" Series by an unknown publisher.

Dean, Frank, R.B.A.　　　　　　　　**fl. 1886-c.1907**
Landscape artist. Exh. R.A. 26. Lived in Leeds until about 1896 when he moved to Arundel in Sussex. He travelled in Egypt and the Sudan. Facsims. of his work were used in Eyre & Spottiswoode's "Woodbury Series". These included watercolour views of Guernsey.

Deane, Barbara　　　　　　　　　　**b.1886**
Actress. P.P. with Ellaline Terriss by Rotary, and with Maisie Ash by Woolstone Bros.

Debenham, A.W.　　　　　　　　　　**pre-1910**
Photographer/publisher, Cowes, I.O.W. R.P.s of yachtsmen including portraits of royalty.

Debenham & Freebody
Advertiser, London. Views of their London stores.

De Reszke. *"Garden Studies. Aubretia and Arabis in Perpendicular Clumps on the Face of a Rock Wall"*. *No. 23 in a series of 30 cards appearing in the larger packets of De Reszke cigarettes.*

Dee, W. Henry
Publisher, Reading, Berkshire. Local views.

"Defco Series"
    See: Delittle, Fenwick & Co.

Deighton, M.S.
Publisher, The Salon, Grayshott, Hampshire. "Salon Series" of Hampshire and Surrey views.

Delgado, G.
Publisher.

Delittle, Fenwick & Co.   **1903**
Printer/publisher, Railway St., York. The firm often used initials only "D.F. & Co.", or the tradename "Defco". They issued coloured views and moonlight scenes, a "Defco Series" of comic cards including satirical sets which made fun of book titles or caricatured Chamberlain and Balfour. They printed many high quality coloured views for other publishers, e.g. Shurey's Publications.

Delivery Rounds
In Edwardian times most tradesmen delivered goods to their customers in horse-drawn vehicles which were sometimes illustrated on cards of local views.

Denney, G.
Photographer/publisher, Teignmouth, South Devon. Local views.

Dennis, E.T.W. (& Sons Ltd.)   **1901**
Publisher, Scarborough and London. Early cards have "E.T.W.D." in very small letters on the picture side. The address side has a rectangle with "Dainty Series" showing a crier with a bell and lantern in what appears to be a snowclad scene. Later cards have an art nouveau-style cartouche enclosing a rectangle with two small girls, the title, and the name of the firm which includes "& Sons Ltd.", with London and Scarborough locations. The output included:
(i)   Views, R.P.s, tinted photographs and facsims. of paintings by well-known artists.
(ii)   Greetings cards.
(iii)   Novelty cards, e.g. pull-outs, and "Mystery Silhouette" hold-to-light cards.
(iv)   Yorkshire Arms, Toasts and Sayings.
(v)   Framed photographic views of Oxford post-1918.
(vi)   "Gertie" cards.
(vii)   Hunting scenes by Warren Williams.

Dent, E., & Co. Ltd.
Advertiser, 28 Cockspur St., and 4 Royal Exchange, London. This firm of clockmakers, who made and installed the clock in the tower of the Houses of Parliament in 1858, issued a card with the tower and clock as an advertisement in Edwardian times.

D.E.R.
David Ewart Relf (q.v.).

D.E.& S., Ltd.
D. Eisner & Son Ltd. (q.v.).

Destroyers
Postcards of destroyers include His Majesty's ships:
    Acasta, disabled Jutland 1916.
    Badger, picked up survivors from H.M.S. *Invincible* 1916.
    Chelmer, picked up survivors from H.M.S. *Triumph,* May 1915.

Fortune, picked up survivors from H.M.S. *King Edward VII* off Cape Wrath, January 1916.
Fury, assisted in attempt to save H.M.S. *Audacious,* October 1914.
Marne, picked up survivors from H.M.S. *King Edward VII* off Cape Wrath, January 1916.
Musketeer, picked up survivors from H.M.S. *King Edward VII* off Cape Wrath, January 1916.
Nessus, picked up survivors from H.M.S. *King Edward VII* off Cape Wrath, January 1916. Sunk at Jutland, 1916.
Nestor, sunk at Jutland, 1916.
Nomad, sunk at Jutland, 1916.
    Ref: Manning, T.D., *The British Destroyer,* 1979.

Dewar, John, & Sons
Whisky distillers, Perth. "Gems of Art" Series with whisky advertisements on the reverse side.

Dexter, Marjorie M.   **fl. c.1925-1939**
Artist who painted child subjects. Facsims. appear in oval frames with a verse beneath on decorative greetings-type cards. Publishers included Salmon and Valentine.

D.F. & Co.
Delittle, Fenwick & Co. (q.v.).

Diabolo
A game with a two-headed top which has to be kept in the air using a string stretched between sticks held in the hands. In 1902 it became a craze which continued for several years. Cards depicting the game were issued by many publishers including: Davidson (Tom Browne), William Ritchie (G.F. Christie) and Tuck (J. Cross, G.E. Shepheard and Louis Wain).
    Ref: Check lists in P.P.M. May 1983, pp. 36-7, 39.

Dialect Cards
Occasionally cards were published with dialect captions, particularly of Devon and Yorkshire dialects.

Diamond Jubilee
A court size postcard was published to commemorate the Diamond Jubilee of Queen Victoria in 1897. It has a portrait

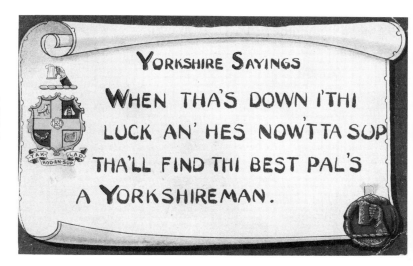

Dialect Cards. *"Yorkshire Sayings".* H.G. Glen & Co. of Leeds. *"Glenco Series".* P.U. 1910.

Dialect Cards. *Devon. "I'm Waitin Fur Some-buddy tew have a Bite With, Will 'ee Cum?" Frith's Series.*

Dialect Cards. *"A Yorkshireman's Advice to His Son", by Jack Broadrick. P.U. 1909.*

of the Queen in the top right-hand corner and vignettes of the Houses of Parliament, Nelson's Column and London Bridge. These cards are rare and have sold for several hundred pounds.

Dickens, Charles   **1812-1870**
Many postcards are associated with Dickens including views of the houses in which he lived, the inns mentioned in his novels, and his characters. Mr. Micawber (q.v.) appears on cards by several publishers including Faulkner and Welch. Tuck issued sets titled "In Dickens Land", which reproduced drawings by Phiz (Hablot K. Browne), a Dickens illustrator.

Dickinson, F.C.
Artist who designed a humorous set for George Pulman & Sons titled "Military Terms".

Dickson
Publisher of coloured Irish views. Trademark a hand with the words "Dickson's Ulster Series".

Diderich, William
Artist who portrayed "Irish Life" in designs for W. Lawrence of Dublin.

Diefenback, Karl Wilhelm   **b. 1851**
Artist who designed glamour cards.

Diemer, Michael Zeno
Versatile artist who painted views of London for E. Wrench.

Dietrich, Marlene   **b. 1904**
Film actress. Scene from *Shanghai Express* with Warner Oland.

Digby, H.C.
Photographer/publisher, Eltham, London, S.E. R.P. local views.

Dinah
Pseudonym of an unknown artist who designed children's cards.

Dirks, Gus
Designer of comic cards.

Disasters
Any disasters which have resulted in injury to people, loss of life or property, have always had news value and many appear on postcards. Photographs were usually by a local photographer.
See: Fires; Flood Disasters; Mine Disasters; Motor Accidents; Railway Disasters.

District Railway
Court size cards with well-known landmarks, e.g. St. Paul's and the Houses of Parliament, were published by the District Railway. They were produced by the Pictorial Postcard Syndicate and the Picture Postcard Company.
Ref: R.O.P.L., No. 16, p. 7.

Diving
See: Pier Divers.

D.M.& W.
Brighton Camera Exchange (q.v.).

Dobbs, Kidd & Co.   **fl. 1902-1906**
Stationer/publisher. A few sets were issued by this firm including one on the occasion of Edward VII's Coronation and one on Ping-Pong.

Dobson, Frank
Publisher, The Photographic Works, Waterloo, Liverpool. Views including a "Velograph" Series.

Dickens, Charles. *"Studies from Life by Charles Dickens. The Artful Dodger"* by Kyd from Oliver Twist. *J. Welch & Sons. P.U. 1906.*

Dickens, Charles. *"The Leather Bottle, Cobham".* No. 1 of a series of 12 published by Hildesheimer for the "Pickwick 'Leather Bottle', Cobham, Kent" Series. Dickens enjoyed taking his friends to this house which was not far from his home at Gad's Hill.

include the following sets:
(i)   Dressing Dolls, 3381.
(ii) Dolls of Many Lands, 3384.
(iii) Dolls' House Furniture, 3398.
(iv) Fairy Tale Dolls, 3385.
(v)   Mechanical Dolls, 3394.
(vi) Swinging Dolls, 3405.

Dolls' Houses
A number of miniature houses appear on postcards. The *Daily Mirror* Pets' House, "Mirror Grange", is an example. It was made as a home for their popular cartoon characters, Pip, Squeak and Wilfred (cards by Tuck, ill. Monahan 42 and 187). More significant were the Queen's Dolls' House (q.v.) and Titania's Palace (q.v.).

Dobson, Henry John, A.R.C.A., R.S.W.   **1858-1928**
Edinburgh painter of homely scenes of Scottish life. Exh. R.A. 6. Some of his work was used in facsims. in Tuck's "Scottish Life and Character".

Dobson, Molle & Co.
Publisher of a "St. Clair War Series" to which Lawson Wood contributed. Ill. Holt 112.

Docker, Edward   **fl. 1883-1908**
Landscape artist. Exh. R.A. 4. Early facsims. with U.B.s.

Dogs
Dog cards can be divided into two main classes:
(i)   Cards with accurate factual information about classes or breeds of dogs, e.g. J. Henderson & Sons "Sporting Dogs" and "Pet Dogs".
(ii) Sentimental series designed to appeal to the general public, e.g. Tuck's "When Dogs are Puppies", 9765.
      See: Colour Plate 13.

Dollman, John Charles, R.I., R.O.I., R.W.S.   **1851-1934**
Genre painter. Exh. R.A. 55. Known for his paintings of birds which appear on postcards issued by the National History Museum, London.

Dolls
Dolls may be seen on many postcards intended for children. The most interesting are the Tuck "Pastime Postcards" which

Dogs. *"Say, Please!"* A sentimental card by Rotary.

Dogs. *Card by an unknown photographer. Was it intended as an advertisement for "Lactol"?*

Domestic Servants. *Posing for a photograph. Photographer unknown.*

Domby, Thomas   pre-1922
Publisher, London and Brighton. General views.

Domestic Servants
Most large houses had domestic servants before W.W.I. While on duty they wore starched uniforms. Occasionally they posed for photographs.

Donadene, Jr.
Animal artist.

Donajowski, Ernest
Publisher, 26 Castle St. East, London, W. Primarily a music publisher but also issued a "Humorous Musical Series" of postcards.

Doncaster Rotophot Co. Ltd.   pre-1923
Publisher, Doncaster. Trademark "D R" within a diamond. Cards carry the description "Dania Glossy Real Photograph". Some photographs were obtained from Judges.

Donkeys
Donkey rides provided one of the main attractions for children on a seaside holiday and were also used to draw carts and invalid carriages. They frequently appear on beach scenes and several publishers featured them in sets, including:
(i) Alpha Publishing Co.
(ii) E.T.W. Dennis & Sons Ltd.
(iii) Photochrom Co. Ltd., "Celesque" cards with such titles as "Forty Winks", "Waiting for Work" and "Learning the Business".

Donlion Productions
Publisher, Doncaster, Yorkshire. Trademark a lion on a plinth carrying the word "Donlion". Output consisted of R.P.s, mainly views which covered a wide area extending as far south as the coast of Sussex.

Dora Street Studios
The London headquarters of Rotary photographic processing.

Dorando, Pietro
Marathon runner who took first place in the Olympic Marathon of 1908; when he reached the Stadium he collapsed but was helped to his feet and completed the course. Although disqualified, the public admired his bravery and Rotary produced a fine photograph of him running in the race.

Doubek, F.B.
Art nouveau artist who painted designs of girls in native costume.

Doughty, M.J.
Photographer/publisher, Milstead, Kent. Local R.P. views.

Douglas, James   fl. 1881-1907
Watercolour artist. Exh. R.A. 4. Contributed several landscape paintings to W. Ritchie's "Waterette" Series, especially views of Edinburgh.

Dover Times
Publisher of a "Dover Times Series" of local views printed above the Dover coat of arms.

Downey, W.D.   pre-1907
Court photographer/publisher, London, S.W. Supplied photographs of royalty to Rotary.

D.P.
Dawkes & Partridge (q.v.).

D.R.
Doncaster Rotophot Co. Ltd. (q.v.).

"Drayton" Series
Black and white London views with narrow white frames.

Donkeys. *"Waiting for Work"*. Photochrom *"Celesque"* Series.

Donkeys. *"Burnham, The Sands"*. Photo by Montague Cooper.

Donkeys. *Donkey-drawn invalid chair*. Photographer unknown.

Drew, John   **pre-1914**
Publisher, Aldershot and Farnborough, Hampshire. Local R.P. views.

Druids Friendly Society, Order of
Advertising cards.

Drummond, J. Nelson   **fl. 1882-1896**
Landscape painter. Exh. R.A. 4.

Drummond, Norah   **fl. c.1905-1930**
Animal artist who painted many sets of Tuck's "Oilette" Series. These included sporting scenes, animal cards and rural landscapes. Some of these were reprinted several times. Sets include:

  In the Hunting Field, 2924, 3296.
  Hunting, 3194.
  The Hunt Day, 9923.
  With Dog and Gun, 9273, 9294.
  On the Moors, 9327, see: Shooting.
  Man's Best Friend, 3052, 3603, 8650, 9561.
  The Friend of Man, 9381.
  Champion Clydesdales, 3109.
  Sporting Dogs, 3219, 3366, 8669, 9105.
  Favourite Dogs, 3184.
  Pet Dogs, 3639.
  Famous British Cattle, 9607.
  The Canadian Rockies, 3350.
  Irish Peasant Life, 9653.
  Rural Life, 9514.
  See: Cowell, L. 'The Postcards of Norah Drummond', P.P.M., February 1982.

D. & S.K.
These initials within a triangle were used pre-1910 by an unidentified firm which produced an "Ideal Series" with a "Rembrandt Oak Frame Border".

Du Cane, Ella   **fl. 1893-1910**
Flower painter of 41 Eaton Place, London, who exhibited at the Fine Arts Society. She illustrated books for A. & C. Black, such as *The Banks of the Nile, Flowers and Gardens of Japan* and *Flowers and Gardens of Madeira*. Her publishers issued some of these illustrations as postcards.

Drummond Norah. *"After the Race"*. R. Tuck & Sons. "Oilette" "Man's Best Friend".

Dunmow Flitch. *"Taking the Oath. Dunmow Flitch. Modern Version"*. P.U. 1906.

Duddle, Josephine
Painter of children's cards.

Dudley, Jessie   fl. c.1900-1914
York landscape artist who painted north country scenes for
J.W. Ruddock & Sons.

Dudley, Thomas   fl. 1879-1910
Painter of landscapes and coastal scenes, mainly in Durham,
Yorkshire, the Lake District and Cornwall. Facsims. of his
works by E.T.W. Dennis and J.W. Ruddock.

Duffett, H.W.   pre-1906
Printer and publisher, High St., Fareham, Hampshire. Black
and white local views.

Dühne, Francisca
Actress. P.P. by Gale & Polden.

Duke, Alfred   fl. 1893-1905
Manchester animal painter. Six facsims. of his work (dog
paintings) were used by George Falkner of that city.

Dumbarton & Balloch Joint Line Committee
Publisher sepia and coloured views of Loch Lomond steamers
and piers.
    Ref: R.O.P.L., No. 12, p. 4.

Duncan, James Allan (Hamish)   fl. pre-1909
Artist who designed humorous cards for Davidson Bros.,
Morison Bros. of Glasgow and for Tuck using the pseudonym
Hamish as his Christian name. He also painted landscapes
which are usually signed J.A.D. Beware the single signature J.
Duncan, which was used by several Edwardian artists.

Dunlop Tyres
Advertising cards.

Dunmow Flitch
One of the rare photographic views (tinted) of a local custom.
The ancient custom of the Dunmow Flitch, originally
connected with the tenure of the abbey lands, is said to have
been instituted by Robert FitzWalter in 1244. It established a
right to a flitch of bacon belonging to the prior and canons to
any married couple who, kneeling on two sharp pointed stones
in the churchyard, swore that they had "not repented them,
sleeping or waking, of their marriage in a year and a day". The
first claim was made in 1445, the sixth in 1771. After that date
the prize was withheld until 1855. Since then the prize has been
awarded several times.

Dunn, Ralph, & Co.
Publisher, 68 Barbican, London, E.C. Multi-views of London
and P.P.s of actresses and cricketers.

Dunning, H.   pre-1905
Publisher, Usk, Monmouthshire. Local black and white views.

Dupuis, Emile
Artist who designed colour series for the Paris firm Color
during W.W.I. titled "Nos Allies", "Nos Poilus", "Leur
Caboches", "Les Femmes Héroïques", etc. Many of these
cards were sent by serving British soldiers from army camps in
Belgium and France.

Durie Brown & Co.
Publisher, 63 Princes St., Edinburgh. Trademark "Pixie"
above a shield with the letters D.B.E. Their output included:
(i)   Photographic views of Edinburgh, e.g. The Princes St.
      Gardens' Floral Clock.
(ii) Watercolour facsims.
(iii) Cards published for the Scottish National Exhibition of
      1908, including a humorous set.
(iv) Cards advertising their tartan souvenirs, ill. Byatt 80.

Dusédau, F   pre-1909
Publisher, 494 Barking Rd., Plaistow, Essex. Black and white
postcards of London in a "Local Series".

Dutch Style Postcards
In early Edwardian times it became fashionable to paint illustrations of children in the dress of Dutch peasant folk. Artists
who exploited this style included Florence Hardy, Ivy Millicent
James and Ethel Parkinson.

Dwiggins, Clare Victor   1873-1958
Artist who designed comic postcards, e.g. "Dry Humour",
for Tuck and used the abbreviation Dwig as a signature.

Dyer, W.H.
Watercolour artist who painted views of Dartmoor and
Exmoor for Salmon.

Dymond, R.J.
Landscape artist who painted moonlight views for Charles
Worcester & Co.

Dysart & Co.   pre-1907
Photographer/publisher, Chelmsford, Essex. "Dysart Series"
of greetings cards and photographs of the Cromer Express
disaster at Witham.

E

E.A.
Edgar Alexander Ltd. (q.v.).

Eagleton, C.D.
Publisher, Post Office, Penshurst, Kent. R.P.s supplied by H. Camburn of Tunbridge Wells.

Earl, Maud   **fl. 1884-1914**
Animal artist who painted a series titled ''Maud Earl's Sporting Dogs'' for E.W. Savory.

Earls Court
Exhibitions were held at this London venue and one of the landmarks was the Great Wheel erected in 1895 and seen on many cards. It carried 40 cars, each built for 40 passengers. The wheel was dismantled in 1906.
    See: Exhibitions.

Earnshaw, Harold C.   **d. 1937**
A versatile landscape and comic artist, the husband of Mabel Lucie Attwell. Designed cards for several publishers including Gottschalk, Dreyfus & Davis, James Henderson & Sons, George Pulman & Sons (ill. Holt 318 and 319), and Valentine.
    See: Colour Plate 14.

E.A.S.
E.A. Schwerdtfeger & Co. (q.v.). The initials are usually enclosed in a heart-shaped outline.

East Coast Express Railway Route
Cards show the ''Flying Scotsman'', King's Cross Station, the Royal Bridge at Berwick and Waverley Station, Edinburgh.
    Ref: R.O.P.L., No. 7, p. 4.

East London Printing Co.   **c.1907**
Publisher, 7 Houndsditch, London, E. This firm was established as printers at least 10 years before it started to issue postcards. Alexander Bloom who ran the business with his sons was a photographer and covered a number of London events. The output was mainly in black and white and sepia, though a few coloured cards were printed in Germany. Some of the photographs were ''staged'' using amateur actors.

Easton, J.B.
Comic artist who designed fiscal cards for W. Ritchie.

E.B.
Initials of an artist whose work was used by Photochrom.

Ebner, Pauli   **fl. 1920s**
Art deco artist who designed greetings cards depicting children at play. Facsims. by M. Munk.
    See: Colour Plate 10.

E. & Co., B.
Edwards & Co., Birmingham (q.v.).

E.C.B.
Edward Coppock, Blackpool.

E.C.G.
Edwin C. Gardner (q.v.).

Edenbridge Chronicle   **pre-1907**
Publisher. R.P. views of Kent.

Edgerton, Linda   **fl. c.1910-1927**
Artist who designed cards with young children for a ''Nursery Rhymes'' Series published by Mansell.

Edison Lamps
Poster-type advertisement cards.

Ediss, Connie   **1872-1934**
Comedy actress who played at the Gaiety Theatre in *The Circus Girl*. P.P. by Philco.

Edmonds & Co.   **pre-1913**
Photographer/publisher, High St., Devizes, Wiltshire. Local R.P. views.

Edward VII
Apart from many postcard portraits published during his reign, two occasions were marked by special issues — his Coronation in 1902 and his death in 1910.
    See: Royalty, British.

Edwards
Photographer/publisher, 16 St. Mary's Rd., Southampton, Hampshire.

Edwards & Co.
Publisher, Edgbaston St., Birmingham. Trademark ''E. & Co. B.'' within a diamond. R.P. views from as far south as Devonshire.

Edwards & Co. *R.P. of ''Mol's Coffee House, Exeter''.*

AN EAST RIDING (YORKSHIRE) LEGEND.

Many years ago a Shepherd was murdered, and was found by his neighbours the next morning with his white dog watching over his dead body. Each anniversary at midnight, near the place where the murder took place, a white dog on guard may be seen. The picture depicts a rider and his horse terrified one night by the apparition.

Edwards, R.R. *"An East Riding (Yorkshire) Legend"* by *Edith Ewen.* *"Many years ago a shepherd was murdered, and was found by his neighbours the next morning with his white dog watching over his dead body. Each anniversary at midnight, near the place where the murder took place, a white dog on guard may be seen. The picture depicts a rider and his horse terrified one night by the apparition".*

Edwards & Son
Photographer/publisher, New St., Worthing. Local R.P.s including some of the Worthing pier disaster.

Edwards, A.R., & Son   **pre-1916**
Publisher, Tower St., Selkirk, Scotland. Local sepia views.

Edwards, C.
Publisher, St. Mildred's Rd., Westgate-on-Sea, Kent. Black and white local views.

Edwards, George Henry   **fl. 1883-1911**
Landscape painter. Exh. R.A. 1. London artist whose work was used by Savory.

Edwards, R.R.
Publisher, 4 Castle St., Salisbury, Wiltshire. Issued sepia views (supplied by Frith), 13 views of the "Old George" Hotel, Salisbury, and at least three "Legend" sets designed by Edith Ewen in black and white.

Edwards & Smith
Photographer/publisher, Fordingbridge, Hampshire.

E.F.A.
Excelsior Fine Art Publishing Co. (q.v.).

Egdell, A. & M.
Publisher, West End Stationery Stores, Lanes St., Morecambe, Lancashire. Local R.P. views.

Eggleton & Co.
Publisher, Fancy Stores, High St., Marlborough, Wiltshire. Local sepia views.

Egyptian Gazette
Publisher, Cairo, Egypt. An English daily newspaper with offices in Cairo. Series of ethnic cards printed by Tuck.

Eisner, D. (& Sons Ltd.)   **c.1912**
Publisher, 42 Mansell St., London, E. This business prospered

under three names:
(i) David Eisner, c.1912-16.
(ii) City Postcard Co., 1916-27.
(iii) David Eisner & Sons Ltd., c.1927-52.
Output consisted mainly of coloured views but some comic cards were also published.

E.J.H.
E.J. Hey & Co. (q.v.).

E.K.
Initials found on ribbon cards of Hugh Rees Ltd. Byatt, p. 229 attributes them to Commander E. Kidner, R.N.

Eland, John Shenton   **1872-1933**
Artist who lived in London from 1895 to 1913. Exh. R.A. 8. Painted Leicester views for J.W. Ruddock & Sons.

Elcock, George A.
Artist who designed cards on the "Rules of Golf" for the North British Rubber Co.

Elgar, Cecil
Publisher, Lymington, Hampshire. Local R.P. views.

Elite Pictorial Postcard Machine
See: Postcard Machines.

Ellam, William Henry   **fl. c.1900-1914**
Versatile artist who painted mainly humorous subjects for the Excelsior Fine Art Publishing Co., famous people in their cars; Faulkner, sets of teddy bears; Hildesheimer; Stewart & Woolf; Tuck, "Breakfast in Bed" and "Pierrot Teddies"; Wrench, political cartoons. He often signed with surname only.

"Ellan Vannin"   **pre-1909**
The Manx name for the Isle of Man which appears on postcards with views of the island. It is associated with the three-legged trademark and the motto "Quocunque Jegeris Stabit".

"Ellanbee"
Tradename used by Landeker & Brown (q.v.).

"Ellanco"   **pre-1933**
Publisher of cards described as "Best Photos. Sepia Tone".

Elliman's Liniment
Advertising cards supplied by Tuck. They depict foxhunting, show jumping and military exercises.

Elliot, Harry
Designer of sporting cards.

Elliott & Fry
Photographer. Portraits of ballet stars for Samuels Ltd., The Strand, London.

Elliott, Mary Gertrude   **1874-1950**
American actress. First appearance on stage 1894. Married Johnstone Forbes-Robertson in 1900. P.P.s by Millar & Lang; Rotary, alone, and with her husband in *The Light that Failed;* Tuck, "Bookmarker" Series IV.

Elliott, Stephen, & Co.
Publisher, 6 Kingly St., Regent St., London, W.1. Firm which specialised in cards of racehorses and mounted jockeys.

Ellis   **pre-1908**
Publisher, Southend-on-Sea, Essex.

Ellis & Walery   **fl. c.1900-1903**
Photographer/publisher, 5 Baker St., London, W. Copyright

P.P.s of actors and actresses were used by postcard publishers such as Beagles and Rotary. They also published a number of their own photographs of actors, actresses and royalty.

Ellum, Owen
Photographer/publisher, Eastchurch, Kent.

E.L.P. Co.
East London Printing Co. (q.v.).

E.L.S.
E.L. Scrivens (q.v.).

Elsie, Lily   **b. 1886**
Actress. First appeared on the stage as "Little Red Riding Hood" and had a great success as *The Merry Widow* in 1907. P.P.s by Ettlinger, "Photocolour Series", and Rotary.

Elsley, Arthur John   **fl. 1880-1927**
Animal, figure and landscape painter. Exh. R.A. 50. Included in Hildesheimer's "Gems of Art" Series, and a Tuck set "Studies in Childhood".

Elwes, Hervey
Watercolour artist who painted a set titled "Tiny Mothers" for Knight Bros.

Emanuel, Frank Lewis, P.S.G.A.   **1865-1948**
London artist who painted in oils and watercolour. Exh. R.A. 38. From 1918 to 1930 he was instructor in etching at the Central School of Arts and Crafts, London. Was for some time President of the Society of Graphic Artists and art critic for *The Architectural Review*. He painted views of Aldeburgh and Lyme Regis for Tuck and also an "Oilette" Series titled "Quaint Corners".

Emberson, Jno.
Publisher, Wimbledon, Surbiton and Tooting.

Embossed Cards
Many greetings cards are embossed featuring angels, cupids or lovers with romantic symbols — a heart or clasped hands. Many such cards were produced in Germany, Austria or Switzerland and imported into Britain. The following firms, many of which had links with Europe, produced embossed cards of various kinds: Beagles, Birn Bros., Blum & Degen, Giesen Bros., Charles Hauff & Co., Meissner & Buch, Millar & Lang, Osnabrucken Paper Co., Philco, Stewart & Woolf, Tuck (Empire Series and U.K. Series), Wildt & Kray, and Woolstone Bros.

Embroidered Silks
These are cards in which a rectangle of stiffened muslin has been embroidered in coloured silks to create a design. The material is backed by card and contained in an embossed frame. Sometimes the silk forms a pocket in which a slip of thin card has been inserted with a printed message, e.g. "With my Best Wishes" or "To My Dear Sister". They were made in France and imported. The first of these cards entered the country about the turn of the century, such firms as Gale & Polden of Aldershot and H.J. Smith of Brighton acting as agents. However, the largest influx was during W.W.I. when British troops sent them home as souvenirs. Many are simply greetings cards for birthdays or Christmas. Then came a flood of patriotic cards which included:
(i)   Naval ships, e.g., the light cruiser H.M.S. *Boadicea*.
(ii) Regimental badges or crests, e.g. Royal Flying Corps (ill. Monahan 100); The City of London Post Office Rifles; Prince Consort's Own Rifle Brigade.

Emanuel, Frank Lewis. *"Low Tide, Tenby Harbour"*. R. Tuck & Sons. *"Oilette"* *"Quaint Corners"*.

(iii) A cross of the allies made up of national flags.
Few of the cards give the name of the publisher though "Brodies 'La Pensee', Paris" has been recorded.
Raphael Tuck & Sons issued a few embroidered cards under the title "Broderie D'Art" in which a small embroidered oval is framed in a card with birthday greetings.

"Emerald Series"
See: Irish Pictorial Post Card Co.

Emery, M.L.
Photographer/publisher, High St., Pinner, Middlesex. Local R.P. views.

"Emm's Series"   **pre-1908**
Framed R.P. views of Hampshire and Wiltshire.

"Empire Series"   **pre-1905**
This title embraces the output of the Pictorial Post Card Co. Ltd. (q.v.).

Embroidered Silks. *"Christmas Greetings"* embroidered in silk with an embossed frame. Such cards were made in France and exported to Britain.

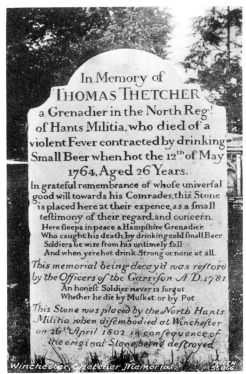

Epitaphs. *Thomas Thetcher Memorial near Winchester Cathedral.* "*In Memory of Thomas Thetcher a Grenadier ... who died of a violent Fever contracted by drinking Small Beer when hot the 12th of May 1764, Aged 26 Years...*
Here sleeps in peace a Hampshire Grenadier
Who caught his death by drinking cold small Beer.
Soldiers be wise from his untimely fall
And when ye're hot drink Strong or none at all."
Frith's Series.

Epitaphs. *Elizabeth Wallbridge, Arreton, Isle of Wight. "To the Memory of Elizabeth Wallbridge, "The Dairyman's Daughter" who died May 30th 1801. Aged 31 years...*
Stranger! if e'er by chance or feeling led,
Upon this hallow'd turf thy footsteps tread,
Turn from the contemplation of this sod,
And think on her whose Spirit rests with God...."
Louis Levy.

Emsley, Walter   **fl. 1883-1927**
Landscape artist. Exh. R.A. 5. Some of his paintings were used in facsims. by Robert Peel of Oxford pre-1910.

Endacott, Sydney   **1873-1918**
Devon artist who spent a short time in America and then returned to live in Exeter where he became an art master. He painted Devon scenes and notable men of Devon, e.g. Sir Francis Drake and Sir Walter Raleigh. The scenes were published by Frith, the historic personalities by Worth & Co., Exeter.

English, Archibald   **fl. c.1905-1920**
Designer of comic cards for Hutson Bros., Mitchell & Watkins, William Ritchie, Thridgould & Co., and Wildt & Kray. He often signed his work A.E.

English Fine Art Co.
Publisher of a "Photo-Colour" Series and a comic series by W. Stocker Shaw.

E.P.
Ernest Pouteau (q.v.).

Epitaphs
Close-up views of gravestones or monuments with unusual epitaphs often appear on postcards.

Epitaphs. *The Sailor's Stone at Hindhead erected by James Stilwell, Esq.*
"*ERECTED In detestation of a barbarous Murder, Committed here on an unknown Sailor; on Sep. 24th, 1786, by Edwd. Lonegon, Michl. Cafey & Jas. Marshall, Who were all taken the same day, And hung in Chains near this place.*"
Frith's Series.

Epp's Chocolate and Cocoa. *Advertising card. P.U. 1909.*

Epps Chocolate and Cocoa   **pre-1909**
Advertising cards. Issued a "Nature Series" of animals,
butterflies, etc.

Erasmic Soap and Dentifrice
Glamorous poster-type advertising cards.

E.R.G.
E.R. Green & Co. (q.v.).

Erotica
Eros was the God of Love, and the word erotica is used here to
describe the category of postcards pertaining to sexual love
and physical desire. Relatively few publishers in Britain
produced cards which can be classed as erotic, though many
comic cards may be termed suggestive. French, German and
Italian cards are more explicit and many such cards were
imported for sale in Britain.
   Ref: The subject is dealt with fully in a well-illustrated book
by Barbara Jones and William Ouellette, *Erotic Postcards*,
Macdonald & Jane's, London, 1977.

E.S.
The "Empire Series" of the Pictorial Postcard Co. Ltd. (q.v.).

E & S. Ltd.   **pre-1925**
Dublin publisher of R.P.s and coloured views in a "Signal
Series".

Esmond, Henry V.   **1870-1922**
Actor and playwright. P.P. by Beagles.

Esperanto
Tuck produced an "Oilette" Esperanto set and photographic

Ethnic Postcards. *Handwritten note on the reverse states
"Ordinary Egyptian women wear this head-dress but usually
the veil is not transparent. The ornament on the nose is felt."*

cards were published when the Third Esperanto Conference
was held in Cambridge in 1906. The publisher of these has not
been identified.

Essex Telegraph
Publisher, Head St., Colchester, Essex. An "Essex
Telegraph" Series of local views.

E.T.B.
Edward Taylor, Beverley (q.v.).

Etches, J.M.
Photographer/publisher, Winton, Bournemouth. Local
photographic views which include the New Forest.

Ethnic Postcards
A category which embraces all cards depicting national charac-
teristics — physical, social and artistic. The only reliable
examples for scientific study are those based on R.P.s.

Ettlinger, Max, & Co. Ltd.   **1901**
Publisher, 10 Long Lane, London, E.C., and New York.
Trademark a script monogram "M.E. & Co." with a ribbon
below with the words "The Royal Series". Much of the output
was of real photographs and various series titles were used,
e.g. "Photolet", "Photocolour", "Lamanet". It included:
(i)   Cards for the Earl's Court Exhibition of 1903
(ii)   Coloured topographical views printed in Germany.
(iii) Hand-coloured brown-toned art studies printed in
       France.
(iv)   P.P.s of actresses (photos by Bassano) and scenes from
       plays, e.g. *Old Heidelberg*.
                                                    continued

(v) Military Series, e.g. "Life in our Army, ill. D. & M. 43: "Troops of the British Empire".

(vi) "The Conquering Hero", cards issued on the return of Joseph Chamberlain from South Africa.

(vii) Framed gallery pictures.

(viii) "Favourite Birds", coloured pictures.

(ix) Novelty cards.

E.T.W.D. & S.
E.T.W. Dennis & Sons Ltd. (q.v.).

Evans, D.
Photographer/publisher, Bournemouth, Hampshire. "Ivory Series" of R.P. views.

Evans, Harry
Artist who painted early motoring scenes for an unknown publisher, c.1907.

Evans, Llew   **pre-1906**
Publisher, Winnington Park, Cheshire. Coloured local views.

Evans, O.   **pre-1908**
Publisher, 10 High St., Conway, Carnarvonshire. Local black and white views.

Evans, R.C.
Publisher, Compton House, Penmaenmawr, Carnarvonshire. Local black and white views.

Everett & Ashdown   **pre-1923**
Photographer/publisher, Tenterden, Kent. Local R.P. views.

Evershed, Sidney
Aldershot artist who contributed comic designs to Joseph Asher's "Kismet Series".

"Everton Series"
See: Thomas Bros. & Co.

E.W.
Ernest Edward Wise (q.v.).

Ewen, Edith
Designer of "Legend" Series for R.R. Edwards of Salisbury Wiltshire (q.v.).

E.W.H.
Ernest W. Haslehurst (q.v.).

E.W.M.
E.W. Mudge (q.v.).

Excavations
Postcards of important archaeological excavations were occasionally issued. The excavations at an Iron Age hill fort at Old Sarum, which later became a Saxon and a Norman settlement, are a good example covered by Frith and by Welch.

Excelsior Fine Art Publishing Co.   **1904-1907**
Publisher, 8 New Coventry St., London, W. Trademark a small girl watching a postman as he empties a letter box. Output included:

(i) "London Theatre" Series, black and white views.

(ii) London Zoo, black and white views.

(iii) Coats of arms and flags.

(iv) "Military Series", ill. D. & M. 47.

(v) Reproductions of gallery pictures.

(vi) Famous personalities in their cars, e.g. Mr. Campbell Bannerman in his Darracq.

(vii) Comic cards.

Exhibitions. *The J. & F. Martell stand at the Franco-British Exhibition of 1908.*

Exhibitions
Every exhibition resulted in a flood of postcards: souvenir cards, advertisers' cards and official cards. A list of exhibitions is given below:

1901 Glasgow International Exhibition.

1902 Cork International Exhibition.
Wolverhampton International Exhibition.

1903 International Fire Exhibition, Earl's Court.
Glasgow East End Industrial Exhibition.
Highland Jacobite Exhibition.

1904 Bradford Textiles Exhibition.
Italian Exhibition, Earl's Court.

1905 Naval Exhibition, Earl's Court.

1906 Austrian Exhibition, Earl's Court.

1907 Irish International Exhibition, Dublin.
Medical Missions Exhibition, Newcastle upon Tyne.
Balkan Exhibition, Earl's Court.

1908 Franco-British Exhibition, White City.
Hungarian Exhibition, Earl's Court.
Scottish National Exhibition, Edinburgh.

1909 American International Exhibition, Earl's Court.

1910 Japan-British Exhibition, White City.

1911 Coronation Exhibition, White City.
Festival of Empire, Crystal Palace.
Scottish Exhibition of History, Art and Industry, Glasgow.

The Lagoon, Japan-British Exhibition

Burma British Empire Exhibition

Exhibitions. *"The Lagoon". Japan-British Exhibition of 1910 at the White City. Valentine Official Card. P.U. 1910.*

1912 Africa and the East Exhibition, Nottingham.
Latin-British Exhibition, White City.
1913 Liverpool Exhibition.
1916 Loos Trenches Exhibition, Blackpool.
1917-18
War Bonds Campaign, Trafalgar Sq., London.
1920 Building Exhibition, Olympia.
Imperial War and Victory Exhibition, Crystal Palace.
1924 British Empire Exhibition, Wembley.
1925 British Empire Exhibition, Wembley.
1928 Wholesale Furniture Trades Exhibition, Glasgow.
1929 North East Coast Exhibition, Newcastle upon Tyne.
1930 Welsh National Exhibition.
1934 Ideal Home Exhibition.
1938 Empire Exhibition, Glasgow.

Refs: No collector of exhibition cards can afford to be without two books which deal with the subject in great detail: Fletcher/Brooks I and Fletcher/Brooks II. Both parts are illustrated and give complete lists of published cards.

Explosions

Serious explosions recorded on postcards include:
1904, Saltley gasometer explosion, Birmingham.
12 December, 1907, powder mill explosion, Worsborough Dale, nr. Barnsley, Yorkshire.
20 February, 1908, colliery explosion, Washington, Co. Durham.
9 April, 1908, colliery explosion, Midsomer Norton, Somerset.

Exhibitions. *British Empire Exhibition of 1938 at Glasgow. "Burma Building ... on the lines of the old royal and sacred buildings of Mandalay", by Charles E. Flower. Facsim. by R. Tuck & Sons. "Oilette".*

28 August, 1908, furnace explosion, Iron Works, Ardsley, Yorkshire.
16 February, 1909, colliery explosion, West Stanley, Durham.
26 August, 1913, boiler explosion, steelworks, Leeds, Yorkshire.
30 May, 1914, colliery explosion, Wharncliffe Silkstone, Barnsley, Yorkshire.
10 August, 1914, boiler explosion, Thornhill Lees, Yorkshire.
2 December, 1914, explosion, Heckmondwike, Yorkshire.

Photographs of most of the above were taken by Warner Gothard of Barnsley for postcard reproduction.
See: Mine Disasters.

Eyre & Spottiswoode Ltd.   c.1902
Publisher, Fetter Lane, London, E.C. This firm had been publishing Christmas cards before the advent of the picture postcard. They entered the postcard field with a "Woodbury Series" which included:
(i) Sepia and coloured reproductions of gallery paintings.
(ii) Coloured views, e.g. "Old Sussex Churches".
(iii) Animals of the London Zoo, photographs by W.P. Dando.
(iv) Rough seas.
(v) Actors and actresses, hand-coloured photographs.
(vi) Watercolour facsims. of paintings of Guernsey, Frank Dean.
(vii) Military cards.
(viii) Views of warships.

Colour Plate 5: Birthday cards

"To My Dear Mother-in-Law on Her Birthday". A typical glossy embossed-border card by Beagles & Co.

"With All Good Wishes From Across the Sea". A shamrock card for the Irish market by the Alphalsa Publishing Co.

"Birthday Greeting". An embossed and gilded card by Gale & Polden. P.U. 1907.

Fabian, Maud　　　　　　　　　　　fl. 1906-1909
Sculptor who also designed advertisements, e.g. for J.S. Fry & Sons.

Fabiano, Fabien　　　　　　　　　　1883-1962
French painter and designer best known for his contributions to *La Vie Parisienne*. His cards were printed in Paris in a series called "Les P'tites Femmes". Each card was framed in a narrow grey border, ill. Monahan 96. He also designed advertising cards for "Evian Cachet".

Fairies
A number of publishers issued sets with fairies, e.g. "Elves and Fairies", seven sets, A. & C. Black; "Fairy Whispers" by A.M. Davis; "Fairies' Friends" by Humphrey Milford; Tuck's "Fairy Tale" Series.

Fairs and Fairgrounds
Fairground postcards fall into three classes:
(i)　The travelling fair which moves from town to town, setting up its roundabout, coconut shies and amusement stalls in a convenient field or open space. They are advertised locally. A message on a card posted in 1906 from the village of Gifford in Scotland states: "There was a fair here last week and a lot of dear little donkeys just going about. The merry-go-round was all horses and Cinderella carriages and I wished you had been there to have a round with me."
(ii)　The traditional town fairs which are organised year after year on a specific date, e.g. St. Giles Fair, Oxford and the Mop Fair at Marlborough.
(iii)　Seaside fairgrounds which cater in summer for an influx of holidaymakers, e.g. at Blackpool with its Joy Wheel.
　　Postcards depicting these fairs are popular. There is a Fairground Postcard Society.

Falkner, George, & Sons　　　　　　　　1903
Printer/publisher, Deansgate Press, Manchester, and 181 Queen Victoria St., London, E.C. Noted mainly for military subjects painted by John McNeill.

"Famous Series"
Coloured views by Tomkins & Barnett of Swindon (q.v.).

Fantasy Cards
These are cards assembled from photographs. Some show impossible situations, e.g. the actress, Zena Dare, seated on a crescent moon, little girls emerging from egg shells, or men on the moon (no longer a fantasy). Fantasy heads are perhaps the best known. They were produced in France and Germany and show a male head against a black background. Closer examination reveals that the head is made up of a number of nude or slightly-clad women in strange postures. Some represent real people, the artist suggesting that they may be prey to lecherous thoughts.
　　Refs: Jones, B., and Ouellette, W., illustrate a number of fantasy heads, including those of Leopold II and Richard Wagner, in *Erotic Postcards,* 1977; a list of personalities caricatured in fantasy cards appeared in an article by Alf Harper in P.P.M., October 1983, p. 30.

Farkoa, Maurice　　　　　　　　　　1864-1916
Actor and vocalist who played in *The Circus Girl* at the Gaiety Theatre in 1896. P.P. by Beagles.

Farmer, C.J.　　　　　　　　　　　pre-1919
Photographer/publisher, Skegness, Lincolnshire. R.P.s of local views including the Skegness Pier disaster of 1919.

Farming
Many topographical views show farm animals and farm workers (then known as farm labourers) but the main object of the photographer or artist was to reflect the atmosphere of the countryside. However, several series aim specifically to reflect work on the farm. These include series by:
(i)　G.P. Abraham Ltd.
(ii)　Judges Ltd., sepia photographs.
(iii)　Photochrom, sepia photographs.
(iv)　E.A. Schwerdtfeger, sepia series, some with a couplet.
(v)　Wildt & Kray, R.P.s with such titles as "Harvestry", "The Reapers", and "The Last Load".
　　Illustrations overleaf.

Father Christmas
Full-length portraits of the Edwardian Father Christmas (little different from his modern counterpart) are commonly found on Christmas greetings cards. He usually wears a red robe though examples are known in blue, brown or green.

"Faulder's Chocolates"
Advertising cards featuring Father Christmas.

Faulkner, C.W., & Co. (Ltd.)　　　　1900 (Ltd. 1905)
Publisher, 79 Golden Lane, London, E.C. Faulkner was in partnership with Albert Hildesheimer in the 1880s, publishing Christmas cards. This partnership continued until 1885. The transition to postcard publishing was therefore relatively simple. Faulkner took over the firm in the 1890s. By 1905, when the firm became a limited company, hundreds of postcard sets had been published and new sets began to appear at the rate of about a hundred a year. The output included almost every type of card. Examples only are given here:
(i)　Comic cards of many types.
(ii)　Patriotic series, ill. Monahan 54.
(iii)　Portraits of the royal family.
(iv)　Portraits of actors, actresses and other celebrities.
(v)　London views, several cathedral sets, and views of North Wales.
(vi)　Countryside views, mainly watercolour facsims.
(vii)　Dogs and cats, including Louis Wain cards.
(viii)　Children's cards, at least 18 sets by Ivy Millicent James, and a "Peter Pan" Series.　　　　　　*continued*

Farming. *"For What We Are About to Receive"*. A halt to feed the horses. E.A. Schwerdtfeger & Co.

Farming. *"A Noonday Halt. At harvest time each fruitful field, A wealth of golden sheaves will yield."* E.A. Schwerdtfeger & Co.

(ix)   Reproductions of gallery pictures.
(x)   Shakespeare's boy characters.
(xi)   Glamour cards, some by Edward Gross and Lester Ralph supplied by the Knapp Co. Inc. of New York.
(xii) Sets of cards by first-class British artists, such as F. Ibbetson and F. Wheatley, e.g. "Cries of London", "London Street Cries", "The London Police".
(xiii) Greetings on stiff card with bevelled edges.
       See: Colour Plate 13.
       Ref: Byatt gives a useful check list of most of the first 262 sets, pp. 344-6.

F.B.
Frances Brundage (q.v.).

Fealy, Maud   1883-1971
Actress. P.P.s by Aristophot, with Pauline Chase and Zena

Dare; Beagles; Pictorial Postcard Co.; Rotary, Bookmarker Series; "Smart Novels" Series, in three poses.

"Feathered World"
Publisher, 9 Arundel St., Strand, London. This firm also published *Canary & Cage Bird Life* (q.v.). Both publications gave away instruction cards which were also issued as postcards.

Feiertag, K.
German artist who designed children's cards for Faulkner.

Felix the Cat
This film cartoon character was advertised in the 1920s on a postcard by the Inter-Art Co. distributed by the Pathé magazine *Eve and Everybody's Film Review*, ill. Monahan 149. Felix also appears on cards by Woolstone Bros.

Feller, Frank   1848-1908
Artist whose work was used by Tuck, in the "Wide Wide World" Series. Exh. R.A. 3.

Fernand, Fernel   fl.c. 1898-1910
French artist who designed cards for a series on racing cars. They are highly prized.

F.F. & Co.
F. Frankel & Co. (q.v.).

F.G.
Fred Gothard (q.v.).

Fidler, Alice Luella
American artist who designed glamour cards, ill. D. & M. 69.

Field, W.A.   pre-1906
Publisher, South Norwood, London, S.E. Coloured views of the London area including three series, each of which covers several hundred localities: "Croydon Series", "Essex Series" and "Surrey Series".

Fielder & Henderson
Publisher, 7 Philip Lane, London, E.C. Framed views of London.

Fields, Grace, D.B.E.   1898-1974
Stage, film actress and vocalist, best known as Gracie Fields or Our Gracie. P.P. by *Picturegoer*.

Fields, J.C. & J., Ltd.
Advertiser of "Fields' Toilet Soap and Candles".

Fields Toilet Soap
Advertising cards stressing its benefit to children.

File & Sons
Photographer/publisher, Boughton, Kent. Local R.P. views, e.g. hop-picking.

Film Actors and Actresses
In the 1920s attention turned from stage personalities to film stars. Many photographic portraits were published by *Film Weekly*, *Picturegoer* and *Pathé Frères*. They are listed individually.

Fine Arts Publishing Co.
Publisher of cards of the National Peace Thanksgiving Service at St. Paul's in 1919, ill. Holt 723, and of cards advertising their art reproductions.

Finnemore, Joseph. *"Emmanuel College, Cambridge". R. Tuck & Sons. "Oilette" "Connoisseur". P.U. 1913.*

Fire Brigades. *A card advertising "British Dominion" Insurance. "A spark neglected makes a mighty fire", Herrick.*

Fireplaces. *"Fireplace — Wagon & Horses Inn, Saltersgate. The fire that never goes out". Photographer unknown.*

Finnemore, Joseph, R.I., R.B.A.   1860-1939

Oil and watercolour artist. Born in Birmingham, he studied at the Birmingham School of Art and then in Antwerp under Charles Verlat. Returned to England in 1881. Exh. R.A. 15. Travelled widely in Malta, Greece, Turkey and Russia. Painted for Tuck's "Oilette" "Connoisseur" Series.

Fire Brigades and Firemen

Apart from rare photographs of firemen in action, two series pay tribute to the service:
(i)   Misch & Co. "The Fire Brigade", 454, designed by Fred S. Howard.
(ii) Tuck "Fighting the Flames", Oilette 6459. Ill. D. & M. 26.

Firemen had a special status in Edwardian times. A postcard message in 1904 reads: "Must tell you that Fred was made a fireman last evening. That's a feather in his HAT. They have their dinner next Wednesday so you must think of them."

Fire Engines

Close up views of fire engines, especially when horse drawn, are keenly sought. They were soon superseded by motor fire engines.

Fireplaces

At least three postcards show the fireplaces of inns in which the fires are said to have burned constantly without being relit for many years. They are:

The Chequers Inn, Slapestones, Osmotherley, Yorkshire.
The Wagon & Horses Inn, Saltersgate, Yorkshire.
Warren House Inn, Dartmoor, Devon.

Fires

Postcards of fires in buildings are not common. Some are photographs taken at the time though police and firefighters make sure that no one comes near enough to impede their work. Others are photographs of buildings as they were before the fire, touched up so that flames appear to be coming from the windows. These are a few examples of fires recorded on postcards:

Annesley Church, Nottinghamshire, 1907.
Bristol, 1905.
Bristol, Merchant Venturer's College, 1906.   *continued*

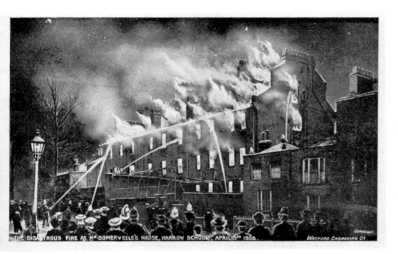

Fires. *"The Disastrous Fire at Mr. Somerville's House, Harrow School, April 3rd, 1908"*. *Watford Engraving Co.*

Bristol, Stokes Croft, 1905.
Dundee, 1906.
Mr. Somerville's House, Harrow School, 1908.
Kirkby Church, Nottinghamshire, 1907.
Leeds, 1906.
Redruth, West End Drapery Store, 1919.
Selby Abbey, Yorkshire, 1906.
Stratford-upon-Avon Shakespeare Memorial Theatre, 1926.
Ware, St. Edmund's College, 1907.
Whiteparish, Wiltshire. "The Old Elms", 1912.
Worthing, "The Great Fire", 1919.

Fiscal Series
Cards in sets dealing with the issue of free trade or protection were published by David Allen, Landeker & Brown, Stewart & Woolf, and Tuck.

Fishing. *"Boats Leaving Harbour, St. Ives"*. *W.G. Peak's "St. Ives Series"*. *Printed by Ettlinger & Co.*

Fiscal Series. *"Free Trade"*. *Published by the National Union of Conservative and Constitutional Associations, St. Stephen's Chambers, Westminster, S.W., and produced by David Allen & Sons. P.U. March 1911.*

Fish, R., & Sons
Photographer/publisher, Eastbourne, Sussex. R.P. views.

Fisher, Harrison   **1875-1934**
American painter of beautiful women for magazine covers, which were published also on postcards for Reinthal & Newman, New York. Ill. D. & M. 60; Monahan 121. His cards were sold in Britain by Beagles and Charles Hauff.

Fisher, Admiral John Archibald (Jacky)
First Sea Lord 1914. Bas-relief portrait (sepia) by Scopes.

Fishing
Views of fishing vessels at sea and in port are not uncommon. Sometimes cards can be found showing fishermen landing their catch at small ports such as St. Ives in Cornwall. At larger east coast ports, Lowestoft and Yarmouth for instance, dockside scenes, such as auctions and fish packing, appear on cards. At one time very large quantities of herring were salted in barrels for export to European markets and views show fisher girls cleaning and packing the fish. The Barbican fish quay at Plymouth also appears on postcards.

Fitzall Bandeau Co.   **pre-1922**
Advertising publisher. Series of "Fitzall Fashions" cards.

Fitzgerald, Florence   **fl. 1884-1922**
Landscape painter. Exh. R.A. 17. Facsims. by Faulkner.

Fitzgerald, Frederick R.   **fl. 1897-1938**
Landscape and marine painter. Exh. R.A. 5. Lived at Boscombe in Hampshire. Facsims. of his work were used by Eyre & Spottiswoode in the "Woodbury Series", c.1906, and by Sydenham & Co. of Bournemouth, c.1907.

Fitzpatrick, Frederick
Dublin designer of comic cards.

Fitzsimmons, Dennis Dorian
Poster artist whose work was reproduced on cards by David Allen, e.g. theatrical posters for *Dick Whittington, Little Bopeep* and *Robinson Crusoe*.

Fishing. *"Herrings. A Fine Haul, Sidmouth"*. Photographer unknown. P.U. 1915.

Fishing. *"Fish Market, Aberdeen"* by Brian Gerald. Facsim. by Valentine.

Fishing. *"A Fish Curer's Yard, Lowestoft"*. Publisher unknown.

Fives
This handball game is traditionally played at some of Britain's leading schools.

F.K.
Kehrhahn, F., & Co. (q.v.).

Flags
Many cards show a flag or flags within the design, particularly the patriotic cards published during W.W.I. Perhaps the most comprehensive series is the "Flag" Series by Aristophot. W.N. Sharpe published "Flags of the Allies" and "Flags of the Empire" and Boots a series of "Regimental Colours".

Flap Cards
See: Novelty Cards.

Fleetway Press Ltd.   **fl. 1917-1929**
Publisher, 3-9 Dane St., Holborn, London, W.C. Concessionaires for the British Empire Exhibition, Wembley, 1924. The photographs were taken by Campbell-Gray. This Press covered other public events such as the Royal Tournament at Olympia and the Tidworth Tattoo.

Fleetwood Motor Passenger Carrying Co. Ltd.
Publisher of advertising cards supplied by William Berry of Bradford, Yorkshire, ill. D. & M. 159.

Flemons, T.A.   **pre-1906**
Publisher, Tonbridge, Kent. Coloured facsims. of local views painted by Warren Williams.

Flemwell, George   **fl. 1892-1910**
Flower and landscape artist who painted a set of "Alpine Flowers" for A. & C. Black. Exh. R.A. 3.

"Fletcher's Sauce"
Advertising card showing their factory.

Fletcher-Watson, P.
Landscape artist whose work was used by Tuck in an "In Dickens Land" Series.

Flett, Henry, & Co.   **pre-1930**
Publisher, 110 Cheapside, London, E.C. R.P. views.

Fives. *"The Fives Court, Shrewsbury School"*. Adnitt & Naunton of Shrewsbury. P.U. 1908.

Flood Disasters. *"Crane Bridge Road, Salisbury, Jan. 1915".*
Publisher unknown.

Fleury, Hermann   fl. 1885-1910
North country artist who designed railway cards for Misch &
Co.'s "Noted Trains" and some comic cards for Gottschalk,
Dreyfus & Davis. Ill. D. & M. 110.
    See: Colour Plate 22.

Flood Disasters
Floods were not uncommon before W.W.I., as small towns
and villages were often without a drainage system. Even some
larger towns were occasionally subject to flooding. Here was
an opportunity for the local photographer to record an event
and many issued photographs of disasters literally on their
doorsteps. Among flood disaster cards are the following:
    Bristol, 1914.
    Clydach Vale, Glamorgan. L. Ladd.
    Codford St. Mary, Wiltshire, 1915.
    Louth, Lincolnshire, 1920. W. Benton Series.
    Norwich, Norfolk, 1912. Jarrold's Series and Valentine.
    Salisbury, Wiltshire, 1915.
    Towcester, Northamptonshire, 1907.
    Standground, St. Ives, Huntingdonshire, 1912.
    Watford, 1906.
    Ref: Holford, I., *British Weather Disasters*, 1976, for
detailed accounts of the Louth and Norwich floods.

Flower, Charles Edwin   1871-1951
Landscape artist who later specialised in architectural subjects.
Exh. R.A. 13. He excelled as a long-distance cyclist. Facsims.
of his paintings were used in over 20 Tuck "Oilette" sets and
these included six sets on English cathedrals. He also did work
for several other publishers, including American scenes.

Flower Farms
Postcards depict flower farms, e.g. daffodil farms in Cornwall
and the Isles of Scilly and tulip farms in East Anglia.

Flower Shows
These tend to be of purely local interest and postcard photographs are not common. A view of Beckenham Flower Show,
1905, has been noted.

Flying Boats
Flying boats or seaplanes were often in the news from 1925

until W.W.II. For the whole of this period the world's speed
record was held by flying boats because they were easier to
take off and land at high stalling speeds.
    Ref: Duval, G.R., *British Flying Boats*, 1973.

Foch, Marshal F.   1851-1929
Commander-in-Chief of the Allied Armies in W.W.I. R.P.
by Beagles in the Victory March of the Allied Troops in
London, July 1919. Ill. Holt 717.

Foden's Ltd.
Advertising cards showing Foden vehicles. The headquarters
of the firm were at Sandbach, Cheshire.

Foley Art China
Advertising cards by E. Brain & Co. Ltd., Foley China Works,
Fenton, Staffordshire, established in 1903.

Folk Dancing
This became extremely popular between the wars as a result of
the work of Cecil James Sharp, 1859-1924, who collected
traditional songs and dances and established the English Folk
Song and Dance Society. Folk dances were performed by both
adults and children in towns and villages, and often at major
pageants. Examples are found in Taunt & Co.'s "English
Country Life" Series.

Folkard, Charles James   1878-1963
Illustrator and cartoonist. Worked as an artist for the *Daily
Mail* and invented the famous mouse, Teddy Tail, who first
appeared in the paper in 1915 and continued to appear for 45
years. He illustrated many books including *Arabian Nights*,
Mother Goose Nursery Rhymes and *Songs from Alice*.
A. & C. Black published some of his book illustrations in sets
of postcards, e.g. "English Nursery Rhymes".
    Ref: Cope p. 9 and ill. p. 40.

Fontan, Léo
French artist who designed glamour and déshabillé cards for a
Paris publisher. Ill. Monahan 99. Some of his cards were
imported into Britain.

Football, Association
Postcards concerning football may be divided into:
(i)   Portrait groups of professional teams, e.g. Bradford City,
     1905-6, ill. Hill p. 86; Sheffield United, 1903; West
     Bromwich, 1910.
(ii) Portraits of individual players, e.g. T. Crayshaw of
     Sheffield Wednesday.
(iii) Amateur teams.
(iv) Women football players when women's football
     flourished (see: Women in W.W.I).
(v) Football grounds and crowd scenes.
(vi) Commemorative cards, e.g. Cup Finals.

Football, Rugby Union and Rugby League
The same classification applies as for Association Football
(above) except that no cards of women's rugby teams have
been noted.

Forbes-Robertson, Sir J.
    See: Robertson, Sir J. Forbes-.

Ford, A.W., & Co. Ltd.
Bristol publisher of a "Celebrated Advertisement Series".

Foreman & Sons
    See: Shakespeare Press.

"Forest of Arden Series"
See: Shakespeare Press.

Forestier, Amadée   **fl. 1903-1922**
Landscape artist. Exh. R.A. 8. Painted sets on Belgian cities for Tuck's "Wide Wide World" Series, 7926-30.

Forres, Kit   **fl. 1926-1938**
Artist who designed comic motoring cards in the 1930s.

Forrest, Archibald Stevenson   **fl. 1893-1909**
Landscape artist who painted sets on "Morocco" and the West Indies in the Tuck "Wide Wide World" Series.

Forrest, T., & Sons
Photographer/publisher, Pontypridd, Glamorgan. Colliery R.P.s.

Forsberg, J.
Artist who painted for Tuck's "View" Series, c.1902.

Fossett, Emmie
Star of Fossett's Grand Circus. P.P. by Senior & Co. of Bristol.

Foster, Gilbert
Landscape artist who contributed to Tuck's "Gem Scenery" and "In the Country" sets.

Foster, R.A. (Mrs.)   **fl. 1898-1939**
Flower painter who exhibited frequently at the Nottingham Art Gallery. She lived at West Bridgford, Nottinghamshire. Facsims. of her work were published by Alpha. Ill. Byatt pl. IA, p.167.

Foulsham & Banfield
Photographer/publisher. R.P. views and P.P.s of actors and actresses. Supplied photographs to Rotary.

Fountains
A category seldom recognised though many are to be found on postcards, e.g "The Fountains, Kensington Gardens", and "The Fountain, Roundhay Park, Leeds".

Foyster, H.A.
Publisher, Worthing. Coloured local views.

Fradkin, E.
Artist who specialised in child subjects.

"Fragments from France"
See: Bruce Bairnsfather.

Framed Cards
Cards in which the picture is surrounded by a border. Such borders vary in width and may be plain, coloured or embossed. Some borders are intended to simulate a wooden frame.

Framed Ovals
Several firms produced cards with a rectangular frame and an oval picture within a mount. They included:
(i) A.C. Redman & Co., Southsea, the outer frame simulating wood.
(ii) Rotary "Real Photographic" Opalette Series, simulated wooden frame with decorated corners, patented 1908.
(iii) R. Tuck & Sons, "Gold Framed Sepia" postcards.
(iv) J. Welch & Sons, Portsmouth.
Illustrations overleaf.

Framed Rectangles
These were used by:
(i) "D. & S.K.", "Rembrandt Oak Frame Border".

Football. *"Newport Intermediate School Association Football Team 1913-14". Photo by J.E. Thomas.*

(ii) Fielder & Henderson, shaded grey-brown frame.
(iii) Portsmouth Postcard Publishers, cream-coloured frame with plate mark.
(iv) Tuck "Oilette" (plate marked) cards with embossed frames, e.g. "Rural England" Series.
(v) Wildt & Kray, gilded greetings cards.
(vi) Woolstone's "Milton" postcards, "Glazette Sunk Mount".
Illustrations overleaf.

Framed Sepia Postcards
Cards produced by Tuck for use by local firms such as Johnson & Sons of Bowness and Windermere.

Francis, E.
Landscape artist who painted Tuck's "Picturesque Durham" set.

Frankel, F., & Co.   **pre-1905**
Publisher, London, W.C. Produced a "Star Series" using the star as a trademark. Issued humorous cards including a set called "The Six Senses".
Illustration p.102.

Franklin & Steinel   **c.1907**
Publisher, 108 City Rd., London, E.C., who issued coloured cards of high quality.

Frascati's
Advertisement card showing this famous London restaurant, ill. D. & M. 21.

Fraser, Mary
Actress. P.P. by Hartmann.

Frater, Ernest
Artist who painted battle scenes of the Russo-Japanese War for Hildesheimer.

Fray-Bentos
Liebig advertisement card for corned beef.

Freeman   **pre-1913**
Publisher, Hungerford, Berkshire. "Freeman's Series" of framed local R.P. views.

Framed Ovals. *"A Mother's Pet"* with simulated wooden *"frame"*, and *"mount"*. Rotary *"Real Photographic"* Opalette Series. P.U. 1909.

Framed Rectangles. *"London. Thames Embankment"* in rectangular *"mount"*. Fielder & Henderson. P.U. 1912.

Framed Ovals. *"View from Clarence Pier, Southsea"* with a *"frame"* and *"mount"*. J. Welch & Sons. P.U. 1910.

Framed Rectangles. *"When All the Fields with Richest Green were Dight — Wordsworth"* by G. Riecke within embossed *"frame"*. Facsim. by R. Tuck & Sons. *"Oilette"* (Plate-Marked) *"Rural England"* Series II. P.U. 1909.

Framed Ovals. *"The Square, Mere, Wilts."* R. Tuck & Sons. *"Gold Framed Sepia"* postcard.

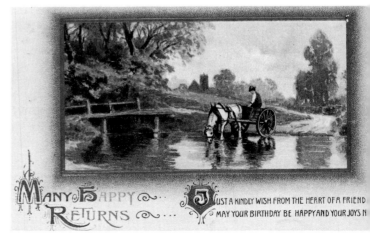

Framed Rectangle. *Wildt & Kray birthday card, printed in Bavaria.*

100

"Pa Has His Bumps Felt". Davidson Bros. P.U. 1906.

"Poor Pa's Troubles. I Won't Be Long Dear". Davidson Bros. P.U. 1906.

"The Adventures of Three Men in a Boat. Over the Weir". Davidson Bros.

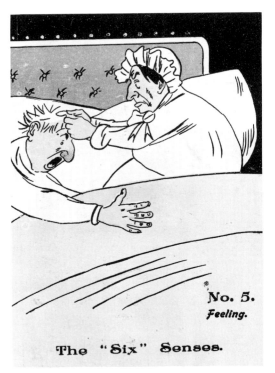

Frankel, F., & Co. *"The 'Six' Senses. No. 5. Feeling"*. *"Star Series"*. P.U. 1908.

Friendly Societies. *"The Order of the Sons of Temperance Friendly Society"*.

French, Annie   **1872-1965**

Glasgow painter and etcher. Exh. R.A. 28. Moved to London shortly before the outbreak of W.W.I. Her work is highly valued.

French, Sir John

Commander of the British Forces in W.W.I. "Bas Relief" card portrait (sepia) by Scopes & Co.

French Topographical Cards

Aware of a potential market, particularly in British resorts such as Bournemouth, Deal and Folkestone, French publishers issued topographical cards for sale in Britain. They bear the words "made in France" in the stamp rectangle. One of the main French publishers to exploit this market was Louis Lévy (q.v.).

Freshwater, Yarmouth & Newport Railway

A single official court size card by the Picture Postcard Co. shows Carisbrooke Castle.

Friendly Societies

These Societies issued postcards to state their objectives and to attract members. Those represented on postcards include the "Hearts of Oak", "Oddfellows", "Rechabites" and "Sons of Temperance".

Frith, F., & Co. Ltd.   **c.1896**

Photographer/publisher, Reigate, Surrey. The business was founded by Francis Frith, see below, to market his photographs in book form. It probably started to issue them in postcard form around the period of his death when his sons were running the business. A few court cards were published, then the larger U.B. cards. From the beginning, the words "Frith's Series" were used to embrace their output but on early cards it is printed in such small letters that they can easily be overlooked. Later cards print this statement in larger type and the sepia output after W.W.I. has "Frith's Series" printed below the words "POST CARD", sometimes even when the cards have been supplied by Frith for official publication by another firm.

Frith's output was mainly of photographic scenes which covered the whole country. They number roughly 75,000.

Apart from photographic views Frith also published some watercolour facsims. including a "Lorna Doone" set, 12. In addition a small number of comic cards were issued.

Ref: The Francis Frith Collection of 60,000 glass negatives is still preserved at the Walworth Industrial Estate, Andover, Hampshire. Recently, the Frith archivist selected 5,000 of the most interesting views which are listed in a booklet published by David & Charles, *The Francis Frith Collection of Victorian Photographs*.

Frith, Francis   **1822-1898**

Born in Derbyshire, educated in Birmingham, apprenticed to a cutlery firm in Sheffield and wholesale grocer in Liverpool. This was the background of Francis Frith who became the most prolific topographical photographer of the 19th century. In the mid-1850s he travelled with his camera and equipment to the Middle East and Egypt and returned to publish books of the photographs taken on his journey. He had established a studio and business at Reigate in Surrey and set out to photograph every part of the British Isles. By the time he died in 1898 he had left over 40,000 negatives. His firm F. Frith & Co. was taken over by his two sons, Cyril and Eustace.

Ref: Jay, B., *Victorian Cameraman. Francis Frith's Views of Rural England, 1850-1898*, 1973.

Fromings, E.
Publisher, Keston, Kent. Local R.P. views.

Frowde, H.
  See: Hodder & Stoughton.

Fruit Farms
Some topographical cards depict fruit pickers of apples or plums on fruit farms in such areas as Kent or the Vale of Evesham, or strawberry trains at Cheddar, Somerset.

Fry, A.H.   pre-1910
Photographer/publisher, Brighton, Sussex.

Fry, John H.
Painter of ships and shipping scenes for Salmon.

Fry, J.S., & Sons Ltd.
Publisher of cards advertising cocoa and chocolate, Bristol and London. There are photographic cards showing the works, exterior and interior. Most cards, however, were specially designed by well-known artists. A few are signed. The copyright was held by J.S. Fry & Sons but several other publishers were given permission to publish for specific purposes. The cards are listed here under their caption wording with some indication of the subjects.
(i) Signed examples
  Tom Browne
    "One Touch of Nature", children outside shop.
    "Highway Robbery", small boy whose chocolate has been snatched.
    "See their Eyes, as she buys Fry's", girl in shop watched by children outside.
    "So near and yet so far", schoolboy outside shop.
  R.C. Carter
    "John Bull says", John Bull.
    No caption, cow being milked.
  Maud Fabian
    "No better food...", polar bear.
  John Hassell
    "Going by leaps and bounds...", Red Riding Hood and dog.
    "Great Scott! What a Find!", burglars and safe.
  Ernest Noble
    "Always merry and bright", boy selling papers.
  Charles Pears
    "Far too good to share", five boys with chocolate.
    "If you feel cold", schoolboy on slide.
    "My Eye!", girl eating chocolate.
    "The Prize Winner", schoolboy with book and chocolate.
(ii) Unsigned cards
    "The best is good enough for me", boy holding cocoa tin.
    "Is the best", lady holding cup.
    "The bloom of health", tramp drinks cocoa.
    "A Perfect Breakfast Table", boy and dog at table made of chocolate.
    "This is my brother Billy", child on stool.
    "With Capt. Scott at the North Pole", sledge and dogs.
    "Avec les Compliments", girl in French costume.
    "With the Compliments of J.S. Fry & Sons", Westminster Abbey, George V Coronation.
    "Disgraced but not defeated", child in dunce's cap.
    "The Diver's Lucky Find", diver in sea.
    "Five Boys", five heads.
    "Five Girls Want", five well-dressed girls.
    "The Five Senses", five girls' heads.

Fry, J.S., & Sons Ltd. *"See Their Eyes, As She Buys Fry's"* by Tom Browne. Celebrated *"Famous Advertisement"* Series.

    "Fry's Cocoa", girl in carriage and several children.
    "Fry's Cocoa", boy with train.
    "Fry's Milk Chocolate", painted on a cow.
    "Fry's Milk Chocolate", boy seated on cocoa tin.
    "Good old Mater", schoolboy with hamper.
    "Hello, Daddy. Guess what I've got", small child makes father guess.
    "I am...", boy in bed.
    "I fully endorse", judge giving verdict.
    "It's worth the risk", children raiding food store.
    "Keeps out the cold", two cards: boy with dog, and lady in furs.
    "The Little Connoisseur", boy holding cup.
    "No better food", highwayman.
    "Right up-to-date", lady and chauffeur.
    "A source of delight", coloured children.
    "Unapproachable", bulldog.
    "Unrivalled", girl in ermine.
    "Whom God Preserve", George V and Queen Mary Coronation.
Publishers who reproduced J.S. Fry designs include Faulkner, Hancock & Corfield, Mansell, Matthews and Tuck. Of the above "Five Boys" and "Hello, Daddy" excelled as items of successful advertising. These were produced under the aegis of Conrad B. Fry who also edited Fry's *The Outdoor Magazine* which was itself advertised on a postcard by Lawson Wood.
  See: Frontispiece.

Fry's Coffee Essence
Advertised by the firm of Charles Fry.

F.S.
Frederick Spurgin (q.v.).

Fuchs, R.
German artist who painted glamour cards.

Fuller, Edmund G., R.B.A.   fl. 1888-1916
Landscape and figure painter. Exh. R.A. 23. Designed cards for Davidson; Henry Moss; Stewart & Woolf; Tuck, "Quaint Holland".

Colour Plate 7:
Watercolour landscape cards

"Woodside, Lymington" by Wilfred Ball.
J. Salmon. P.U. 1922.

"Rye, From the Military Canal" by
W.H. Borrow. Water Colour Post Card
Company. P.U. 1915.

"Holyrood Palace, Edinburgh" by
W. Carruthers. J. Salmon.

Fuller & Richard
Publisher, Great Windmill St., London. Issued two sets of "Alice in Wonderland" cards based on Tenniel's illustrations in the book.

Fuller, T.L.
Publisher, Amesbury, Wiltshire. Local black and white and sepia views, e.g. a plane flying over Stonehenge; Park House Camps, Salisbury Plain.

Fuller's Photo Service
Photographer/publisher, Westerham, Kent.

Fulleylove, John, R.I., R.O.I.   **1845-1908**
Landscape painter and illustrator. Vice-President of the Royal Institute of Oil Painters, 1906, although he painted mainly in watercolours. Using London as a base, he travelled widely, mainly in Belgium, France, Greece, Italy and Palestine, illustrating books such as *The Stones of Venice,* 1900, and *The Holy Land,* 1902, for A. & C. Black. A number of these illustrations were used by Tuck. He also painted a set on "Old Oxford" for Robert Peel and a London set for the Regal Art Publishing Co.

Fullwood, A. Henry   **fl. 1882-1926**
Painter and etcher of landscapes and architectural subjects. Born in Birmingham, he studied at the Birmingham School of Art. In 1881 he went to Amsterdam where he designed cards

Fulleylove, John. *"Edinburgh — The National Monument on Calton Hill". Facsim. by R. Tuck & Sons. "Oilette".*

Funerals. *Horse-drawn hearse and procession leaving Broadlands, Hampshire. Photo by Test Valley Studio, The Hundred, Romsey, Hampshire.*

for the Orient Shipping Line. In 1889 he returned to London. Exh. R.A. 21. Travelled widely in the U.S.A., Australia, New Zealand and South Africa and contributed to Tuck's "Wide Wide World" Series.

Funerals
Several publishers issued cards for the funeral of Edward VII, 1910, using *Daily Mirror* photographs. Cards are known of the funeral of the Duke of Devonshire in March, 1908.

Furness Railway
Lakeland views supplied by McCorquodale and 21 sets by Tuck.
    Ref: R.O.P.L., No. 4.

Furniss, Harry   **1854-1925**
Born in Ireland, he moved to London and contributed to several illustrated journals. In 1880 he joined the staff of *Punch* and remained as a political cartoonist until 1894. One of his poster designs advertising soap was included in Tuck's "Collector's Postcard Series" and John Walker (q.v.) used his cartoons for a series on free trade.

Futcher, F.
Photographer/publisher, 18-19 Fisherton St., Salisbury, Wiltshire. Issued R.P.s of local events including the railway disaster at Salisbury on 1 July, 1906.
    See: Railway Disasters.

G

G.A. & Co. Ltd.
G. Ajelli & Co. Ltd. (q.v.).

Gabriel, Edward
Architect of 42 Old Broad St., London. Exh. R.A. 2. In 1904 he painted the Cunard liner S.S. *Etruria* for Tuck's "Celebrated Liners", 6230.

Gaiety Girls
These glamorous girls were extremely popular. They included such stars as Gladys Cooper, Phyllis Dare, Gertie Millar, Marie Studholme and Ellaline Terris, all constantly photographed.
Ref: Hyman, A., *The Gaiety Years,* 1975.

Gaines, W. & T.   fl. c. 1902-1934
Printer/publisher, Bankfield Works, Kirkstall Rd., Leeds. Trademark an owl overprinted "W. & T. Gaines, Leeds". This firm issued a few cards of local events.
See: Shops and stores.

Gale, B.A., & Co.
Publisher, Premier Penny Bazaar, Portsmouth and Southampton. The postcards show the bazaar from the street and were obviously printed for publicity purposes.
See: Shops and stores.

Gale & Polden Ltd.   fl. c.1901-1968
Printer/publisher, 9 Wellington St., Aldershot; 2 Amen Corner, London, E.C.; Portsmouth; Chatham. This printing firm had been established in Chatham in 1885 but Aldershot became the main centre when *The Military Mail* was published at the turn of the century. It started to publish picture postcards in 1901 and specialised in military subjects but did not confine the output to this field. Some of the early cards included publicity for their army journal. Output included:
(i)   Views of London, e.g. "The Tower" and "Kew Gardens".
(ii)   Views of the provinces and towns abroad, mainly of centres with some military significance, e.g. Bisley, Woolwich and Gibraltar.
(iii) "Wellington Series", the tradename for their "Real Photograph" Series; the series name appears on a shield surmounted by a crown and flanked by pennants.
(iv)   Regimental cards, e.g. "The Rifle Brigade", "R.A.M.C.", "The Devonshire Regt." etc.; half the picture side depicts the uniform in colour; the other half shows the regimental badge in outline and gives the "Battle Honours" and "History and Traditions" of the regiment. Ill. D. & M. 45.
Ref: Check list, Byatt p. 317.
(v)   Naval cards including battleships at sea.
(vi)   "History and Traditions" Series; mainly regimental
(vii) Coloured reproductions of well-known gallery pictures, e.g. "The Vigil".
(viii) "Regimental Badges".
(ix)   "Regimental Pets", ill. Byatt col. pl. IVR.
(x)   Series of humorous sets, e.g. "Naval Nicknames".
(xi)   Event cards, e.g. "Aldershot Tattoo Series", 1928.
(xii) "Nelson Series", scenes in the life of Nelson's navy.
(xiii) "Tower of London" Series.
See: Colour Plates 4 and 5.

Gallery Reproductions
Several publishers produced series reproducing art gallery pictures including:
(i)   Eyre & Spottiswoode Ltd., sepia reproductions.
(ii)   Gale & Polden, the "Wellington Series", coloured.
(iii) Misch & Stock, "From the National Gallery" and "Turner Masterpieces".
(iv)   Photochrom, series including pictures from the Tate Gallery.
(v)   Tate Gallery Series published by the Gallery.
(vi)   Wrench "Famous Pictures Series".

Gallon, Robert   1845-1925
Landscape and coastal painter. Exh. R.A. 32. Lived in London but travelled widely in Britain. His work was used by Hildesheimer in such series as "Cornish Views" and "Thames Views" printed in Bavaria. W.S. Cowell of Ipswich used Gallon's paintings of East Anglia.

Galyons   1902
Publisher, 61 Paternoster Row, London, E.C. A firm which appears to have issued postcards for little more than a year. A set titled "The King's Subjects" was tied to the Coronation of Edward VII and a humorous set, "Ping-Pong", was published in the same year.

Gambling
Rarely reflected on postcards but a card has been noted

Gallon, Robert. *"Langdale Pikes". Facsim. by S. Hildesheimer.*

showing a roulette wheel with instructions on "How to Play One's Stakes".

Garages
These were few and far between in Edwardian times and even in the 1920s. Garage postcards are rare.
   See: Motor Cars.

Garaway & Co.
Publisher, Durdham Down Nurseries, Bristol. Coloured cards of roses used to acknowledge orders.

Garbo, Greta (Greta Louisa Gustafsson)   **b. 1905**
Swedish film actress. Appeared in her first film in 1922. Later went to Hollywood and starred in many films including *Mata Hari*, *Anna Christie* and *Anna Karenina*. P.P.s with John Gilbert and John Barrymore by *Film Weekly*.

"Garden Series"
   See: Alden & Co. Ltd.

Gardener, G.C.
Publisher, 7 Barton St. and 150 High St., Tewkesbury, Gloucestershire. Local sepia views.

Gardner, E.
Publisher, High St., Selsey, Sussex. Framed local photographic views supplied by Valentine.

Gardner, Edwin C.
Landscape artist who sometimes signed with initials only. Exh. R.A. 3.

Gardner, Sidney V.   **fl.1891-1927**
Landscape artist. Exh. R.A. 5. Painted a set on St. Albans for Tuck.

Gardner, William Biscombe   **c.1849-1919**
Landscape artist. Exh. R.A. 44. Lived for some time in London but later moved to various places in the south-east of England, where most of his landscapes were painted. He illustrated books for A. & C. Black and the publishers later issued some of these illustrations in postcard form, e.g. views of Canterbury.

Garner, Henry   **fl. c.1903-1909**
Photographer/publisher, 45 Parkenhoe St., Leicester, and later at 18 London Rd. He named his firm "The Living Picture Post Card Co." and the trademark consisted of a camera on a stand overprinted with the letters "H.G.L." Above this mark, or sometimes elsewhere on the cards, are the words "Living Picture Series". Although local photographic views were used, the main output consisted of contrived photographs to illustrate a song, a hymn, a proverb, humorous comment, romantic idea, or a well-known saying. These were the "Living Pictures" photographed with amateur models or actors. There were also sets on "The Language of Precious Stones", "The Language of Flowers", etc. A few comic cards by F. Macleod were also published. Most of Garner's cards were printed by Shaw & Leathley Ltd., of Shipley.

Garratt
Photographer/publisher, Bristol. Local R.P. views.

Gassaway, Katherine
American designer of cards for Tuck, e.g. "Quaint Children".

Gaston, R.
Artist who painted for Hildesheimer.

Gates, W.V.
Printer/publisher, Tadworth, Surrey. Tinted local views.

Gay, Cherry
Artist who specialised in child subjects.

Gazettes Ltd.   **pre-1928**
Publisher, 22 Beach Rd., Littlehampton, Sussex. Local black and white views.

G.B. Co.
Giesen Bros. & Co. (q.v.).

G.D. & D.L.
Gottschalk, Dreyfus & Davis, London (q.v.).

Gear, Mabel   **fl. 1920s**
Painter of animals and birds. Exh. R.A. 11. Noted for a "Mabel Gear Series" of horse studies published by Valentine.

"Gee-Tee"
Signature used by George Teale (q.v.).

Geiger, R.
French artist who designed glamour cards used by Pascalis, Moss & Co.

Geiger, W., & Co.   **1898**
Publisher, 6 Carey Lane, London, E.C. London views under various conditions — "by daylight", "by moonlight", "snow scenes." These were followed by sets for resorts such as Brighton and Southend. In 1899 they published a standard size set of some of the main architectural features of London, e.g. The Natural History Museum.

G.E.L.
George E. Lewis (q.v.).

"Gem Series"
   See: Grand & Lewis.

General Elections
Postcard publicity was used locally during general elections. This usually consisted of photographs of candidates or light-hearted statements of policy. Nine election cards are ill. by Brian Lund in P.P.M., May 1983, pp. 22-3.
   Illustration overleaf.

Geographia Ltd.
Publisher, 55 Fleet St., London, E.C.4. Trademark a small girl studying a globe. Issued a series of cards with horses by Eileen Hood.

George & Son
Publisher, Brecon. "The Real Photographic Series".

George, Marie   **1879-1955**
Actress. P.P.s by Dainty Novels; Rotary; Rotophot; Tuck, "Celebrities of the Stage".

Gerald, Brian
Landscape painter who was the official artist for the Empire Exhibition, Glasgow, in 1938. His views were published by Valentine in an "Art Colour" Series.

Gerbault, Henri   **b. 1863**
French artist who contributed humorous illustrations to many periodicals some of which were reproduced as postcards.

Gerrards Ltd.   **1903**
Publisher, 411a Harrow Rd., London, W. Issued a few sets of cards with political themes, e.g. "Two Loaves" contrasting the policies of free trade and tariff reform.

Gervèse, H.
French artist who designed cards of "Our Sailors" with English and French captions. They were published in Toulon.

GENERAL ELECTION

DECEMBER 16th, 1910.

'Ere Christmas comes, with all its joys,
Election comes on by surprise ;
Who shall you send to Parliament ?
Why, Eustace Fiennes, of fine descent.

This gentleman, once our M.P.,
Suffered defeat by R. Brassey ;
But still, he's coming on again,
With fervent zeal and active brain.

They say he stands a clinking chance,
And means to make the Tories dance,
And, leading on the Liberal Band,
Will sing again " God gave the Land."

Now Eustace Fiennes has nobly said
That he will fight for cheaper bread ;
And, by his colleagues' valued aid,
Will advocate again Free Trade.

The Band, with Eustace at the head,
Is marching on with colours red,
And eager, anxious for the fray,
Will make a charge on Polling Day.

And when the Flag of Freedom flies,
And cheers ascend towards the skies,
'Twill be a day of letters red,
And " Brittain's " subjects will be fed.

When Eustace Fiennes regains his seat,
The Band will play and drums will beat,
And then the Radicals will shout
" Tariff Reform is up the spout."

Composed, Printed and Published by W. West, North Newington, Banbury

General Elections. *A light-hearted election manifesto. Composed, printed and published by W. West, North Newington, Banbury, in 1910.*

G.F.C.
George Fyffe Christie (q.v.).

Ghosts
Several cards show see-through figures in interior scenes produced by trick photography.

Gibbs, F.H.   **pre-1928**
Publisher/stationer, Fleet St., Torquay, Devon. Local sepia views.

Gibbs, H.R.   **pre-1916**
Publisher, London and Pirbright. Photographer to the Brigade of Guards.

Gibson & Son
Publisher, Hexham, Northumberland. Black and white views of Hadrian's Wall.

Gibson & Sons   **pre-1914**
Photographer/publisher, Penzance and Isles of Scilly. Local R.P. views including several shipwreck scenes.

Gibson, Charles Dana   **1867-1944**
New York pen and ink artist who portrayed an American girl as healthy, refined and dignified. She came to be known as The Gibson Girl and was based on Irene Langhorne, the sister of Nancy Astor, who became Gibson's wife in 1895. She appeared in many magazine illustrations, particularly in *Life*. Ten sets of these Gibson illustrations were reproduced c.1902 by James Henderson & Sons who published the magazine *Snap-Shots* which carried Gibson illustrations. Gibson also designed fantasy and golfing cards.

Giesen Bros. & Co.   **fl. 1902-1909**
Publisher, 28 Monkwell St., London, E.C. Trademark a monogram "G.B.Co." on a square box held by a lady. The firm was closely linked with the Rotophot Co., Berlin, and P.P.s of actors and actresses were grouped in a "Rotophot" Series. They produced some "Book/Post" cards which were called "Giesen's Panel Cards" with photographs of stage celebrities but they were of rather poor quality.

Many embossed greetings cards were published. Various series bear their trademark: a "Baby Series", "Enamelette" Series, "National Dog Series", "Motor Series" and "Parliament Series".

Gift House   **pre-1938**
Publisher, 3-5 Pier Av., Clacton-on-Sea, Essex. Local R.P. views.

Gilbert & Clarke
Publisher, Buntingford, Hertfordshire. Photographic views of the county.

Gilbert, John   **fl. 1885-1915**
Cork artist who designed cards for Purcell & Co. including one for the Cork Exhibition of 1902.

Gill, Arthur
Designer of humorous cards for Tuck including "Seaside Sketches" and "Leap Year".
    See: Colour Plate 14.

Gill, Basil   **1877-1955**
Actor. First London appearance 1898. P.P. as Ferdinand in *The Tempest* by Beagles.

Gill, Gordon, Ltd.   **pre-1903**
Publisher, 78 Old Bond St., London, W. Black and white vignette views of London on U.B.s.

Gill, J.R.
Publisher, Kingsbridge, Devon. Local photographic views.

Gillson   **pre-1924**
Photographer/publisher, Ipswich. Local photographic views, series over 900.

"Gilmour"
Signature of a designer of comic cards.

THE GHOST AT HAMPTON COURT PALACE.

Ghosts. *"The Ghost at Hampton Court Palace". Photograph by J.S. Catford, Morland Studio, Kingston-upon-Thames.*

Gibson, Charles Dana. *"When Doctors Disagree". James Henderson & Sons. P.U. 1903.*

Gilmour, John   **pre-1910**
Publisher/stationer, Cupar, Fife. "Strathenden Series" of photographic views by R.J.F. Spence, in oval frames.

Gilmour Thomson Whisky
Advertising card in the Tuck "Celebrated Poster" Series.

Gilson, T.   **fl. c.1913-1939**
Artist who designed comic cards mainly for:
(i) Alphalsa.
(ii) Marcus Day.
(iii) E.J. Hey.
(iv) Salmon, "She loves me, she loves me not".

Gilyard Bros.
Publishers, North Gate, Bradford, Yorkshire. This firm produced several sets of cards for the Bradford Exhibition of 1904, including moonlight views.

Girls' Own   **pre-1902**
A magazine which issued "The Girls' Own Picture Postcards", e.g. U.B. card in colour showing "Pigeons on the Editor's Window Sill".

Gladwin, May
Artist who painted children's cards for Tuck, e.g. "Little Hollander".

Glamour Cards
Cards of beautiful women were produced in large numbers, especially during W.W.I. when they were used as pin-ups by the troops. Most of them were produced in France and Italy but Rotary issued some photographic examples in the style of the French cards.
  See: Colour Plate 15.

Glanville
Artist's signature on comic W.W.I. cards by Millar & Lang titled "Active Service". Ill. Holt 380 and 382.

Glass, John Hamilton   **fl. 1890-1925**
Edinburgh watercolour painter who contributed Scottish scenes for a series published by George Stuart & Co.

Glasgow & South Western Railway
The main view cards were produced by McCorquodale,

Maclure Macdonald and Tuck. Hotel cards were also issued by McCorquodale and Tuck.
  Ref: Check lists in R.O.P.L., No. 12, pp. 10-14.

"Glaxo"
Advertising cards by Joseph Nathan & Co. include sepia groups of a nurse with six children of various ages all "brought up on Glaxo from one week old."

Glen, H.G., & Co. Ltd.   **pre-1900**
Publisher, 20 Basinghall St., and 133 Park Lane, Leeds. R.P. Yorkshire views, comic and greetings cards and "Yorkshire Savings" in a "Glenco Series". Some comic cards were based on photographs of amateur actors posing for such cards as "Going to the Dogs" and "Washing Day".

Goat Carts
Small carts drawn by goats used in Edwardian times to give children rides at seaside resorts. They are sometimes seen on topographical cards.

Goff, Col. Robert Charles   **1837-1922**
Landscape artist. His work was reproduced in the Medici Society "Old Master Series".

Golay, Mary   **fl. c.1910-1914**
Artist who designed cards for Faulkner, e.g. "Cardinal Birds", and still-life pictures for Ernest Nister.

Goldwin, J.H.
Publisher, The Library, Rochester. Issued a series of cards of places in the Rochester area associated with Charles Dickens, e.g. "The Leather Bottle" at Cobham and Gad's Hill where Dickens lived.

Glamour Cards. *In the style of French glamour cards. Rotary Photographic Series.*

Golliwog. *"Golliwog Rescued" by Florence K. Upton. Facsim. by R. Tuck & Sons. "Christmas" Post Card. P.U. 1904.*

Golf

In 1894 the Open Golf Championship, previously held in Scotland, was held for the first time on an English links. There were three great rivals: James Braid of Scotland, J.H. Taylor of England. and Harry Vardon of the Channel Islands. Portraits of these players and others, with general views of courses and tournaments, appear on postcards. They include links at Alnmouth, Cruden Bay, Grange-over-Sands, Seascale and Turnberry. Valentine issued a set of "Famous Golfers".

Golf provides a subject for a number of humorous cards, e.g. Davidson Bros. "Spooning on the Links" by Tom Browne.

Ref: Henderson, I.T. and Stirk, D.J., *The Compleat Golfer,* 1982.

Golliwog

A black child character invented by Florence K. Upton (q.v.).

Good, Lady

See: Prisoner of War Fund.

Goodall, F.   pre-1923

Publisher, hairdresser and tobacconist, 27 Hart St., Henley-on-Thames, Oxfordshire. Sepia photographs of the town.

Goodman Bros.   pre-1911

Publisher, 104 High St., Southend-on-Sea, and 8 King's Rd., London, S.W. Coloured views.

Goodman, Maude (Mrs. Scanes)   fl. 1880-1920

Painter of humorous studies of children. Exh. R.A. 52. Illustrator of many books. Postcards by Hildesheimer, "Gems of Art" Series, and Tuck.

Goodrich Tyres

Advertising cards. Mountain scene with car.

Gordon, A., & Co.   pre-1901

The Brewery, Lyndhurst Rd., Peckham, London, S.E. Decorative order form postcards.

Gordon, Kitty   d. 1974

Actresss. P.P.s by Davidson Bros., Pictorial Postcard Co.

Goss, P.

Publisher, 2 The Crescent, Morthoe, Devon. Local sepia views.

Goss, William Henry, Ltd.   fl. 1862-1944

Advertiser of armorial porcelain made at the Falcon Pottery, Stoke on Trent. Small souvenir pieces were made, mainly for sale to visitors to seaside and tourist resorts. Many were based on the shapes of early Roman or medieval vessels in museums and each one was printed in colour with the coat of arms of the town in which they were sold. The trade started in the 1880s and continued for nearly 50 years. In 1905 William Goss collaborated with S. Oates & Co., a postcard publisher in Halifax, Yorkshire. Six postcards were produced showing souvenirs against a dark green ground. Each shape could be overprinted, as with the original porcelain souvenirs, with the coat of arms of any town where a sufficiently large order could be guaranteed. So the six original cards have many variants.

Gossages

Advertisers of carbolic soap on poster-type cards. Ill. D. & M. 80.

Gotch, Phyllis M.   fl. c.1902-1905

Designer of humorous cards for Charles Voisey including a series of 15 telling the life story of a chicken.

Gothard, Fred   1882-1977

This part-time designer worked in a bank and supplied Thomas Hine, a Huddersfield publisher, with comic drawings signed "F.G." or "Spatz". After W.W.I. he moved to London and began to design for other publishers including Mack, Photochrom, Salmon, Tollit & Harvey and Tuck,

Goss, William Henry, Ltd. *Loving cup with the arms of the City of London. Published for Goss by S. Oates & Co., Halifax.*

though only a single Tuck example has been recorded.

Ref: Lacy, R., 'Uncle Fred (Gothard)', P.P.M., March 1982, p. 4.

Gothard, Warner   **1835-1909**
Photographer/publisher, 6 Eldon St., Barnsley, Yorkshire. A specialist in disaster photographs, especially multi-view types. The firm covered a number of railway accidents between 1905 and 1916 and many colliery disasters. Gothard died in 1909 and the business was carried on by his four sons.

See: Explosions; Mine Disasters; Railway Disasters; Shipping Accidents and Wrecks.

Ref: An article on 'Warner Gothard of Barnsley' in P.P.A., 1982, states that a total of 59 Gothard cards have been noted covering 40 events. There is also a useful check list.

Gottschalk, Dreyfus & Davis   **c.1904**
Publisher, 4-5 Bunhill Row, London, E.C. Trademarks:
(i) The initials "G.D. & D.L." within a six-pointed star sometimes surmounted by an eye.
(ii) A second mark showing a small girl posting a letter in a pillar box was used from time to time after 1908.
(iii) Cards simply marked with "The Star Series. G.D. & D. London".

The output was mainly of fine quality coloured views printed in Bavaria but also included:
(i) Real photographs of views, railway engines and ships.
(ii) Photographs of actresses (in colour).
(iii) Coloured views of landscapes and ocean liners with inset flags and/or coats of arms.
(iv) Photographs of Members of Parliament.
(v) Comic cards by such artists as H.C. Earnshaw, H. Fleury and H. Parlett. One series signed "K.S." deals with occupational statements in verse, e.g.

    "The Chemist explained to his daughter!
    This stuff that you see in this mortar
    You can sell for a cough
    Or to take a corn off
    By adding a little more water."

Gouldsmith, G.
Photographer/publisher, Bexhill-on-Sea, Sussex. Local views.

Govey, Lilian   **1886-1974**
Designer of postcard sets for Humphrey Milford under the general title "Postcards for the Little Ones", and also for Wildt & Kray.

Ref: Cope p. 10, ill. p. 41.

Gowland Bros.   **pre-1904**
Publisher, Eastbourne. Local views.

Gozzard, J.W.
Landscape artist.

G. & P.
Gale & Polden Ltd. (q.v.).

G.P. Government Tea   **1902**
Set of six cards advertising tea. They were not complete individually, but were designed to make a composite portrait of King Edward VII. The cards were issued at the time of his Coronation.

Grace, Dr. William Gilbert   **1848-1915**
Cricketer. Played for Gentlemen v. Players 1865-1906. He was England's supreme batsman from 1866-76, scoring 400 in a single innings in 1876. His aggregate was 54,896 runs and 2,876

wickets. Captained England in 13 Tests against Australia. P.P. by Wrench.

Graeff, Gustave   **pre-1910**
German portrait painter who contributed to a humorous series by Valentine.

Graf, Marte
Art deco artist who designed silhouette postcards.

Graham, Duncan   **fl. c.1909-1914**
Designer of cards for the Cynicus Publishing Co.

Grand & Lewis
Publisher, Newcastle upon Tyne, Northumberland. Issued a "Gem Series" printed in Hessen.

Grant, Carleton, R.B.A.   **fl. 1885-1901**
Landscape painter. Exh. R.A. 10. His paintings were mainly of scenes in the Thames valley.

Grant, W.H., & Co.
Publishers of woven silk postcards, Foleshill, Coventry. This firm was making woven silks in the 1880s, and probably started to mount silks as postcards in 1902 when the divided back was allowed. Many woven silk postcards carry greetings but there were also views: Blarney Castle, Anne Hathaway's Cottage, The High Level Bridge at Newcastle; portraits: Sir John French, and Lord Kitchener; exhibition postcards: Cork 1902, Bradford 1904, Dublin 1907, Glasgow 1911.

Ref: A detailed account of W.H. Grant's woven silk postcards is given in Godden, G.A., *Stevengraphs and other Victorian Silk Pictures*, 1971, pp. 435-68.

Graphotone Co.
Publisher, London, E.C., and Enfield, Middlesex. Glossy sepia views. This firm also issued a "Grant Card" (per ½d. post) which measured 12¼ × 8½ ins.

Grasset, Eugene Samuel   **1841-1917**
Swiss artist who was trained as an architect and noted as an illustrator. He was particularly known for his poster designs which were exhibited in 1894. These were reproduced as postcards which are highly prized.

Ref: Maindron, E., *Les Affiches Illustrées 1886-1895*, Paris, 1896.

Gratton, B.
Publisher, Bakewell, Derbyshire. Local tinted views.

Gravely, Ethel Marion   **fl. c. 1904-1910**
Pen and ink artist who made drawings for Charles Worcester & Co. (q.v.).

Gray, Campbell-, Ltd.   **pre-1911**
Photographer. Issued views of the Crystal Palace and grounds for the Festival of Empire, 1911, and was official photographer for the British Empire Exhibition at Wembley in 1924.

Gray, J.P.
Publisher, Cambridge. Views of Cambridge colleges in a "Cantab Series".

Greagsby, A.W.
Publisher, Surrey. "Real Photo Series".

Great Central Railway
Two sets of views including abbeys, castles and churches, and a set by Photochrom of scenes at Immingham Deep Water Dock. A series of over 30 R.P. views, which also appear in W.H. Smith & Sons "Kingsway Series", was also issued.

Ref: For check list see R.O.P.L., No. 6, pp. 3-6.

Great Eastern Railway Co. **1905**
Official series included sets on "Watering Places on the East Coast", "Cathedrals", "Cambridge Colleges", the "Norfolk Broads", "Locomotives" and general views. The publishers producing cards covering the area included Faulkner, Jarrolds and Tuck. There were many poster reproductions including Hassall's "Come and Join Us on the East Coast".
Ref: Complete details with check list in R.O.P.L., No. 8, 'Picture Postcards Officially issued by the Great Eastern Railway Company'.

Great Northern and City (Electric) Railway
This underground railway opened in 1904 and issued a few cards. The railway was taken over by the Metropolitan Railway in 1913.
Ref: List of cards issued in R.O.P.L., No. 16, p. 8.

Great Northern, Piccadilly & Brompton Railway
This line opened in December, 1906. Previously Hartmann had issued cards showing the construction work. Two sets by the Locomotive Publishing Co. were issued in 1906 and 1907 respectively. They show cars, stations, a signal cabin and a power house.
Ref: R.O.P.L., No. 16, p. 9.

Great Northern Railway **1903**
Official cards include Photochrom coloured sets of "Famous Abbeys", "Noted Cathedrals", "Historic Castles", "Stately Homes" and various types of G.N.R. locomotives. Many views of Great Yarmouth were published and some of Great Northern Hotels in London, Bradford, Leeds and Peterborough. A few court cards by the Picture Postcard Company were also used.
Ref: For check lists see R.O.P.L., No. 6, pp. 7-12.

Great Western Railway
Locomotives are depicted on cards by the *Locomotive Magazine*, e.g. "The Flying Dutchman", and by Tuck in their "Famous Expresses" Series. A very large number of official cards were published.
Ref: For complete check lists see R.O.P.L., No. 9.

Greaves & Co.
Publishers, 5 and 58 High St., Stamford, Lincolnshire. Output

Great Western Railway. *"Old Yarn Market, Conegar Tower, Dunster". Official card. G.W.R. Series.*

included:
(i) Greetings cards for Christmas, Easter, New Year and birthdays.
(ii) Views with embossed frames.
(iii) Facsims. of paintings overprinted with greetings.

Green, Edward Rhodes, & Co. **pre-1907**
Publisher, Victoria St., Blackpool, Lancashire. The output, which consisted almost entirely of comic cards, was sold under the general title "Victoria Series".
See: Teddy Ashton.

Green, Mabel **b.1890**
Actress. P.P.s by Davidson Bros., Giesen Bros. (Enamelette), Palatine Pictorial Co., Philco, Pictorial Postcard Co., Rapid Photo Printing, Rotary and Woolstone Bros.

Green, Roland, F.Z.S. **fl. c.1926-1932**
Painter of animals and birds who worked at the Ruskin Studio, 6 New Court, Lincoln's Inn, London. Designed postcards for the Ruskin Studio Art Press and illustrated books for A. & C. Black. Some of his illustrations were reproduced by this publisher as postcards, e.g. "Birds One Should Know".

Green, W.T.
Publisher, Winchester. Issued black and white views of the Wolvesey Pageant of 1908.

Greenaway, Kate **1846-1901**
Artist and illustrator. Her drawings of children in early 19th century costume made her famous. She contributed to many magazines, illustrated over 30 books and designed Christmas cards for Marcus Ward. However, she never designed postcards, and "Kate Greenaway postcards" are all reproductions of her book illustrations or Christmas cards.
Refs: Buday, George, *The History of the Christmas Card,* 1954, pp. 227-9, gives an account of her Christmas card work; Engan, R., *Kate Greenaway,* 1981; Moore, A.C., *A Century of Kate Greenaway,* 1946; Spielman, M.H., *Kate Greenaway,* 1905.

Greene, Evie **1876-1917**
Actress and vocalist noted for her part in *The Country Girl,* 1902. P.P.s by Beagles, Byers, Rotary and Tuck.

REAT NORTHERN PICCADILLY & BROMPTON Ry. SHIELD *used in* CONSTRUCTION.

Great Northern, Piccadilly & Brompton Railway. *"Shield Used in Construction". Official card. P.U. 1907.*

LUCKY DOG!

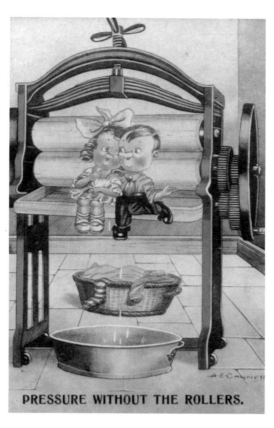

PRESSURE WITHOUT THE ROLLERS.

**Colour Plate 8:
Carnell, Ludgate and
Clearwell cards —
were they all by the
same artist?**

*"Lucky Dog" by Albert
Carnell. Valentine. P.U.
1923.*

*"Pressure Without the
Rollers" by A.E. Carnell.
Photochrom. P.U. 1930.*

*"Ain't it Rural?" by
Ludgate. E.J. Hey & Co.*

*"I Didn't Serve an
Apprenticeship in France
for Nothing" by Clearwell.
E.J. Hey & Co.*

"AIN'T IT RURAL?"

I DIDN'T SERVE AN APPRENTICESHIP
IN FRANCE FOR NOTHING

Greetings Cards

These were designed for many occasions including birthdays, Christmas, Easter, Hallowe'en, the Jewish New Year, Leap Year, St. Patrick's Day, Thanksgiving Day, twenty-first birthdays, Valentine's Day, wedding anniversaries and wedding days. Most publishers issued greetings cards, if only as overprints, and they exist in infinite variety. Some of the better known publishers were:

Alpha/Alphalsa Publishing Co., coloured "Across the Sea" cards.

Bamforth, R.P.s with embossed tulip frame.

Beagles, R.P.s with flowers.

Birn Bros., Valentine cards, ill. Monahan 161.

E.T.W. Dennis, embossed cards with coloured insets and embossed frame.

Ettlinger, sold Schwerdtfeger greetings cards from 1901. Ill. D. & M. 182.

Giesen Bros., pre-W.W.I.

Inter-Art Co., birthday cards by Barribal. Ill. Monahan 191.

J.J. Keliher, "Shamrock Series" coloured floral cards.

E. Mack, humorous cards by Reg Carter.

Philco, R.P.s with embossed frame, printed in Italy.

Regent Publishing Co., R.P.s using heads of actresses.

Rotary, R.P.s using heads of actresses in lettering. Embossed ivy frame.

E.A. Schwerdtfeger, Father Christmas Cards. Ill. D. & M. 178.

H.J. Smith, Brighton, importer of greetings cards from Europe.

Thridgould & Co., sold Schwerdtfeger stock of birthday cards after outbreak of W.W.I.

Greetings Cards. *"A Merry Xmas. XV Divn. Loos. Sept. 25, 1915"*. Christmas card in satirical vein. Publisher unknown.

Tuck, Easter cards, birthday cards, Christmas and New Year cards. Ill. D. & M. 173 and 174.

Many cards with flowers were still based on the "Language of Flowers" published in many small handbooks in Victorian times, e.g. in Warne's *Bijou Books,* 1883. The commonest flowers all reflect aspects of love. Forget-me-nots, which appear frequently, mean True Love; Pansies — Thoughts; Purple Lilac — First Emotions of Love; Roses — Love.

Embroidered silk greetings cards were popular during and after W.W.I. Ill. Monahan 103, 105-7.

See: Colour Plates 5, 10 and 11.

Greiner, M.
Designer of cards with children.

Gretna Green
A number of publishers have issued special series about the village in Dumfriesshire because of clandestine marriages which were said to be held in the Blacksmith's Shop. Lord Russell in Edinburgh in 1939, however, rules the legend to be unfounded. The following have been noted:
(i) Hayton & Son of Carlisle, view of the old Blacksmith's Shop with Thos. Johnston, the old Priest.
(ii) Tuck "Oilette" Series, "A Gretna Green Elopement".
(iii) Valentine "Art Colour" Series with a caption on the face of each card.

Gretty, G.
Landscape artist who painted for Tuck.

"Greys" Cigarettes   **1920s**
Publisher of two series of 48 cards each entitled "Beautiful Britain".

Gribble, Bernard Finegan   **1873-1962**
Marine painter who was trained as an architect. Exh. R.A. 66. From 1912 was marine painter to the Worshipful Company of Shipwrights. He contributed to the Tuck set "History in the Making". Also painted "Saved", a scene in which a lifeboat has just rescued crew and passengers from a sinking ship.
See: Royal National Life-Boat Institution.

Griffiths, S.G.   **pre-1930**
Publisher, Haverfordwest, Pembrokeshire. Local views.

Griggs, H.B.
American artist who designed humorous cards with children.

Grocock, A.
Publisher, Croydon, Surrey. Local R.P. views.

Gronvald, Henrick   **1858-1940**
Bird artist in Denmark. Moved to England 1893. Employed by Natural History Museum. Illustrator of books on ornithology.

Gross, Edward, Co.
American firm which used the Alphalsa Publishing Co. as its agent in Britain.

Gross, H.
Photographer, Calne, Wiltshire.

Grossmith, George   **1847-1912**
Actor. P.P.s in Play Pictorial Series by Tuck.

Grossmith, George Jr.   **1874-1935**
Actor in musical comedy and revue. P.P. by Beagles.

"Grosvenor Series"
See: W. Ashton & Sons Ltd.

The famous old Blacksmith's Shop, Gretna Green,
Thos. Johnston, the old Priest, ready for a Motor Run. He has been responsible for many romantic marriages in the old Smithy Buildings.

Gretna Green. *"The Famous Old Blacksmith's Shop ..."* Hayton & Son, Carlisle.

Grosze, Manni
Designer of art deco silhouette postcards.

Grove, William Henry   fl. pre-1914
Chelsea artist who designed posters. His work is included in Tuck's "Celebrated Posters" Series.

Groves, Robert E.   fl. c.1887-1939
Landscape and figure painter of St. Albans. Painted series of the St. Albans' Pageant for Tuck.

Grube, H., Ltd.   1910
Publisher, 12a Paternoster Row, London, E.C. Issued a "Blow" postcard with a small bag which could be inflated to show views of London.

Grunevald
Isaac and Sigrid Grunevald were husband and wife and signed work with the surname only. They were both born in Sweden, Sigrid in 1885 and Isaac in 1889.
    Isaac painted marine subjects, still life and theatrical scenery; Sigrid painted portraits of children.

Gruss Aus Cards
These words are the German for "greetings from". They were used on German postcards early in the 1890s when coloured views were printed on U.B. cards, leaving about one-quarter of the picture side blank on which the sender could write a message. When picture postcards were allowed in Britain the same style was adopted. Indeed, most of the early British cards were printed in Germany. Such cards are usually described as of the Gruss Aus type.

Guernsey Press Co. Ltd.
Publisher, St. Peter Port, Guernsey, C.I. Guernsey views.

Guerzoni, Stephanie   b. 1887
Viennese artist who moved to Switzerland at an early age and made her name as a painter. She designed glamour cards.

Guigesse, Ada
Actress. P.P. by Rotary.

Guillaume, A.   b. 1873
French figure painter who designed seaside comic cards which were imported by Pascalis, Moss & Co.

Guinness Brewery
Advertiser, Dublin. Direct postcard advertising and R.P. views of the brewery yard, horse drays, etc.

Gummery & Blackham   pre-1905
Photographer, Droitwich, Worcestershire.

Gunn, Archie   b. 1863
Artist who specialised in glamour and W.W.I. patriotic cards.

Gunn, G.L.
Publisher, Fine Art Gallery, Valley Rd., Lynton, Devon. Tinted matt-surfaced local views.

Gunter, W., & Son
Publisher, Tenby, Pembrokeshire. Composite local view photographic cards.

Gurnsey, C. & H.   fl. c.1905-1941
Publisher, 23 Walterton Rd., Paddington, London, W.9 until 1913. Thereafter there were various moves (Byatt p. 108). Henry Gurnsey was the businessman, Charles the artist. The output was mainly of comic cards.

Gurnsey, Charles Joseph
Artist who designed a "Gurnsey Series". See previous entry.

Gusteeson, P.C.
Publisher, Esplanade Tobacco Stores, Ventnor, I.O.W. Sepia views.

Guy, Herbert F.
Publisher, Surrey.

Guy, T.
Artist who painted architectural landscapes of Durham Castle and York for E.T.W. Dennis's "Dainty Series" and views of York for J.W. Ruddock.

Gwennet, W. Gunn   fl. 1903-1940
Landscape artist who also designed some humorous cards for Philco. Exh. R.A. 8.

G.W.W.
G.W. Wilson & Co. (q.v.).

Gypsies
Views of gypsy encampments with horse-drawn caravans, or gypsies on the road, are not common but represent a romantic aspect of rural life which attracts many collectors.

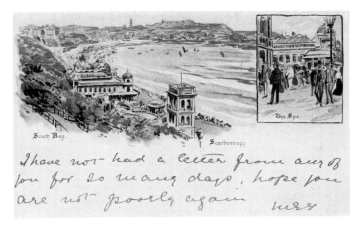

Gruss Aus Cards. *"South Bay. Scarborough"*. *Gruss Aus type card by an unknown publisher. P.U. 1902.*

Hacker, Arthur   **1858-1919**
Painter of an "English Beauty" Series for Faulkner.

Haddow, William   **pre-1909**
Publisher, Tipton, Staffordshire. "Haddow Series" of black and white views of an area extending west from Staffordshire to the Welsh coast.

Hagelberg, Wolff   **1902**
Publisher, Bunhill Row, London. Trademark "WH" within a shield. A Berlin firm which introduced hold-to-light cards.

Hager, Nini
Art nouveau artist whose cards are highly valued.

Haig, General Sir Douglas   **1861-1928**
Succeeded Sir John French as Commander-in-Chief British Forces in 1915. R.P. by Beagles. Ill. Holt 61.

Haigh Bros.
Photographer/publisher, Barnsley, Yorkshire. North country views.

Hailey, Clarence   **pre-1905**
Photographer, Newmarket, Suffolk. Racehorse photographs.

Hale, B.   **pre-1919**
Publisher, High St., Amesbury, Wiltshire. Local sepia views.

Hall, Bernard P., & Co.   **c.1904**
Art publisher, Bakewell, Derbyshire. Published two main types of card:
(i)   "Water Colour" cards, serial nos. to over 600.
(ii) "Horticultural" cards in the form of flowers which could be coloured in by hand.

Hall, C.A.
Painter of sets of "British Wild Flowers" for A. & C. Black.

Hall, Sydney Prior   **1842-1922**
Portrait painter who contributed to *The Graphic*. One of his views of an Oxford Degree Ceremony was published by George Davis.

Hallet, A.R.
Photographer/publisher. Sturminster Newton, Dorset. Local R.P. Views.

Halstan, Margaret   **b. 1879**
Actress. First appearance at Haymarket Theatre in 1896. Played in the film *Drake of England* in 1935. P.P. by Davidson.

Hamel, E.   **pre-1909**
Publisher and printer, Nottingham. Calendar advertisements.

Hamilton, E.
Marine artist who designed advertising cards for the Union Castle Shipping Line showing ships used on their services.

Hamilton, T.M.   **fl. 1920s**
Artist who lived in Dublin and designed comic cards.

Hamilton's Postcards   **pre-1920**
Publisher, 24 Queen's Rd., Brighton, Sussex. Trademark "H" on a circular medallion with a flower. Beneath the medallion are the words "Hamilton's Quality". R.P. views of Sussex.

Hamish
Pseudonym of James Allan Duncan (q.v.).

Hammick, Joseph William   **fl. c.1907-1912**
Artist. Exh. R.A. 4. Lived at Mount Ephraim, Tunbridge Wells, and painted glamour postcards for Photochrom under such titles as "The Motor Girl".

Hammond, Davy   **pre-1907**
Flower painter. Set of facsims. by the Ruskin Studio Art Press.

Hammond, J.D.
Publisher, 1-2 Westonville Promenade, Margate, Kent. Coloured local views. "British Throughout".

Hamon, Horace J.
Publisher, Jersey, C.I. Coloured Jersey views.

Hampshire, Ernest Llewellyn   **fl.1907-1938**
Landscape painter. Exh. R.A.3. Facsims. of garden scenes by Salmon.

Hampson, W.
Publisher, Bettws-y-coed. North Wales views in a "Snowdonia Series".

Hampstead Tube
This London underground line was opened in June 1907. Three sets of cards cover places of interest reached by the line. Two were printed by Weiners (q.v.) and one by Photochrom.
  Ref: Check lists in R.O.P.L., No. 16, p. 10.

Hamptons   **pre-1908**
Photographer/publisher, Argyll St., Glasgow. R.P.s of local events, e.g. launching of Sir Thomas Lipton's *Shamrock*.

Hanbury, Hilda
Actress. P.P.s by Rotary, Rotophot and Tuck.

Hanbury, Lily   **1875-1908**
Actress. P.P. on Rotary Bookmarker card.

Hancock & Corfield Ltd.   **1905**
Publisher who specialised in views of old coaching inns in a "Gems of Art" Series, having taken over from the Art in Commerce Co. in 1905. The cards, which had U.B.s, were printed in America. The artist was John Charles Maggs who had painted the scenes in Victorian times.

Hand-decorated Postcards
Many an aspiring artist has decorated his or her own cards. Some have real appeal. One early Edwardian artist who signed them "Amy" is particularly sought after.

Hannaford, Charles E., R.B.A.   1863-1955
Landscape painter. Exh. R.A. 1, but over 80 at R.B.A. Facsims. by E.T.W. Dennis & Sons.

Hansteen, A.
Animal painter who designed cards with dogs for Tuck.

Harbour, Jennie
Artist who designed "Oilette de Luxe" sets for Tuck, titled "Early Victorian", 3801 and 3803.

Harbours
Harbour scenes are among the most attractive of postcard views. They range from the small fishing port to the city harbours used by ocean-going vessels and often show dockside workings, e.g. Princes Dock, Govan.

Hardings   pre-1906
Publisher, Bristol and Cardiff. "Britannia Series" which included framed views of South Devon and coloured multi-view cards of the Clifton Zoological Gardens, Bristol. One card shows views of a chimpanzee, cockatoo and a kiwi; others show a single animal such as a tiger. The name "Britannia Series" was also used by Boughton & Sons of Thetford (q.v.).

Hardman, E.   pre-1920
Stationer/publisher, Torquay, Devon. Local sepia views.

Hardy, Dudley, R.B.A., R.I.   1866-1922
Artist whose main work was for illustrated magazines and theatre advertisers. Exh. R.A. 33. Designed humorous cartoons, also published in *Punch,* for Collins, Davidson, Faulkner, Hartmann, H.J. Smith, Tuck, Valentine and Wrench. His poster work is included in Tuck's "Celebrated Posters" Series.
Ref: For a check list of Dudley Hardy postcards see P.P.A. 1984, p. 79.

Hardy, F.C.   fl. pre-1901
Black and white artist whose sketches of horses, e.g. Royal Horse Artillery, were reproduced by Hildesheimer, but in colour on U.B.s.

Hardy, Florence   c.1860-1933
Artist. Exh. R.A. 36. Her Christmas card and postcard designs were mainly of children dancing and in fancy dresses. She worked mostly for Faulkner.

Hardy, Heywood   1842-1933
Animal and sporting painter. Exh. R.A. 30. His work was used by Langsdorff & Co.

Hardy, Paul
Historical artist. Exh. R.A. 1. His black and white drawings were adapted for Tuck's "Old English Sports".

Hargrave, W.   pre-1915
Photographer/publisher, 82 Preston St., Faversham, Kent. Local R.P. views.

Harper, Henry Andrew   1835-1900
Landscape painter of scenes in the eastern Mediterranean. Exh. R.A. 10. His work was used by the Scripture Gift Mission.

Harrap, J., & Sons
Publisher, Holborn Buildings, London, E.C.

Harris, Charles
Photographer/publisher, 77 London Rd., Dover. R.P.s of the Dover Pageant of 1908.

IN THE HARBOUR, ST. IVES   37317

Harbours. *"In the Harbour, St. Ives".* E.A. Sweetman. *"Solograph" Series De Luxe Photogravure.*

Harris, Claude
Photographer who worked for Faulkner, Hildesheimer, Rotary, and Wildt & Kray.

Harris Cycle Co.
Publisher. Advertising cards.

Harris, James Taylor   pre-1910
Photographer/publisher, Counterslip, Bristol. P.P.s at the 1910 aviation meeting at Bournemouth.

Harris, Percival   pre-1919
Publisher, High St., Barnstaple, Devon. Local R.P. views.

Harrop's Ltd.   pre-1905
Publisher, Liverpool. "Cable Series" of coloured views. R.P.s of local celebrities.

Hart Publishing Co. Ltd.
Publisher, London, E.C. Trademark a small heart, often on the picture side. Firm which specialised in R.P.s including views and greetings cards.

Hart, W., & Son (Saffron Walden) Ltd.
Publisher of local sepia views supplied by Frith.

Hartland, F.
Painter of glamour cards for Tuck.

"Hartley's Jam"
Advertising cards showing their works at Aintree.

Hartmann, Frederick   fl.1902-1909
Publisher, 45 Farringdon St., London. Trademark a lady holding an artist's palette and brushes. F. Hartmann was very unhappy about the U.B. and was convinced that room could be made for a message on the address side leaving one side available for a picture. He put the case very strongly to the British Post Office and succeeded with his argument. He then introduced the divided back. The Hartmann output included:
(i)   High quality coloured views printed in Saxony which covered most of Britain, including the Channel Islands.
(ii)   Photographs by C. Reid of Wishaw of Scottish scenery and people.
(iii)   Photographs of royalty and various celebrities. *continued*

Hassall, John. *"What Every Woman Knows!"* Facsim. by *Inter-Art Co.*

(iv) "Miniature Series", multi-view cards with up to 12 views on each card.
(v) Coloured photographs of children and animals.
(vi) Famous cricketers in action.
(vii) Bathing beauties.
(viii) Express trains and underground railways.
(ix) Famous liners.
(x) Public schools.
(xi) Breeds of cattle.
(xii) Cartoon cards on the free trade issue.
(xiii) Famous battles, Caton Woodville.
(xiv) Hold-to-light transparency cards.
(xv) An "Aquarelle" Series of facsims. including work by Jotter.
(xvi) "Sporting Cats" by Louis Wain.

Apart from the above, Hartmann imported a great many cards from Europe, mainly glamour, especially from Trenkler & Co. of Leipzig, for whom he was the British agent.

Hartnoll   **pre-1905**
Publisher, Bank St., Newquay, Cornwall. A "Hartnoll Series" of Cornish views. Some cards were supplied by Frith.

Harvey, F.B.
Publisher, Andover, Hampshire. Local R.P. views.

Harvey, Sir John Martin   **1863-1944**
Actor-manager. Joined Henry Irving's company at the Lyceum in 1882 where he remained until 1896. In 1899 he took over the management of the Lyceum where he played Sidney Carton in *The Only Way* with great success. In 1901 he played in *A Cigarette Maker's Romance*. In 1921 he was knighted.

P.P.s by Beagles; Ellis & Walery; London Stereoscopic Co.; Rotary, ill. Hill p. 54.

Harvey, Len   **b. 1907**
Boxer. British Heavyweight Champion. Retired in 1942. P.P. by George Spearman.

Haslehurst, Ernest William   **1866-1949**
Landscape artist. Exh. R.A. 18. Painted Cotswold scenes for Salmon and Valentine.

Hassall, John, R.I., R.M.S.   **1868-1948**
Illustrator, watercolourist and poster designer, particularly remembered for The Great Northern Railway poster of the jolly fisherman with the "Skegness is so Bracing" caption. Exh. R.A. 12. His first postcard work was for write-away cards at the turn of the century. Hassall's interests went beyond the bounds of graphic art. He was a collector of Mesolithic flints and his collection, with the exception of one flint, is now in the Fitzwilliam Museum, Cambridge. The single flint was buried with him. He decided he would confuse any archaeologist who might dig him up in the 2000s!

Hassall's comic cards are highly prized. He designed for Davidson Bros., Faulkner, Inter-Art, Savory, Tuck, Valentine and Wrench. His theatre posters for comedies and pantomimes were reproduced as cards by David Allen, ill. Byatt, col. pls. IIH and J. He designed many advertisements and at least 10 have appeared on postcards.

Hauff, Charles Henry, & Co.   **c.1901**
Importer/publisher, 69 Great Russell St., London, W.C. Issued series of cards by Agnes Richardson (q.v.) but nearly all his output consisted of cards imported from abroad, particularly from Italy and from Reinthall & Newman of New York.

Haviland, Frank
Artist who designed glamour cards.

Haviland, William   **1860-1917**
Actor-manager. P.P. by Beagles.

Hawke, A.H.
Photographer/publisher, Helston, Cornwall.

Hassall, John. *"Peace is Not Always Found in Solitude".* *Davidson Bros.*

Hawke, M.B., Baron 1860-1938
Cricketer. Captain of Yorkshire for 28 years. P.P.s by
S. Cambridge. Ill. Byatt 49.

Hawker, S.
Publisher, Post Office, Bradninch, Devon.

Hawkins
Photographer/publisher. P.P.s of cricketers.

Hawley
Photographer/publisher, Sheffield.

Haworth, Paul
See: Elmer Keene.

Hawthorn, Leslie, & Co.
Crane builders, Newcastle. Advertising cards.

Hawthorne, Lil b.1882
Actress. P.P. by Ralph & Co.

Hay, Beryl
Artist who designed a "Fairy Whispers" Series for A.M. Davis
& Co.

Hay, W.J.
Publisher, John Knox's House, Edinburgh. Trademark John
Knox's House. Local Edinburgh views.

Haydock, W.T., & Sons Ltd.
Publisher, Soho, London. Photographic portraits.

Hayes, Frederick William, F.R.G.S. 1848-1918
Landscape and coastal painter. Born in Cardiff and studied
watercolour painting in Liverpool. Designed cards for Inter-
Art, Meissner & Buch, and Tuck. A Tuck "Oilette" Series on
North Wales is curiously without locality captions.

Hayes, Sydney fl. 1906-1924
Animal painter. Exh. R.A. 6. Painted "Oilette" sets for Tuck,
e.g. "Chums" and "Share and Share Alike".

Hayes, W.
Publisher, York.

Hayes, W.R.
Athlete who undertook to trundle a pair of carriage wheels
from Portsmouth to Newcastle upon Tyne and back in 100
days. Souvenir postcards by Mezzotint Co. (q.v.).

Haylock, E.C. pre-1910
Publisher, March, Cambridgeshire. Coloured views by a local
photographer.

Hayton & Son
Publisher, Carlisle. Trademark two heraldic shields with the
inscription "Success Series. H. & S." below. Black and white
views of Carlisle and district, including Gretna Green.

Hayward & Son
Publisher, Stourport, Worcestershire. "Sabrina Series" of
R.P. views.

H.B.
Hutson Bros. (before 1919) (q.v.).

H.B. Ltd.
Hutson Bros. Ltd. (after 1919) (q.v.).

H.B. & S.
Harvey Barton & Son (q.v.).

H.B. & S. Ltd.
Harvey Barton & Son Ltd. (q.v.).

H.B. & S.B.
Harvey Barton & Son, Bristol (q.v.).

H.C.
H. Coates (q.v.).

Head, Arthur William fl. 1886-1929
Landscape painter. Exh. R.A. 4. His work was used by Tester,
Massy & Co., in their "Gold Framed Postcards".

Head, Edward Joseph fl. 1889-1929
Landscape painter. Exh. R.A. 18. His work was used by
Tester, Massy & Co. in their "Gold Framed Postcards".

"Health & Strength" Series
Sepia portraits of boxers issued with the magazine.
See: Tommy Burns.

Hearn, Nancy
Actress. P.P. in "Lilywhite Photographic Series".

Hearts of Oak Benefit Society
Publicity cards.

Heath Robinson, W.
See: W.H. Robinson.

Heavy Goods Vehicles
Commercial vehicles form a specialist category for postcard
collectors.
Refs: Baldwin, D., *Heavy Goods Vehicles, 1919-1939*, 1976;
Klapper, K.F., *British Lorries, 1900-1945*, 1974.

Hebblethwaite, Sidney fl. 1899-1908
Artist who worked for *Pick-Me-Up* and *The Graphic*, mainly
in black and white. He designed comic cards for Tuck "Racing
Illustrated" and "Comic History".

Heinke's Diving-Gear Pump
Advertising card showing a ship in Tilbury Docks.

Heinz, H.J., & Co.
Poster-type cards advertising canned foods.

Hellier, V.G. pre-1912
Photographer/publisher, Bexhill-on-Sea, East Sussex. Local
R.P. views.

Hellier's Locomotive Series 1903
Express trains on cards printed in Germany. Very few have
been recorded.

Hely's Ltd. pre-1910
Publisher, Dublin. Photographs of the Easter Rising.

Henckle, Carl
Painter of military subjects.

Henderson, Alex. D.
Publisher, 90 High St., Maybole, Ayrshire. R.P. views
including some supplied by Valentine.

Henderson, James, & Sons Ltd. 1903
Publisher, Red Lion Court, Fleet St., London, E.C. Best
known for cards by the American artist Charles Dana Gibson
who created the Gibson Girl. The drawings were taken from
magazine illustrations and there are over 60 of these black and
white cards. Other Henderson cards include:
(i)   Sepia views.
(ii)   Greetings cards including "Children's Birthdays".
(iii) "Aqualette" watercolour facsims. series.
(iv)   "Humour" and "Pictorial Comedy".
(v)   "Gem Picture Series" of book illustrations. *continued*

(vi)   Ladies' heads, Emil Vernon.
(vii) Horses' heads, Gilbert Wright; Hunting Series.
(viii) Toy models including cut-outs.
(ix)   British Sporting Birds Series.
    See: Colour Plate 14.

Hensman, J.M. (Miss)
Designer of a playing card series for Stewart & Woolf.

Heraldic Cards
These are to be found with single and multiple coats of arms, coats of arms of towns or counties with an appropriate view, and coats of arms of families with tartans. Publishers include:
(i)   Brown & Rawcliffe "Camera" Series, civic heraldry with views.
(ii)   W.E. Byers.
(iii) Excelsior Fine Arts Co., arms and flags of many countries.
(iv)   C.W. Faulkner & Co., U.B. cards with views and coats of arms.
(v)   W.H. Goss, coats of arms on ceramics.
(vi)   Gottschalk, Dreyfus & Davis, Scottish coats of arms on views of Scotland.
(vii) Hartmann, views with embossed and gilded coats of arms.
(viii) "Ja-Ja" Heraldic Series, Stoddart & Co., specialists in heraldic cards.
(ix)   Jarrold & Son.
(x)   Rapid Photo Printing Co.
(xi)   Rattray "Photo and Arms Series".
(xii) W. Ritchie & Sons.
(xiii) A. Savage, "Arms of the Oxford Colleges".
(xiv) Scott Russell & Co.
(xv)   A. Smee.
(xvi) R. Tuck & Sons, coats of arms on multi-view "Glosso" cards and coats of arms of other countries.
(xvii) Valentine, multiple coats of arms of Oxford and Cambridge colleges.
(xviii) E. Wrench, Oxford and Cambridge colleges.
    Ref: Scott-Giles, W., *Civic Heraldry of England and Wales*, 1953.

Herouard, Mathilde Angeline
French figure painter who designed glamour and déshabillé cards for a Paris publisher. Ill. Monahan 98.

Hervé, G.
French artist who designed glamour cards. Ill. Monahan 129.

Hewerdene, M.B.
Artist who painted dancers and pierrots for Faulkner sets.

Hey, E.J., & Co. (Ltd.)   fl. 1908-1921   (Ltd. from 1917)
Publisher/importer, 57-9 Ludgate Hill, London, E.C. Tradename "Ludgate Series". A series of comic cards was issued by such artists as T. Gilson and Fred Spurgin. German glamour cards were imported in the closing years.
    See: Colour Plate 8.

Hey, Paul
German artist who designed cards which were imported into Britain, e.g. "Sommermorgen", Wintersonne", and some cards for children.

Heyermans, Jean Arnould   fl. c.1881-1902
Belgian figure painter who moved from Antwerp to London in the 1890s and did some postcard work for Tuck, e.g. "English Cottage Homes", "Tower of London".

Heraldic Cards. *London coat of arms from a "Heraldic" Series by "Ja-Ja". P.U. 1906.*

H.G.L.
Henry Garner, Leicester (q.v.).

Hibberds Ltd.
Publisher, Tisbury, Wiltshire. Local views printed in Treves, Germany.

Hickling, P.B.
Designer of romantic cards for Lawrence & Jellicoe.

Hickman, C.
Newsagent/publisher, 651 Romford Rd., Manor Park, Essex. Framed coloured photographic views.

Hicks, Sir Seymour   1871-1948
Actor-manager and author. Wrote and acted in *The Cherry Girl,* 1903, and *The Gay Gordons,* 1907. He was responsible for the building of the Aldwych Theatre and was knighted in 1935. P.P.s by Beagles, with Zena Dare; by Rotary, with Ellaline Terris in *Bluebell.*

Hickson
Artist who designed at least one anti-Kaiser card for Photochrom.

Hier, Van
    See: Van Hier.

Higgs, J.   fl. pre-1920
Designer of comic cards for the British Art Co. "Britart Series".

Higgins, Sydney B.   pre-1906
Publisher, Henley-on-Thames, Oxfordshire. Local coloured views printed in Germany.

Heraldic Cards. *"Bognor". Valentine's Series. P.U. 1908.*

Heraldic Cards. *Cambridge colleges. Valentine's Series.*

Heraldic Cards. *"Margate. The Oval. Cliftonville". Brown & Rawcliffe's "Camera" Series.*

Heraldic Cards. *"Torrington". Twiss Bros. "County Arms" Series.*

Highams 1905
Photographer/publisher, Woodford Green, Essex.

Highland Railway Co.
For a relatively small railway a remarkable number of official view cards were issued. They were produced by Valentine — at least 38 collotype sets between 1902 and 1910 with many reprint variations, some photographic views, c.1906, and some coloured views, c.1908; McCorquodale & Co. produced some hotel cards.
Ref: Full details with check list are given in R.O.P.L., No. 14, pp. 4-21.

Hildebrand, Fritz
Designer of a "Teddy Bear" "Oilette" Series for Tuck.

Hildesheimer, Albert
Poster artist whose work is included in Tuck's "Celebrated Posters" Series.

Hildesheimer, Siegmund, & Co. 1900
Publisher, 14-16 Silk St., and 8 Chapel St., London, E.C., 63 Miller St., Manchester; premises in New York. This firm was producing high quality Christmas cards as early as 1876 and appears to have started to produce picture postcards in 1900. After about 1905 a monogram trademark was used with the initials "S.H. & Co." within a circle, sometimes with a series name beneath. Output included:
(i) "Gems of Art", a series reproducing the work of living artists such as Laura Epps (Lady Alma Tadema).
(ii) "London by Twilight" Series, by A.G. Pirkis.
(iii) Write-away cards based on motoring episodes by Pirkis.
(iv) Black and white series including "Famous Horses".
(v) Humorous cards, e.g. "Heads and Tails They Tell".
(vi) Various art nouveau cards, e.g. "The Seasons".
(vii) Photographic portraits.
(viii) "Fac-simile" sets based on paintings by various artists. These coloured views, with serial nos. over 5,000, were printed by chromolithography "in our Works in Germany". The following selection shows the range of these views with the name of the artist when known.

5171 North Wales, E. Longstaffe.	5382 Algerian Views.
5186 Scotland, E. Longstaffe.	5391 Thames Views.
5189 Scotland, E. Longstaffe.	5392 Bournemouth.
5229 Ireland, E. Longstaffe.	5395 Salisbury.
5248 Surrey, L. Staples.	5401 Surrey Views, pre-1907.
5275 Cathedrals, A. Payne.	5409 English Lakes.
5292 London Views.	5416 On the Severn.
5310 Langdale Pikes, R. Gallon.	5420 Yorkshire.
5324 Fifteenth-century London, A. Payne.	5430 Views of Chingford.
	5431 North American Indians.
5353 Goring.	5433 Orkney Isles.
5362 North Devon.	5445 Scenes in Surrey.
5363 Shakespeare Country.	5456 Canterbury.
5364 Norfolk Broads.	5457 British Navy, Past and Present, R. Gallon.
5366 Ruined Abbeys.	
5367 Norfolk Broads.	5485 Views of Waltham.
5370 Scottish Lochs.	5489 Epping Forest.
5376 In the Trossachs.	5492 Wanstead & Leytonstone.
5377 Cornish Views.	5494 Views of Bristol.
	5521 Views of Oxford.

See: Colour Plate 20.

Hill Figures
See: White Horses and Hill Figures.

Hill, G., & Son
Publisher, Stanley St., Leek, Staffordshire. Views of the Manifold Valley.

Hill, Mary fl. 1912-1928
Watercolour artist. Exh. R.A. 3. Painted street scenes in Hampstead where she lived. They were used in facsims. by an unknown publisher.

Hill, R.H.O.
Publisher, Blackpool. Coloured views.

Hills & Co.
Publisher, Sunderland, Durham. Tradename "Hill's Aquatint Series", in a rectangle with a lady holding palette and brush. Coloured views of Scotland and the Lake District, some supplied by MacPherson Bros. of Invergordon, Ross and Cromarty.
See: John MacPherson.

Hills & Co. Ltd. fl. 1903-1905
Publisher, London. Issued a "For the Empire" Series embracing the following types:
(i) Pictorial comments on newspaper advertisements.
(ii) Glamour girls' heads.

Hilton, Alfred E.
Designer of comic cards who contributed sets with naval or military titles to Modena & Co.'s "Ducal Series", e.g. "Illustrated Army Orders".

Hind, Thomas fl. c.1908-1910
Printer/publisher, 31 John William St., Huddersfield, Yorkshire. Comic cards mainly using the work of Fred Gothard who used the initials "F.G." or the pseudonym Spatz. Many make fun of roller-skating in a set titled "On the Rink".

Hindenburg, Paul von 1847-1934
German soldier and President of the German Republic. After successful campaigns against the Russians he was given supreme command of the German Field Army on the Western Front in 1916. He became President in 1925. P.P.s by several publishers.

Hines, Frederick fl. c.1880-1905
Landscape painter. Exh. R.A. 13. Rural scenes for Ernest Nister.

Historic Houses
These appear on topographical cards by a number of publishers. It seems to be a neglected field as far as collectors are concerned but one with considerable interest, particularly as so many of these houses are disappearing. Old photographs are often the only records left of those that have been demolished. In Edwardian times very few were open to the public. The following have been noted, but there must be many more:
Arundel.
Burghley House, Greaves & Co.; Photochrom; Radermacher, Aldous & Co.
Chatsworth House.
Eaton Hall, Hartmann.
Haddon Hall.
Hamilton Palace, unknown publisher, U.B.
Hampton Court Palace, Morland Studios.
Hatfield House, Photochrom.

Historic Houses. *"Burghley House, Stamford". Greaves & Co.*

Historic Houses. *"Longleat House". R. Wilkinson & Co.*

Historic Houses. *"Scone Palace, near Perth". "Woodall" Series.*

Hinchingbrooke House, Photochrom.
Knebworth House, Photochrom.
Longleat House, R. Wilkinson & Co.
Mere Hall, Valentine.
Newstead Abbey, Photochrom.
Orwell Park, W.S. Cowell.
Osborne House.
Penshurst Place.
Sandringham, Photochrom; Salmon.
Scone Palace.
Wilton House, R. Wilkinson & Co.

In addition Tuck produced an "Oilette" Series on "Historic Houses".

Refs: *Historic Houses, Castles and Gardens,* published annually; Ware, D., *A Short Dictionary of British Architects,* 1967.

Hitch, Edward
Publisher, 4 St. Mary St., Weymouth, Dorset. Views of Portland, e.g. "St. Peter's Church built by the convicts".

H.L.
Hugo Lang (q.v.).

H.M. & Co.
Henry Moss & Co. (q.v.).

Hoare, Florence E.   fl. c.1915-1923
Artist who painted a view of Church St., Bexhill, which was used in facsim. by an unknown publisher.

Hobbs & Sons   pre-1937
Publisher, Blandford, Dorset. Local R.P. views.

Hobbs, Sir John Berry (Jack)   1882-1963
The cricket career of Jack Hobbs spanned the years from 1905 to 1934. He was a brilliant batsman, making an aggregate of 61,237 runs (average 50.65) with 197 centuries.

Hobley, Edward George, A.R.C.A.   1866-1916
Landscape painter. Exh. R.A. 5. In 1898 he became art master at Queen Elizabeth Grammar School, Penrith. In 1909 the Ullswater Navigation and Transit Co. commissioned him to

Hobley, Edward George. *"Well-end Bridge, Deepdale". Facsim. by Ruddock of Lincoln for the Ullswater Navigation and Transit Co.*

Hockey. *Sheffield University Team, 1927-8, the author stands on the extreme left.*

paint 24 pictures of the Lake District for postcard reproduction by Ruddock of Lincoln. He also painted a set of 12 for Photochrom. His cards were sold on board the Ullswater pleasure boats.

Ref: Birkbeck, A. 'The Gentle Artist: Edward George Hobley', P.P.M., November 1982, p. 33.

Hockey
The Men's Hockey Association in England was formed in 1886, although hockey has never proved as popular as football. England won the hockey tournament at the Olympic Games in 1908 and 1920.

Hodder & Stoughton   **fl. c.1908-1920**
Publisher, London. This firm, jointly with H. Frowde, issued several sets of paintings by Eileen Hood. During W.W.I. they produced patriotic cards.

Hodge, David T., & Co.   **pre-1907**
Publisher, Kingsmead St., Bath, Somerset. Black and white views.

Hodges, R., & Co.   **pre-1907**
Photographer who covered the rail disaster at Shrewsbury in 1907.

Hodgson, A.
Stationer/publisher, 64 Victoria St., Bristol. R.P.s of Bristol and Clifton.

Hodgson, G.
Publisher, Brampton, Cumberland. "Arty Series" of coloured local views.

Hodgson, George   **1847-1921**
Watercolour landscape painter. Exh. R.A. 4. Facsims. of the country around Nottingham in J.W. Ruddock's "Artist Series".

Hodgson, H.   **pre-1918**
Photographer/publisher, Cleckheaton, Yorkshire. R.P. views of the Huddersfield district.

Hodgson, William Scott   **fl. 1900-1927**
Landscape and coastal painter. Exh. R.A. 2. Lived for a time at Whitby, Yorkshire.

Hodgson's Library
Publisher, Seaford, Sussex.

Hoey, Iris   **b.1885**
Actress. P.P.s by Beagles, and Rotary.

Hoffman, C.R.
Tobacconist and "Shipping Photo-Card Publisher", No. 1 The Docks, and 44 Oxford St., Southampton, Hampshire. The photographs cover not only battleships and the largest liners such as the *Mauretania* but also the Southern Railway channel steamers.
    See: Shipping.

Hoffman, H.W.
Watercolour landscape painter who lived in London.

Hoffman, Josef   **1870-1956**
Art nouveau artist particularly associated with the Wiener Werkstätte which he helped to found in 1903. Some of his work was published by Philipp & Kramer.

Hoffman, Maud
Actress. First stage appearance in 1890. P.P. in Shurey's "Yes and No" Series.

Hoggarth, Arthur Henry Graham   **1882-1964**
Watercolour artist who lived at Petersfield. Exh. R.A. 10. Painted a number of scenes of the Oxford Pageant of 1907 for Davis's Oxford Post Cards.

Hohenstein, A.
Art nouveau artist.

Holbrooks Ltd.
Advertisers of sauces.

Hold-to-light Cards
    See: Novelty Cards.

Hole, H.H.   **pre-1913**
Publisher, Williton, Somerset. Local R.P. views.

Holiday Camps
There were relatively few holiday camps before W.W.I. Two camps on the Isle of Man feature on postcards — Howstrake Camp, near Groudle Glen, pre-1903, and Cunningham Camp which opened in 1907. Pre-W.W.I. postcards show the Cunningham Camp with rows of bell tents in which campers slept. After W.W.I. the holiday camp industry in Britain expanded rapidly and by 1939 over 200 had been established.

Holloway & Bible   **pre-1907**
Publisher, Weston-super-Mare, Somerset. Coloured local views.

Holloway, Edgar A.   **fl.1934-1940**
Military artist. Exh. R.A. 6. Painted regimental cards for Gale & Polden in the 1930s. Ill. D. & M. 41.

Holloway, W.H.J.   **pre-1917**
Printer/publisher, 40 Denison Rd., Brentham, Ealing, Middlesex. Produced cards supporting the War Bond Campaign of 1917.

Hollyer, Eva   **fl. c.1889-1904**
Figure painter. Exh. R.A. 3. Her paintings of small girls in the style of Kate Greenaway were used in facsims. by Birn Bros. and Langsdorff & Co. She occasionally used the pseudonym Alice Martineau.

Holman, F.G.

Publisher, Reculver, near Herne Bay, Kent. Local black and white cards with historical notes. Fred Holman was born in Reculver in 1840 and lived into his '80s when the postcard business was continued by his daughter, Mary Helen Holman.

Holmes & Son   **pre-1914**

Publisher, High St., Andover, Hampshire. Local views.

Holmes, F.

Photographer/publisher, Mere, Wiltshire. Photographs of early motor cars.

Holmes, George Augustus, R.B.A.   **d. 1911**

Genre painter. Exh. R.A. 20. Facsims. by Hildesheimer.

Holmes, W., & Co. Ltd   **1903**

Publisher/stationer, Glasgow. This firm was established in the 19th century and started to publish postcards in early Edwardian times. In 1913 it adopted a trademark of a herald within a circle.

   Output included:
(i)   Real Photo Series, Scottish views.
(ii) Comic cards.

Holt, Christopher, & Co.

Printer/publisher, Sutton and Carshalton, Surrey. General views printed in Saxony.

Home, Gordon   **b. 1878**

Landscape painter. Exh. R.A. 1. Set on "Picturesque Yorkshire — the N.E. Coast" for Tuck, 7557.

Homewood, A.H.   **pre-1905**

Publisher, Burgess Hill, Sussex. Trademark an art nouveau-style hand mirror with twisted handle and the name and address on the frame. The mirror reflects a view. Coloured views were, in fact, the main output covering most of Sussex and Kent, but a special interest seems to have been taken in trams, trains and especially railway stations.

Honiton Lace

Frith's issued a card showing Honiton lace against a black background and a lacemaker at work. It was retailed by Pollard's Ltd. of Exeter.

Honiton Lace. *"Honiton Lacemaker and Lace"*. *Frith's Series.*

Hop Picking. *"Hop-Picking-Londoners"*. Young & Cooper, Maidstone, Kent.

Hood & Co.

Publisher, Middlesbrough, Yorkshire. Trademark a church spire with the words "Sanbride Series". Views including cards for the West Clare Railway in Ireland. The firm also obtained some Hampshire photographs from Judges.

Hood, Eileen   **fl. 1916-1924**

Animal painter who contributed horse studies to a "Geographia" Series on "Polo Ponies" and also to a "Wild Life" Series published by Humphrey Milford. She painted a dog series for Frowde/Hodder & Stoughton.

Hood, H.D.   **pre-1913**

Publisher, The Abbey, Melrose, Roxburghshire.

Hooke, William H.

Publisher/stationer, Abingdon, Berkshire. Local sepia views supplied by R.A. (Postcards) Ltd.

Hooper   **pre-1910**

Photographer/publisher, Cromwell St., Swindon, Wiltshire. Local views including the cottage in which Job Franklin was murdered by his brother.

Hop Picking

Scenes in the Kent hopfields were published by Young & Cooper of Maidstone.

Hope, Lt. Col. P.M., O.B.E.

Publisher, Keswick. Postcard map of the English Lake District.

Hopkins, C.R.   **pre-1932**

Watercolour artist who painted a number of Thames views for Salmon, e.g. "Woolwich Reach".

   Illustration overleaf.

Hopkins, Everard   **1860-1928**

London illustrator who contributed to many magazines. His black and white drawings for *Punch* were coloured and used by Tuck "Oilette", 4516.

Horder, J., & Son

Publisher/wholesale stationer, Wellingborough, Northamptonshire. Photographic views.

Hopkins, C.R. *"Upper Pool"*. *Watercolour facsim. by J. Salmon.*

Hornby, W., & King, J.W.   pre-1909
Publisher, Ilford. Facsims. of unattributed paintings. Cards supplied by Wildt & Kray.

Horniman's Tea
Advertiser. One postcard shows King Edward VII in military uniform holding a cup with the caption "A Right Royal Drink". Some Horniman's Tea cards may be sold as postcards, though they are, in fact, usually slightly smaller and the backs are completely covered with advertising material.

Horowitz, Helena   fl. 1889-1920
London miniature painter. Exh. R.A. 33. Her postcard work is usually classed under glamour.

Horrell, Charles A.   fl. 1895-1918
Artist who painted young ladies, often with a dog. They were W.W.I. pin-ups published by James Henderson.

Horrocks & Co. Ltd.   pre-1906
Advertising publisher, Ashton-under-Lyne. This firm issued postcards which advertised the Wood-Milne Rubber Heel, a circular rubber which could easily be screwed into a leather heel without resorting to a cobbler. The firm used a drawing of the heel as a trademark. The cards are mainly coloured views of Lancashire towns, though seaside views of Scarborough and Whitby have been noted. Each card carries a number and the series appears to have had 40 cards in all.

Other advertising cards were issued for various northern firms, including some facsims. of watercolours.

Horse and Dog Cards
A large number of postcards feature both horses and dogs in the same setting. Publishers include:
(i)   Alpha Publishing Co., horses in stables with dogs.
(ii) Hildesheimer & Co., horses in stables with cats or dogs.
(iii) Tuck & Sons, set titled "Faithful Friends", Norah Drummond; set called "Stable Chums".

A considerable number of similar cards were imported from Italy (A. Traldi of Milan) and distributed in Britain by the Alpha Publishing Co.

Horse Racing and Racehorses
Horse racing cards were published by:

Horse and Dog Cards. *"In the Stable". Alpha Publishing Co.*

(i)   Blum & Degen, a "Kromo Series" of racehorses each captioned with the names of sire and dam, e.g. "Sceptre" by "Persimmon-Ornament".
(ii) Stephen Elliott & Co., a specialist publisher in this field. Postcards of racehorses and mounted jockeys in tear-off booklets.
(iii) M. Ettlinger & Co., "The Royal Series", racing scenes, e.g. "Tattenham Corner, Epsom, during a race".
(iv) Hildesheimer, "Famous Horses".
(v)   Millar & Lang, "The National Series", cards of Derby

Horse Racing. *"First Past the Post" by Ludwig Koch. R. Tuck & Sons. "Oilette".*

Horse Shows. *Horse decorated for show. Photographer unknown.*

Horse-drawn Transport. *A baker's cart in Hampshire. Photo by Thatcher & Son, Basingstoke.*

winners with and without jockeys.

(vi) Rotary Photographic Co., photographs of racehorses, e.g. "Littleton" (Derby Cup Winner), and "Isinglass and St. Marlow", thoroughbred stallions.

(vii) R. Tuck & Sons, horse racing sets including "A Trial Gallop", "The Preliminary Canter" and "Leading in the Winner", also sets with famous racehorses, e.g. "Popular Racing Colours".

(viii) Valentine, racehorses photographed by Clarence Hailey of Newmarket.

(ix) Wildt & Kray "Racing Colours" Series, facsims., the cards give the owners' names.

(x) Wrench, views of racehorses, e.g. "Sceptre".

Horse Shows
Cards show the Champion Cart Horse at Lewisham, 1907, owned by a firm of coal merchants.

Horse-drawn Transport
In Edwardian times commercial and passenger transport was mainly by horse-drawn vehicles. Many people had a horse and trap; others used an open horse brake, a vehicle which could carry 8-10 passengers, and in large towns and cities there were open-topped horse buses, run by a number of companies of which the largest was the London General Omnibus Company. These were drawn by two horses and the sides carried advertisements, ill. Hill p. 72. Over 3,500 horse buses were still operating in London in 1900, each bus carrying about 26 people. For commercial transport there were horse-drawn milk floats, bread carts and coal drays. Removal vans were also drawn by horses.

All forms of horse transport are well represented on postcards.

Ref: Parry, D., *English Horse Drawn Vehicles,* 1979.

Horses
Postcards depicting horses fall naturally into two groups: the realistic and romantic. Realistic types show horses at the circus, on the farm, racing or being ridden. Romantic cards show the head of a horse, sometimes caressed by a glamorous lady, or posed with dogs under such captions as "Faithful Friends".

Realistic cards were published usually in sets or series by:

(i) G.P. Abraham, series with shepherd on horseback.

Horse-drawn Transport. *Horse Bus. "Piccadilly Circus. London". London Pavilion in background. Publisher unknown. P.U. 1906.*

(ii) Alpha Publishing Co., coloured pictures of stallions.

(iii) Beagles & Co., "Real Photographs" of farm horses.

(iv) Cynicus Publishing Co., coloured scenes with horses and foals.

(v) Geographia Ltd., facsims. after Eileen Hood of various breeds.

(vi) F. Hartmann, views with such titles as "Farm Horses" or "Suffolk Mares and Foals".

(vii) S. Hildesheimer & Co., "Famous Horses" Series including successful racehorses, e.g. St. Maclon, Sceptre, Scullion, Solicitor.

(viii) Judges, photographs of horses and ponies in natural settings, e.g. "Dartmoor Ponies".

(ix) Knight Bros., groups of black and white horses in a "Knight Series".

(x) Photochrom Co., coloured set of farm horses at work and a sepia set of "New Forest Ponies".

(xi) Rotary Photographic Co., a series of photographs including shire stallions, hacking mares and many race-

Horses. *Shire horse. R.P. by Wildt & Kray.*

horses, sometimes overprinted with greetings. Also a "Radio Series" of framed photographs of individual farm horses.

(xii) E.W. Savory, "Photogravure Series" titled "Studies of Horses".

(xiii) Schwerdtfeger & Co., photographs of working horses.

(xiv) Tuck & Sons, "Horse Studies" and "By Mead and Stream", facsims. after Harry Payne; "The Horse" and "On the Land".

(xv) Valentine & Sons, R.P.s of horses and foals.

(xvi) Wildt & Kray, photographs of shire horses at work, facsims. of horses, and a series showing individual horses with descriptions on the address side, e.g. "Shire Stallion. Hendre Champion. Sold for £1,550. Owned by Leopold Salomons, Esq."

Romantic scenes with horses, sometimes in the form of a greetings card were published by:

(i) Faulkner & Co., facsims. after Florence E. Valter and a series of birthday cards of framed scenes with horses.

(ii) J. Henderson & Sons, horses' heads, a set by Gilbert Wright.

(iii) Inter-Art Co., horses with lovely ladies.

(iv) W.E. Mack, horses' heads in circular frames with birthday wishes in verse beneath.

(v) Mansell & Co., two series, one of horses looking over stable doors or stiles; the other of horses' heads.

(vi) Humphrey Milford, two series by Eileen Hood; one with young girls feeding and stroking horses, each with a two-line verse beneath; the other titled "The Farm Team".

(vii) Photochrom Co., a "Celesque" set of horses' heads by G. Vernon Stokes.

(viii) Pictograph Publishing Co., "Friends" set.

(ix) J. Salmon, facsims.: after George Rankin of horses' heads in profile; after C.T. Howard of glamorous ladies holding horses' bridles; after Gordon Gray with such titles as "Mutual Understanding".

(x) Tuck & Sons, set by Norah Drummond titled "Man's Best Friend" and two sets by Hilda Walker, "Horses Heads" and "Bit and Bridle".

See: Colour Plate 16; Blacksmiths; Horse-drawn Transport; Horse Racing and Racehorses; Horse and Dog Cards; Hunting; Racecourses; Steeplechasing.

Horsfall, Mary   fl. c.1900-1914
Painter who lived in St. John's Wood, London. Exh. R.A. 1. Designed cards for Carlton Publishing Co., William Ritchie of Edinburgh and for Tuck, e.g. "Maidens Fair" and "Your Fortune". Some of her cards dealt with women's suffrage.

Hospitals. *Appeal Card. "The Queen's Hospital for Children, Hackney Rd., London, E ... 130 beds always full and over 74,000 outpatient attendances annually. Urgently in need of funds". Philco Publishing Co. P.U. 1910.*

Hospitals. *"The New Royal Infirmary, Manchester. Front Entrance". William Ashton & Sons. "Grosvenor Series". P.U. 1909.*

Hotels, Inns and Public Houses. *"The 'Cat and Fiddle' (1,765 feet above sea level) Buxton"*. *Stengel & Co. U.B.*

Hotels, Inns and Public Houses. *"Dungeon Ghyll Hotel"*. *Stengel & Co.*

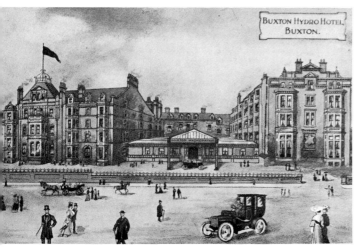

Hotels, Inns and Public Houses. *"Buxton Hydro Hotel"*. *A hotel publication.*

Hotels, Inns and Public Houses. *"The Hawthorns Hotel, Bournemouth. South Front"*. *Photochrom "Celesque" Series. P.U. 1917.*

Hospitals and Infirmaries
Exterior views and photographs of the wards in hospitals are fairly common; operating theatres, operations and patients receiving treatment are rare on postcards though some do exist. A Tuck "Oilette" set was issued to raise money for the Elizabeth Garrett Anderson Hospital, since hospitals depended largely on voluntary contributions before the days of the National Health Service.

H.O.T.
H.O. Taylor (q.v.).

Hotels, Inns and Public Houses
This is a vast field. Virtually every hotel keeper was anxious to have postcards of his hotel to sell to visitors. It was excellent free publicity. Collectors no doubt choose a limited field. Cards can be divided very roughly into the following categories of which a few examples are given.

(i) Large seaside hotels, e.g.
   Hotel Metropole, Bexhill-on-Sea.
   Metropole and Grand Hotels, Brighton.
   Metropole and Grand Hotels, Folkestone.
   Empire Hotel, Lowestoft.
   Grand Hotel, Eastbourne.
(ii) Railway Hotels (q.v.), e.g.
   Midland Hotel, Manchester.
   St. Enoch's Hotel, Glasgow.
   Many of the early railway companies established hotels near their mainline stations. They all appear on postcards.
   Ref: Mainline station hotels are listed in detail in R.O.P.L., Nos. 2, 6, 8, 9, 10, 11, 12, 13 and 19.
(iii) Large London hotels, e.g.
   Hotel Cecil, ill. D. & M. 14, interior view.
   Grafton Hotel, Tottenham Court Road.
   Imperial Hotel, Russell Square. *continued*

129

(iv) Historic inns, e.g.
> The Pilgrim's Inn, Glastonbury.
> The New Inn, Gloucester.
> The Feathers, Ludlow.
> The Greyhound, Corfe Castle.
> The Talbot, Oundle.
> The Mermaid, Rye.
> The George & Dragon, Hurstbourne Tarrant.

A great many of these inns on the old coaching roads have survived. Many have been modernised and still provide accommodation.
> Ref: Coysh, A.W., *Historic English Inns,* 1972.

(v) Small country inns and hotels, e.g.
> Dungeon Ghyll Hotel, Westmorland.
> The Ship Inn, Porlock.
> The Keigwin Arms, Mousehole.
> The Cat and Fiddle, Buxton.

Some of these have ceased to cater regularly for overnight visitors and are used mainly as locals, where people meet for a drink and a talk.

(vi) Temperance Hotels. These were mainly associated with the Temperance Movement which flourished in Victorian and Edwardian times, though there is a postcard showing the "Old Temperance Hotel of 1400" at Aber Conway.
> See: Hydros.
> Ref: 'Tourist Guide to Britain's Hotels', P.P.M., April 1982.

Hough   **pre-1910**
Publisher, Douglas, I.O.M. R.P. views.

Hough, W.
Jeweller/publisher, Amesbury, Wiltshire. Coloured local views.

Houghton, Jane
Artist whose drawings were used by the Art Ray Co.

Howard, Charles T.   **fl. 1897-1930s**
Artist who painted landscapes and military scenes used in facsims. by Photochrom and Salmon. He also designed a few comic cards for Salmon.

Howard, F.M.
Publisher, Lyndhurst, Hampshire. Photographic views.

Howard, Fred S.
Designer for Misch & Co.'s "The Fire Brigade", 454.
> See: Colour Plate 16.

Howe, Ian A.
Artist who designed comic cards during W.W.I.

Howe, Jean
Designer of a "Tiny Tots Series" for Valentine.

Howe, Vertigen & Co.   **1904**
Publisher, Guildhall Chambers, Basinghall St., London, E.C. A short-lived partnership which broke up in 1906 leaving the firm as H. Vertigen & Co. The main output consisted of coloured views under a general title "Picturesque England". There were also scenes in Europe and Japan. Novelty cards were a speciality.

H.P.
Harry Parlett (q.v.).

H. & R. Ltd.
Liverpool publisher of photographic views covering the city and parts of north Wales.

H.S.   **pre-1910**
Publisher, Margate. "Marine Series" of comic seaside cards, and framed local views.

H. & S.
Hayton & Son (q.v.).

H.T.B.
Publisher of a "Sunny South" Series.

Huardell, P.G., & Co.   **fl. 1899-1904**
Publisher and fine art dealer, 18-19 Cranbourn St., London. Primarily importers of postcards from all over Western Europe including cards by such artists as Mucha and Cassiers. They also published various scenes of London involving flowergirls, policemen, cab drivers, etc.

Hubner, Peter Paul   **fl. 1908-1913**
Designer of cards with children for the Inter-Art Co. Exh. R.A. 3.

Huddlestone
Publisher, Orwell, Suffolk. Issued a "Huddlestone Series".

Hudson Bros.   **pre-1925**
Publisher, London, E.C.1. Specialist in birthday cards printed in Italy.

Hudson, Isabel
Artist who painted comic cards of children for the Inter-Art Co.

Hudson, Roy, Photos Ltd.   **pre-1939**
Photographer/publisher, 12 Terminus Rd., Eastbourne, Sussex. Local R.P. views with serial nos. over 5,000.

Hughes, Annie   **1869-1954**
Actress. P.P.s by Philco, and Tuck "Bookmarker" Series V.

Hughes, C.R.
Bookseller/publisher, West Gate, Tenby, Pembrokeshire. Local R.P. views.

Hughes, Lloyd
Designer of comic cards for Valentine.

Hughes, Robert Morson   **1873-1953**
Landscape painter who lived in Kent until 1909 and then moved to Cornwall. Exh. R.A. 13. Facsims. by Gale & Polden.

Huke's Library
Publisher, Chester. The "Cestrian Series" of Chester views.

Hull & Barnsley Railway Co.
Publisher. Issued two sets, one of the Alexandra Docks, Hull; the other of stations on the line.

"Humber Bicycles"
Advertising card shows Ellaline Terris (q.v.) with a "Humber" machine.

"Humorous"
A set designed by Graham Hyde for Tuck showing figures in an inn, e.g. "Ye Huntsmen", "Ye Host", etc.

Humphrey, J.E.
Photographer/publisher, Wick, Sutherland. Local R.P. views.

Hunt, Edgar   **1876-1953**
Painter of animals and farmyard scenes.

Hunt, J.E., & Son
Photographer, London. Publicity portraits.

Hunt, Muriel   **fl. c.1900-1906**
Animal artist who lived in Torquay.

Hunt, Philip G.   **c.1905**
Publisher, 34 Paternoster Row, London, and at Manchester.
Photographic views printed in his own works at Balham, the
London Photo Printing Co. A view of Worthing, 21316, is
described as "specially for the Y.M.C.A.".

Hunt, Terry B.   **pre-1920**
Photographer/publisher, Vyne Rd., Basingstoke, Hampshire.
Local black and white views.

Hunter, Mildred C.
Animal painter.

Hunting
Red-coated huntsmen, well-groomed horses and baying
hounds provide the ideal picture for a postcard. Most of the
major publishers issued hunting sets. They include:
(i)   Carlton Publishing Co.
(ii)   E.T.W. Dennis, hunting scenes by Warren Williams.
(iii)   Faulkner & Co., hunting scenes by John Sanderson
        Wells.
(iv)   J. Henderson & Sons, hunting sets and some coloured
        vignettes.
(v)   Vivian A. Mansell, hunting scenes sometimes over-
        printed with greetings.
(vi)   Meissner & Buch, framed hunting scenes by John
        Sanderson Wells in a "Highest Award" Series.
(vii)   Millar & Lang, tinted photographs in their "National
        Series".
(viii) Pictorial Stationery Co., views of the Minehead
        Harriers in their "Peacock Series".
(ix)   J. Salmon, several hunting series by George Rankin, D.
        Manzoni and an unknown artist.
(x)   E.W. Savory, facsims. of unsigned hunting paintings.
(xi)   R. Tuck & Sons, four early cards and a number of
        "Oilette" sets:
        In the Hunting Field, Norah Drummond, 2924 and
        3296.
        Fox Hunting, Gilbert Wright, 3579.
        Hunting in the Shires, 3596.
        Fox and Stag Hunting, 8778.
        Hunting, 8899.
        The Hunt Day, Norah Drummond, 9923.
(xii)   Unknown publisher of an "Owl" Series, a white-framed
        set of hunting scenes which would appear to have been
        based on early 19th century hunting prints. This
        publisher may have been W. & T. Gaines whose trade-
        mark was an owl.

Huntley & Palmer   **pre-1905**
Advertiser of biscuits. Cards include a view of their Reading
factory. U.B.s.

Huntsman, Maud   **fl. c.1897-1910**
Artist who painted landscapes, especially woodland scenes.
Facsims. by Suttley & Silverlock of London.

Hurley, N.   **fl. c.1911**
Artist who lived at Hove, Sussex. Exh. R.A.1. Painted
children dressed as soldiers. Facsims. by Photochrom, nos.
937-42.

Hurst & Co.
Photographer/publisher. Fine Art Warehouse, Cornmarket,

Hurst, Hal. *"The Skipper's Christmas Dinner". From a black
and white drawing. R. Tuck & Sons. "Oilette" "Ye Mariners
of England".*

Belfast. Local R.P. views including shipbuilding scenes and a
"Fine Art Series".

Hurst, George Herbert   **1871-1954**
Professional all-round cricketer for 40 years. Player in 24 Tests
between 1897 and 1909. Highest score 341. P.P.s.

Hurst, Hal, R.B.A., R.O.I., V.P.R.M.S.   **1865-1938**
Portrait painter. Exh. R.A. 19. Spent some time in America
where he was influenced by Charles Dana Gibson. Tuck used
coloured versions of his black and white drawings in a series on
"Ye Mariners of England".

Hutchinson, F.A.
Photographer/publisher, Dittons, Pevensey, Sussex.

Hutchinson, Frances
Watercolour artist who painted for J.W. Ruddock's "Artist
Series", especially views of Lancashire and Cumberland.
    Illustration overleaf.

Hutchinson, W.J.
Publisher, Wolverton, Buckinghamshire. Views of railway
works.

Hutson Bros. (Ltd.)   **1908 (Ltd. 1919)**
Publisher, 15 Red Lion Sq., London, W.C. Two brothers,
P. & H. Hutson, took over the Pictorial Postcard Co. in 1908
and continued the business (Percy Hutson had travelled for the
Company before its bankruptcy). After 1915 the firm moved
to 53 Aldersgate St., in the late 1920s to 64-8 Whitecross St.,
then to 48 Great Sutton St., and in the late 1930s to Seward
St., Goswell Rd.
    The firm had a close association with Donald McGill and his

Colour Plate 9:
Cards with children

"THAT'S THE WORST OF THEM
CHEAP SOCKS!"

A SPOT OF LEAVE, CHEERIO !

"That's the Worst of Them Cheap Socks!" by Mabel Lucie Attwell. Valentine's "Attwell" Series. 1924.

"A Spot of Leave, Cheerio!". Agnes Richardson War Humour Series. Exclusive Celesque Series by Photochrom.

"LET 'EM ALL COME"

LOVE MAY COME AND LOVE MAY GO.
BUT THIS GOES ON FOR EVER.

"Let 'Em All Come" by F.P. Kinsella. Langsdorff & Co. P.U. 1907.

"Love May Come and Love May Go But This Goes on Forever" by Freda Mabel Rose. Publisher unknown. P.U. 1932.

132

Hutchinson, Frances. *"The Guildhall, Boston"*. *Facsim. by J.W. Ruddock in the "Artist Series"*.

GLORY SONG.

When all my labours and trials are o'er,
And I am safe on that beautiful shore,
Just to be near the dear Lord I adore,
Will thro' the ages be glory for me.

Oh, that will be . . . glory for me, . . .
Glory for me, . . . glory for me, . . .
When by His grace I shall look on His face,
That will be glory, be glory for me!

Hymn Cards. *"Glory Song". Photo by Bamforth.*

cards must have provided them with a large proportion of their output. McGill and other comic cards were their main stand-by until W.W.I. when wartime themes were taken up.

See: Colour Plates 12 and 14.

Hutton, Thomas S.   **fl. 1887-1906**
Newcastle upon Tyne watercolour landscape artist who painted views of Berwick upon Tweed and Dunbar for William Ritchie & Sons of Edinburgh.

H.V. & Co.
H. Vertigen & Co. (q.v.).

Hyde, Graham   **fl. c.1900-1916**
Artist who designed "Humorous" sets for Tuck, e.g. Coons and "In Our Village".

Hydros
In 1864 Dr. James Manby Gully published a *Guide to Hydro-*

Therapeia: The Water Cure in Acute Disease. Thereafter interest rapidly spread and people not only flocked to the spas (q.v.) but also to special hydropathic establishments or hydros which were set up to cater for those who wished to take the cure. These continued to flourish well into Edwardian times and they are often seen on postcards, sometimes for advertising purposes. Examples include:

Chesterfield House Hydro, Matlock.
Cleveleys Hydro, West Lancashire.
Torquay Hydro-Hotel, sepia view from the air.
Oldham House Hydro, Matlock, Photochrom Sepiatone.
The Hotel Hydro, Peebles.
The Worcestershire Brine Baths Hotel, Droitwich, published by the hotel.

Hymn Cards
These were published by Bamforth (q.v.). They consisted of posed illustrative photographs with the words of a hymn.

I

I.A. Co.
International Art Co. (q.v.).

Ibbetson, Ernest   **fl. c.1903-1918**
Figure painter of Ilkley, Yorkshire. Exh. R.A. 1. Designed several sets of cards for Faulkner, e.g. "The London Police", and military cards for Gale & Polden, e.g. "The King's Royal Rifle Corps".

I.C.
Ingram Clark (q.v.).

Illingworth, Thomas, & Co.
Photographic suppliers. Their initials "T.I.C." within a horseshoe appear on the stamp rectangle of many R.P.s It is believed they supplied the cards for printing.

I.M.J.
Ivy Millicent James (q.v.).

Imperial Tobacco Co. Ltd.
Advertiser of W.D. & H.O. Wills' "Westward Ho!" Smoking Mixture on U.B. cards showing Indians smoking "The Pipe of Peace". Also, at a later date, "Three Castles Tobacco and Cigarettes".

In Memoriam Cards
Until the 1920s it was customary to have black-edged "In Memoriam" cards printed and sent to friends and relatives when someone in the family died. The cards were sometimes printed postcard-size so that they could be sent through the post.

In Memoriam cards also covered royalty and public figures in all walks of life.

Industrial Scenes
Views of coal mines, cotton mills, steel works and quarries are featured on many cards but interiors are seldom seen, though there are views of the Royal Mint, cotton mills and of the Vickers Works at Barrow. Most industrial scenes were taken by local photographers sometimes with groups of workers. Publishers reflecting industry include Tuck, "British Industries"; Valentine; Wrench. Industries on cards include, e.g.:

Arsenal, Woolwich.
Brass foundry, Woolwich.
Breweries, Dublin.
Lace making, Long Eaton.
Naval construction, Vickers of Barrow.
Printing works, Preston Hall.
Royal Mint, London.
Steel works, Black Country, and Sheffield, Cammell Laird.
Tobacco works, R. & J. Hill.
Wheel works, Coventry, Dunlop.
Illustration overleaf.

Ingall, E. Marjorie   **fl. 1925-1939**
Birmingham artist who painted for Salmon, e.g. a rugby player on the field.

Inge & Co.   **pre-1906**
Publisher, Haslemere, Surrey. Coloured, sepia and black and white local views in an "Inge's Series".

Inglis, Alex A.
Photographer/publisher, Calton Hill, Edinburgh. Local R.P.s.

Inglis, Francis Caird
"Photographer to His Majesty at Edinburgh" and publisher. Trademark a castle with thistle scrolls and "Ingle Series" on a ribbon.

Illustration overleaf.

Ingram, Clark & Co. Ltd.   **pre-1906**
Publisher, Ilfracombe. Photographic views. Trademark "Britannia Series" with a coin showing a seated Britannia. This firm covered the Salisbury rail disaster in 1906.

Innes, John
Edinburgh painter who exhibited at the Royal Scottish Academy in 1939.

Inns
The dictionary description of an inn states that it is "for lodging travellers, smaller and less pretentious than a hotel and usually in the country or small town". Those which appear on postcards are usually the more attractive old coaching inns. Some inns advertised "Good Motor Accommodation" or adopted the name of "Cyclist House".

Illustration overleaf.
See: Hotels, Inns and Public Houses.

Inskip, John Henry   **fl. c.1886-1940**
Landscape painter. Exh. R.A. 32. Painted a set on "Arundel" for Tuck, 7479.

Insurance Post Card Series
See: Langsdorff & Co.

International Art Co.   **1909**
Publisher more frequently known as Inter-Art Co. Addresses: from 1909 at Southampton House, 317 High Holborn, London, W.C.; from 1914 at Kinofilm House, 6 and 7 Red Lion Sq., London, W.C., with a warehouse at Florence House, Barnes, London, S.W.

No trademark appears to have been used until 1922 when the initials "I.A. Co." were carried on a shield surmounted by a lion.

The output was considerable:
(i)   "Photogravure Series" including cards by Hassall.
(ii)   Comic cards including a "Katchy Kids" Series, and a long-running "Comique Series" to which McGill and

continued

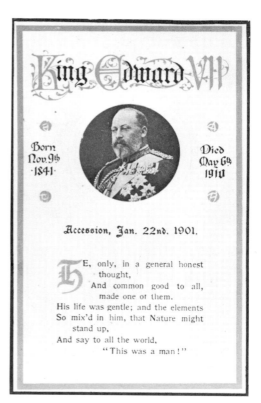

In Memoriam Cards. *"Victoria The Good"*. R. Tuck & Sons.
Empire Postcard. U.B. P.U. 1901.

In Memoriam Cards. *"King Edward VII"*. C.W. Faulkner.

In Memoriam Cards. *"England's Greatest Actor. Sir Henry Irving"*. Rapid Photo Printing Co. *"Silverprint"* Series.

In Memoriam Cards. *"Queen Alexandra's Letter to the Nation"*. C.W. Faulkner.

Industrial Scenes. *"Silver Melting House (1911). The Royal Mint". Royal Mint Provident Society.*

Inglis, Francis Caird. *The "Banqueting Hall, Edinburgh Castle". "Ingle" Series.*

Inns. *"Bideford, Old Ship Tavern. Family, Commercial and Cyclist's House. Charles Kingsley's Historic House. Where the Brotherhood of the Rose was Founded". "Frith's Series". P.U. 1909.*

Fred Spurgin contributed.
(iii) Coronation Series with a Union Jack border, mainly child studies.
(iv) W.W.I. cartoons.
(v) W.W.I. "Patriotic Series" and "Terrier Series", ill. Monahan 91.
(vi) Facsims. of paintings by Arthur Butcher in a "Ten-Nine-Eight" Series, a "Song" Series, a romantic series featuring wounded soldiers and their nurses, and a series with captions in both English and French, e.g. "The Girl behind the Man behind the Gun". Also some glamour cards by Barribal.
(vii) "Artistique" Series including close-ups of horses' heads.
(viii) The "Eleven-o-Four" Series of child subjects starting with the serial number 1104.
(ix) "Sentinel" Series, 1194.
(x) "Glamour Fireflies".
(xi) "Relation Birthday" Series.
(xii) "Oilart" Series and "Artcolour" Series.
(xiii) "Colour Gravure" Series.
(xiv) "Holborn" Series.
(xv) "Holiday Series".
(xvi) "Rembrandt Gravure", hand coloured.
See: Colour Plates 13 and 18.

International Horse Show, Olympia
Advertising cards, 1908.

Invergarry & Fort Augustus Railway Co.
Cards of a Highland Railway Series by Valentine overprinted in red.
Ref: R.O.P.L., No. 14, p. 22.

Irish Nationalism
A number of postcard photographs reflect the demand for Irish Home Rule and the opposition to it, e.g. strike in Belfast, and opposition Orange marches. There are postcards of the opponents John Redmond and Sir Edward Carson. The Easter Rising of 1916 in Dublin is reflected in postcards by Hely's, Rotary, and Valentine.
See: Sinn Fein.

Irish Pictorial Post Card Co. 1903
Publisher, 9 and 10 Maylor St., and Eagle Works, South Mall, Cork, Ireland. Tradename "Emerald". The name embraced view cards and comic cards "designed, made and printed in Ireland". The views are mainly Irish but some London views are included. Comic cards were also published including cartoons of "Parliamentary Candidates". Ill. Byatt 141.

Irish Railways
Most of the Irish Railways issued a few cards. They included these lines:
(i) Belfast & County Down, several hotel cards.
(ii) Cork, Bandon & South Coast, Tuck "Oilettes", "Sunnyside of Ireland".
(iii) Cork, Blackrock & Passage, paddle steamer "Audrey".
(iv) Dublin & South Eastern, Rathdrum Station card.
(v) Dublin, Wicklow & Wexford, a few cards by the Pictorial Stationery Co. Ltd. in their "Peacock Series".
(vi) Northern Counties Committee, a few view cards and L.M.S. hotel cards.
(vii) Great Northern Railway (Ireland), a few cards by W. Lawrence of Dublin.

(viii) Great Southern Railway, hotel cards by W. Lawrence.

(ix) Great Southern & Western and Midland Great Western Joint Railways, postcards for British Empire Exhibition, 1924.

(x) Great Southern & Western Railway, various views including Tuck "Oilettes", and hotel cards by Lawrence of Dublin and by Jotter.

(xi) West Clare, cards in Hood & Co.'s "Sanbride Series".
Ref: For check lists see R.O.P.L., No. 10.

Irvine's Ltd.   pre-1916
Publisher, 19 Buckingham St., Strand, London, W.C. An addressing firm that published a few postcards including a set titled "The Destruction of a Zeppelin" and some greetings cards. Trademark "IV" within a circle. The title "Irvine Series" embraced their output.

Irving, Ethel   b. 1869
Actress. First appearance in Gaiety Theatre in 1885. Career lasted over 45 years. P.P. by Rotary.

Irving, Sir Henry   1838-1905
Actor-manager. First stage appearance 1856. In 1878 he became lessee and manager of the Lyceum Theatre, London, and began a long association with Ellen Terry (q.v.) playing Hamlet to her Ophelia. P.P.s by Beagles, (ill. Hill p. 54), Rotary and Tuck.
Ref: Bingham, H., *Henry Irving and the Victorian Theatre,* 1978.

Irwin, Jean H.   fl. c.1930-1940
Glasgow watercolour artist. Painted card of Peace Pavilion, Empire Exhibition, Glasgow, 1938.

Irwin, Madelaine   fl. 1881-1906
Portrait and figure painter. Exh. R.A. 10. Contributed paintings for Jarrold & Sons.

Isle of Man Government
The I.O.M. Government issued 30 postcard views of the island at the British Empire Exhibition, 1924.
Ref: For check list see Fletcher/Brooks II, p. 53.

Isle of Man Railways
Two railways covered this relatively small island:
(i) Manx Electric Railway; nearly 100 different cards were issued including coloured views, framed views and R.P.s.
(ii) Douglas Southern Electric Railway. Twelve views by Hildesheimer.
Ref: Full details in R.O.P.L., No. 10.

Isle of Man Steam Packet Co.
Regular services have operated between Liverpool and the port of Douglas in the Isle of Man for passengers, mail and cargo for very many years. The fleet was operated by the Isle of Man Steam Packet Co. and included the steamers "Prince of Wales", "Mona", "Mona's Isle", "King Orry", "Empress Queen", "Queen Victoria" and "Viking". All Tuck cards.

Isle of Wight Railway
Court cards have been recorded with views of Ryde, Shanklin and Ventnor. They were produced by the Picture Postcard Co. Two full-size views also exist.

IV
See: Irvine's Ltd.

"Ivanhoe Series"
See: Crowther J. Cox.

Ives, H.M.   pre-1910
Publisher, Suffolk. Coloured photographic views.

"Ivory Series"
See: D. Evans Ltd.

IXL Series   pre-1905
Publisher unknown. Coloured views of London and East Anglia.

"Izal"
Advertising cards designed by W. Heath Robinson (q.v.).

J

J.A. & Co.
J. Alderton & Co., or J. Asher & Co. (qq.v.). Alderton published write-away cards (q.v.), c.1903; Asher cards are later, after 1906.

Jackson, Helen　　　　　　　　　**fl. 1884-1906**
Figure painter and illustrator. Exh. R.A. 7. Designed children's cards for Tuck.

Jackson, James Eyre　　　　　　　**fl. 1882-1906**
Designer of a series of cards depicting antique pottery and porcelain published by R. & J. Lea of Manchester. Exh. R.A. 4.

Jackson, J.M., & Son (Gy) Ltd.　　　　　　**1914**
Publisher, Grimsby, Lincolnshire. Trademark "JAY-EM-JAY SERIES" within a circle with the letters "GY". The initials are those of John Middleton Jackson. Gy for Grimsby indicates the main premises; the firm had a branch office in Bradford. Noted for multi-view cards, often coloured photographic views of eastern counties, but their views range over most of England.

"Jackson's Faces"　　　　　　　　**pre-1919**
Photographer/publisher, 10a South Terrace, Weston-super-Mare, Somerset, who inset a photograph of the buyer on view cards of the locality. The cards often included a greeting and a verse.

Jackson's Hats and Boots
Advertising cards by Louis Wain showing cats in hats and boots.

Jacobs, Helen Mary　　　　　　　**1888-1970**
Painter and illustrator of children's books. Exh. R.A. 5. Her children's cards were mainly of fairy-type and were published by Faulkner. She was the sister of W.W. Jacobs, the author of *The Monkey's Paw, Odd Craft* and many other books.
　Ref: Cope p. 13 and ill. p. 44.

Jacobs, J.
Publisher, Caerphilly, Glamorgan.

Jacobus　　　　　　　　　　　　**fl. pre-1918**
Pseudonym of an artist who painted children and animals at play for Woolstone Bros.

Jacques, J. Jr.　　　　　　　　　**pre-1918**
Publisher, Broadway, Worcestershire. Coloured local views.

J.A.D.
James Allan Duncan (q.v.).

"Ja-Ja"
The trademark registered in 1905 by Stoddart & Co. Ltd. (q.v.).

Jalland, G.H.　　　　　　　　　**fl. c.1888-1910**
Punch artist whose black and white drawings were coloured

and used in Tuck's "Motoring Jokes from *Punch*".

James, Frank　　　　　　　　　**fl. 1888-1910**
Landscape painter who exhibited at the R.A. in 1888 and 1890.

James, Ivy Millicent　　　　　　　**1879-1965**
A figure painter who lived at Weston-super-Mare, Somerset. She was trained in London and in 1901 started to design for Christmas card publishers. This led to painting scenes with children for postcards published by Faulkner, ill. D. & M. 188. She started on this career in 1907 and travelled on the Continent, particularly the Low Countries. Her children often wear clogs. Some of her cards were also published by M. Munk (q.v.).
　Ref: An excellent booklet by Cole, D. and P., *Ivy Millicent James 1879-1965,* appeared as a Woodspring Museum Publication in 1980. It reproduces some of the postcard work from the museum collection and gives a check list of titles of the cards in many Faulkner sets.

James, Ivy Millicent. *Scene with children. Facsim. by M. Munk of Vienna.*

James, Julia
Actress. A Gaiety Girl who became a leading lady. Appeared in the Novello/Kern *Theodore & Co.* in 1916. P.P. by Philco.

Jamieson, James C.
Designer of maps painted in watercolours for Valentine, e.g. The Firth of Forth.

Jane & Gentry
Publishers, Margate. Cards of the German air raids of 1917.

Jarach, A.
French designer of déshabillé cards.

Jarrold & Son(s) Ltd.   c.1898
Printer/publisher, 3 Cockney Lane, Norwich, and London. Output included:
(i)   "Jarrold's Series", coloured views of East Anglia.
(ii)   "Pageant Series".
(iii)   Flower sets, e.g. "Poppyland" and "Wild Flowers".
(iv)   Flag/portrait cards.
(v)   "Great War Series".
(vi)   Heraldic cards with the appropriate views.
(vii)   "Punch War Cartoons" and other patriotic sets.
(viii)   "New Autograph Postcard".
(ix)   Views by Hayward Young, using his own name (he usually used the pseudonym Jotter).
   Ref: Gowan, B., 'The Jarrold Story', P.P.M., November 1983.

Jarvis, Maggie
Actress. P.P. by Aristophot.

Jay, Miss Cecil, R.M.S.   fl. 1902-1928
Miniature painter who designed glamour cards. Exh. R.A. 18.

Jay-em-Jay (Gy)
J.M. Jackson & Son, Grimsby (q.v.).

Jay, Florence   fl. 1905-1920
Animal artist. Exh. R.A. 4. Painted "Dogs at Play" set for the Medici Society.

Jay, Isabel   1879-1927
Actress and vocalist. Noted for performance as "Miss Hook of Holland". P.P.s by "Dainty Novels", Foulsham & Banfield; Philco; Rotary with Bertram Wallis; Wrench. Became Mrs. Cavendish; there is a Rotary P.P. of her with her daughter.

J.B. & Co.
J. Beagles & Co. (q.v.).

Jefferies & Co.
Publisher, Goodmayes, Essex. "The Essex Artistic Series" of R.P.s. Series nos. exceed 1,700.

Jefferies, Maud   1869-1946
Actress. P.P.s by Beagles, Philco and Rotary.

Jellicoe, Admiral Sir John R.   1859-1935
Supreme Commander of the Home Fleet in W.W.I. until after the Battle of Jutland in 1916. P.P.s by Rotary; Scopes bas-relief; Sport & General; F.W. Woolworth. Many portraits on patriotic cards and those of wartime leaders.

Jenkins, F.   1904
Photographer/stationer/publisher, 94 High St., Southwold, Suffolk. The output comprised:
(i)   Photographs of local events including a visit by the Prince of Wales to Southwold in 1906.

(ii)   Photogravure Series of Suffolk views.
(iii)   "Sylvester Stannard" Series, facsims. of local views painted by this artist (q.v.).
(iv)   "Studio Series", paintings by Sylvester Stannard.
(v)   *Punch* cartoons reproduced in black and white.

Jenkins, G.H. Jr.
Landscape painter of Devon views. Facsims. were published by Tuck in sets titled "Clovelly", "Dartmoor", "Picturesque Dartmoor" and "Picturesque Devon".

Jenkins, H.
Photographer/publisher, 2 Pier Terrace, Lowestoft, Suffolk. Black and white local views.

Jennings & Hill
Publisher, Lewisham, London. R.P. views.

J.H.W.
John Henry Waterhouse (q.v.).

J.J.K. & Co. Ltd.
J.J. Keliher & Co. Ltd. (q.v.).

J.M. Co., Go. E.
J.A. McCulloch & Co., Gorgie, Edinburgh (q.v.).

J.M. & Co. Ltd.
J.A. McCulloch & Co. Ltd. (q.v.).

J.M.S.
Initials of the artist who designed the *Western Mail* "Colliery Series" (q.v.).

Jockeys
   See: Horse Racing.

Joffre, J.J.C.   1852-1931
French General. Many W.W.I. portraits.

John o' Groats
This caption appears on a number of cards. The John o' Groats Hotel, Caithness, and the John o' Groats Tea Rooms published cards in the 1930s. Used cards often carry a circular rubber stamp or cachet with the words "John o' Groats House" in addition to the postmark.

Johnson Ltd.   pre-1906
Publisher, Keighley, Yorkshire. Heraldic cards.

Johnson & Sons
Publisher, Bowness and Windermere. "Framed Sepia Photographs of the Lake District". Cards supplied by Tuck.

Johnson, Ben
Publisher, York. Local historical series covering events from 800 B.C. to A.D. 1642.

Johnson & Doyle   pre-1905
Publisher, Manchester. Silvered local views.

Johnson, M.
An artist who painted "The Guildhall, London" for a Tuck "Oilette" card. As there were several artists named Johnson with the initial M it is not possible to identify with certainty.

Johnson, S.
Landscape artist who painted a set on "South Devon" for Tuck, 7279.

Johnston, R., & Son   pre-1915
Publisher, Gateshead, Durham. "The Monarch Series" of

local R.P. views, serial nos. to 4275, includes at least three railway cards.

Johnston, W. & A.K., Ltd.   1901
Publisher, Edinburgh and London. The Edinburgh printing centre was the Edina Works in Easter Road. The firm, which for nearly a century had been concerned with cartography, started printing postcards for other publishers before 1900. By 1901 they were printing and selling their own cards. The first U.B. cards were on the Scottish clans, each one in colour with a strip of tartan and a coat of arms. Later issues included:
(i)   Sets of "Clanswomen".
(ii)   Set for the Glasgow Exhibition, 1901.
(iii) Coloured views of Edinburgh, "gruss aus" type, and general coloured views of Scotland.
(iv) Black and white views of Edinburgh.
(v)   Boer War Series, "Peace with Honour".
(vi) Scottish Regiments.
(vii) Robert Burns sets, at least 12.
(viii) Humorous cards with Scottish flavour.
(ix) Ocean liners.
(x)   National dances.
    Most of the cards have a strong Scottish flavour.
    Ref: Byatt lists a number of individual sets, p. 144.

Johnston's Patent Corn Flour
Court size advertising cards. A series of cards on "Methods of Travelling".

Joint South Western & Brighton Railway   c.1900
Six cards with views of Southsea, Portsmouth and the Isle of Wight supplied by the Picture Postcard Co.
    Ref: Check list in R.O.P.L., No. 11, p. 8.

Jones, A.V.N., & Co.   pre-1908
Publisher, Fore St., London, E.C. The best known cards by this firm were reproduced from *Queen Alexandra's Gift Book*. The series was called "Queen Alexandra's Photographs". Other cards included characters from Dickens and a number of comic cards.

Jones, Bayard
Artist who designed golfing cards, e.g. "He should have used his iron".

Jones' Flour
Advertising cards.

Jones, Hugh
Publisher, "Advertiser" Office, Llangollen. Coloured local views.

Jones, M.
Publisher, Cowes and East Cowes, I.O.W. Local views supplied by Valentine.

Jones' Sewing Machines   pre-1918
Advertising cards published in Leicester. Line drawings with captions, e.g. "Runs as smoothly as an airship and is as strong as a dreadnought". Cards were also published in sets, e.g. "Flags of Britain's Allies" and "Flags of the British Empire".

Jozsa, Karoly   b. 1872
Watercolour artist and illustrator who worked in Budapest and Munich. Best known for "Sirens and Circes" and "World of Fairy Tales" in the art nouveau style.

Jotter (Walter Hayward Young)   1869-1920
A prolific artist who almost invariably signed his work Jotter. He was a great traveller, painting landscape and coastal scenes but also designed some comic and patriotic cards. He was clearly much in demand and as a freelance did work for a great many firms including:
(i)   Boots Cash Chemists, set of 24 Cambridge colleges and sets of 12 cards of the Isle of Wight, Kent, Sussex and Yorkshire. Several sets of six cards including the New Forest.
(ii)   A. Burkart & Co., a firm which produced hotel cards for railway companies and individual hotels. A few view cards were also issued. About 80 "Jotter" cards in all.
(iii) E.J. Barrow, a hotel card.
(iv) Collector's Publishing Co., views of Wimbledon Common.
(v)   Cynicus Publishing Co., general views.
(vi) Max Ettlinger & Co., at least nine sets, some views and a few comic.
(vii) F. Frith & Co., scenes in the West of England.
(viii) F. Hartmann, 16 sets of six cards in an "Aquarelle" Series depicting scenery ranging over every part of the British Isles.
(ix) Charles Martin, views of Hampstead, etc.
(x)   Misch & Stock, six sets of country cards in the "Nature Miniatures" Series.
(xi) D. Napier & Sons Ltd., card advertising the "Napier Motor Carriage" signed Hayward Young.
(xii) Philco, a few comic cards.
(xiii) Photochrom, some views, humorous black and white sketches for "The Wedgwood Series" and a series on "Dutch Children".
(xiv) Pictorial Stationery Co., framed views.
(xv) E. Gordon Smith, "Pinachrom" Series, mainly views. At least 10 sets.
(xvi) Tuck. At least 27 "Oilette" sets of six cards including "Derbyshire Dales", "Lynton", "County Antrim" and the "Picturesque Counties" of Cornwall, Devon and Kent.
(xvii) Wildt & Kray, two sets on "Constable's Country".
(xviii) Woolstone Bros.   *continued*

Jotter. *"The Hotel Metropole, Brighton". Published for the hotel by A. Burkart & Co.*

"Bonne Année" by Adolfo Busi. P.U. 1925.

"Joyeux Noël" by Carlo Chiostri. P.U. 1929.

"Bonne Année" by Pauli Ebner.

A few cards were designed for other publishers, mainly later than most of those listed, e.g. for Jarrold, Mansell ("Kute Kiddies") and Thridgould (greetings cards).

See: Frontispiece and Colour Plate 17.

Ref: A more detailed check list is given in an article on Jotter in P.P.A., 1982, pp. 44-6.

J.S.
J.J. Samuels. (q.v.).

J.T. & Co.
John Thridgould & Co. (q.v.).

Judd, A.H., & Co. pre-1908
Publisher, Southend-on-Sea, Essex. Local R.P.s and coloured views.

Judges (Ltd.) 1904 (Ltd. from 1910)
Photographer/publisher, Hastings, Sussex. A firm founded by Frederick Judge (b. 1872) in Hastings in 1902. Postcards were certainly produced by 1904 and bear the name "Judges' Photo Stores". The first issues were in colour and were processed in Germany. Local events were soon being photographed as were views of the Hastings sea coast. Fred Judge appears to have worked by himself for a considerable period. It has been stated that photographs with a serial number below 7,400 were taken by him. He also published some watercolour and pencil sketches signed with his initials, but these are hard to find.

The firm grew and other photographers were recruited. In the 1920s shops were opened in Ludgate Hill, London, and in seaside resorts. London views were added to the output and these bear the prefix "L".

Judges are best known for their sepia views with a matt finish, though some were black and white collotype.

There is a Judges' Study Group carrying out research into the output of this firm which still flourishes.

Juggins pre-1906
Photographer, Birmingham.

Jukes
Photographer/publisher, Wilton, Wiltshire. Local black and white views.

Jungman, Nico W. 1872-1935
Landscape artist. Exh. R.A. 7. Born in Holland, he became a naturalised British citizen. He painted a "Wide Wide World" set on Holland for Tuck, 7556.

J.W.B.
J.W. Bland (q.v.).

J.W.S. or J.W. & S.
J. Welch & Sons (q.v.).

Judges. *"Torpedo Boats' Searchlights"*. *Sepia print.*

Judges. *"A New Forest Road"*. *Sepia print.*

K

Kammerer, R.
Landscape painter.

Karactus
Pseudonym of an unknown artist who designed comic cards for the Crown Publishing Co.

Karsavina, Tamara   **1885-1978**
Russian ballerina who made her debut at the Marinsky Theatre in 1902 and became a prima ballerina in 1907. She married an Englishman and settled in Britain where she gave invaluable encouragement to British ballet. P.P. by Samuels Ltd., The Strand, London (photo by Elliott & Fry).
   Ref: *Theatre Street*, 1930, Karsavina's memoirs.

Kaufmann, J.C.
Painter of animals, especially horses.

Kaye, Frederick   **1855-1913**
Actor. Played Lord Coodle in *A Runaway Girl* at the Gaiety Theatre in 1898. P.P. by Rotary.

Keats, John   **1795-1821**
From 1818 to 1820 the poet Keats lived at Wentworth Place, Hampstead. Portraits of the poet and views of his home (now open to the public) appear on postcards.

Keeling Press Ltd.   **pre-1924**
Publisher, 3-7 Dane St., Holborn, London, W.C.2. A firm which held the sole concession for printing and publishing postcards of the British Empire Exhibition, Wembley, 1924.

Keene, Charles Samuel   **1823-1891**
Humorous artist who was on the staff of *Punch* over a long period. His work in black and white was used by F. Jenkins of Southwold and in the Wrench series "Pictures from Punch".

Keene, Elmer   **fl. c.1895-1914**
Landscape painter who lived in Leicester. Exh. R.A. 1, 1895. He sometimes used the pseudonym of Paul Haworth. He painted moonlit views of lakes, e.g. Buttermere, Coniston and Windermere, and buildings, Holyrood Palace, Melrose Abbey and Warwick Castle. His work was used by Barton Harvey & Son, E.T.W. Dennis, C.W. Faulkner, E.W. Savory, Tuck, and C. Worcester & Co.

Keene, Minnie
Animal painter, especially of cats and kittens.

Keenes, J.A.   **pre-1908**
Publisher, Woking, Surrey. Local views.

Keeping, F., & Co.   **pre-1916**
Printer/publisher, Weston-super-Mare, Somerset.

Keesey, Walter Monckton   **fl. c.1912-1937**
Watercolour painter. Exh. R.A. 16. Was a teacher of art and in the 1930s designed a series of postcards for Trust Houses Ltd. which was published by Radermacher, Aldous & Co. He

was also responsible for two sets of cards on Cambridge.

Kehrhahn, F., & Co.   **pre-1905**
Photographer/publisher, Bexley Heath. R.P.s of Bexley, Kent, and London.

Keiller, James
Advertiser of his marmalade and other preserves.

Keliher, J.J. *Trademark of their "Shamrock Series".*

Keliher, J.J., & Co. Ltd.   **pre-1910**
Publisher. Trademark with initials followed by "Shamrock Series. Printed in London". The firm appears to have specialised in army cards (ill. Byatt 159), especially regimental uniforms but coloured floral birthday cards were also published.

Kelly, Edith
Actress. Tuck "Celebrities of the Stage", 4712.

Kelly, Robert George Talbot   **1861-1934**
Landscape artist. Exh. R.A. 12. Travelled in Burma and painted two sets on that country for Tuck's "Wide Wide World" Series, 7866-7.

Kendal, J.H.   **pre-1912**
Publisher, Shield St., Allendale, Northumberland. R.P. views.

Kennard, Julie
Actress who played Lady Isobel in *East Lynne* in 1908. P.P. by Lyne Opera House, Hammersmith.

Kennedy, A.E.
Painter of animals, theatrical subjects and comic cards. Designed a set called "Three Bears" for Faulkner.
   See: Colour Plate 13.

Kennington, Thomas Benjamin, R.B.A., R.O.I.   **1856-1916**
Genre painter. Exh. R.A. 72. There is a collection of his work in the Tate Gallery. One of his paintings of an impoverished family was reproduced as a postcard overprinted "Free Trade".

Kent and East Sussex Railway
One set of official cards with well-known landmarks in the area. Each card states the nearest station.
   Ref: Check list in R.O.P.L., No. 18, p. 5.

Kent, F.
Publisher, Piccadilly, Manchester. Lancashire views.

Colour Plate 11: Christmas cards

"Teddy Cooks His Xmas Dinner". Wildt & Kray. P.U. 1915.

"All You Wish, I Wish For You...". Christmas card with verse by E. Blomfield. R. Tuck & Sons. "Christmas Fun".

"May Happy Folk Join You in Your Fun..." by Phyllis Cooper. R. Tuck & Sons. "Oilette" Happy Land Series. P.U. 1929.

Kent, T.
Photographer/publisher who issued cards showing "The German Fleet at Scapa Flow, 28 Nov. 1918".

Kerin, Nora   **b.1883**
Actress. P.P. by Beagles, and Rotary (with Lauderdale Maitland).

Keulemans, J.C.
Illustrator of J.L. Bonhote's *Birds of Britain*, A. & C. Black. The illustrations were used by the publishers on postcards.

Kew Gardens
The Chinese pagoda, erected 1761, is 163ft. high and features on postcards.

Keystone Art Co. Ltd.   **pre-1921**
Publisher, South Norwood, London, S.E. Floral cards.

"Kia-Ora"
In 1912 this soft drinks firm appears to have sponsored the visit of a troupe of Maori entertainers to Britain. They toured various towns, including St. Albans, and for each town a coloured postcard was printed advertising the visit. The picture showed the troupe of 23 artists and the advertisement of the entertainment included the words "Kia-Ora Greetings from Maori Land".

Kilburne, George Goodwin
There were two artists with this name, father and son. The father lived from 1839 to 1924, the son from 1863 to 1938, so one cannot be certain which painted the sets for Tuck depicting literary men. It was probably the son who exh. R.A. 24.

Kew Gardens. *"The Pagoda. Kew Gardens". Gale & Polden. "The Wellington Series".*

King, Edward R. *"Under Reserve. He: Darling, will you share my lot? She: Yes, Charlie, if it really is a lot". R. Tuck & Sons. "Oilette". "Good Jokes from Punch". P.U. 1906.*

King Bros.   **pre-1926**
Publisher, Hastings and St. Leonards, Sussex.

King, Alfred, & Son   **pre-1913**
Publisher, Oundle and Thrapston, Northamptonshire. Local R.P.s.

King, Alice Price   **fl. c.1907-1922**
Landscape and flower painter.

King, Edward R.   **fl. 1884-1924**
Figure and landscape painter. Exh. R.A. 54. Some of his black and white drawings in *Punch* were coloured and used in Tuck's "Good Jokes from Punch".

King, Gunning   **1859-1940**
Painter and illustrator. Exh. R.A. 47. He painted for Hildesheimer and several Tuck series including "Flowers in Vases".

King, Jessie Marion   **1876-1949**
Scottish graphic artist who studied at the Glasgow School of Art, and became a well-known illustrator and designer of silver and fabrics for Liberty. She worked in the art nouveau style and some of her nursery rhyme illustrations were used by Millar & Lang in a "National Series". Ill. Cope p. 45.

King, John
Stationer/printer/publisher, Southall, Middlesex. Coloured local views.

King, John H.
Publisher, Birmingham. "Forward Series" of comic cards.

King, John W.   **fl. 1893-1924**
Artist who painted scenes from the Oxford Pageant of 1907
for Tuck. Exh. R.A. 6.

King & Wilson   **pre-1924**
"Photographers & View Publishers", 8 Pier Arcade, Bognor,
Sussex. Local R.P.s. Serial nos. to 659 have been noted.

Kingsley, Frank
Pseudonym occasionally used by Percy Tarrant (q.v.).

Kingsway Real Photo Series   **pre-1910**
  See: W.H. Smith.

Kinnear, James   **fl. 1880-1917**
Edinburgh landscape painter. Exh. R.S.A. 80, R.A. 7. He
painted a Tuck "Oilette" set on "Old Edinburgh".

Kinsella, Edward Patrick
Versatile Irish artist who designed posters and comic cards
with child subjects. His best known cards shows a small boy
with a white hat playing cricket and a small girl playing tennis.
These sold in great numbers and must have been a major
source of income to Kinsella's publishers, Langsdorff & Co.
He also painted a "Diabolo" Series. Some of his theatre
posters were reproduced as postcards by David Allen.
  See: Colour Plate 9.

Kipper, L.J.
An artist who designed an "Errand Girl" card in a series for
E. Nister (q.v.).

Kirchner, Raphael   **1876-1917**
Born in Vienna, he worked as a portrait painter and illustrator
in America and moved to Paris in 1905 where he contributed
to Paris journals including *La Vie Parisienne*. His postcard
work falls into four periods:
(i) Pre-1900, noted for "Leda" Series by Philipp & Kramer.
(ii) c.1900-1903, art nouveau cards including such sets as
    "Fleur d'Amour", "Les Cigarettes du Monde", "Les
    Enfants de la Mer", "The Geisha", "The Mikado" (ill.
    D. & M. 56), and "San Toy". These were chromolitho-
    graphed U.B.s. Several British publishers imported these
    sets including Henry Moss, H.J. Smith, E. Taylor; Tuck
    included Kirchner in his "Continental" Series.
(iii) 1903-1914. During this period Kirchner turned to
    designing glamour cards, his wife Nina sometimes acting
    as his model, and also to painting children, e.g. sleeping
    under a Christmas Tree, 1905. Many of these cards were
    promoted by the Bruton Galleries in London.
(iv) 1914-1917, Kirchner designed wartime glamour cards.

Kirk & Sons
Publisher, Cowes, I.O.W. "Shamrock Series" of views. Cards
supplied by J.J. Keliher & Co.

Kirk, A.H.
Landscape painter. Painted a Tuck set on London, 7257.

Kirk, Charles
Publisher, 156 Sauchiehall St., Glasgow. "Wild Birds at
Home" Series showing birds in their natural surroundings,
e.g., guillemots on Ailsa Craig.

Kirkland Emporium   **pre-1911**
Publishers, Eaglesham, Renfrewshire. R.P. views.

Kirkpatrick, Ida Marion   **fl. 1888-1927**
Landscape and flower painter who studied in Paris and
exhibited mainly at the Alpine Club Gallery and the S.W.A.
Facsims. by Faulkner.

Kirmse, Persis   **fl.1920s**
Animal painter who exhibited at Walker's Gallery, London, in
the late 1920s. Painted cat and dog series for Photochrom and
for Tuck's "Lucky Playmates".

Kissogram Cards
A Valentine patent of 1906 (application no. 1677) which shows
a face with enormous red lips. The sender is asked to "Moisten
the Lips" and "Kiss the Gentleman", then to impress the lips
on a blank space below. This process removed a red pigment
from the lips on the card and impresses the lips of the sender in
the form of a "kiss".
  See also under Novelty Cards.

Kitchener, Field Marshal Earl   **1850-1916**
Kitchener was Secretary of State for War during the early part
of W.W.I. In 1915 his call for volunteers recruited over
1,700,000 men and Kitchener became a household name with
the famous poster "Your King and Country Need You".
P.P.s by Rotary; Scopes & Co., bas-relief; Valentine.

Kitchener, Field Marshal Earl. *Birn Bros. Photo by Bourne & Shepherd, Simla.*

Kitto, Fred, & Son
Photographer/publisher, Fowey, Cornwall. Local R.P. views.

Klein, Christina   **fl. c.1900-1914**
German artist who painted birds, butterflies, flowers and fruit.
She provided material for Alpha, ill. D. & M. 191; Birn Bros.;
Hildesheimer; Meissner & Buch; Millar & Lang; Stiebel; Tuck,
over 20 sets; and Wildt & Kray.
  Ref: A brief list is given by Holt, T. and V., 'A Bunch of
Flowers', P.P.M., May 1982, p. 26.

Klein, Richard
Nazi propaganda artist of the late 1930s, some of whose cards found their way to Britain.

Klempner, Ernest Sigmund
Designer of humorous cards for Olney Amsden & Sons. All his titles deal with money in some form.

Klio Post Card Co. Ltd.   **1905**
Publisher, 118 City Rd., London, E.C. This firm appears to have been in business mainly as importers of postcards though it used its own trademark "Klio". The leading figure was Maxim Niven whose activities are described by Byatt p. 146.

Knight Bros. (Ltd.)   **fl. 1904-1908 (Ltd. 1906)**
Publisher, Dyer's Buildings, Holborn Bars, London, E.C. Trademark a chess knight. Having had previous experience of the postcard business with Wrench their firm developed rapidly to include:
(i)   The "Map of Truelove River", an extraordinarily successful card which sold nearly 250,000 copies, followed later by "Chart of Betrothal Bay".
(ii)   A "Mirror" Series of views.
(iii)   "Beautiful Britain".
(iv)   Photographs of prominent figures in politics, science, the army, etc.
(v)   "Royal Navy" Series and a Nelson centenary card.
(vi)   "Sweet Old Stories", a series for children.
(vii)   "The Spirit of the Past", silhouettes of ancient monuments and buildings against a blue moonlit background. This series was designed by W. Stocker Shaw (q.v.).
(viii) London theatres at night.
(ix)   Children and dolls, a series titled "Tiny Mothers".
(x)   "Knight Collection of British View Cards", coloured views printed in Germany.
(xi)   "Knight Series" of black and white portraits of horses.
(xii)   Railway cards, one British set and one European. Complete list in Picton, 1982.
(xiii) Cavalry regiments.
(xiv)   Greetings cards.

Knight, Ethel   **fl. 1899-1918**
Artist who lived at West Bridgford, Nottinghamshire. Painted local views for J.W. Ruddock & Sons.

Knight, John
Manufacturer of "Knight's Family Health Soap" advertising cards with children, some carrying the slogan "What Mother Orders".

Knight, Mary Foster
Artist who painted a set of "Baby Birds" for the Medici Society.

Knight, W.I.
Publisher, Olney, Buckinghamshire. Local coloured views.

Knowles, Davidson   **fl. 1880-1898**
Landscape painter. Exh. R.A. 14. His work was used by Hildesheimer.

Knowles, George Sheridan, R.B.A., R.I., R.O.I.   **1863-1931**
Artist who was included in Boots' "Famous Pictures" Series. Exh. R.A. 28.

Koch, Ludwig   **1866-1934**
Painter of "Horse Racing" scenes for Tuck, 9871, including "Saddling Up in the Paddock", "A Good Start", "First Past the Post" and "Leading the Winner".

Koch, Walter   **fl. c.1894-1904**
Figure painter who lived at Bushey, Hertfordshire. Designed a winter sports series which was lithographed in Zurich.

Kodak   **pre-1911**
Publishers of R.P.s, Kingsway, London.

Koehler, Mela   **fl.c.1908-1921**
Designer of many cards, mainly for the Wiener Werkstätte, and some fashion models and glamorous ladies in the art deco style.

Koekkoek, H.W.
Artist who contributed to a war series published by Hildesheimer.

Kokoschka, Oskar   **1886-1980**
Austrian artist who painted for the Wiener Werkstätte. His postcards are very highly valued.

Konopa, Rudolf   **b. 1864**
Art nouveau figure and landscape painter.

Kramer, W.
Austrian artist who painted an "Oilette" set for Tuck titled "Winter Landscapes".

Kubelik, Jan   **1880-1940**
Czech violinist. Composer of violin concertos. He became a naturalised Hungarian. P.P. by Rotary, with his wife Countess Csaky Szell. Ill. Hill p. 48.

Kurt, Erna M.
Designer of cards used for anniversaries.

Kurton, Peggy
Actress. Played the part of Lady Pussy Preston in *Tonight's the Night* at the Gaiety Theatre in 1916. P.P.s by Lilywhite, Rotary.

Kyd
Pseudonym of Joseph Clayton Clarke (q.v.).

"Kyle Pharmacy Series"
Sepia views of the Kyle of Lochalsh.

L

Lace
   See: Honiton Lace.

Ladd, Levi   **pre-1921**
Photographer/publisher, Tonypandy, Glamorgan. Local R.P. views including the floods in the Clydach Vale and the coal strike of May, 1921.

Ladies of Llangollen
   See: Association Cards.

Lady Godiva
According to legendary history Lady Godiva released the townsfolk of Coventry from heavy taxation imposed by her husband Leofric, by riding through the town clothed only in her long hair. The townsfolk agreed not to watch her progress except for Peeping Tom who is seen at a window on cards depicting the ride.

Lafayette
Photographers who supplied material for the Photochrom "Photogravure Series".

Lamb, Eric
Landscape painter.

Lancashire & Yorkshire Railway Co.
Many sets of official cards were used, 14 sets of views, six sets of locomotives, trains, etc., and three sets of steamers.
   Ref: Check lists in R.O.P.L., No. 3.

Lancaster, P., & Co.
Publisher, Tunbridge Wells.

Lady Godiva. *"Lady Godivas Equestrian Statue, Coventry"*. *Valentine's XL Series.*

Lancaster, Percy, R.B.A., R.I.   **1878-1951**
Landscape and figure artist. Exh. R.A. 20. Designed cards of monks in comic situations.

Lance & Lance   **pre-1916**
Stationer/publisher, Waterloo House, Weston-super-Mare, Somerset. Local R.P. views.

Landeker & Brown   **1903-1906**
Publisher, 28-30 Worship St., London, E.C. These were fine art publishers and turned their attention to picture postcards for less than three years. During this time they used the trademark "Ellanbee" with a statue of Venus. Later the word "Oilosimile" appeared. Most of their cards were printed in Vienna. Output included:
(i)   Humorous cards, "Ellanbee" and "Ellanbee Quotation" sets.
(ii) Miscellaneous series including "Dutch Art", "Fiscal", "Seascape" and "School Rhymes".

Lander, Capt. Edgar   **fl.c. 1910-1936**
Watercolour artist. Exh. R.A. 4. Facsims. of his work used by Faulkner.

"Landor's Studies"
Black and white studies of children by an unknown publisher with such titles as "Tired Out", "Tea and Scandal" and "Tub Night".

Land's End
Views of the cliffs at Land's End and of the "First and Last House" are relatively common.

Landscape, Photographic and Fine Art Publishers
Llandrindod Wells, Radnorshire. Trademark a shield containing a statue of "Hygena" with "Llandrindod Wells" below and "The Spa Series" above. Hygena was the goddess of health, an appropriate symbol for a spa.
   Output included:
(i)   Coloured views of North Wales.
(ii) Sets with a Welsh content, e.g. "Welsh Costume".
(iii) Humorous "Scenes at Llandrindod".

Lanfier
London photographer who supplied photographs to Rotary.

Lang, Hugo, & Co.   **1901**
Publisher, 14 Church St., Liverpool. A few local views were issued but the main business of this firm was the importation of cards from America and Europe.

Lang, Matheson   **1878-1948**
Actor-manager. First appeared on London stage as Montjoy in *King Henry V,* 1900. Acted in films from 1916. P.P. by Beagles.

Land's End. *"Lands End"*. Printed and published by The First and Last House in England.

Land's End. *"First and Last House. Lands End"*. Valentine *"Sepiatype"* Series. P.U. 1927.

Langlands
Publisher, Dumbarton. Multi-view tartan scenes.

Langsdorff & Co.   fl. c.1905-1914
Publisher, 19 City Rd., London, E.C. Trademark a seated figure with a bird at his feet above the names "Zeus" and "Jupiter". The bird is symbolic of a messenger.

Output consisted mainly of coloured views by landscape artists and of humorous cards, particularly very successful sporting children by E.P. Kinsella (q.v.). The most famous card, which sold in vast numbers, was called "The Hope of His Side". It shows a small boy in a floppy white hat playing cricket. This was followed by a tennis girl, "Let 'Em All Come". Langsdorff & Co. held the copyright of an "Insurance Post Card Series". Each view card had a printed coupon in the address space which insured the addressee for £50 in the event of death from accident as a passenger "on train, public omnibus (motor or horse), tramcar or four-wheeled or hansom cab (driven by a licensed driver plying for public hire)". The cover held good for seven days "from the time printed by the Post Office cancelling stamp". The scheme ceased on 31 December, 1909.
See: Colour Plate 9.

Larbalestier, Thomas Charles. *"Elizabeth Castle, Jersey"*. Facsim. *"Oilette"* by R. Tuck & Sons.

Lankester, P., & Co.   1904
Publisher who specialised in topical postcards, e.g. the Witham train disaster. They also sold machines, one for printing cards and a penny-in-the-slot automatic machine for selling them.

Larbalestier, Thomas Charles
Jersey landscape and seascape artist who lived in St. Helier.

Larcombe, Ethel   fl. c.1902-1910
Landscape artist whose paintings were used by Savory.

Larne & Stranraer Steamship Co.
A company in which several railways had a financial interest. Their Royal Mail steamers included *Princess Maud, Princess May* and *Princess Victoria*.

Lasalle, Jean
Designer of Tuck "Oilette de Luxe" sets "Golden Dawn" "Golden Hours" and "Dreamland Gardens".

Lascelles, Thomas W.   fl. 1885-1914
Painter and etcher who lived at Cookham Dean, Berkshire. Exh. R.A. 7. Coloured cards in Tuck's "Fighting the Flames" set are described as "after black and white drawings".

Latter, J.
Photographer/publisher, Wallingford, Berkshire.

Lauder, Charles James, R.S.W.   fl. 1890-1920
Watercolour painter of landscapes and architectural subjects. Studied in Glasgow and then travelled widely before returning to Scotland.

Launchings
The launching of ships, especially liners, is sometimes recorded on postcards, e.g. the *Mauretania* in 1906 and the *Queen Mary* in 1934.

Lautrec, Henri de Toulouse
See: H. de Toulouse-Lautrec.

Lawes, Harold   fl. 1890s
Landscape artist whose work was used by Salmon. He lived at Primrose Hill, London.

Lawn Tennis
In Edwardian times lawn tennis was becoming a popular game. The All England Championships were well established and

Launchings. *"Launch of Cunard White Star Liner* Queen Mary. . . *Clydebank, September 26th, 1934." Central Press.*

Lawn Tennis. *A ladies' lawn tennis club before W.W.I. Photographer unknown.*

many of the star players appear on postcards. It proved a splendid opportunity for a local photographer, E. Trim of Wimbledon.

The well-known players who won the Men's Championship were:

J. Borotra, 1924, 1926.
W.E. Brookes, 1907, 1914.
J.D. Budge, 1937-8.
H. Cochet, 1927, 1929.
J. Crawford, 1933.
H.L. Doherty, 1902-6.
A.W. Gore, 1901, 1908-9.
W.M. Johnston, 1923.
R. Lacoste, 1925, 1928.
G.L. Patterson, 1919, 1922.
F.J. Perry, 1934-6.
R.L. Riggs, 1939.
W.T. Tilden, 1920-1, 1930.
E.H. Vines, 1932.
A.F. Wilding, 1910-13.
S.B. Wood, 1931.

Women champions included:
Frl. C. Aussem, 1931.
Miss D. Boothby, 1909.
Mrs. Lambert Chambers, 1910-11, 1913-14.
Miss D.K. Douglas, 1903-4, 1906.
Mrs. L.E. Godfree, 1924, 1926.
Miss Hilyard, 1900.
Miss H. Jacobs, 1936.
Mrs. Larcombe, 1912.
Mlle. Lenglen, 1919-23, 1925.
Miss A. Marble, 1939.
Miss M.E. Robb, 1902.
Miss D. Round, 1934, 1937.
Mrs. Sterry, 1901, 1908.
Miss M.L. Sutton, 1905, 1907.
Miss H. Wills, 1927-30, and as
    Mrs. H. Wills Moody, 1932-3, 1935, 1938.
See: 'The Ladies of Wimbledon', P.P.M., December 1983, pp. 4-5.

Lawrence, Gertrude   **1898-1952**
Actress who played in many parts in London and New York. She started a film career in 1929 but returned to the stage, playing in Noël Coward plays.
Ref: Reminiscences, *A Star Danced*, 1945.

Lawrence & Jellicoe Ltd.   **c.1907**
Publisher, Henrietta St., Covent Garden, London, and later at Bedford St., Strand, London. Cards by this firm are by no means common yet their serial nos. exceed 5,000. They are mainly comic cards and a number of well-known artists, including P.B. Hickling and Lawson Wood, were involved. In some cases cartoons were used which had appeared in print elsewhere.

Lawrence, W.   **pre-1900**
Publisher, Dublin, Ireland. The output of this publisher falls into five main categories:
(i)   Views of Irish scenery, mainly in sepia.
(ii) Irish humour.
(iii) People, their occupations and way of life.
(iv) Motor racing at such localities as Athy Junction, Ballitore, Kilcullen and Kilrush Hill.
(v)   Cards for Great Northern Railway, Ireland.

Lawrence, W.B.   **pre-1905**
Photographer/publisher, Tonbridge, Kent. Local R.P. views.

L.B.
L. Bompard (q.v.).

L. & B.
Landeker & Brown (q.v.).

L.E.
Linda Edgerton (q.v.).

Lea, R.J., Ltd.
Publisher, Manchester. Advertiser of tobacco in a Chairman "Cigarette" Series, including 24 cards on "Old English Pottery and Porcelain" painted by James Jackson. Ill. Byatt col. pl. IVS. This firm issued them as cigarette cards.

Leader, Benjamin Eastlake   **fl.1900-1916**
Exh. R.A. 26. His work was used by Hildesheimer.

Leahy, Margaret   **fl. 1920s**
Actress described as the "Daily Sketch Girl". P.P. by Rotary.

Lea, R.J., Ltd. *"Old English Pottery and Porcelain"*. One of a set of 24 cards issued by Chairman Cigarettes in 1912.

Lealman, W.S.
Photographer/publisher, Kirkby Moorside, Yorkshire.

Lee, Auriol   **b. 1880**
Actress and producer. First London appearance at Drury Lane 1900. P.P. by Beagles.

Lee, Frederick Richard, R.A.   **1798-1879**
Landscape artist who worked with T.S. Cooper, an animal painter. A joint landscape "River Scene with Cattle" was reproduced in Photochrom's "Gallery Reproduction Series".

Lee, Mark (Fred Lee, Proprietor)
Stationer/printer/publisher, 24 Market Sq., Aylesbury, Buckinghamshire. Coloured local views.

Lee, Nicholas
Stationer/publisher, Wendover, Buckinghamshire. Local sepia views.

Lee, W.H.
Publisher, 4 Fife Rd., Kingston upon Thames, Surrey. Cards supplied by Wildt & Kray.

Leek and Manifold Valley Light Railway
This short line which linked Leek and Waterhouses opened in 1904, was absorbed by the L.M.S. Railway in 1923 and ceased to carry passengers in 1934. Although privately owned it was operated by the North Staffordshire Railway which issued eight sets of cards with views of the Manifold Valley. These were numbered 3, 4, 10, 11, 14, 16, 20 and 21. Two main pub-

Le Mair, Henriette Willebeek. *"Baby's Breakfast"*. Augener's *"English and Dutch Rhymes"* Series. P.U. 1938.

lishers were involved — G. Hill & Sons and William Shaw of Burslem.

Refs: Check lists may be found in P.P.M. November 1981, pp. 20-1, and December 1981, p. 17.

Leete, Alfred   **1882-1933**
Educated at Weston-super-Mare, he went to London at an early age and established himself as a poster artist and cartoonist. He designed the well-known W.W.I. Kitchener poster "Your Country Needs You". He painted a few comic cards including "Sensation at Weston-super Mare", the startling discovery of a German about to shell Madeira Cove. He also produced a watercolour scene for a black and white facsim. of the Grand Pier at Weston.

Legarde, Millie
Actress. P.P. by Rotary.

Leggatt, T.N.
Publisher, Halifax, Yorkshire. Heraldic and Yorkshire dialect cards.

Legrand, P.
French artist whose cards were imported by Edward Taylor.

Lehmann, Felix
Designer of sporting cards.

Leicester Rubber Co.
Advertisers of John Bull tyres.

Leigh, Conrad
Painter of sporting subjects.

Leighton, Frederick   **fl. c.1900-1903**
Designer of heraldic cards for Faulkner. Exh. R.A.1.

Leighton, Queenie
Actress who started at Drury Lane as a principal boy and played a Spanish beauty in *The Toreador* at the Gaiety in 1901. P.P. by Aristophot.

Le Mair, Henriette Willebeek 1889-1966
Dutch artist and illustrator of children's books. Her postcards, published by Augener Ltd., included "Little Folk", "Little Songs of Long Ago", "Old Nursery Rhymes" and "Small Rhymes for Small People".
  Illustration previous page.
  Ref: Cope, p.30, ill. p. 64.

Leman, General 1851-1920
Belgian General noted for his defence of Liège against the Germans in W.W.I. P.P. by Beagles. Ill. Holt 38.

Lembe, Capel
Designer of the "Pictorial Itinerary Postcard".
  Ref: Byatt pp. 204-5.

Lendon, Warwick William b. 1883
A Bath artist who designed cards for the First United Kingdom Aerial Post in 1911.

"Lennards"
  See: Public Benefit Boot Company

Leno Dan 1861-1904
Comedian. P.P.s by Biograph Studio, U.B., in Rotary Bookmarker Series; Rotophot.

Leominster News
Publisher of a "Leominster News Series".

Leroy, A. 1908
Publisher, Witham Close, Winchester, Hampshire. Winchester Pageant scenes.

"Lesco Series" 1900
  See: London Stereoscopic Co.

Lessieux, Ernest Louis 1848-1925
Landscape and marine painter especially of scenes in Spain and the Mediterranean countries. He designed opera postcards for "G. & D.", Paris, which were imported into Britain by H.J. Smith of Brighton.

Lessing, Madge
Actress. P.P.s by Ralph Dunn & Co., and Rotary.

Lester, Adrienne
Animal painter who designed postcards for Faulkner.

Lever Bros. Ltd.
Soap manufacturers. Several series of "Pictorial Post Cards of Port Sunlight", facsims. of paintings by J. Hughes Clayton (q.v.) and monochrome views. Some Lever Bros. cards in green frames were supplied by Valentine.

Lever, S.I. pre-1918
Publisher and fine art dealer, Burton upon Trent, Staffordshire. Local sepia views in an "S.I.L. Series".

Lévy, Louis, Sons & Co. c.1905
Publisher, 118-22 Holborn, London, and in Paris. Trademark "L.L.", sometimes within a circle. The output consisted of black and white, sepia and coloured views. They were mainly of London and seaside resorts in the south and east, for these were profitable markets, but the territory covered extended as far north as a line joining the Wash to the Severn, north of Gloucester. Each town or river valley had its own serial number. The same applied to gallery reproductions, each gallery having its own set of serial numbers. A few event cards were also issued. The Louis Lévy Collectors Society operates a postal service.

Libraries. *"The Library, Ancient House, Ipswich ..." by Howard Penton, 1905. Facsim. by Ancient House Press.*

Lewin, Frederick George fl. 1902-1930
Book illustrator and designer of comic postcards. He worked from Redland, Bristol, for the Inter-Art Co., contributing to their "Artistique" Series, and also for Salmon and for Savory. Some Easter cards were designed for W.E. Mack.

Lewis Bros.
Bath. Official photographers for Bath Historical Pageant of 1909.

Lewis, C. & A.G. pre-1924
Publisher, Nottingham. General views of high quality.

Lewis, F.C. pre-1906
Publisher, Horsham, Sussex. "Bon Marché Series" of local photographic views and "Lewis's Copyright Series" of coloured views.

Lewis, George E.
Photographer/publisher, 62 Dudley St., Birmingham, and at Wolverhampton. Local street scenes and a "Wulfruna Series" covering Wolverhampton.

L.G.
William Lyon, Glasgow (q.v.).

Liberty & Co.
London and Paris. Fashion advertising cards designed by H.T. Miller (q.v.).

Libraries
Libraries are often featured on postcards, ranging from large libraries, such as the Bodleian at Oxford, to small libraries in churches, clubs, and private houses.

Lifeboats
Views with lifeboats, lifeboat crews, boathouses and lifeboat events, e.g. "Lifeboat Saturday", are keenly sought. Elmer Keene (q.v.) painted a scene showing rescues from the *Coupland* off Scarborough in 1861. Wrench produced a card showing the "Wreck of the Ryde Lifeboat" in 1907, and the local photographer, Matthews, issued an R.P. of the victims' grave.

"In the Evening, By the Moon-Light Dear Louise!" by Comicus. Hutson Bros. P.U. 1913.

"The Last Train from Selsey" by Cynicus. Cynicus Publishing Co. P.U. 1907.

"Mixed Bathing at Boscombe" by Cynicus. Cynicus Publishing Co. P.U. 1908.

153

Libraries. *"Oxford. Bodleian Library."* Frith's Series.

Libraries. *"The Chain Library. Wimborne Minster".* J. Welch & Sons.

"Life's Comedy" Series
Framed humorous cards by James Henderson & Sons.

Lighthouses and Lightships
Under this heading may be included lights and other devices designed to guide and safeguard mariners, e.g. buoys, fog horns, harbour lights, pier lights. There are between 150 and 200 lighthouses around the coast of Britain and most of them are to be found on postcards. Examples include:

   Beachy Head, Eastbourne.
   Bell Rock, or Inch Cape, off the east coast of Scotland.
   Bull Point, north west coast of Devon.
   Corbière, Jersey.
   Dovercourt, Essex.
   Eddystone, S. Devon.
   Fastnet, off coast of Co. Cork, Ireland.
   Flamborough Head, Yorkshire.
   Lizard, Cornwall.
   Longships, Land's End, Cornwall.
   The Needles, Isle of Wight.
   New Brighton, Wirral, Cheshire.
   Porthcawl, Glamorgan.
   Portland Bill, Dorset.
   Roker, Near Sunderland.
   St. Anthony's, Falmouth, Cornwall.
   Shoreham Harbour, Sussex.
   South Stack Rock, Holyhead, Anglesey.
   West Usk, near Newport, South Wales.
Ref: Mead, H.P., *Trinity House,* n.d.

Lilywhite Ltd.   fl. c.1910-1939
Publisher, Triangle, York, and Dunkirk Mills, Halifax, Yorkshire. After 1932 the firm had a branch at Sowerby Bridge, Yorkshire. Output included:
(i)   "Lilywhite Photographic Series" of views which concentrated on Wales and the north of England, but also covered more distant parts.
(ii) Portraits of theatre and cinema stars.
(iii) Boxing. Lilywhite had the sole rights to photograph the Championship of Europe fight in 1919 between Joe Becket and Charles Carpentier.

Libraries. *"The Library, Thoresby".* Woolstone Bros. Milton *"Artlette"* Series.

(iv) Greetings cards and verses.
(v) "Lilywhite Humour".

   Lilywhite Ltd. described their firm as "High Grade Color Printers and Publishers" [*sic*]. They supplied photographic views to small publishers all over England.

Limericks
In 1903 William Lyon of Glasgow published a number of limerick cards. Interest in limericks grew and by 1908 the craze swept the country, encouraged by postcard publishers who ran competitions for a good "last line" and incidentally boosted their sales.

   Ref: An article by Evan Poole, P.P.M., April 1983, pp. 6-7, lists 20 designers of limerick cards and 29 publishers.

Lindley, H.   pre-1905
Publisher, Nottingham. Cards of the 1905 Test Match v. Australia at Lords.

Lighthouses. *"Gorleston, the Jetty and Lighthouse"*. Photochrom *"Sepiatone"* Series.

Liptons. *"Tea Factory, Bunyan Estate, Ceylon"*. Photochrom. *P.U. 1909*.

Lindsay, James   **fl. 1881-1906**
Scottish artist who exhibited at the Glasgow Institute of Fine Arts. Painted scenes for Valentine.

Lindsell, L.
Watercolour artist who painted sets for Tuck, e.g. "The Carnival".

Linear Collection
This term is used for a collection of views along the course of a river or along a particular road or railway, e.g. The Dover Road, the Great North Road or the Roman Watling Street.

Liners
   See: Shipping.

Lipton, Sir Thomas
   See: Yacht Racing.

Liptons   **pre-1909**
Advertiser of tea. A "Lipton Series" was published by the Photochrom Co. showing the tea plantations and the tea warehouses at Bunyan Estate, Ceylon. The word "LIPTON" appears on each card on the roof of a building. Another series of coloured cards was published by Faulkner, e.g. "Plucking tea, Dambateune Estate, Ceylon".

Literary Personalities
Poets and novelists are commemorated on postcards. There are portraits, views of their homes and of their memorials. Sometimes postcards of the characters in their works are to be found. They are recorded individually in the dictionary.

Little, Fred
Photographer/publisher. Multi-view cards of the "Great Fire at Bristol", 1905.

Littlebury & Co. Ltd.
Publisher, The Worcester Press, Worcester. Facsims. of paintings of Worcestershire by E.A. Phipson.

Liverpool Daily Post & Mercury Ltd.
Publisher of two sets of cards by the artist Samuel John Milton Brown (q.v.).

Living Picture Post Card Co.
   See: Henry Garner.

Livingstone, David, LL.D., D.C.L.   **1813-1873**
Traveller and missionary who explored the interior of Africa between 1849 and his death in 1873. P.P. by Knight Bros.

L.L.
Louis Lévy (q.v.).

Lloyd
Publisher, Albury, Surrey. General views.

Lloyd George, David   **1863-1945**
Prime Minister 1916-22. P.P. by Philco. Ill. Hill p. 15.
   Illustration overleaf.

Lloyd & Langston
Publisher/stationer, Chatham, Kent. General views and birthday cards.

Lloyd, Marie   **1870-1922**
Music-hall comedienne. P.P. by Rotary.

Lloyd, T. Ivester
Painter of military subjects for W.N. Sharpe of Bradford.

Llythyr-Gendyn
The Welsh language name for postcard used on a series published by the Western Mail Ltd., Cardiff and on "The Strand Series" published by W.H. Smith & Son in Cardiff pre-1905.

Loader's Photo Stores   **pre-1937**
Photographer/publisher, Worthing, Sussex. Local R.P. views.

Local Customs
These are sometimes recorded on postcards, e.g. the Dunmow Flitch (q.v.), and "Wayfarers' Dole, St. Cross Hospital, Winchester".
   Illustration overleaf.

Local History
Some local history groups take a particular interest in old postcards which reflect life in their area as it was over 50 years ago;

Lloyd George, David. *"The Rt. Hon. D. Lloyd George & Miss Megan"*. *Frith's Series*.

Local Customs. *"Wayfarers' Dole, St. Cross Hospital, Winchester"*. *Frith's Series*.

one of the most enterprising is in the Somerset village of Banwell. The Banwell Society for Archaeology Reproduction is concerned with reproducing views of Old Banwell from early postcards.

Local View Publishing Co.
Several views have been noted by this publisher, all photographs of Brockwell Park, Lambeth.

"Lochinvar" Series
See: Nicholson & Carter.

Locomotive Publishing Co. Ltd.   c.1900
Publisher of railway material, 102 Charing Cross Rd., London, W.C. until 1903, thereafter at 3 Amen Corner, London. Cards of every type were issued, black and white, sepia and coloured. Many postcards were prepared for *The Locomotive Magazine,* published by the same company, but unfortunately a great number have no titles. The firm also supplied cards to other publishers.
    Ref: Picton 1982, p. 58 *et seq.*

Loffler, Berthold   fl.c.1908-1913
Wiener Werkstätte artist.

Lomax, John Arthur   1857-1926
Genre painter. Exh. R.A. 56. Facsims. by Hildesheimer.

London, Brighton & South Coast Railway
The cards issued by this railway include some sepia vignette views by the Picture Postcard Co., and six sets printed by

Waterlow & Sons Ltd. in 1907. These all have views, though two include cards of motor rails and the turbine steamship *Brighton*. Three sets deal with special subjects, railway river bridges, churches, and castles.
    Ref: Full check lists in R.O.P.L., No. 11, pp. 4-5.

London, Chatham & Dover Railway
Vignette views of Canterbury, Dover and Margate by the Picture Postcard Syndicate.
    Ref: R.O.P.L., No. 11, p. 13.

London County Council
Publisher of reward cards which were given to schoolchildren for good attendance, etc.

London, Midland & Scottish Railway
Most L.M.S. cards relate to their hotels and their recreational facilities for golf and tennis. They were supplied mainly by Tuck and McCorquodale. Photochrom, McCorquodale and the Locomotive Publishing Co. supplied some views of locomotives, and the shipping links with Ireland.
    Ref: Check lists in R.O.P.L., No. 17, pp. 4-12.

London Missionary Society
Publisher, 16 New Bridge St., London, E.C. The Society had a Picture Post Card Dept., managed by the Rev. Chas. H. Vine, which issued coloured cards, e.g. "Women in Madagascar", and black and white portraits, e.g. James Chalmers (1841-1901) who was murdered by cannibals.

London, Midland & Scottish Railway. *"Gleneagles Hotel in Perthshire. Britain's Premier Sports Hotel"*. *Published by R. Tuck & Sons for L.M.S. Hotel Services.*

London & North Eastern Railway

This railway used postcards to draw attention to their hotels and shipping services. Over 20 hotels served the area between London and Aberdeen and 10 steamships used Harwich for services to Antwerp, Hook of Holland and Zeebrugge.

Ref: Check list in R.O.P.L., No. 17, pp. 13-17.

London & North Western Railway   pre-1910

This railway used several types of card. The trademark was a seated Britannia within concentric circles which carry the company name. This is often found on the picture side as well as on the address side. Cards included:

(i)   Advertising cards supplied by the Locomotive Publishing Co., of trains, locomotives, etc. Diamond Jubilee card ill. D. & M. 134.

(ii) Views of the area served by the railway which is said to have sold over 11 million cards by 1914. Many were supplied by McCorquodale.

(iii) "Railways in the Thirties", a series of black and white pictures of railways as they were in the 1830s.

Other publishers issued cards relating to the railway, e.g. J.W. Bland's "Irish Mail Train" and Tuck's cards which included Edward VII's sleeping compartment.

Ref: Check lists in R.O.P.L., No. 19.

London Photo Printing Co.

See: Philip G. Hunt.

London Society for the Promotion of Christianity amongst the Jews

Publisher. Postcards made comparisons between Old and New Testament quotations.

London Stereoscopic Co. Ltd.   1900

Publishers, 106-8 Regent St., London. Noted for R.P. cards, especially of cathedrals.

London View Co. Ltd.   pre-1909

Coloured views of Brighton, Hastings and other south coast resorts.

Long, Lady Mary   1789-1875

Amateur landscape painter whose work was used by Tuck in facsims. of European scenes.

Longley, Chilton   fl. 1920s

Art deco artist who painted glamour cards.

Longmire, R.O.   fl. 1903-1924

Liverpool artist who designed comic political cards.

Longstaffe, Edgar   fl. 1884-1906

Landscape painter. Exh. R.A. 6. His oil paintings were used in facsims. by Hildesheimer and Tuck. They mainly included landscapes in Ireland and Scotland.

Lonsdale & Bartholomew Ltd.   pre-1927

Publisher, Accrington, Lancashire. Hand-painted greetings cards. Serial nos. exceed 1,000.

Loosley & Sons   pre-1906

Stationer/publisher, Berkhamsted, Hertfordshire. Local views.

Lord Mayor's State Coach

A view taken by the London Stereoscopic Co.

Love, Blanche

Actress. P.P. by Davidson.

Love, Mabel   1874-1953

Actress. First London appearance in *Alice in Wonderland* at the Prince of Wales Theatre in 1886. She continued as an actress for 25 years and then became a teacher of dancing and elocution. P.P.s by Rotary.

Love, Montague   b. 1877

Military artist who worked for David Allen and designed regimental cards for Blum & Degen. He served in the Boer War and then became a professional actor, first on the London stage and later in many American films.

Lovegrove, C.A.   pre-1909

Publisher, 5 Market Place, Clevedon, Somerset.

Lovering & Co.

Publisher, 24 Yeoman's Row, London. See next entry.

Lord Mayor's State Coach. *"The Lord Mayor's State Coach, London"*. *London Stereoscopic Co. P.U. 1907.*

Lovering, Ida   **fl. 1881-1915**
Versatile painter. Exh. R.A. 14. Decided to design and publish
her own postcards and those of her artist friends. She
therefore formed Lovering & Co. (q.v.). Many of her cards
depict the front doors of the houses of literary people. Some
are of effigies of nobilities buried in Westminster Abbey. She
also painted views of south east England.

Low, Claude
Photographer, 72 Princes St., Edinburgh. Studio postcards.

Lowe
Publisher, Patterdale, Westmorland. Local views. Serial nos.
to over 3,800.

Lowe, J.T.
Publisher/stationer, 18-20 The Arcade, Bedford.

Lowe, Meta
Painter of child subjects.

Loy, Myrna   **b. 1905**
Film actress. Scene with Ramon Novarro in *A Night in Cairo*.
P.P. by Film Weekly.

L.P. & Co. Ltd.
L. Pickles & Co. Ltd. (q.v.).

L.P. (L.P. & F.A.P.)
Landscape Photo, or Landscape Photographic and Fine Art
Publishers (q.v.).

L.S. & S.   **pre-1904**
Initials of an unknown publisher of Scottish views.

Lucas, E.F.
Publisher, Cobham, Kent. General views printed in Trèves,
Germany.

Lucy & Co.
Photographer/publisher, Marlborough, Wiltshire. Local
photographic views.

Ludgate
    See: Albert E. Carnell.

Ludgater, A.
Publisher, Braintree, Essex. Photographic views.

Ludlow, Henry Stephen   **fl. 1888-1928**
Portrait painter and illustrator. Exh. R.A. 35. Signed his work
Hal Ludlow. Painted the Tuck sets "For the Dear
Homeland", 8846, and "Lucky Dogs", 2981.

Ludovici, Albert Jr., R.B.A.   **1852-1932**
Painter. Born in Prague but lived mainly in Paris. Exh. R.A.
15. "Scenes from Dickens" and political cartoons for
Davidson Bros.

Luke, William
Belfast artist who designed comic cards for Tacon Bros. of
Manchester.

Luminous Print Co.
Publisher of floral cards in which the design was outlined in
luminous paint so that it glowed in the dark.

Lumley, S.
Designer of military cards for Gale & Polden.

Lyle's Golden Syrup
Advertising cards which feature bears. A card with two bears,

LORD ROSEBERY at Sheffield: "There are those who,
like Mr. Chamberlain, went the whole hog, and might be
expressly denoted by the title of whole hoggers."

Ludovici, Albert. *Fiscal Cartoon. Davidson Bros.*

one with its nose in a tin of syrup, the other watching, is
captioned "A Sister to Assist Her".

Lynton & Barnstaple Railway
Set of 12 coloured cards of stations and general views was
produced by the Pictorial Stationery Co.
    Ref: Check list in R.O.P.L., No. 18, p. 6.

Lyon, William   **1900**
Publisher, Glasgow. Trademark a shield with the letters
"L.G." Output included:
(i)   U.B. cards with Scottish views.
(ii)   U.B. cards for the Glasgow Exhibition, 1901.
(iii)   Write-away cards.
(iv)   "Popular Songs Illustrated".
(v)   Comic cards in a "Premier Series", e.g. "Juvenile
        Smokers".
(vi)   Map series which included not only Scottish country but
        the Lake District, the Isle of Man and the river Thames.
(vii)   Events, e.g. America's Cup Yacht Race, 1901.

Lyons, J., & Co. Ltd.
Advertising cards, e.g. R.P. of the London Oxford St. Corner
House with the "Mountview Cafe".

Lyons, John
Artist who painted comic situations for an "XL Series".

Lytton, Sir Henry A.   **1867-1936**
Leading member of the D'Oyly Carte Opera Company, 1894,
1897-1903, 1908-34. Wrote two books on his experiences,
Secrets of a Savoyard and *A Wandering Minstrel*. P.P. by
Parkslee Pictures.

M

M. & Co.
Misch & Co. (q.v.).

"Mac"
Pseudonym used by Lucy Dawson (q.v.).

McCarthy, Lillah   1876-1960
Actress. Married H. Granville Barker. Divorced 1918 and married Sir Frederick Keeble. Played with the Ben Greet and Wilson Barrett companies. P.P. in Tuck's "Bookmarker" Series IV.

Refs: *My Life*, 1930; *Myself and My Friends*, 1933, autobiographies.

McCaw, Stevenson & Orr Ltd.   1903
This firm based in Belfast took over Marcus Ward & Co., the Christmas card publishers in 1899, and when they started to publish postcards they named them the "Marcus Ward Series". Output included:
(i)   "The Silent Highway", a set depicting the River Thames.
(ii) Children's cards.
(iii) "Dainty Damsels" and "Beauty's Daughters" sets.
(iv) Sets covering sports; cricket, golf, etc.
(v)   Advertising cards for the Provident Association of London.

McClinton's Soap Co.
This company built an Irish village, "Ballymaclinton", at the Franco-British Exhibition of 1908 to advertise their soap. Ill. Hill p. 42.

McCormick, Arthur David, R.B.A., R.I., R.O.I.   1860-1943
Painter who was born in Ireland but spent most of his life in London. Exh. R.A. 49. He illustrated a book on *The Alps* for A. & C. Black and facsims. of the illustrations were used in Tuck's "Wide Wide World" Series on "Switzerland".

McCorquodale & Co. Ltd.   fl.c. 1900-1930
Publisher of cards of trains, stations, etc., used as official issues by several railway companies.

McCrum, R. & L.
Robert and Louisa McCrum founded the Inter-Art Co. in 1909. After 1921 the company was owned by Robert McCrum. Some cards bear the words "Copyright by Robert McCrum".

McCulloch, J.A., & Co.   1903
Publisher, Hillside Printing Works, Delhaig, Gorgie, near Edinburgh. Trademark a shield with "J.M." surmounted by a stag's head and with "Caledonia Series" beneath. Ill. Byatt p. 310. Output consisted mainly of sepia and coloured views of Scotland. The photographs were mainly by Reid of Wishaw and the cards were printed in Saxony.

Macdonald, A.K.   fl. c.1900-1910
Art nouveau artist who made pen and ink drawings for Henderson and designed exhibition cards for Valentine.

McClinton's Soap Co. *"Colleens Dancing, Ballymaclinton"*. *P.U. 1908.*

Macdonald, Greenlees & Williams (Distillers) Ltd.
Leith, London and Glasgow. Advertisers of whisky including "Claymore, Old Parr, Sandy Macdonald Scotch Whiskies" at the Empire Exhibition, Wembley, 1924, using "Defenders of the Empire" cards supplied by Tuck.

Macdonald, James Ramsay   1866-1937
Prime Minister 1924, 1929 and 1931-5. P.P. by unknown publisher. Ill. Monahan 47.

Macfarlane Lang & Co.
Biscuit makers. Advertising cards included a "Sultana Sandwich Series", ill. D. & M. 78.

McGill, Donald   1875-1962
Prolific watercolour painter who provided a very large number of comic postcards which have been used from the early years of this century to the present day. He started his working life in the office of a naval architect and was 30 before he produced comic pictures for postcards. There followed a seemingly unending output. He worked for several publishers:
(i)   1905-1908, cards mainly for the Pictorial Postcard Co.
(ii) c.1906-1914, cards were designed for Joseph Asher & Co., printed in Germany or Holland; Thridgould & Co.; Woolstone Bros.
(iii) c.1908-c.1935, Hutson Bros. who took over the stock of the Pictorial Postcard Co. and continued the connection with McGill.
(iv) c.1913-1935, Philco, Thridgould & Co., and Woolstone Bros.
(v)   1914-1932, Birn Bros. and Inter-Art "Comique Series", ill. Monahan 82, 84.   *continued*

159

LIAR!

McGill, Donald. *"Liar!" Inter-Art "Comique Series". P.U. 1919.*

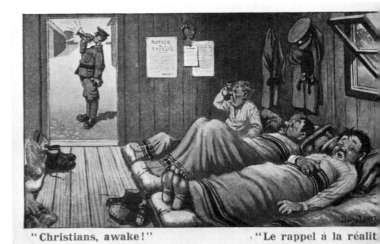

"Christians, awake!"   , "Le rappel à la réalit

McGill, Donald. *"Christians, Awake!"* Caption also in French. Inter-Art *"Comique Series"*.

McIntyre, R.F. *"Isleworth on Thames"*. Facsim. by R. Tuck & Sons. *"Oilette"*. *"The Picturesque Thames"*. P.U. 1906.

(vi) 1938 *et seq.*, D. Constance Ltd., "The New Donald McGill Comics". These cards are revised editions: some of them have been redrawn.

See: Colour Plate 18.

Refs: Calder-Marshall, A., *The Art of Donald McGill*, 1966; Tickner, M., and Buckland, B.N., *The World of Donald McGill, 1875-1962*, 1974.

MacGillivray
Publisher, The Stores, Rosemarkie, Ross and Cromarty. Local sepia views supplied by R.A. Postcards Ltd.

McGurk, C.D.
Designer of cards for Davis's "British Commercial Aircraft" Series.

McIntyre, Robert Finlay   **fl. c.1895-1910**
Landscape painter. Exh. R.A. 2. Painted Tuck "Oilette" sets "Happy England" and "The Picturesque Thames".

McIsaac & Riddle   **pre-1924**
Publisher, Oban. Local R.P. views.

Mack, Robert
Landscape artist who painted for Salmon.

Mack, W.E.   **fl. 1903-1940**
Publisher, 52 Park Row, Bristol, and from c.1908 at 102 King's Rd., Hampstead, London, N.W.3. This firm was producing biblical text cards in the 1890s. The transition to postcard publishing followed naturally. Output included:

(i)   Greetings cards, romantic and humorous, including examples by F.G. Lewin.
(ii)   Photographs of aeroplanes.
(iii)   Photographs of railway engines, post-1921.
(iv)   "Satin" Series of photographs of racehorses and jockeys, both named. Each card has a descriptive paragraph on the address side.
(v)   Fashion cards including a series with large hats.
(vi)   W.W.I. patriotic cards, e.g. "Flags of the Allies".
(vii)   "Bluette" Series of humorous poems.
(viii) Comic cards.
(ix)   Composite sets, e.g. "The Elongated Dachshund".

In the 1920s W.E. Mack had a close association with J. Salmon of Sevenoaks who printed a number of Mack cards. On some cards both names appear. See Byatt p. 178.

Mackain, F.   fl.c.1914-1918
Painter of a humorous "Sketches of Tommy's Life" Series
during W.W.I. which included sets of eight cards each with
such titles as "At the Base", ill. Monahan 88, "In Training",
"Out on Rest" and "Up the Line". These were also issued as
Christmas postcards. They were published by Savigny of
Paris.

Mackenzie, James Hamilton, R.S.W.   1875-1926
Painter and etcher. Exh. R.S.A. 49. Etched cards for the
Scottish Exhibition of 1911.

McKenzie, William, & Co.   1905
Printer/publisher, 48-52 Banner St., London, E.C. Some of
their postcards were in an "Artistic Series". Output included:
(i)   Greetings cards.
(ii)   Hunting scenes, example ill. Byatt 183.
(iii) Political caricature of the Pears' "Bubbles" advertise-
       ment.
(iv)   Several sets of cards by Harry Payne issued in 1922.
(v)   Vignette-type comics. Ill. D. & M. 106.
(vi)   Views including Scotland.

MacKinder, Arthur   fl.c.1904-1918
Artist who painted views of Lincoln used by J.W. Ruddock in
the "Artist Series".

McLagan & Cumming
Publisher, Edinburgh. Issued a card on 19 June, 1915, in aid
of disabled soldiers of the Scottish Lowland Regiments. Ill.
Monahan 64.

Macleod, F.
Painted comic subjects in the style of Tom Browne, for H.
Garner of Leicester.

McLove, M., & Co.   1916
Publisher, Imperial House, Kingsway, London. "Imperial
Series". Some of their cards were reproduced by agreement
from an American "Klever Kards" Series.
     See: "Klever Kards" under Novelty Cards.

McNeill, John
Military artist who designed cards for George Falkner & Sons,
and Gale & Polden.

MacPherson, John
Publisher/stationer, Invergordon, Ross and Cromarty. Issued
a "MacPherson's Art Series" of coloured views, a tartan
series and a "Hill's Aquatint Series". At one period a partnership was formed with a brother and the firm became
MacPherson Bros., with a branch at Beauly in Inverness-shire.

Madden, Admiral C.E.   1862-1935
Took a prominent part in naval design under Lord Fisher
when the *Dreadnought* was laid down. Became Commander-
in-Chief of the Grand Fleet after W.W.I. Bas-relief card by
Scopes.

Maddison, A., & Son
Publisher, Hounslow, Middlesex. R.P. views.

Maggi
Advertiser of their soups. Give-away view cards.

Maggs, John Charles   1819-1896
Painter of old inns and coaching scenes who taught art in Gay
St., Bath. Facsims. of his paintings were published by
Hancock & Corfield in a "Gems of Art" Series.

Macleod, F. *"When the Gentle Breezes Blow. Hold Your Hair
On!" Henry Garner, Leicester. P.U. 1910.*

Maguire, Bertha   fl. 1881-1904
Flower painter in watercolour. Exh. R.A. 4.

Maguire, Helena J.   1860-1909
Animal painter, sister of Bertha Maguire. Exh. R.A. 13.
Painted for Hildesheimer and Tuck, mainly animal studies.

Mailick, A.   fl. c.1900-1918
German art nouveau artist who designed embossed religious
cards for Giesen Bros., e.g. "Faith", "Hope" and "Charity",
each with a glamorous lady standing before a cross. He also
painted military subjects during W.W.I., e.g. "The Charge",
which depicts a mounted cavalry officer in action. Som Alpine
landscapes and Christmas greetings cards have also been
noted.
     Illustration overleaf.

Mair, L.   pre-1911
Publisher/stationer, Andover, Hampshire. Framed local
views.

Maitland, Beatrice
Painter of cards with children.

Maitland, Lauderdale   1877-1929
Actor. P.P. with actress Nora Keren by Rotary.

Major, Fred   fl. c.1910-1920
Photographer/publisher, Bisley-with-Lypiatt, Gloucestershire.
     Ref: Merrett, W., 'A Village Photographer', P.P.M.,
March 1983, p. 11.

Mallet, Dennis   **fl. 1930s**
Designer of comic cards for Tuck.

Mallett & Son
Publisher, Tewkesbury, Gloucestershire. Firm which advertised "2,000 different views".

Mallett, Beatrice   **fl. c.1900-1918**
An artist who designed children's cards for Tuck's "Kute Kiddies" Series.

Manavian, V.
Designer of comic cards titled "Egyptian Humour".

Manifold Valley Light Railway
See: Leek and Manifold Valley Light Railway.

Manley, J.
Photographer/publisher, Windsor, Berkshire. Local sepia views.

Manly, Alice Elfrida   **fl. 1880-1917**
Figure and landscape painter who designed for E.W. Savory. Exh. R.A. 16.

Mansell, Vivian A., & Co.   **pre-1910**
Fine art publisher, Chapel St., and Silk St., London, E.C. Specialised in artistic work using facsims. of paintings, and prepared advertising cards for such firms as J.S. Fry & Sons and the Indian Tea Association. They issued series of hunting and glamour cards.
    See: Frontispiece.

Manx National Postcard, The
Manx postcard firm with the trademark of a Scandinavian sailing ship. The cards which are mainly coloured views of the Isle of Man are headed "YN KAART MANNINAGH".

Manzoni, D.
Painter of hunting scenes for Salmon.

Mapple, A. Nelson
Guildford artist who painted local scenes for Biddles, a Guildford publisher.

Maps
The following publishers issued postcard maps:
(i)   G.N. Bacon & Co., county maps.
(ii)   F. Bauermeister, map of Arran.
(iii) M. Ettlinger & Co., postcard guides which included a local map.
(iv) W. Holmes & Co., map of Arran, a set titled "Tramping in Arran".
(v)   P.M. Hope (Lt.-Col.), Lakeland maps.
(vi) W. & A.K. Johnston, maps to illustrate special events, e.g. The Royal Visit to Edinburgh in 1903.
(vii) William Lyon, maps of Scotland, the Lake District, the Isle of Man and the Thames Valley.
(viii) J.A. McCulloch, Scottish maps.
(ix) R. Tuck & Sons, map of Russo-Japanese War zone.
(x)   Valentine & Sons, an "Art Colour" Series of maps.

Mailick, A. *"Happy Christmas". Giesen Bros. & Co. Embossed.*

Mapple, A. Nelson. *"The Royal Grammar School, Guildford". Facsim. by Biddles Ltd.*

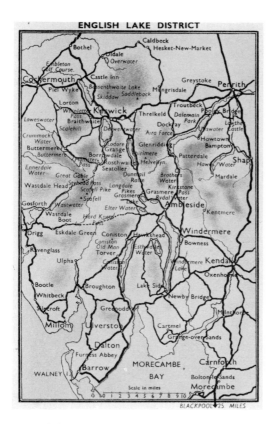

Maps. *"English Lake District". Published by Lt.-Col. P.M. Hope, O.B.E., Keswick.*

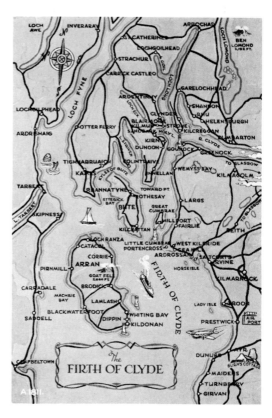

Maps. *"The Firth of Clyde" by James C. Jamieson. Valentine "Art Colour".*

(xi)   J. Walker & Co., "Walker's Geographical Postcards". Issued a complete set covering England and extended this with the aim of covering most of the world, maps engraved by J. Bartholomew & Co.

Marcuse, Day & Co. Ltd.   **pre-1920**
Publisher, London. Trademark "MD" in monogram form within a circular belt, sometimes with the words "A Mark of Quality". Greetings cards, children's cards, seascapes and comic animal cards.

Margetson, Hester   **1890-1965**
Designer of cards for children published by V. Mansell, and of a single set, "Fairy Wings" by Humphrey Milford.
   Ref: Cope p. 14, ill. p. 46.

"Marine Series"   **pre-1910**
Comic seaside cards published by a firm with initials "H.S."

Marion & Co. Ltd.
Publisher of a card of the late King Edward VII lying in state, 16 May, 1910.

Markets
Several types of market appear on postcards:
(i)   Cattle markets.
(ii)   Street markets, e.g. Petticoat Lane, London.
(iii)   Undercover markets, e.g. Covent Garden.
(iv)   Wholesale markets, e.g. Wolverhampton, ill. Hill. p. 92.

Markham
Publisher, Oundle, Northamptonshire. "Oundle Series" of local views.

Markino, Yoshio   **fl. 1904-1928**
Japanese artist who worked in Britain for Delittle, Fenwick & Co.

Marks, Benjamin, & Co.   **1907**
Publisher, 7 Brushfield St., Bishopsgate, London, E.C. Published hold-to-light cards designed by Henry Clayton. A special set was issued for the Franco-British Exhibition of 1908.

Marks, S., & Sons   **1907**
Publisher, 72 Houndsditch, London, E.C.

Marriner, Mary
The smallest barmaid in the world. Age 22. Height 3ft. Card published by Joe Haynes, proprietor of "The Monarch Tavern", Chalk Farm Rd., London, N.W., where she served.

Marsden, G., & Son
Publisher, Wirksworth, Derbyshire, and London. Derbyshire "Artistic" Series of coloured views.

Marsh, W.P., & Son
Publisher, Southgate, Chichester, Sussex. Local R.P. views.

Marshall
Publisher, Sudbrook, Monmouthshire. Black and white local views.

Marshall, Sons & Co. Ltd.
Maker and advertiser of thrashing machines, Gainsborough, Lincolnshire.

Marshall, Charles Edward, R.B.A.   **fl. 1880-1920**
Figure painter. Exh. R.A. 30. His work was used by Langsdorff & Co.

Marshall, H.
Photographer/publisher, 77 London Rd., Waterlooville, Hampshire. Local R.P. views.

Marshall, Keene & Co.
Photographer/publisher, Hove, Sussex. Local sepia views.

Marshall, Lily
Artist who designed comic cards for Boots Cash Chemists.

Markets. *"The Cattle Market, Ipswich." "The Christchurch Series". P.U. 1908.*

Markets. *"Rochford Market". "The Bell Series", Leigh-on-Sea.*

Marsh-Lambert, H.G.C. (Mrs.)   **fl.c.1914-1918**
Designer of comic series for A.M. Davis, e.g. "Nursery Rhymes", and of W.W.I. cards for Faulkner.

Martin, Charles   **fl. 1903-1912**
Publisher, 49 Aldermanbury Rd., London, E.C. Views of London and its suburbs, especially the suburban railway stations. A few early cards are of views of the Sussex coast. Many of his cards were printed in Prussia. There were also facsims. of paintings by Jotter.

After several years Martin appears to have moved to Ponders Green and to have covered some of the country north of London.

Martin, G.H.   **pre-1907**
Publisher, 217 Clapham Rd., London, S.W. Black and white London views.

Martin, L.B.
Designer of comic cards.

Martin, Rita
Photographer for Beagles and Rotary.

Martineau, Alice
See: Eva Hollyer.

Martyn, A.   **pre-1905**
Photographer/publisher, Hoylake, Cheshire. Local R.P. views.

Martyn, C.W.
Landscape painter who contributed to Ruddock's "Artist Series".

Maryport & Carlisle Railway
A single map card has been recorded.

Mascots
See: "Service Pets".

Mason, Delia
Actress. P.P. by Misch & Co.

Mason, Finch
Artist. Designed a "Sporting Notions" Series for J. Alderton, and a "Hunting Series" for F.C. Southwood.

Mason's Alpha Series
Photographic views of Cornwall.

Masters, F.N.D.
Painter who contributed to a Tuck "Oilette" Series of "Sport Impressions".

Mataloni, Giovanni
Art nouveau artist.

Matania, Fortunino, R.I.   **1881-1963**
Historical painter born in Naples. Settled in London before W.W.I. and joined the staff of *The Sphere*. Paid great attention to accuracy and, perhaps for this reason, was invited to illustrate scenes on royal occasions, e.g. the Coronation of George V and the marriage of Kaiser Wilhelms's daughter. Many contributions he made to *The Sphere* were reproduced as postcards.

Ref: Bradshaw, P.V., 'Fortunino Matania and His Work' in *The Art of the Illustrator, 1916-17.*

"Matheson's Tea"
Advertising cards showing the packing and tasting of tea.

Mathieson, T. pre-1903
Bookseller/publisher, Lerwick, Shetland Isles. Local views.

Matthews
Publisher, Bradford, Yorkshire. Supplied cards of camping coaches to the L.M.S. Railway.

Matthews, Ethel
Actress. P.P. in Tuck's "Celebrities of the Stage".

Matthews, Jessie 1907-1982
Actress and dancer. P.P. by De Reszke.

Matthison, William fl. 1883-1923
Landscape painter. Exh. R.A. 2. Illustrated a book on Cambridge, 1905, published by A. & C. Black. Some of his illustrations were reproduced in four Tuck "Oilette" sets on Cambridge. He also painted a "London" set for Tuck and views of Oxford and Whitby for Robert Peel.

Matthison, William. *"St. Paul's Cathedral, London. From Ludgate Hill".* R. Tuck & Sons. *"Oilette" "London".* P.U. 1910.

Maude, Cyril 1862-1951
Actor-manager. Haymarket Theatre, London. P.P. by Rotary.

Maule, S. pre-1908
Stationer/publisher, 67 Clarence St., Kingston upon Thames, Surrey.

Maurice, Reg fl. c.1905-1920
Prolific artist who painted comic cards for the Regent Publishing Co.
    See: Colour Plate 14.

Mauzan, Achille 1886-1940
Italian artist who made his name during W.W.I. designing posters for the Italian National Savings Movement. He designed postcards both glamour and déshabillé which were published in Milan and exported all over Europe.
    See: Colour Plate 15.

May, Edna b. 1878
Actress and vocalist. Started her career in New York but played in a number of London theatres. P.P.s by Ellis & Walery, Pictorial Post Card Co., Rapid Photo, Rotary (with her husband Oscar Lewisohn) and Woolstone.

May, M.F. fl. c.1900-1910
Landscape painter. Exh. at the S.W.A. in 1902 and 1903. Lived in Marlborough, Wiltshire, and an unknown publisher used facsims. of "Long Harry Avenue" in Savernake Forest and "Penny's Yard Marlboro".

May, Olive fl. 1901-1935
Gaiety Girl. P.P. by Aristophot and in Tuck's "Bookmarker" and "Celebrities of the Stage" Series.

May, Philip Williams, R.I. 1864-1903
Phil May, as he was generally known, was born on the outskirts of Leeds. He was engaged to paint scenery in the Grand Theatre, Leeds, and later moved to London where he started to contribute drawings to illustrated papers. In 1885 he went to Australia, returning in 1888. Joined the *Punch* table in 1895 and carved his name between those of W.M. Thackeray and Gerald du Maurier. Was a superb draughtsman, using great economy of line, and his drawings of the social life of the 1890s reflect the working class cockney with accuracy and humour. His drawings were used on postcards by Davidson Bros., black and white with red frame; Tuck; Valentine; Wrench.
    See: Colour Plate 23.
    Ref: Cuppleditch, D., *Phil May: The Artist and his Wit,* 1981.

May, William, & Co. Ltd. fl. c.1912-1926
Photographer/publisher, 45 High St., Aldershot, Hampshire. Noted for photographs of early aircraft published before W.W.I.

Mayall & Co.
Photographer. A firm established at 224 Regent St., London by the American photographer John Jabez Mayall (1810-1901) with a studio at Brighton.

Maybank, Thomas fl. c.1898-1925
Illustrator noted for his drawings of fairies in *Punch*. His designs with dancing girls were used on postcards by M. Munk.

Maybury
Publisher, Swindon. Coloured local views.

Maycock, F.A. pre-1925
Photographer/publisher, Polzeath, Wadebridge, Cornwall. "West Ray Series" of photographs of Cornish views, including the launching of a lifeboat at Port Isaac.

Maydell, E.
Artist who designed comic cards for the Medici Society.

Mayer, Henry b.1868
Designer of humorous cards for Ernest Nister.

Maypole Margarine
Advertising card with a view of the works at Southall, Middlesex.

Maypoles
Dancing round the maypole on May Day is a custom which now survives only in a few rural districts. A limited number of topographical postcards show the festivities, e.g. a photograph of children around the maypole at Selly Oak in 1905.

Maysons   **pre-1929**
Publisher, Keswick, Cumberland. A "Maysons Series" of local R.P.s includes a portrait of Hugh Walpole and his dog Bingo.

M.B.
Meissner & Buch (q.v.).

M.D. & Co.
Marcuse, Day & Co. (q.v.).

Meadows, Charles
Designer of an Inter-Art "Today's Weather" set.

Medals
Several firms issued cards with medals, notably Wildt & Kray who published a set with notes on their history.

Medici Society   **c.1912**
A Society founded in 1908 to provide reproductions of famous paintings at a reasonable cost. Within a few years postcards were issued in a number of sets reflecting works in the National Gallery and National Portrait Gallery. The scope

Maycock, F.A. *"Cornwall's Wave-beat Shore". A typical photograph of the Cornish coast. P.U. 1936.*

widened after W.W.I. to include modern painters and also natural history cards. There were many cards for children or about children designed mainly by Margaret Tarrant and Margaret Tempest. These were published in the 1930s and were reprinted many times.

Meissner & Buch   **fl. c.1900-1914**
Publisher, 121 Bunhill Row, London, E.C. This Leipzig firm published Christmas cards from 1884 which they marketed through an agent in Fleet Street. Their colour printing was of a very high quality. Output was limited mainly to:
(i)   Greetings cards.
(ii) Ladies posed as fashion models.
(iii) Children.
(iv) Views.
   The cards were often highly decorated with frames and embossed margins.

Meissonier, Jean Louis Ernest   **1815-1891**
French painter whose military pictures were reproduced on postcards by Eyre & Spottiswoode.

"Meldon Series"
A series of R.P. views by "A.M.H." of South Shields, Durham. Meldon is a village in Northumberland.

"Mellin's Food"
Poster-type advertisement card for baby food.

Mellor, Jack   **1900-1971**
Photographer/publisher, 26 Aked's Rd., Halifax, Yorkshire. He also lived at 9 Brunswick St. at some time in his career. A journalist who issued fairground postcards in a "Sepia Series" and a "Mel-lo-tone Series". He included earlier photographs in these series and most of them give the name of the show-man.
   Ref: White, S., 'Jack Mellor', P.P.A., 1983.

"Melox Marvels"
Poster-type advertisements for dog food.

Memorials
These were usually erected to commemorate an outstanding event, the life of a prominent citizen, or a highly respected group such as a lifeboat crew, either shortly after death but often many years later. They may take the form of a statue carved as a likeness or a memorial stone. Examples are often seen on postcard views, e.g. The Cook Memorial at Whitby, the Lifeboat Memorial at Margate, and, in London, the Albert Memorial, the Cenotaph, the Monument, the Nelson Column, and the Queen Victoria Memorial.
   See: Epitaphs; Statues; War Memorials.

Menpes, Mortimer   **1860-1938**
Australian artist who studied under James Whistler. Exh. R.A. 42. He was an artist-war correspondent in South Africa during the Boer War where he sketched the leading political and military personalities. Worked as an illustrator for A. & C. Black and many of his book illustrations were used as postcards, e.g. "World's Children", for Wrench. His work also appears in Tuck's "Wide Wide World" Series, e.g. "Fair Japan" and "Native Life in India".

Meras, Rene
Glamour artist whose work was published by Alphalsa.

Mercer, Joyce   **1896-1965**
Designer of children's art deco cards for Faulkner in the 1920s.
   Ref: Cope, p. 15, ill. p. 47.

Memorials. *"Nelson Monument, Trafalgar Square, London"*. Designed by Sir Gilbert Scott and erected in 1872. Gottschalk, Dreyfus & Davis.

Memorials. *"The Albert Memorial, London"*. Publisher unknown. P.U. 1906.

Memorials. *"Queen Victoria Memorial, London"*. Rotary Photographic Series.

Memorials. *"The Monument, London, Commemorating the Great Fire of London"*. Gottschalk, Dreyfus & Davis.

Meredith, Jack
Designer of a set of comic cards titled "Spoons" for W. Ritchie & Sons.

Meredith, William   fl. 1882-1926
Painted a set on "Barmouth" for Tuck.

Mersey Railway
A series of at least nine cards by Wrench depict the stations and electric trains.

Merté, O.
German animal painter who contributed studies of horses' heads for a Tuck "Oilette" set. During W.W.I. he designed propaganda cards showing German troops and zeppelins attacking targets in Britain.

Meschini, G.   fl. c.1914-1926
Art deco artist who designed cards in Italy.

Messages
Most collectors of postcards do so for the picture, the postmark or the postage stamp. However, the messages have a fascination all their own, reflecting as they do the attitudes, customs, habits, pleasures and tribulations of their period. The following extracts give some of the flavour of the times:
Hackney Dec. 1902
> This is the first time I have written on one of these cards which invite you to write on the side which used to be reserved for the address, though I believe they have been out for a long time.

Siracusa, Italy, 22 April, 1903
> After a very rough passage of 8½ hours in the steamer *Peloro* we arrived here at 6.30 p.m. yesterday. King Edward had preceded us as we found his yacht in the harbour with 4 cruisers. He left this morning for Naples.

Bayswater, London, 3 December, 1904
> Nearly buried in fog all this week.

Reigate, February 1905
> Sending card for collection. Hope you will like it. Any card will be acceptable of Britain or any place. Album will hold 160 more.

Messages. *Italian card from Siracusa. The message on this U.B. card refers to King Edward and "his yacht in the harbour with 4 cruisers". P.U. 1903.*

Reigate, 22 January, 1906
> Liberal returned. Majority 219.

New Milton, 23 January, 1906
> Hobart. 48 majority. "Hurrah".

New Milton, 12 April, 1906. 12.45 p.m.
> Will you please bring my green tie? It is in the drawer in J's room. Arrived about 8 p.m. fairly dusted by motors. Will meet train this evening. Hope this will be in time. M.
> [It was delivered in Hordle, some three miles distant, the same day.]

Gifford, 1906
> Dear Willie,
> This is the school, and the village green goes all along the street and past our window. There was a fair there last week and a lot of dear little donkeys just going about. The merry-go-round was all horses and Cinderella carriages and I wished you had been there to have a round with me. I wonder how your silkworms like to be without you. Yours, Anna.

London, 1906
> The last 2d gone! Borrowed ½d for stamp. Governor's got a swollen head. I'm tired. Ink's bad. Fire's gone out. I feel very worried about a certain little girl, and altogether am feeling very rotten. Have just lost the post. Have stuck my pen in my hand and there's no soap to wash with.

Leicester, 1907
> I have just about settled down. I saw Zena Dare down at Leicester about six weeks ago with Seymour Hicks in two or three little plays. I think she is ripping. Kind regards to Grace. Tell her I have had my photo taken but don't like it so am having another.

Hammersmith, 1907. 8.45 a.m.
> If it would not be troubling you too much could you or little 'Cissey' bring round the Trumpet and rubber tube tonight, or tomorrow?

Sandown, Isle of Wight, August 1919
> I hope you found the tennis net and posts, Molly put them in the coach house.

Broadstairs, St. Mary's Home, June 1921
> I have sent a photo of the home from an aeroplane as I thought you would like to see it. Thank you very much for your shilling. It came in very handy.

Newbury, 5 December, 1921. 8 p.m.
> Just a line hoping to find you all well. I quite thought I should have had a line from you by now. I hope Jim is still in work, it's dreadful the unemployment.

St. Mary's Scilly, August 1928
> Started 9.30 a.m. Got here 1.15 p.m. Alf seasick twice — was very rocky. Only about a dozen people that wasn't sick. Catching the boat back 4.15 p.m.

Messer, C.
Photographer/publisher, 20 Castle St., Salisbury, Wiltshire.

Methodist Publishing House
Publisher of cards relating to Methodism, including chapels, events and portraits of well-known methodists.

Metlicovitz, L.
Art nouveau artist who designed a set of cards to illustrate Puccini's opera, *Tosca*.

Meunier, Henri George Jean Isodore   1873-1922
Belgian art nouveau artist who contributed to a number of Paris journals, painting ladies in the latest fashions. His postcards are highly prized.

Micawber, Mr. *By Kyd. Tuck's "Dickens" Postcard Series.*
U.B.

MR. MICAWBER.
FROM THE DRAWING BY F. BARNARD.
"His clothes were shabby, but he had an imposing shirt-
collar on. He carried a jaunty sort of stick, with a large pair
of rusty tassels to it, and a quizzing-glass hung outside his
coat."—DAVID COPPERFIELD.

Cassell's Art Postcards.

Macawber, Mr. *By F. Barnard. Cassell's Art Postcard.*

Meunier, Suzanne
Figure artist who is described as having painted "pretty
nudes", often with cupids.

Mex Motor Spirit
Advertising cards by the Bowring Petroleum Co.

Mezzotint Co. pre-1902
Publisher, York Hill Rd., London, N., and Brighton, Sussex.
U.B. views of Brighton and Worthing.

Micawber, Mr.
Cards from different publishers are known of the popular
Dickens' character Mr. Macawber, from *David Copperfield*.
They illustrate the artists' different interpretations.

Mickey Mouse
Cartoon character invented by Walt Disney. Made his début in
the cartoon film *Steamboat Willie* in 1928.

Micklewright, G.P.
Artist who painted locomotives for the Ruskin Studio Art
Press.

Middlesex & Buckingham Advertiser
Publisher, Uxbridge, Middlesex. Local black and white views.

Midland Picture Postcard Co. 1909
Publisher, 77 Finsbury Pavement, London, E.C. Greetings
cards and comic cards designed by Comicus. The name was
later changed to the Midland Pictorial Postcard Co.

Midland Railway Co.
Cards by the Locomotive Publishing Co. with views of Midland express trains and locomotives. Ill. D. & M. 133.

Micawber, Mr. *By A.C. Stewart & Woolf. Printed in Bavaria.*
U.B.

Midwinter & Co. Ltd.
Publisher of photographic cards.

Miles & Co.
Publisher, 68-70 Wardour St., London, W. Specialist in cards advertising theatrical performances.

Miles, Violet   **b. 1884**
Designer of embossed cards featuring children, signed V.S.M. It has been suggested that her cards, which were printed in Germany, had hidden messages within the pictures included for her Serbian tutor, Arthur Thiele, who wished to communicate with compatriots without arousing the suspicion of Kaiser Wilhelm's security police.

Milford, Humphrey   **1917**
Book publisher, London. This firm used facsims. of paintings by well-known women artists including:
(i)   Barbara Briggs, "Our Dogs".
(ii)   Eileen Hood, horse studies.
(iii) Ruth Sandys, "Old Street Cries".
(iv) Millicent Sowerby, "Fairies' Friends", "Flower Children", "Happy as Kings".
(v)   Dorothy Wheeler, "Snow Children".

Military Leaders
Portraits of W.W.I. army leaders were produced by several firms including Beagles & Co., Gottschalk, Dreyfus & Davis, and Rotary. They included Marshal Foch, Sir John French, Sir Douglas Haig, General Joffre, Earl Kitchener, Field Marshal Methuen, General Pershing, Earl Roberts.

Military Subjects
Cards in this area cover a wide field including battles, life in the army, mascots, regimental uniforms, army history, etc. The main publishers were:
(i)   Blum & Degen, early U.B. cards by F.O. Beirne.
(ii)   Excelsior Fine Art Publishing Co.
(iii) G. Falkner & Sons, cards by John McNeill.
(iv) Gale & Polden, specialised in cards relating to the British Army.
(v)   F. Hartmann, "British Battles".
(vi) Photochrom, "On Active Service" Series.
(vii) Ritchie & Co., "Our Highland Regiments".
(viii) Salmon, military cards including many by C.T. Howard.
(iv) W.W. Sharpe, "Our Friends and Allies".
(x)   Tuck, many military subjects including facsims. of Harry Payne's work.
(xi) Valentine, "The King's Army", etc.
    See: Flags; Regimental Badges.
    Ref: Carman, W.Y., *Uniforms of the British Army,* 1982.

"Milkmaid Milk"
Advertising cards with a "Too Good for Cats" slogan.

Millar, Gertie   **1879-1952**
Actress. First stage performance in Manchester 1892. Made her name in pantomime and musical comedy, and was one of the best known of the Gaiety Girls. Later became the Countess of Dudley. P.P.s by Aristophot, Beagles, Philco, and Rotary.

Millar & Lang (Ltd.)   **1903 (Ltd. 1905)**
"Art Publishers" and printers, Glasgow, and 49 Queen Victoria St., London. Trademark "National Series" within a shield surmounted by a lion. This firm had a very large output which continued into the 1940s. The range included:
(i)   High quality coloured views.

Military Leaders. *"Marshal Foch, Sir D. Haig, General Pershing". P.P.s by Beagles & Co.*

(ii)   Greetings cards.
(iii) Aviation subjects.
(iv) Coloured animal and bird photographs, some unfortunately untitled.
(v)   Many sets of comic cards, e.g. "Commercial Traveller" and a "Seasick Series".
(vi) W.W.I. caricatures of the Kaiser.
(vii) Heraldic cards.
(viii) Paintings reproduced in facsims. by the "New Color-Crayon Process".
(ix) Scottish subjects including cards for the Scottish Exhibitions of 1908 and 1911.
(x)   P.P.s, mainly of actresses.
(xi) Novelty cards.
(xii) Ocean liners.
(xiii) Political subjects.
(xiv) Staged romantic scenes.
(xv) Franco-British Exhibition, 1908 (photo by Wakefield of Ealing).

Millard, Evelyn   **1869-1941**
Actress-manageress. First stage appearance at the Haymarket Theatre, London, in 1891. P.P.s by Beagles, Millar & Lang, and Rotophot.

Miller, Hilda T.   **1876-1939**
Painter. Exh. R.A. 1. Designed cards with children and fairies for Faulkner, e.g. "Fairy Visions", and advertising cards for Liberty & Co.
    Ref: Cope, pp. 17 and 48.

Mills, Harry (Brusher). *"Brusher Mills, New Forest, Snake Catcher". His hut. F.G.O. Stuart.*

Miller, Phil   **fl. c.1925-1939**
Cartoonist who designed comic cards for Eisner & Son and D. Constance.

Miller, William   **1796-1882**
Black and white artist whose sketches of Edinburgh were used by George Stewart & Co.

Millière, Maurice   **b. 1871**
French painter and illustrator who contributed to *La Vie Parisienne* and exhibited at the Salon des Humoristes. His postcards were mainly published during W.W.I.

Mills
Publisher, Portsmouth. Shipping views.

Mills, Arthur Wallis   **1878-1940**
Designer of a "Prehistoric Sports" Series for William Collins. He also worked for William Lyon.

Mills, Harry (Brusher)   **1838-1905**
Born at Lyndhurst in the New Forest, he became a snake catcher at an early age and lived for over 20 years in a cone-shaped hut built of branches and turf. He was greatly respected, renowned for his honesty, though people found him hard to understand for he had a cleft palate. When bitten by a snake he treated himself, cutting out the affected part with his pocket knife and applying his own ointment. Many of the snakes were sent to the zoological departments of universities.

The nickname Brusher Mills was given to him because he regularly brushed the cricket pitch at Balmer Lawn, Brockenhurst, with a besom. One day in 1905 he went to the Railway Inn at Brockenhurst for some bread and pickles and a pint. Later the landlord found him lying in an outhouse where he had died of heart failure. Postcards by F.G.O. Stuart.

Mills, John W.
Publisher, The Arcade, Portsmouth. Naval ships.

Mills, R.H.
Photographer/publisher, Peabody Road, Farnborough, Hampshire. R.P.s of local events.

Mills, Harry (Brusher). *F.G.O. Stuart.*

Milner, E.
Publisher, Finchley, London. R.P.s of W.W.I. preparations, ill. Holt 492, and postcards of the Building Exhibition, Olympia, 1920.

Milton, Alf
Designer of comic cards for an unknown publisher, e.g. "Our Navy" set.

"Milton Post Card"
   See: Woolstone Bros.

Mine Disasters
Coal mining was a particularly dangerous occupation before W.W.I. when safety precautions were not so strictly observed as they are today. When a disaster occurred, photographs were often taken locally, but one particular photographer, Warner Gothard (q.v.), was usually on the scene in record time. "In Memoriam" cards were often available soon after the event.

   The following mine disasters have been recorded on R.P.s:
   15 November, 1907, Barrow Colliery, Barnsley, Gothard.
   23 November, 1907, Silkstone Colliery, Hoyland, Yorkshire, Gothard.
   20 February, 1908, Glebe Colliery, Washington, Co. Durham, Gothard.
   4 March, 1908, Hamstead Colliery, Great Barr, Birmingham, Gothard.
   9 April, 1908, Midsomer Norton, Somerset, Gothard.
   18 August, 1908, Maybole Colliery, Abram, Wigan, Gothard.
   16 February, 1909, West Stanley Colliery, Durham, Gothard.
continued

"Please, Lord, Excuse Me a Minute While I Kick Fido". Inter-Art Comique Series". P.U. 1919.

"I've Got the Distemper!" by A.E. Kennedy. C.W. Faulkner. P.U. 1921.

"There's Nothing Like Meeting a Few Old Friends" by George Willis. Valentine's "Chummy" Series. P.U. 1936.

1910, Whitehaven Colliery, Cumberland.
October, 1913, Senghenydd Colliery, nr. Caerphilly, S. Wales, W. Benton.
30 May, 1914, Wharncliffe Silkstone Colliery, Barnsley, Gothard.

The toll of life in some of these disasters was high. At West Stanley Colliery 168 miners lost their lives and there were only 30 survivors.

See: Explosions.

"Miniature Post Cards"

See: Rotary Photographic Co.

Minns, Fanny M.   fl. c.1881-1905

Landscape watercolour artist who lived at Newport, I.O.W. She painted views of Dorset and the Isle of Wight for J.W. Ruddock's "Artist Series" and views of "Old Edinburgh" for George Stewart.

Minter, May Miles

American actress. R.P.s by Rotary and Tuck.

Miracle, The

A mime play produced by Max Reinhardt for C.B. Cochran at Olympia in 1911 and revived at the Lyceum in 1932. Scenes from the Olympia production were published in a postcard set by Gale & Polden.

Misch & Co. (Misch & Stock until 1905)   c.1903

Publisher, Cripplegate St., Golden Lane, London, E.C. This firm was producing Christmas cards in the 1890s and turned to postcards soon after the turn of the century. The trademark was three bells carrying the initials "M & S" or "M & Co." Many series were produced, most of them designed in England and printed in Saxony. Many generic names were given, e.g. "Messograph", "Aerotint", "Camera Graphs". The range included:

(i) Coloured views.
(ii) Sepia views.
(iii) Greetings cards including a "Birthday Wishes" Series and a "Christmas Post Card Series".
(iv) "Nature's Miniatures", views in an early series, nos. 170-230.
(v) "Reutlinger Series" of stage personalities.
(vi) Glamour series, e.g. "Famous Beauties", "Stage Beauties" and "Summer Beauty".
(vii) Hand-painted postcards, e.g. "Violet Series" and "Pansy Series".
(viii) Gallery reproductions, e.g. "The Great Masters"; "Millet's Masterpieces", works by Jean François Millet; "Imperial Frescoes"; "World Galleries".
(ix) "The Holy Scripture", several series of 12 similar to the Gallery reproductions.
(x) Classic Rome, coloured vignettes.
(xi) Comic series, e.g. "Agony Column", ill. D. & M. 104-5; "Addled Ads"; "Comic Cricket"; "Dogs and Their Owners"; "At our Concert"; "Railway Travellers".

continued

Minns, Fanny M. *"The Keep, Corfe Castle"*. Facsim. by *J.W. Ruddock. "Artist Series"*.

The Miracle, Olympia.—The Abbess, Francisca Dühne.

Miracle, The. *"The Miracle, Olympia — The Abbess, Francisca Dühne."* Gale & Polden.

173

(xii) Railway cards, e.g. "Noted Trains" Series, H. Fleury.
(xiii) "The Fire Brigade", Fred S. Howard.
(xiv) Sporting series, e.g. "With the Hounds", ill. D. & M.
       88.
     See: Colour Plates 16 and 22.

Missionary Societies
Postcards were published by missionary societies to promote their work abroad. These include:
(i)   Baptist Missionary Society; Medical Auxiliary in China (two series).
(ii) Church Missionary Society.
(iii) London Missionary Society (q.v.).
(iv) Scripture Gift Mission.
(v)   South American Missionary Society.
(vi) Universities Mission to Central Africa.

Mitchell & Butler
Advertiser of beer, Birmingham area. Cards show a view of Camp Hill Brewery.

Mitchell & Watkins   1904
Publisher, 63 St. Paul's Churchyard, London. Tradename "Canon Series". Output consisted mainly of views of London. A number of comic cards were also produced.

Mitchell, W. Fred.
Artist who painted a card of *The Titanic* for Salmon.

M.J.R.B.
M.J. Ridley, Bournemouth (q.v.).

M. & L. or M. & L. G.
Millar & Lang (q.v.).

Models
The outstanding example is the Queen's Dolls' House (q.v.) but there are cards of other models including "Heath Robinson's Ideal Home", shown at the Ideal Home Exhibition of 1934, and cards showing models of aeroplanes, railways and ships published by museums.

Moden, Harry Allan
Cartoonist and owner of the Cambridge Picture Post Card Co. (q.v.).

Modena, C., & Co.   fl. c.1902-1912
Publisher/stationer, 46-8 Sun St., London, E.C. Tradename "Ducal Series". The output consisted almost entirely of comic cards concerning the armed services, e.g. "Illustrated Army Orders".

Moet & Chandon
Advertising card for champagne by Alphonse Mucha which carried Christmas and New Year greetings.

Molassine Meal
Animal food advertisements.

Molle, Dobson & Co. Ltd.   1914
Publisher, London and Edinburgh. "St. Clair War Series".

Molyneux & Co.   pre-1906
Publisher, London. "Molyneux Series" of R.P. views of London.

Monbard, Georges   1841-1905
French artist who became a naturalised Englishman in the 1880s. He worked for *The Illustrated London News* and some of his Boer War pictures were used by the Picture Postcard Company.

HOME TO THE FOLD.
A Scene in Palestine.

Missionary Societies. *"Home to the Fold"*. Scripture Gift Mission.

Monestier, C.
Italian artist who designed glamour cards towards the end of W.W.I.

Montague, Alfred, R.B.A.   fl. 1880-1888
Coastal and landscape painter.

Montague, R.
Seascape artist who painted sets titled "Sea and Sky" and "The Busy Ocean" for Tuck.

Montedoro, M.
Italian art deco artist who designed glamour cards.

Monument
This fluted Doric column, 202ft. high, commemorating the Great Fire of London, was designed by Christopher Wren and erected in 1671-7. Heraldic card by G.D. & D.L.
     See: Memorials.

Moody, Fannie   fl.1880-1940
Animal painter. Exh. R.A. 38. Her work was reproduced in Boots Famous Picture Series and she painted dogs for the Alpha Publishing Co.

Monestier C. *Glamour pin-up.*

Moonlight Views. *"London. — The Houses of Parliament from the River". R. Tuck & Sons. "Raphotype". U.B.*

Moonlight Views. *"Clifton Bridge from Leigh Bank" by J. Stanley Thornton. Facsim. by Burgess & Co. "Bee" Series.*

Moonlight Views
Many publishers issued moonlight views, including Burgess, Davidson, Huardel, Knight Bros., Tuck, Valentine and Woolstone Bros.

Moore, A. Winter   **fl. c.1908-1916**
Nottingham artist, who painted views for a Tuck "Oilette" set on "Picturesque Whitby".

Moore, Carrie   **1883-1956**
Actress. P.P. by Pictorial Postcard Co.

Moore, E.   **pre-1908**
Publisher, 2 Stuart St., Pontlottyn, Glamorgan. Coloured local views in grey oval frames.

Moore, Frank   **fl. 1910-1939**
Painter of railway subjects. Exhibited mainly at the Royal Cambrian Academy.

Moore, Mary (Lady Wyndham)   **1862-1931**
Actress-manageress. P.P. by Beagles.

Moore & Wingham   **c.1919**
Publisher, 39 East St., Chichester, Sussex.

Moorehouse, E.T.
Publisher, 102a King St., Egremont, Cheshire.

Moreland, Arthur   **fl. c.1895-1906**
Cartoonist of *The Morning Leader*. Designer of comic cards with historical or political overtones, e.g. "John Bull" and "Fiscal Speeches" Series for Faulkner, "Humours of History" for Eyre & Spottiswoode.

Morgan & Sons
Photographer/publisher, Sheffield, Yorkshire.

Morgan, F.E.
Designer of cards for George Pulman & Sons "Quaint" Series, and of comic cards for Salmon.

Morgan, Frederick   **1856-1927**
Artist whose work was included in Hildesheimer's "Gems of Art" Series. Exh. R.A. 50. Signed his work "Fred Morgan".

Morgan, R.T., & Co.
Publisher of a woven silk postcard of the Crystal Palace in black and white, sold in the Arcade of the Crystal Palace in

1903. It was woven by Thomas Stevens (q.v.) but does not bear his name.

Morgan, William Edward
Poster artist whose work was reproduced on postcards by David Allen & Sons.

Morison Bros. c.1900
Publisher, Buchanan St., Glasgow. Output mainly local views, some R.P.s, others based on watercolour drawings. In addition, a few comic cards by J.A. Duncan (Hamish).

Morland Studios
Publisher, Kingston upon Thames, Surrey. "Morland Series" of local sepia views.

Morrell & Sons pre-1905
Publisher, 17 Alexandra Rd., Morecambe, Lancashire. "Crown Series" of coloured local views.

Morrell, Olive
Actress who played opposite George Grossmith Jr. in *The Spring Chicken* in 1905. P.P.s by Philco, Pictorial Postcard Co., and Tuck's "Bookmarker" Series II and IV.

Morris & Co. pre-1911
Publisher, Liverpool. Local and Isle of Man framed views and shipping.

Morris, M.
Landscape and animal painter. The signature M. Morris was used by several artists of the pre-W.W.I. period. It appears on A.G. Taylor and Tuck cards.

Morris & Yeomans pre-1917
Needle manufacturers, Astwood Bank, Redditch, Worcestershire. Advertisers of "Kaurkuk" crochet hooks which were used for Berlin woolwork.

Morrow, Albert 1863-1927
Watercolour artist. Exh. R.A. 9. Designed a card to advertise Edgar Wallace's *Four Just Men* published in 1905. He was a poster artist and a number of his theatre posters were reproduced as postcards by David Allen.

Morse
Photographer, Putney, London. R.P.s of the Oxford and Cambridge Boat Race.

Mortan, Fred
Poster artist whose work was included in Tuck's "Celebrated Posters" Series.

Mortimer, Betty Florence fl. c.1904-1914
Designer of an anti-suffragette card for Worcester & Co. of Bristol.

Moser, Koloman 1868-1918
Art nouveau artist born in Vienna. He helped to found the Wiener Werkstätte (Vienna Workshops) with Josef Hoffman in 1903. He painted for postcard reproduction including a card to mark the Jubilee of Emperor Franz Joseph in 1908. His work is highly prized.

Moss, Henry, & Co. 1902
Publisher, 8 Cheapside, London, E.C. This firm continued the business of Pascalis, Moss & Co., at a new address. Cards were still imported from Europe, mainly the art nouveau work of Mucha and the landscapes of Cassiers. Output included:

(i) Coloured views.
(ii) "Expresses of the World", 24 U.B. watercolour facsims., unsigned.
(iii) "The Courtship and Marriage of Mr. Thomas".
(iv) "Hobbies, Postcard Collecting".
(v) "Famous Posters".
(vi) "Musical Terms Up-to-date".
(vii) Later sets with serial nos. over 4,000 included:
Language of Flowers, 4135. Roumanian National
Months of the Year, 4154. Types, 4294.
Billiard Players, 4181. Soap Bubbles, 4351.
Skating Girls, 4216. Playwrights, 4431.
Louis Wain Series, 4249. Motors and Hunting, 4442.
Many novelty cards were also produced by this firm.

Moss, W. Dennis pre-1906
Photographer/publisher, Cirencester. A "Cecily Series" of local black and white and sepia views.

Mostyn, Dorothy fl. c.1904-1925
Landscape painter who designed glamour series for Tuck "Oilette" Connoisseur Series, e.g. "The Six of Us", "My Mascot", and "My Heart".

Mostyn, Marjorie fl. c.1904-1921
Portrait and flower painter who designed glamour cards for Tuck, e.g. "Girls of Today", "Jewel Girls", "Fair of Feature", "Fair Daughters of Eve" and "A Dream of Fair Women".

Mothers' Union
Publisher, Westminster, London. Cards were published for special occasions, e.g. the Jubilee Celebrations at Winchester Cathedral, a card showing the flying buttresses built in 1912, two of which were given by the Mothers' Union members in memory of Bishop Sumner.

Motor Accidents
Cards of motor accidents are uncommon; the wreckage was often cleared from the road before the arrival of a photographer. Several cards were published of a Vanguard motor omnibus accident at Handcross in Sussex in July 1906, ill. Hill p. 37.

Motor Buses
Motor buses began to replace horse-drawn buses in London before W.W.I. Some cards are coloured but there are also many R.P.s. They were mostly taken in such places as Constitution Hill, Holborn, Hyde Park Corner, Ludgate Hill, Oxford Street, Regent Street, and the Royal Exchange.

Motor Cars
Motor cars of the pre-1939 period are now classed as veteran cars and are either museum pieces or have been restored and tended with care by collectors. Cards depict veteran cars, usually in street scenes, but sometimes specially photographed with their owners, drivers or mechanics. R.P.s are desirable and the use of a magnifying glass will often reveal significant detail. If the number plate can be deciphered it is possible to date the car by referring to the original registration authority since records have almost invariably been retained.
See: Colour Plate 19.
Refs: Georgiano, G.N., *A Source Book of Vintage and Post-Vintage Cars*, 1974; Munro, C., *A Source Book of Motor-Cars*, 1970; Sedgwick, M., *Early Cars*, 1962, 1972 ed.

Motor Cars. *A Rover 12 h.p. which was introduced in 1911 and was Rover's sole production in the period just before W.W.I. R.P. P.U. 1913.*

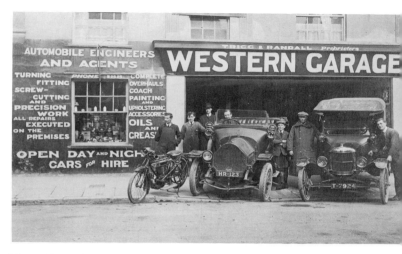

Motor Cars. *A garage in Andover with a Model T Ford.*

Motor Cars. *Left, an early Lanchester in which the chauffeur sits beside the engine; right, Humber, c.1910.*

Motor Cars. *A motoring cartoon. "Our First Halt" by Pirkis. S. Hildesheimer.*

Motor Cycles

These were not common until after W.W.I. Cards of events, e.g. The Isle of Man T.T. Races, are to be found.

Ref: Hough, H., and Setright, C.T.K., *A History of the World's Motor Cycles,* 1977.

Motor Racing

Motor racing cards often include both the car and a portrait of the driver, e.g. Sir Henry Segrave with Golden Arrow. There is a card showing Dorothy Levitt in her Napier racing car at Blackpool, c.1905.

Mount Everest Expedition

Official cards were published on the occasion of the 1924 Mount Everest climb.

Mounter, H.G.   pre-1905

Publisher, 64 Alfred St., Burnham, Somerset. Tinted local R.P.s taken by H.M. Cooper of Burnham. Red captions.

Mouton, George L.   fl. 1893-1920

Painter who specialised in portraits of children.

M. & S.

Initials used by Misch & Stock (q.v.), and possibly Morgan & Sons of Sheffield (q.v.).

M.S.O.

McCaw, Stevenson & Orr (q.v.).

Mucha, Alphonse   1860-1933

Czech art nouveau painter and poster designer who worked in Paris from 1887. Postcard reproductions of his posters were published by Champenois before 1900, ill. D. & M. 55.

By 1909 Mucha had returned to Prague. His work is very highly valued. Importers included P.G. Huardel, Henry Moss, H.J. Smith, and F.C. Southwood.

Ref: Mucha, J. Alphonse, *Mucha, His Life and Art,* 1966.

I DON'T SPECT I'LL GET MUCH
POCKET MONEY NOW.

Murnaghan, Kathleen Irene. *Comic card. Millar & Lang's "National Series". P.U. 1926.*

Mudge, E.W.
Photographer/publisher, The Studio, Fawley, Hampshire. Local R.P. views of an area bounded by the Beaulieu River and Southampton Water.

Muller, Augustus
German artist who painted dogs, particularly dachshunds, for Hildesheimer.

Multi-message Cards
Valentine published postcards in which half of the usual picture side was printed with possible messages, e.g. "I spend the time ... Golfing, Bathing, At Tennis, Boating". All the sender had to do was to put a cross against items which were applicable. Ill. Monahan 151.

Multi-view Cards
Cards in which several views have been arranged to form a pattern, usually photographic views of a particular town or district.

Munk, M.
Publisher and printer, Vienna, who exported to Britain and published cards by British artists, which were printed in Vienna for Landeker & Brown and for Henry Moss who almost certainly acted as Munk's agent. Cards invariably bear the imprint "M.M. Vienna" or "M. Munk". It is interesting to note that those painted in the Dutch style by Ivy Millicent James (q.v.) of children in a lighted street bear her initials "IMJ" but no captions. These may have been omitted so that the cards might be sold in several different countries without special printings.

Multi-view Cards. *"Plymouth". F. Hartmann. P.U. 1905.*

Multi-view Cards. *"Sandown, I.W." Salmon. P.U. 1919.*

Munro, H.
Publisher, Birmingham. Local R.P. views.

Murder
A card by Hooper of Swindon, P.U. 1910, shows the cottage of Job Franklin who was murdered by his brother at Lyneham.

Murnaghan, Kathleen Irene   **fl. 1920s**
Painter who contributed pictures of children to Millar & Lang's "National Series".

Murray, Andrew   **fl. 1930s**
Poster artist whose work was reproduced on postcards by David Allen.

Murray, James, & Sons
Advertisers of "Jasmine Self-Raising Flour". Card designed by Percy Carr.

Museums. *"The National* [sic] *History Museum, London".*
Hartmann. P.U. 1904.

THE COWPER AND NEWTON MUSEUM, OLNEY. Cowper's Home from 1767-1786.

Museums. *"The Cowper and Newton Museum, Olney,*
Cowper's House from 1767-1786." W.I. Knight, Olney.

Murray, Tom E.
Musical comedy actor. P.P. by J. Baker & Son.

Museums
Many of our museums were built shortly before the postcard
age. Views of the building were sold in the museums, together
with cards of some of the exhibits. The Natural History
Museum in London was opened in 1881 and Aston Webb's
extension to the Victoria and Albert Museum in 1909.
Museums in smaller towns were often established in older
buildings, sometimes in places with particular associations.
The museum at Olney, Buckinghamshire, for example, was the
home of William Cowper from 1767 to 1786; Dove Cottage
Museum at Grasmere was the home of Wordsworth from 1799
to 1808.
   Ref: *Museums and Art Galleries in Great Britain and
Ireland,* published annually.

MISCHA ELMAN.

Copyright *London Stereoscopic Co.* No 204.

Musicians. *"Mischa Elman". Born 1891, world famous at the
age of 13. London Stereoscopic Co. P.U. 1907.*

Musical Post Card Syndicate   1903
Publisher of cards with greetings and messages set to music.

Musicians
There are P.P.s of many musicians, some in a Valentine
Series, "Famous Composers". The following have been
noted:
   Backhaus, Wilhelm: Rotary.
   Beethoven, Ludwig van: Valentine.
   Cherubini, Maria Luigi: Rotary.
   Chopin, Frederick: Rotary.
   Elgar, Edward: Breitkoff & Hartel.
   Elman, Mischa: London Stereoscope.
   German, Edward: Rotary.
   Handel, George F.: Rotary; Valentine.
   Hoffman, Joseph: Rotary.
   Kubelik, Jan: Tuck.
   Mendelssohn, Felix: Valentine.
   Meyerbeer, Giacomo: Rotary.
   Mozart, Wolfgang Amadeus: Valentine.
   Paderewski, Ignacy: B.K.W.I.; Rotary.
   Ronald, Landon: Breitkoff & Hartel.
   Schubert, Franz: Rotary, Valentine.
   Strauss, Richard: Breitkoff & Härtel.
A series of cards by Blum & Degen shows portraits of
musicians side by side with views of their homes.
   Refs: Isaacs, A.T., and Martin E., (eds.), *Dictionary of
Music,* 1982; Scholes, P., *The Concise Oxford Dictionary of
Music,* 1952.

"Nabob Sauce"
Advertising cards.

Nadin, C.H.   **pre-1907**
Publisher, West Bars, Chesterfield, Derbyshire. Christchurch Pictorial. Local R.P. views and events.

Naillod, Charles, S.   **fl.c.1906-1920**
Painter of glamorous ladies.

Nam, Jacques Lehmann   **b.1881**
Animal painter and illustrator.

Name Cards
Rotary designed Christian name cards made up from photographs of attractive ladies.

Nanni, Giovanni   **1888-1969**
Italian artist who painted fashion models and sporting girls, sometimes cuddling dogs, against a plain background. Cards were printed in Milan during W.W.I.

Nannies
Most well-to-do parents employed a nanny to look after their children but in the nature of things they were self-effacing, though an occasional private postcard does turn up. They are seen in the background in a Hill ill. p. 88.

Nansen, Fridtjof   **1861-1930**
Norwegian explorer and scientist. Cards were published depicting his Arctic journeys.

Nap
Pseudonym of an unidentified artist who designed comic cards for Robert Peel of Oxford.

Napier, D., & Son Ltd.   **pre-1920**
Advertiser, 14 New Burlington St., London, W.1. Card to advertise the Napier six-cylinder motor carriage. Designed by Walter Hayward Young and signed with his name.

Nash, Adrienne A.   **fl.c.1914-1939**
Watercolour figure painter of scenes with children. Exh. R.A. 5. Early work during W.W.I. by Inter-Art carried both English and French captions. Later work was used by James Henderson, e.g. "Children's Birth Days", seven cards for the days of the week.

    Illustration overleaf.

Nash, J.T.
Publisher, Northbrook St., Newbury, Berkshire. Local views.

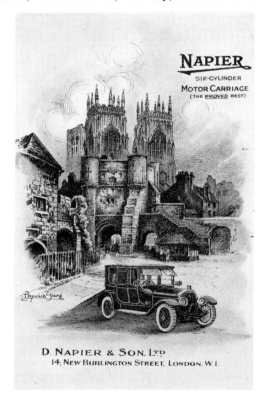

Name Cards. *Rotary Photographic Series.*

Napier, D., & Son Ltd. *Advertisement card signed by Walter Hayward Young, who usually used the pseudonym Jotter. P.U. 1920.*

*"I've Given Up
Smokin', Donald..."
by Archie Cameron.
Hutson Bros. P.U.
1917.*

*"How to Keep Fit..."
by Harold
C. Earnshaw.
J. Henderson.*

*"Leap Year. Why
Won't the Girls
Propose?" by Arthur
Gill. R. Tuck & Sons.
"Oilette".*

*"A Jolly Little Tart and
a Large Welcome
Awaits Your Return"
by Reg Maurice. Regent
Publishing Co. P.U.
1918.*

Nash, T.J. pre-1909
Publisher, High St., Battle, Sussex. Black and white local views.

National Federation of Discharged and Demobilised Sailors and Soldiers
Publisher of wartime scenes in France during W.W.I.

National Free Church Council
Publisher of portraits, e.g. Gypsy Smith.

National Institute for the Blind
Publisher, Gt. Portland St., London, W. Coloured postcards of soldiers blinded in battle in W.W.I. were issued with an appeal for funds for the St. Dunstan's Training Centre in Regent's Park.
See: Richard Caton Woodville.

National Insurance
There was considerable opposition to Lloyd George's National Insurance Act, which was eventually passed in 1911, and this was reflected in postcard satire expressed in such captions as "The stamp that takes a bit of licking".

"National Series"
Tradename used by Millar & Lang (q.v.).

National Union of Conservative and Constitutional Associations
Publisher, St. Stephen's Chambers, Westminster, London, S.W. Political cards printed by David Allen. These showed pictures of poverty overprinted with the words 'Free Trade'' suggesting that preferential tariffs would raise the standard of living.

National War Bonds
In 1917 the Prime Minister, the Rt. Hon. David Lloyd George, launched a National War Bonds campaign. Publicity followed and an army tank was placed in Trafalgar Square.

National Women's Social and Political Union
Publishers, 4 Clement's Inn, Strand, London, W.C. "Votes for Women" propaganda cards. Ill. Holt 531.

Natural Features
Some cards which show the natural features of particular types of country — chalk hills of the south, limestone country of the Pennines, and the elevated tracts of older rocks in Wales, the Lake District and Scotland — have a special interest for geographers and geologists. Coastal scenes show the rocks exposed in cliffs and islands.
See: Caves.

GIVE ME A SOLDIER, NOW!

Nash, Adrienne A. *"Give Me a Soldier, Now!"* W.W.I. card by Inter-Art Co.

Natural Features. *"Castle Rock & Pinnacles, Cheddar Gorge."* R.P. by E.A. Sweetman & Son.

Natural Features. *"The Caves, Swanage". Wrench.*

Natural Features. *"Last Ascent on to Scawfell Pike". G.P. Abraham Ltd.*

Natural Features. *"Arched Rock, Freshwater Bay." Hartmann. P.U. 1907.*

Natural Features. *"The Buckstone, Monmouth". Publisher unknown. U.B.*

"Naturette Pictorial Post Cards"
Set of views in C.H. Nadin's "Christchurch Series".

Naval Postcards
Views of individual ships have been covered under Battleships, Cruisers and Destroyers. The following publishers issued cards dealing with life in the Navy:
(i)   Blum & Degen, early sets of 12 cards titled "Her Majesty's Fleet".
(ii)   Boots Cash Chemists.
(iii) E.T.W. Dennis.
(iv)   Eyre & Spottiswoode, many warship cards, British and foreign.
(v)   Gale & Polden, "Life in the Navy", series 42-90, 1340-1398, 1400-1440, and various humorous sets, e.g. "Jack Ashore" and "Jack's Leisure Moments", and "Types of the Navy".
(vi)   Gottschalk, Dreyfus & Davis, warships.
(vii) S. Hildesheimer, "British Navy, Past & Present", 5457, facsims. of paintings by R. Gallon.
(viii) C.R. Hoffman, warships.

(ix)   Knight Bros., "Royal Navy" Series.
(x)   Photochrom Co. Series included: "Britain's Bulwarks" with a detailed description of each ship on the address side; "Britain Prepared", a general series with close-up views of deck activities on battleships; a "Duo-type Process" Series in black and green.
(xi)   Pictorial Stationery Co., "Bulwarks of Empire".
(xii) G.A. Pratt, R.P.s of naval ships.
(xiii) A. Reid & Co., coat of arms series using battleships and a scenic background.
(xiv) Rotary, R.P.s of naval vessels. Inset portraits of George V and others. Captions state power, speed and armament of each ship.
(xv)   Salmon, views of ships.
(xvi) Singer Sewing Machines, "Our Ironclads".
(xvii) Tuck, many sets under such titles as "Empire Series", "Our Ironclads", "Our Navy" and "The Fleet in the Far East".
(xviii) Universal Photo-Printing & Publishing Co., set on "Battleships".

continued

Colour Plate 15:
European glamour cards

"Anniversaire" by E. Colombo.

Glamour card by Achille Mauzan. P.U. 1920.

"Coquetterie" by Xavier Sager.

Naval Postcards. *"Dockyard Gate, Chatham"*. Naval card by *Valentine*.

(xix) Valentine, naval cards include a set on the surrender of the German Fleet in 1919, and views of naval dockyards.

(xx) J. Welch & Sons, photographs of naval vessels.

Nazi Propaganda

A number of German cards designed by Richard Klein were issued shortly before W.W.II. with maps of "Greater Germany" and inset portraits of Hitler.

Neilson, Julia. *"Miss Julia Neilson in* Henry of Navarre*"*. Beagles. P.U. 1909.

N. & C.
Nicholson & Carter (q.v.).

Neame, Elwin
Photographer who provided Philco with portraits for their birthday cards.

Neaves Baby Food
Poster-type advertisements.

Neeson, Andrew L.
Artist who designed a card showing Britain and Ireland threatening one another while the Kaiser, representing Germany, looks on.

Negri, Pola
Daughter of a Polish nobleman, Pola Negri went to Hollywood in 1922 and became a star in such films as *Forbidden Paradise,* 1924, and *Woman of the World,* 1926. P.P.s by *Picturegoer.*

Neilson, Harry B.   **fl. 1895-1905**
Birkenhead artist who designed early cards for William Lyon and Charles Voisey.

Neilson, Julia   **1868-1957**
Actress. First London appearance at the Lyceum in 1888. Played with Fred Terry in *The Scarlet Pimpernel,* 1905. Scene from *Henry of Navarre* by Beagles. P.P. by Ellis & Walery.

Nelson, Horatio   **1758-1805**
A number of cards were issued to mark the centenary of Nelson's death and the Battle of Trafalgar. Publishers included:
(i)   Cassell & Co. Ltd.
(ii)   J.J. Corlyn, card of Nelson's column.
(iii)   Gale & Polden, "Nelson Series".
(iv)   Knight Bros., multi-view card with portrait.
(v)   Rotary, "Life of Nelson".
(vi)   Tuck, "Nelson Centenary".
(vii)   Woolstone, set portraying events in the life of Lord Nelson. The stamp space on these cards states: "Printed and Copyrighted by J.J. Keliher & Co., Ltd., London, by permission of the Lords Commissioners of the Admiralty."

Nelson, Horatio. *"Nelson's Old Flagship* The Victory *in Portsmouth Harbour"*. A Nelson Centenary card. R. Tuck & Sons.

Nelson, J.W. pre-1913

Photographer/publisher, Glasgow. Street scenes in the city.

Nesbit, T. pre-1908

Photographer/publisher, Blandford, Dorset. Coloured local views.

"Nestlé's Swiss Milk"

Advertising cards including U.B. vignettes and poster-type cards. One card shows two cats in conversation:

"Thanks for your feed of Nestle's Milk,
It did me good, my coat's like silk
And now I'm sound in wind and brain
I'll never drink skim milk again."

A set of four cards, "Types of the British Army", was offered in exchange for labels from Nestlé products.

Nethersole, Olga Isabel, C.B.E. 1870-1951

Actress-manager. First appeared in London at the Grand Theatre, Islington in 1887. Manager of Royal Court Theatre, 1893. P.P. by Rapid Photo and Rotary.

Netherwood, N., A.R.C.A. fl.1920s

Publisher, Llandudno Junction, Carnarvonshire. Watercolour views printed in sepia.

Newbury, Thomas

Newbury, 41 Sidbury, Worcester. Local sepia views.

Newby & Son

Publisher, Bicester, Oxfordshire. Photographic views.

Newham, Theodore T. fl. 1930s

Landscape artist who lived and exhibited in Leicester. Facsims. by H.A. Bennett.

Newman Bros.

Publisher, Glasgow. The cards by this publisher have a silvered background and were printed in Switzerland. Many of them have a Scottish flavour with heather, tartans or thistles.

Newman, Wolsey & Co. pre-1932

Publisher, Leicester. "Country Series" of coloured views sometimes overprinted with greetings.

Newport, Godshill & St. Lawrence Railway

Two court size cards by the Picture Postcard Co. have been recorded.

Newton, G.E.

Landscape and marine artist. Painted some early "Rough Sea" cards for Tuck and "St. Anthony's Lighthouse" in their "Bookmarker" Series, XV.

Nicholls, Horace

Photographer for Philco.

Nichols & Son

Photographer/publisher, Wantage, Berkshire. Local R.P. views.

Nicholson, A.W.

Publisher, Wells Rd., Bristol.

Nicholson & Carter pre-1911

Publisher, Carlisle. Issued a "Lochinvar" Series of coloured local views.

Nickson, H.H.

Publisher of Lancashire views in the "H.H. Nickson's Series".

Nielsen, Vivienne

Animal painter.

Nigh, W.J., & Sons Ltd. pre-1929

Publisher, Ventnor, I.O.W. Sepia views in "Photogravure Postcard" and "Real Hand-Coloured Photo-Cards" Series. Multi-view cards were also produced each with a central coat of arms. Range extended into mainland Hampshire.

Nimmo

Publisher, Leith, Edinburgh.

Nister, Ernest fl.1898-1917

Publisher, 24 St. Brides St., London, E.C. German publisher of Nuremberg who established a branch in England and, after some years of fine art printing, started to publish coloured postcards of London scenes. Many were painted by a watercolour artist, C. Schmidt. Further series of cards followed including birds and animals, still life, an Aesop's Fables Series and some humorous cards, e.g. "The Animals' Trip to Sea" (ill. D. & M. 111), "The Animals' Picnic" etc., and a "Jumbo" elephant series. The firm had a close association with E.P. Dutton & Co., New York.

"Nixey's" Black Lead

Advertising card.

Nixon, Kathleen fl. 1920-1927

Artist who painted *Alice in Wonderland* cards for Faulkner in the 1920s. She also designed a few postcards of animals.
   Ref: Cope p. 18 and ill. p. 49.

Noble, Ernest

Designer of W.W.I. comic cards.

Noble, John Edwin. *"Guildford. Castle Arch"*. Facsim. by A.G. Curtis.

Noble, John Edwin, R.B.A., F.L.S.   fl.1898-1930
Animal and landscape painter. Taught at Calderon's School of
Animal Painting from 1914-21. Moved to Guildford and
painted local views for A.G. Curtis.

"Norman".
See: Shoesmith & Etheridge Ltd.

Norman, Carl, & Co.   pre-1903
Publisher. A company which was absorbed by Photochrom
some time after 1909 when Carl Norman became
Photochrom's manager. Previously his company had
produced fine photographic views of Kent.

Norman, Parsons   1840-1914
East Anglian landscape and coastal painter. Exh. R.A. 3.
Painted a "Parsons Norman" Series for W.S. Cowell, a
"Durham" set for Tuck, and views for J.W. Ruddock.

North British Railway Co.   c.1903-1910
Publisher of views of the area served by the railway, e.g. The
Forth Bridge.
  Ref: Full details in R.O.P.L., No. 13.

North British Rubber Co.
Cards advertising their golf balls.

North Eastern Railway
"Panoram" view cards were published from 1903 (40 in all)
and Photochrom supplied 20 poster cards in 1908. A number
of cards advertised the steamers of the Hull-Rotterdam service
and also "Picturesque Holland". The Alphalsa Publishing
Co. also issued cards of the N.E.R., e.g. "East Coast Express
leaving Waverley Station, Edinburgh".
  See: Colour Plate 22.
  Ref: Check lists of "Panoram" and Photochrom cards in
R.O.P.L., No. 7.

North Staffordshire Railway
Issued 23 sets of views of the area served, some by
McCorquodale, othes by Wildt & Kray, and by Wood,
Mitchell & Co.
  Ref: Check lists in R.O.P.L., No. 1.

Norman, Parsons. *"Driven Ashore". Facsim. by R. Tuck &
Sons. "Aquarette".*

"North Star"
Publisher of the *Halfpenny Morning Paper,* Darlington,
Durham, who issued cards of the Durham County Show, July
1913.

Norwich Union Insurance Co.
Advertisement card issued on the occasion of the Coronation
of George VI in 1937.

Norwood, Arthur Harding   fl.1889-1893
London landscape painter.

Noury, Gaston   b.1866
French illustrator and poster artist.

Novarro, Ramon   1899-1968
Film actor, P.P.s by *Film Weekly* and *Picturegoer,* including a
scene with Myrna Loy from *A Night in Cairo.*

Novello, Ivor   1893-1951
Actor-manager, author and composer. Well known on stage
and in films. P.P. Foulsham & Banfield.

Novelty Cards
Competition in the postcard industry was intense. Every
publisher strained to produce something unique which would
attract the customers. As a result all kinds of ingenious ideas
gave rise to the novelty card. They are listed here under the
titles by which they are best known:

(i)   Aluminium cards. These cards could only be sent
        through the post in an envelope. The Palatine Pictorial
        Co. therefore produced an "Alumino" card which
        had only the appearance of aluminium.

(ii)   Appliqué cards. All kinds of materials were glued to
        the surface of postcards. Real hair was stuck on heads
        and on animals, feathers on birds, ill. D. & M. 116,
        shamrocks on Irish cards, and heather or pieces of
        tartan on Scottish cards. The Cynicus Publishing Co.
        went to extremes, using pieces of canvas, coal,
        celluloid, granite, leather and rice. Oates & Co. of
        Halifax stuck small fragments of watercolour paint on
        their cards so that the recipient, using a little water,
        could paint in an outline picture printed on the card.

(iii)   Button cards. The Cynicus Publishing Co. introduced
        "The Bachelor's Button" which consisted of a button
        on a strip of elastic which related to the picture on the
        card.

(iv)   Calendar cards. Some postcards published by Percy
        Redjeb had a calendar attached which, when out-of-
        date, could be detached, leaving an ordinary postcard.

(v)   Celluloid cards. Celluloid is a plastic material made
        from nitrocellulose and camphor. It can be produced
        in very thin sheets and was used for postcards.
        Unfortunately it cracks rather easily.

(vi)   Cigar and cigarette cards. Cards with a figure and
        either cigarettes or cigars attached in transparent paper
        were sold by Max Ettlinger. Retailers prepared to sell
        enough were provided with a licence to sell tobacco.

(vii)   Composite cards. A set of several cards which fit
        together to form a picture. Charles Voisey sold a set of
        four cards which, when fitted together, produced an
        "Elongated Dachsund". Other composite cards depict
        Sarah Bernhardt, a map by Tuck, and there is an
        advertising composite for "G.P. Tea".

(viii) Cork cards. Thin slices of cork were sometimes printed
        with views. Such cards are not very durable.

(ix)   Cut-out cards. Instructions are given to cut the card where indicated so that a figure in the picture can be made to sit or stand up. Some cut-out cards by Tuck were made as children's playthings and are therefore rare since most of them were destroyed in use. Some Tuck butterfly cards can be cut out so that the wings stand out.

(x) Fab cards. These were published by W.N. Sharpe of Bradford as "The Patent 'Fab' Patchwork Cards". Small pieces of bright coloured cloth and even portraits on cloth were attached to postcards. These could be detached to make patchwork, pin cushions, etc.
Ref: A full account of their origin is given in Byatt pp. 248-9.

(xi) Flap cards. Cards with small flaps that cause movement on the card when lifted were made by Woolstone Bros. A "Gaping" Series causes mouths to open on humans or animals. When the flap is used on cards in a "Transformation" Series the character or occupation of the figure is changed. See Lever Cards below.

(xii) Gramophone record cards. Ettlinger introduced a "Discophone Postcard" in 1905, and Tuck produced a number of "Gramophone Record" cards in 17 series. These included vocal, instrumental solos, orchestral pieces, piano solos, hymns, carols and nursery rhymes.
Ref: A full check list is given in Byatt p.320.

(xiii) Hold-to-light or HTL cards. These were introduced by W. Hagelberg of Berlin. The cards look like ordinary view postcards but when held to the light (as instructed) the view changes. The War Puzzle Picture Co. used the technique during W.W.I. on cards with zeppelins, warships and submarines.

(xiv) Kaleidoscope cards. These were published by Alpha. The cards have revolving parts so that colours can be changed.

(xv) Kissogram cards. A face appears on this type of card with the rather large lips impregnated with colouring. When the sender of the card kisses the face he or she can transfer the "kiss" to a space at the base of the card with a message "A kiss from....." or "A kiss to....."

(xvi) "Klever Kards". Cut-out cards with lines indicating where the cards should be folded so they could be made to stand up like small tents to form the background for cut-out figures.

(xvii) Leather cards. These very occasionally appear in Britain but they were mainly made in America. The material is most unsuitable because of its flexibility.

(xviii) Lever cards. These are sometimes included under mechanical cards. The movement of a cardboard lever changes the picture. A girl is made to put her tongue out, E.T.W. Dennis's "Saucy Girl"; people change clothes, S.J. Payne & Co.; or move a head to take a drink, C.R. Pinchbeck.

(xix) Luminous cards. Luminous paint, in the outline of a flower or view for example, was applied to cards by one or two publishers. The Luminous Print Co. issued some remarkable cards which, after having been exposed to a bright light and then looked at in the dark, produce a glowing outline.

(xx) Magic cards. These cards by Valentine have a white centre. The viewer is asked to hold it close to his face for a short time and then hold it close to the fire. The heat produces a portrait.

(xxi) Magic stereoscopic cards. These are based on the principle behind the stereoscope. The eyepieces for viewing are cut from the card.

(xxii) Mechanical cards. Cards designed to produce movement, e.g. the opening of a fan or a book, the turning of clock hands or a wheel, the movement of a head, or a flapper dancing the Charleston.

(xxiii) Panoramic cards. Large cards (9¾ x 3¾ ins.) with a coloured view pasted on board. They could be sent by Halfpenny Packet Post but no message other than a signature was allowed. The illustration on p. 196 shows a view in the Forest of Dean. It was sold by S.J. Cooksey of Cinderford.

(xxiv) Peat cards. Paper made of peat was manufactured at a mill near the River Liffey, west of Dublin in Ireland. Cards of peat were printed with Irish subjects and verses.

(xxv) Photographic insert cards. Cards in which there is a slit into which a small photograph can be inserted. They were made by the Pictorial Postcard Co. as "Midget Postcards", and also by Schofield & Co.

(xxvi) Pop-up cards. Cards in which people or animals appear when a flap is raised. A series by E.T.W. Dennis.

(xxvii) Pull-out cards. These cards had a major central feature in the design which was made into a flap which could be lifted to reveal a folded strip of up to 12 views. The cards could be used for any tourist centre or resort because the name was overprinted and the views inserted before the cards were despatched. One Valentine card is headed "Your Fortune in a Teacup"; when the teacup flap is raised 12 diagrams of cups with tealeaf patterns are revealed each with a paragraph which describes "The Reading of this Fortune". Valentine and Photochrom were the main publishers, though a few were published by E.T.W. Dennis who called them "Pocket Novelty Cards", and by Solomon Bros. An unusual pull-out card was produced by Woolstone Bros.; known as a "Coon" Series, a character in top hat is attached to the card by paper concertina-type legs and arms which expand when the head is pulled. One multiple view card by Photochrom involved pulling a photograph from a frame.

(xviii) Puzzle cards. A number of publishers issued puzzle cards including the Puzzle Post Card Co.; Tuck; Valentine, puzzlegrams; and Wrench, Instalment Puzzle Cards. Relatively few of these have survived. Some were returned to publishers in the hope of winning a prize offered for the solution, others were damaged through too much handling, and a few were sent in instalments and were seldom assembled.

(xxix) Real dress cards. A series by Howe, Vertigen & Co., with figures in cloth clothing.

(xxx) Reversible cards. Cards on which the view changes when they are held upside down.

(xxxi) Sand pictures. Cards which have had the coloured sands of Alum Bay in the Isle of Wight applied to a local view as souvenirs. Some cards have certain areas with applied sand to be used for striking matches, e.g. the seat of a teddy bear, ill. D. & M. 120.

(xxxii) Scented cards. Cards impregnated with perfume.

(xxxiii) Squeakers or pinch-and-squeak cards. These cards

Novelty Cards. *Sand picture "arranged with sands from the coloured cliffs of Alum Bay". "An Isle of Wight Curiosity" by T.E. Porter, The Arcade, Sandown, I.O.W.*

Novelty Cards. *"Kippax Church", Yorkshire, outlined in tinsel and with a tinsel greeting. E.J. Bloor, Castleford.*

were made in two layers with a squeaking device inserted between them. There is a small hole on the address side from which air is expelled. When the card is pinched between thumb and fingers it omits a squeak. The cards were designed to appeal to small children, often with a design based on a nursery rhyme printed below, e.g. "Goosey, goosey gander". Many such cards were issued by Ettlinger.

(xxxiv) Tinsel cards. Tinsel or glitter was much used on greetings cards and some publishers even outlined features on a scene with tinsel, e.g. the Gateway of Carisbrooke Castle, a painting by Jotter published in

facsim. by E. Gordon Smith in a "Pinachrome" Series.

(xxxv) Toy model cards. Postcards which children could turn into cardboard toys were made by several publishers including David & Carter, steamers; Henderson, "Characters for a Young Folk Model Theatre"; Salmon, "Miniature Models"; Tuck, "Dressing Dolls".

(xxxvi) "Wagger Cards". A series of animal cards by Hutson Bros., with "H.B. Wagger Card" in place of the usual "Post Card". Dogs or other animals were fitted with coiled springs for tails which popped out when the card was removed from the envelope in which it was sold.

(xxxvii) Wooden cards. These were produced by the Pictorial Postcard Co., and H.J. Smith of Brighton had fantasy cards engraved on wood.

(xxxviii) "The X-Ray Illusion Postcard". A card with a hole through which one looked at one's hand held about a foot from a bright light, preferably against a window, when the bones of the hand were seen as in an X-ray photograph.

Novelty Post Card Co. pre-1906
Publisher, 15 Lord St., Liverpool, Lancashire, and later at 62 Victoria St. Output included:
(i) Coloured views of Lancashire and North Wales.
(ii) Greetings cards.
(iii) "Sentimental Series".
(iv) "Letterbox Series", ill. Byatt 213.
(v) "Enamelette" postcards, portraits of actresses.

N.P.C. Co.
Novelty Post Card Co. (q.v.).

N.P.G.
Neve Photographische Gesellschaft. German cards imported into Britain.

Nudes
Cards with nudes are usually photographs, since few British artists painted nudes for postcard reproduction. A small quantity only in either medium was produced in Britain, but they were imported in considerable quantities from France, Germany and Austria.

Ref: Nude cards are fully discussed and displayed in Jones and Ouellette's *Erotic Postcards,* Macdonald & Jane's, London, 1977.

Nursery Rhymes
Many publishers included nursery rhymes in their cards. A.M. Davis & Co. published a special series.

Nurses
Many cards show nurses in hospitals, including posed group photographs of nursing staff. They are also seen in action in W.W.I. photographs; Arthur Butcher painted a series of romantic cards of nurses with wounded soldiers for Inter-Art.

Nystrom, Jenny 1857-1946
Swedish painter and illustrator who designed greetings and banknote postcards.

Oates, Sarah, & Co   pre-1905
Publisher, 6 The Arcade, Halifax, Yorkshire. Issued coloured cards of armorial souvenir wares made by William Henry Goss (q.v.), who is acknowledged on each card. Mrs. Oates, the founder of the firm, was primarily a fine art dealer and it is not surprising that she should devise a card in the style of a child's drawing book. Each card has an outline to be filled in with colours adhering to the card. All that is needed is a brush and a little water.

Oatey, J.E.
Photographer/publisher, Wadebridge, Cornwall. Cornish views.

Obermeyer, H.F.
Landscape artist who painted European views for Tuck.

O'Connor, Fergus, & Co.
"Publisher to the Trade", Dublin. Trademark an Irish harp surmounted by a crown.

Oddfellows, Grand United Order of
Friendly Society publicity cards.

Odol
Publisher, The Odol Chemical Works, London and Paris. Advertisement cards for mouthwash and dentifrice. Glamorous ladies and several actresses who used their products were photographed pouring Odol into a glass. There is a signed postcard of Ellaline Terris using Odol, and Philco produced cards of Billie Burke on which a rubber stamp states: "I have been using your Odol dentifrice for years and I don't think I could possibly do without it either at the Theatre or at home", P.U. 1908. Camille Clifford, Zena Dare and Marie Studholme all advertised Odol on postcards.

O.F.
O. Flammger, the British agent for Stengel & Co. Ltd. The initials are found before the firm's name which is printed in brackets.

Odol. Advertising card by the Odol Chemical Works, London and Paris.

"Oilette". "Ryde, Spencer Avenue, I.o.W." by R. Esdaile Richardson, 1905. R. Tuck & Sons. P.U. 1921.

Order Form Postcards. Fine Art Corporation Ltd. The reverse side advertises "High class engravings" for 2s.6d. each and leaves a space for name and address if a catalogue or print is required.

Offor, Beatrice   **fl. 1887-1917**
Figure painter. Exh. R.A. 14. Designed cards for Mitchell & Watkins.

Ogden's Cigarettes and Tobacco
Advertising card in Tuck's "Celebrated Posters" Series.

"Ogden's Series"
Publisher, Morton Lane, Manchester. R.P. views.

O. & G.L.
Ormiston & Glass, London (q.v.).

"Oilette"
Type of card introduced by Raphael Tuck in 1903 with an irregularly embossed surface designed to simulate the brush strokes on an oil painting. Very many "Oilette" cards, however, have a smooth surface and it became the generic term for a card which was the facsimile of an artist's work.

"Oilograph"
Type of card used by Max Ettlinger & Co.

Oilosimile
Registered series by Landeker & Brown, 1904, usually referred to as an "Ellanbee Oilosimile" clearly imitating the Tuck "Oilette".

"Old Bill"
The W.W.I. character invented by Bruce Bairnsfather (q.v.).

Oliver, Ethel
Actress. P.P. by Philco.

Oliver Typewriters
Advertising cards. "Writing through the Ages".

Olney Amsden & Sons Ltd.
Importer/publisher, 9-11 Falcon St., London, E.C. This firm published a few cards designed by Ernest Klempner. They dealt with humorous aspects of money, e.g. "A Farthing Change", "Cabby's Fare" and "Including Costs".

Owen, Will. "Humorous" postcard by R. Tuck & Sons. "The Humour of Life." Facetious Doctor: "These on the walls are your failures, I suppose?" Dyspeptic Artist: "Yes, that's where you doctors have the pull over us. You can bury yours".

O'Neill, Rose   **1874-1944**
American artist who designed cards which were used by McLove & Co. They depicted cupids ("Kewpies"). She also designed greetings cards.

Opera
Photo-portraits of opera stars are found on postcards, e.g. Clara Butt, Enrico Caruso and Nellie Melba. Pictures of stage performances, amateur and professional, were also issued. Faulkner produced an "Opera Scenes" Series; and Tuck published a "Wagner" Series with scenes from *Lohengrin* and other operas.

O.P.F.
Osnabrücker Papiervaarem Fabrik.
  See: Osnabrücker Paper Manufacturing Co.

Order Form Postcards
Several firms, such as the Fine Art Corporation Ltd. of 64 High Holborn, London, W.C., printed cards advertising a product, in this case "high class engravings". A potential customer had merely to fill in a name and address, stamp the card and post it. He was then sent a catalogue, a specimen engraving and a coupon for a competition. An order could be placed by filling up a similar card.

Orens, Denizard
French artist who specialised in political satire. He signed his work Denizard or Godillot.

Orme, Denise   **1884-1960**
Actress. Played at Daly's in *The Lady Dandies,* 1906. P.P.s by Davidson and Rotophot.

Ormiston & Glass Ltd.   **1905**
Publisher, London. Trade initials "O. & G.L." Message cards with some printed material and spaces left for the sender to fill in.

Osborne, E., & Co.
Photographer/publisher, Alresford, Hampshire. Local R.P. views.

Osnabrücker Paper Manufacturing Co.   **c. 1901**
Publisher, 304 High Street, Holborn, London, W.C. A branch of a Berlin firm using the trade initials O.P.F. The early U.B. cards show a view through a window with the words "Souvenir of London" above the message space. The firm published many greetings cards, some embossed.

Outcault, Richard Felton   **b. 1863**
American artist who contributed to *The New York Herald.* He designed comic postcards, especially those with children.

Outhwaite, Ida Rentoul   **1889-1961**
Australian illustrator of children's books. Some of her illustrations were reproduced as postcards by A. & C. Black in the 1920s, e.g. "Elves and Fairies".
    Ref: Cope p. 19 and ill. p. 50.

Ovaltine
Advertising cards. A card designed by Phyllis M. Cooper shows a mother with two children and a tin of Ovaltine in the foreground, ill. Monahan 141. Another shows a maid in cap and apron holding a tin of Ovaltine in one hand and a basket showing its natural ingredients in the other.

Over, George
Publisher, Rugby. Local coloured views, e.g. bust of Dr. Arnold in New Big School, Rugby.

Overprinting
Printing superimposed on an original printing. It converted an ordinary pictorial card into a greetings card by overprinting such words as "Merry Christmas" or "Happy Birthday". Sometimes overprinting was done in two stages. A card would be printed with such words as "Arrived at ..." or "Mixed Bathing at ..." and when the destination of the card was known the name of a town would be added making it read "Arrived at Blackpool" or "Mixed Bathing at Margate". This was often done on Cynicus cards.

Owen, Will, R.C.A.   **1869-1957**
Artist and caricaturist. He illustrated the books of W.W. Jacobs and contributed humorous sketches to *Punch, The Strand Magazine* and *The Graphic.* His cartoons are found on postcards by Davidson Bros., Meissner & Buch, Tuck, and Wrench. David Allen reproduced his theatre posters on postcards.

Ox Roasts
At country gatherings and fairs an ox was sometimes roasted on a spit over an open fire. Cards may sometimes be found depicting this ceremony, e.g. at Stratford-upon-Avon.

Oxford Colleges
Views of the Oxford colleges were published by:
(i)   Frith & Co., black and white views.
(ii) Robert Peel.
(iii) Penrose & Palmer.
(iv) Alfred Savage.
(v) Taunt & Co.
(vi) Valentine.

Oxford Times Co. Ltd.
Publisher. Local views in a "Carbon Glosso" Series.

Oxford Varsity City
Words on a ribbon in the trademark of Alfred Savage Ltd. of Oxford (q.v.).

Oxo
Advertising postcards sometimes depicting events, e.g. Shackleton's *Nimrod* or an aeronautical event at Blackpool in 1909. Others are humorous, one showing a small boy in a kilt with the caption: "Ma mither winna gie me ony mair Oxo, it mak's me grow oot o' ma claes".

Oystow, George   **fl. c.1891-1897**
Landscape painter whose work was used by Tuck in "The Blush of Eve" set.

P

P. Co.
Photochrom Co. Ltd. (q.v.).

Packer, Frank
Photographer/publisher, Chipping Norton, Oxfordshire. Local R.P. views.

Paddle Steamers
Paddle steamers were the forerunners of screw-driven steamers but they persisted as excursion steamers well into the 20th century because they were fast and easily managed. They operated in estuaries and coastal waters to serve the holiday trade. Steamer trips were very popular and many piers were built in seaside resorts as landing stages, though many of these also became pleasure piers. Excursion trips in the Bristol Channel operated from Bristol to Minehead and South Wales, on the River Clyde, and along stretches of the east and south coasts.

Postcard views with close-ups where the name of the steamer can be seen are particularly desirable. Among the named steamers are:

Atlanta.
Audrey.
Barry, P. & A. Campbell.
Bickerstaffe.
Bilsdale.
Brighton Queen.
Britannia, P. & A. Campbell.
Cardiff Queen, P. & A. Campbell.
Devonia.
Glen Sannox.

Golden Eagle.
Greyhound.
Ivanhoe.
Juno.
Lady Evelyn.
Lady Moira.
London Belle.
Marchioness of Lorne.
Prince of Wales, I.O.M. S. Pk. Co.
Ravenswood.
Royal Eagle.
Waverley.
Westward Ho, P. & A. Campbell.
Ref: Cox, B., *Paddle Steamers,* 1979.

Padgett, A.J.
Publisher, Leigh-on-Sea, Essex. "Haven Series" of R.P. views, serial nos. to 6031.

Page, Ernest
Artist and publisher, Iwood, Warbleton, Sussex, who published his own work. Children's cards bear the trademark "An Ernest Page Picture Postcard" with a figure of a page-boy.

Page, K.
Publisher, 21 Newgate, Walton-on-the-Naze, Essex.

Pageants
Pageants which illustrated local history and involved many local people in acting roles and processions were enormously popular before W.W.II. and were all subjects for postcard illustration. They included the following:
1905 Sherborne (official cards by R. Wilkinson & Co., Trowbridge).
1906 Sheffield (Chadwick & Allan).
      Warwick (Water Colour Post Card Co.)
1907 Bury St. Edmunds, I.O.W., Liverpool (G.G. Walmsley).
      Oxford (3 sets by Tuck).
      Porchester, Romsey, St. Albans (2 sets by Tuck).
1908 Bradford, Chelsea, Dover (W.H. Smith).
      Gloucester (Debenham).
      Gorleston, Pevensey, Winchester.
1909 Bath (Lewis Bros., and R. Wilkinson).
      Pageant of Wales.
      York (G.G. Walmsley).
1910 Army Pageant, Chester, Ilford, Pickering.
1911 Carshalton, Festival of Empire, Crystal Palace (Bemrose & Sons).
      West Dorset.
1912 Scarborough.
1919 Peace Pageant.
1922 Kingston, Madame Tussaud's (Tussaud's).
1924 Lullingstone, Peace Pageant, Pageant of Empire.

continued

Paddle Steamers. *"Southsea. — On Clarence Pier. — Arrival of the Boat."* Louis Lévy. P.U. 1912.

Colour Plate 16: Horse cards

"The Royal Horse Guards... Passing Buckingham Palace" by Harry Payne. R. Tuck & Sons. "The Military in London". Series II.

"The Return to the Stables". R. Tuck & Sons. "Oilette" Connoisseur "Coaching". Series II.

"Hi! Hi!!" by Fred S. Howard. Misch & Co. "The Fire Brigade" Series. P.U. 1906.

194

Pageants. *Dover, 1908. "An Elder Knight of King Arthur's Round Table". Photo by Charles Harris, Dover. P.U. 1908.*

Winchester Pageant. 1908.   Gandy, Copyright
EMPRESS MATILDA. (MISS MOSS.)

Pageants. *"Winchester Pageant, 1908. Empress Matilda (Miss Moss)". Gandy.*

1925 Nutfield.
1926 Chester (Phillipson & Golder).
1927 Bideford, Rillington.
1928 Carlisle, Westcroft Park.
1929 Ashdown Forest.
1930 Warwick Castle.
1931 Bradford, Newcastle upon Tyne (Johnstone & Sons Ltd.).
Tewkesbury.
1932 Battle Abbey, Rochester.
1934 Runnymede (Fleetway Press).
1935 England.
1937 Surrey.
1938 Birmingham.
1939 Kenilworth.

Some publishers issued sets of cards reflecting a number of scenes in a pageant. Tuck, for example, issued three sets for the Oxford Pageant of 1907, 2783-5.

Pageant Queens were also the subjects of photo-portraits as were some of the other leading players.

Palace Book Depot
Publisher, 37 White Rock, Hastings. Glossy sepia local views.

Palatine Pictorial Co. Ltd.   **1905**
Publisher, 14 Cumberland St., Manchester. Registered trademark "Photinotype". The main output consisted of views. The most interesting cards are those which have the name "Alumino" and look as though they were printed on a thin sheet of aluminium.

Pageants: *"Oxford Pageant 1907. Official postcard. The Expulsion of the Fellows of Magdalen by King James II, 1687". R. Tuck & Sons. "Oilette". "Oxford Pageant" Series III.*

Panoramic Cards. *"Forest of Dean, near Speech House." S.J. Cooksey, Cinderford.*

Palethorpe's Sausages & Pies
Poster-type advertisement in Tuck's "Celebrated Posters" Series.

Palmer, Harry Sutton, R.B.A., R.I.   **1854-1933**
Landscape painter in watercolour. Exh. R.A. 33. Illustrated books for A. & C. Black; some of these illustrations were used as postcards by Tuck, e.g. "Bonnie Scotland — The Trossachs", and Salmon. A. & C. Black also published postcards of his illustrations to books on North and South Devon and Surrey.

Palmer, J.
Publisher, Durham.

Palmer, Minnie   **1857-1936**
Actress and vocalist. P.P. in Tuck's "Bookmarker" Series IV.

Palmer, Phyllis M.
Painter of child subjects.

Palmer Tyres
Advertising cards.

Panel Cards
These are cards printed on board, often with a bevelled and gilded edge. Wildt & Kray published a panel card c.1915, and Faulkner a "Panel Greeting Card" c.1919.

Pankhurst, Christobel   **1880-1958**
Organising Secretary of the National Women's Social and Political Union (q.v.). R.P. by the Union taken by Kay of Manchester.

Pannett, R.
Artist who specialised in glamour and the theatre. His cards are highly prized.

Panoramic Cards
Three publishers issued long panoramic views on stiff card:
(i) S.J. Cooksey, Stationer, Cinderford, Gloucestershire; card with a view of the Forest of Dean pasted on green surfaced card.
(ii) Photochrom Co.; an example noted posted in 1909.
(iii) Tuck; the "Oilette Panoramic Card" measured 11 × 3½ins. Several cards are included with numbers between 6636 and 6642. A view of Glasgow is ill. in an article by

David Penfold, P.P.M., March 1982, p. 5.
    These panoramic cards could be sent by Halfpenny Packet Post provided they carried a signature only. If a message was included the postage was one penny.
    See also under Novelty Cards.

Pan-Yan Pickle
Advertising card by Maconochie Bros. of London; it features Studdy's "Bonzo" who is sitting in pickle. Caption: "You're in a fine pickle!"

"Paquebot"
Stamp cancellation used on cards posted on ships at sea.

Parades
Military parades were held particularly at memorial services, e.g. after the death of Edward VII, ill. Hill p. 46, and as a regular part of military training.

Parbury, F.G.
Artist who painted scenes in India for Tuck's "Wide Wide World" cards.

Parades. *"Argyle [sic]* and Sutherland Highlanders, Edinburgh Castle". Hartmann.

Parks. *"Manningham Park, Bradford"*. Woolstone Bros. Milton *"Glazette"*. P.U. 1916.

MORNING IN THE PASTURE.

Pastoral Scenes. *"Morning in the Pasture"*. Davidson Bros. P.U. 1911.

Parisian Studios   **pre-1908**
Publisher, Gillingham, Kent. Black and white local views.

Park Drive Cigarettes
Poster-type advertising cards by Gallaghers.

Parker, N.
Animal painter.

Parkinson, Ethel   **fl. c.1900-1910**
Artist who painted children in the Dutch style, ill. D. & M. 187. Her cards often have a verse below the picture. Noted particularly for a "Coon Series". Cards for Faulkner included "Cleaning Day" and "Mending Day".

Parkinson, Roy
Publisher, Leeds. Local views.

Parks
Municipal parks often feature on postcards. The more interesting show some form of activity, e.g. boating on a lake.

Parkslee Pictures
Publisher of theatrical portraits.

Parlett, Harry   **fl. c.1909-1916**
Designer of comic cards for Gottschalk, Dreyfus & David, e.g. "How to Behave". He painted chubby-faced children for Tuck and, using the pseudonym Comicus, designed cards for Hutson Bros., the Midland Pictorial Postcard Co., and A. & G. Taylor.

Parr & Son
Publisher, Newmarket, Suffolk. Coloured local views.

Parr, Doreen M.
Artist who designed cards with animals dressed as children.

Parrs (Stationers) Ltd.
Publisher, Knaresborough, Yorkshire. Local R.P. views.

Parry's
Publisher, Penmaenmawr, Carnarvonshire. "Parry's Series" of coloured views.

Parsons, A.
Photographer/publisher, Church St., Hungerford, Berkshire.

Parsons, F.J.
Painter who specialised in scenes on the London, Brighton and South Coast Railway.

Partridge, Sir Bernard   **1861-1948**
Painter and illustrator who was on the staff of *Punch* from 1891 to 1906. Exh. R.A. 18. Some of his political cartoons were published by Wrench.

Partridge & Love
Bristol printer of advertising cards for Schweppes.

Pascalis, Moss & Co.   **fl. 1900-1902**
Publisher, 4 and 5 Mason's Ave., Coleman St., London, E.C. A firm which imported cards from the Continent, including cards by Kirchner which proved to be extremely popular.

 Two of the most interesting series were "The Post in all Nations" and "Cyclists of all Nations".

 C.H. Pascalis left the partnership in 1902 and the firm became H. Moss & Co. (q.v.).

Passmore, Walter   **1867-1946**
Actor and vocalist. First appearance on London stage 1890. Built a solid reputation as a singing comedian. P.P. in "Yes and No" Series.

Pastel Publishing Co.   **1908**
Publisher, 6 & 7 Gough St., Fleet St., London, E.C. The company flourished on lithographs drawn by Thomas Way (q.v.). The sets were mainly of London scenes, often at twilight or by moonlight. One set covered Brighton.

Pastoral Scenes
These are found as photographs and as facsims. of paintings. Sometimes a locality is given but often they simply show an attractive rural scene.

Patella, B.
French art nouveau artist.

Paterson, Vera
Painter who designed comic cards with animals or children for the Regent Publishing Co. Ill. Monahan 130. A few have a golfing interest.

 Illustration overleaf.

197

SCRATCHING REAL HARD FOR A LIVING

Paterson, Vera. *"Scratching real hard for a living"*. *Regent Publishing Co.*

Pathé Frères Cinema Ltd.
Publisher of a series of film star portraits.

Patten, Leonard   **fl. c.1889-1903**
Marine artist. Exh. R.A. 1, 1889. Painted seascapes for M.J. Ridley of Bournemouth.

Patterson, George Malcolm   **fl. 1921-1938**
Pencil artist who lived in St. Andrews, Scotland. Exh. R.A. 7. Designed a set of cards on St. Andrews for A. & C. Black.

Patton, H.F.
Publisher, 27 Arnwell End, Ware, Hertfordshire. Local sepia views.

Pavièr, Leslie
Landscape painter. Facsims. of Oxford views published by F. Cape & Co.

Pavlova, Anna   **1881-1931**
Famous Russian ballerina. First danced outside Russia in 1907 and from 1912 made her home in Hampstead, London. P.P. by Rotary.

Payne, Arthur Charles   **1856-1933**
Brother of Henry Payne (q.v.). Painter who specialised in architectural subjects. Facsims. by Hildesheimer, e.g. "Fifteenth Century London"; J.W. Ruddock, "Lincoln Castle"; Tuck, six sets on cathedrals. Sometimes he worked with his brother.
See: Colour Plate 20.

Payne, Arthur Charles. *"Greenwich"*. *S. Hildesheimer & Co.* *"London On Thames" Series. P.U. 1911.*

Payne, Edmund   **1865-1914**
Actor. P.P. in Tuck's "Bookmarker" Series VI.

Payne, G.M.
Painter of comic and glamour subjects for Gale & Polden and the London View Co.

Payne, Henry Albert, R.W.S.   **1858-1927**
Portrait and landscape painter usually known as Harry Payne. Brother of Arthur Payne (q.v.). Born in Birmingham, studied and later taught for 18 years at the Birmingham School of Art. Exh. R.A. 22 but mainly at the Royal Society for Painters in Watercolours. Started a long association with Tuck when he designed Christmas cards for the firm in the late 1880s. He was a prolific and versatile artist and designed postcards for a number of firms including:
(i)   A.M. Davis, "War Bond Campaign Postcard".
(ii) Gale & Polden, military subjects.
(iii) S. Hildesheimer, country scenes, e.g. "Farm Life Series".
(iv) W. Mackenzie, mainly rural subjects after 1921.
(v)   Stewart & Woolf, military subjects.
(vi) Raphael Tuck for whom he painted postcards from 1900 to 1921. Sets were produced in a steady stream with two main themes: military, both current and historical, including action pictures of engagements such as the charge of the First Life Guards, Waterloo, 1915; rural scenes of farm life.
See: Colour Plates 16 and 20.
Refs: Several of Payne's Christmas cards for Tuck are illustrated in George Buday's *The History of the Christmas Card*, 1964, pl. 200; Harry Payne's life work has been well documented by M. Cane in *The Career of Harry Payne, Military Artist, 1850-1927*, privately printed, 1977. This contains a check list of his postcards; Picton 1981 contains a Harry Payne Supplement.

Payne, S.J., & Co.   **fl. 1903-1904**
Publisher, 3 and 4 St. George's Ave., Aldermanbury, London, E.C. Output included views, military cards and novelty cards.

Payne, S.M.
Comic artist who designed sets for Blum & Degen, e.g. "Hints to Girls", and for Gale & Polden, e.g. Naval Nicknames.

Payne, Henry Albert. *"Defenders of the Empire."* R. Tuck & Sons. *"Oilette"*. A card issued in aid of The Prince of Wales' National Relief Fund, and also as a Zag-Zaw Puzzle.

Payton, R.B.M.
Landscape artist who painted London views for Eyre & Spottiswoode in the 1920s.

Peacock, J.
Publisher, Sutton, Surrey. "Photo Series".

"Peacock Brand"
　See: Pictorial Stationery Co. Ltd.

Peak, W.G.
Publisher, St. Ives, Cornwall. Local R.P. views.

Pearce, H.G., & Co.　　　　　　　　　　**pre-1912**
Printer/stationer/publisher, 23 Cannon St., and 48 Newgate St., London, E.C. Collotype views of London.

Pearce, Thirkell　　　　　　　　　**fl. c. 1929-1937**
London artist who painted an impression of Edward VIII in coronation robes which was issued by the Crown Publishing Co. before the coronation which did not, in fact, take place.

Pearce, W.　　　　　　　　　　　　　**pre-1914**
Photographer/publisher, 14 High St., Shirley, Southampton, Hampshire. Local R.P. views.

Pearks
Advertisers of butter and tea. Military cards (e.g. Battle of Waterloo) and coloured scenes with children.

Pears, Charles　　　　　　　　　　　**1873-1958**
Painter who was an official naval architect in W.W.I. and

Pears, Charles. *Designer of the "Far Too Good to Share" card for J.S. Fry & Sons Ltd.*

again in 1940. Exh. R.A. 9. Designed advertising cards for J.S. Fry & Sons Ltd. (q.v.).

Pears Soap　　　　　　　　　　　　　**pre-1908**
Advertising cards by the manufacturers, A. & F. Pears, using the famous painting "Bubbles".
　Illustration overleaf.

Pearse, Alfred　　　　　　　　　　　**1854-1933**
Black and white artist. Exh. R.A. 1. Designed cards of heroic wartime scenes for War Photogravure Publications, ill. Holt 608-13, and cards of the Italian Army for Tuck.

Pearse, F.　　　　　　　　　　　　　　**1906**
Publisher, The Andover Bazaar, 63 High St., Andover, Hampshire. Matt-surfaced coloured local views supplied by Photochrom and photographs taken by the firm.

Pearse, Susan Beatrice　　　　　　**fl 1910-1937**
Designer of children's cards for Faulkner; Humphrey Melford, "Postcards for the Little Ones"; M. Munk.
　Ref: Cope p. 20 and ill. p. 51.

Pearson & Co. Ltd.
Publisher, London and Mitcham. Comic cards with children advertising "Lactagol" for nursing and expectant mothers.

Pecket, David
Photographer/publisher, Scarborough, Yorkshire. Local R.P. views.

Peckett & Sons Ltd.
Advertiser of tank locomotives, Bristol.

"BUBBLES."
By Sir John Millais, Bt., P.R.A.
After the Original in the possession of Messrs. Pears

Pears Soap. *"Bubbles". Advertisement card reproduction of Sir John Millais' famous painting.*

Peddie, George Salmond
Edinburgh artist who painted for Valentine.

Peek Frean
Message advertising cards.

Peel, Robert
 See: Robert Peel Postcard Co.

Peele, Freda
Figure painter who designed glamour cards for Photochrom.

"Peerless Erasmic Soap"
Advertising cards.

Pelaw Metal Polish
Poster-type advertising cards.

Pelham Post Card
 See: Boots Cash Chemists Ltd.

Peltier, Leon
French figure painter of déshabillé cards.

Penley, Edwin A.   fl. c. 1853-1881
Landscape watercolour artist whose work was used by Tuck in a set on "Scottish Lochs".

"Penny Post Series"   1903
Series by E. Blackwell of Northampton sold in aid of the Rowland Hill Benevolent Fund.

Penrose & Palmer   pre-1928
Publisher, Oxford. Sepia views of the Oxford colleges.

Percival, E.D. *"Hillsboro' & Lantern Hill, Ilfracombe". Facsim. by Twiss Bros. P.U. 1911.*

Penton, Howard   fl. c. 1900-1910
Artist who painted views of the Ancient House and St. Lawrence Church, Ipswich, for the Ancient House Press.

Pépin, Maurice
French artist who contributed to a "Post Bonheur" glamour series published in Paris, ill. Monahan 97.

Percival, C.A.
Stationer/publisher, Gold St., Kettering, Northamptonshire. Local R.P. views.

Percival, E.D.   fl. c. 1881-1908
Landscape painter who lived at Ilfracombe, Devon, from c. 1901. He contributed views of the county to a Tuck "Aquarette" set, a Regent Art Co. set, "Delightful Devonshire", and a local view to Twiss Bros. of Ilfracombe.

Percival, Maude
Actress. P.P. by Rotary.

Perkins, G., & Son
Publisher, Lewisham, London. Local views. The firm was later known as Perkins & Sons.

Perlberg
German landscape artist. Most of his work was done in Palestine and the Levant.

Perrier Table Water
Advertising cards showing the Perrier Pavilion at the Franco-British Exhibition, 1908.

Perry, Arthur W.   fl. c. 1900-1910
Landscape artist who lived at Prospect House, Seaton, Devon. Painted for Worth & Co. of Exeter.

Pettitt's   pre-1929
Publisher, Keswick, Cumberland. R.P.s in "Pettitt's Prize Medal Series".

"Peveril" Series   pre-1910
Tradename used by an unknown publisher who covered the Derbyshire/Nottinghamshire area. Coloured and R.P. views.

Pfaff
Pseudonym of an unidentified landscape painter.

Philco Publishing Co.   **fl. 1906-1934**

1-6 Holborn Place, London, W.C. Trademark "PPC" monogram in a rectangle with "Philco Series" below in a larger rectangle. Series included:

(i)   "Photogravure" sepia views of London.

(ii)   Tartan series of Scottish views.

(iii)   Facsims. of watercolour landscapes and hunting scenes.

(iv)   Glossy coloured views printed in Germany, sometimes overprinted with greetings.

(v)   "Philco Series" of framed photographs of domestic animals.

(vi)   P.P.s of actors, actresses and sportsmen.

(vii)   Black and white cat cards by Louis Wain.

(viii)   "Comic" Series by Donald McGill and others.

(ix)   Patriotic glamour cards during W.W.I.

(x)   Greetings cards which included sets of embossed cards printed in Germany and a "Photo Birthday Series" printed in Italy.

(xi)   "Faith, Hope and Charity". Philco seems to have made a speciality of these cards, publishing three different sets of three and two single cards displaying the three virtues. The symbols of the cross, anchor and heart feature largely.

(xii)   "The Lord's Prayer", set of six coloured embossed cards.

Phillimore, Reginald P.   **1855-1941**

Landscape painter who worked in oil and watercolour. Exh. R.A. 1. Born in Nottingham but spent a good deal of time with grandparents at Bridgnorth in Shropshire where he painted scenery for over 20 different facsims. Phillimore & Co. was set up in North Berwick, to which Phillimore moved soon after the turn of the century. The cards he published reveal his interest in history, i.e., Bass Rock, Dryburgh Abbey, Dunolly Castle, Fair Maid's House at Perth, Shakespeare's House at Stratford-upon-Avon and Mol's Coffee House in Exeter. Many of his cards are from a "Historical Series".

Ref: For check list see *Picture Postcard Collector's Gazette*, May and July 1975.

Phillips

Publisher, Pewsey, Wiltshire. "Pewsey Vale" Series of black and white local views.

Phillips, Albert

Photographer/publisher, Wells, Somerset. Local R.P. views. His negatives, photographs and postcards are preserved in the Wells Museum.

Phillips & Lees

Photographer/publisher, High St., Ilfracombe. R.P.s of passengers on the Bristol Channel paddle steamers, e.g. P.S. *Barry*.

Phillipson & Golder

Bookseller/publisher, Chester. Local R.P. views.

Philps

Photographer/publisher, Truro, Cornwall. "Philps Photo Series" of local views.

Phipson, E.A.   **fl. 1897-1910**

Worcester watercolour artist who painted town scenes as he imagined they might have appeared many years before, e.g. "The Commandery, Worcester", for J. Littlebury, and Small St., Bristol, for Salmon. He also painted views of the Welsh border country for L. Wilding & Son of Shrewsbury.

Illustration overleaf.

I'VE SEEN A RAILWAY LINE   AND I'VE SEEN A TRAMWAY LINE

I'VE SEEN A FISHING LINE

AND A CLOTHES LINE

BUT I'VE NEVER SEEN **A LINE FROM YOU**

Philco Publishing Co. *"I've Seen a Railway Line; and I've Seen a Tramway Line. I've Seen a Fishing Line and a Clothes Line. But I've Never Seen a Line From You".* Philco *"Comic" Series.*

Phoebus Studio   **pre-1905**

Publisher, Bradford on Avon. Local collotype views, e.g. Farleigh House, Farleigh Hungerford, Somerset.

"Phoenix Photo Series"

See: Brittain & Wright.

Phoenix Poultry Foods

Advertising cards by Walker, Harrison & Garthwaite.

Photochrom Co. Ltd.   **fl. from 1896**

Publisher, 121 Cheapside, London, later at Hosier Lane, Snow Hill and, by W.W.I., at 7-11 Old Bailey. Their Graphic Studios were at Tunbridge Wells, Kent. This firm, which became one of the major postcard publishers, was producing Christmas cards from 1896 and entered the postcard business c.1903 for none have been recorded with undivided backs. The postcard trademark varies. One consists of a bear and staff; another is the head of a bulldog; a third shows an art nouveau-style "P" and the words "All British Production"; a fourth "P. Co." within two concentric arches. Output included:

(i)   Rural scenes in colour, untitled.

(ii)   Named views in colour, "Exclusive Photo-Color Series".

(iii)   "Grano Series" of black and white views.

(iv)   "Sepiatone" Series, photographic views.

(v)   "Photogravure Series" and "Photogravure Velvet Finish" Series.

(vi)   "Carbofoto" Series, R.P. views.

(vii)   "Duotype Process" Series of views.

(viii)   "Wedgwood Series" of comic cards.

continued

Phipson, E.A. *"The Commandery, Worcester"*. Facsim. published by Joseph Littlebury.

(ix) "Lipton Series", coloured views advertising Lipton's Tea.
(x) "Celesque" Series which covered a wide range of subjects. Some are views, others are named sets such as "London Types", e.g. Chelsea Pensioner Recruiting Sergeant, etc.
(xi) "Famous Picture" and "Gallery Reproduction" Series.
(xii) "Agnes Richardson War Humour Series".
(xiii) "British Bulwarks", W.W.I. naval ships each described on the address side.
(xiv) "Lorna Doone" Series.
(xv) "Silhouette Series" and "Camp Silhouette Series", ill. Holt 372-4.
(xvi) Special Constable Series, silhouettes.
(xvii) Panoramic cards.
      Series nos. exceeded 44,000.
      See: Colour Plates 8 and 9.

"Photochromie"
Continental cards designed for the British market. Not to be confused with Photochrom Co. Ltd. cards.

Photographic Printing & Publishing Co.   fl. 1904-1921
Publisher, 24 London Rd., Croydon, Surrey. A firm known for coloured London views and for "The ABC Postcards" published in 1906. Each card carries a large letter in red and a coloured cartoon of an occupation for which this is the initial.
    Ref: Check list in P.P.A., 1982.

Photo-Precision Ltd.
Publisher, St. Albans, Hertfordshire. Trademark a Tudor rose. An "English Series" of coloured views.

Physical Culture
Rotary issued a series of cards titled "Ideal Physical Culture" of 12 exercises with photographs and instructions designed to banish obesity and improve health.

Pickford, Mary   1893-1979
Actress who appeared on the stage at the age of five, spent another 15 years as a stage actress and then started a film career in 1913. She made a film for the Biograph Company

under D.W. Griffiths and soon became a star of the silent film. In 1920 she married Douglas Fairbanks Sr. P.P. by Beagles, "Famous Cinema Stars Series", ill. Monahan 154.

Pickfords
Advertiser of their transport services. Early cards have been reprinted.

Pickles, L., & Co. Ltd.
Publisher, Bradford, Yorkshire.

Pictograph Publishing Co.   fl. c. 1919-1920
71 Lincoln's Inn Fields, London, W.C. This firm published postcards for a short period soon after W.W.I. They printed "Oilographs" to simulate oil paintings and produced a series of glamour cards with black backgrounds in an "Artistique" Series and a "Chick" Series of birthday cards.

Picton, Frank
Artist who designed comic cards for Bamforth's "Holiday Series".

"Pictorchrom"
See: Pictorial Stationery Co. Ltd.

Pictorial Centre   pre-1911
Publisher, 7 Grand Junction Rd., Brighton. Black and white and sepia views of the Brighton area printed in Germany. Issued over 50 sets.

Pictorial Postcard Co. Ltd.   fl. 1903-1908
Publisher, Red Lion Square, London. Cards were issued under the general title "Empire Series", sometimes abbreviated to E.S. They included:
(i) Comic cards by Donald McGill, among his earliest postcard designs.
(ii) "Pictorial Itinerary" cards.
(iii) P.P.s of actors and actresses.
(iv) Novelty cards.

Pictorial Postcard Syndicate   1898-1899
A few early court cards printed in Germany with London views were used by railway companies.
    Refs: R.O.P.L., No. 11, p. 22, and No. 16, p. 7.

Pictorial Stationery Co. Ltd.   fl. 1897-1914
Publisher. This firm moved premises several times but during its most active period was at 23 Moorfields, London. Trademark a peacock with feathers displayed on which "Peacock Brand" is printed. Production started with court-size cards printed in Holstein. Many types of card followed: "Autochrom Series", "Pictorchrom Post Cards", "Platino-Photo" cards and "Platino-Frosted" on which the surface resembled frost crystals on a window, "Stylochrom" cards, printed in Leipzig, and a "Black Frame" Series.

   Most of the firm's output consisted of views, either R.P.s or facsims. of paintings, e.g. Jotter painted scenes in Cornwall, Wales and Warwickshire. A few general series were also issued including "Bulwarks of Empire", "Familiar Figures of London", and some humorous cards by Kyd. The latest cards to be published coincided with the opening of the "New Gough's Caves" at Cheddar, Somerset, in 1908, for which some sepia cards were produced.

Picture Postcard Co. Ltd.   fl. 1899-1901
Publisher, 6 Draper's Gardens, London, E.C. This firm continued the business of the Pictorial Postcard Syndicate (q.v.),

Pictograph Publishing Co. *"Mickie"*. *Glamour card.*
"Artistique" Series.

reproducing view cards for the use of railway companies.

Ref: Details are given, with check list, in R.O.P.L., No. 11,
pp. 22-3.

In addition, five sets of Boer War cards were published in
1899, with views of places in the news, and portraits of
personalities involved in the war.

Ref: Greenwell, R., 'The Picture Postcard Company's Boer
War Cards', P.P.M., July 1983.

Picturegoer

Film magazine which published P.P.s of film stars.

Pictures Ltd.

85 Long Acre, London, W.C.2. Portraits of film actors and
actresses.

Pier Divers

Pier divers or "ornamental swimmers" gave displays on
seaside piers, diving from high poles, from the roof of a
pavilion, or at night with illumination. Cards record these
men, sometimes with a portrait inset. They called themselves
"Professor".

Ref: P.P.M., September 1982, p. 16.

Pierrots

These itinerant minstrels, with their whitened faces and loose
white clothing, provided summer seaside entertainment at
many resorts before and after W.W.I. The best known were
Catlin's Royal Pierrots. Cards show them entertaining crowds
on the beach at such towns as Bournemouth and Withernsea.

Piers and Pier Disasters

Piers originated as purpose-built jetties on which to land

Pierrots. *"Blackpool Pierrots"*. *Publisher unknown.*

passengers and cargoes at seaside resorts. They were soon used
as promenades and in Edwardian times became pleasure piers
with pavilions for dancing and entertainment. They are now
decreasing in number as the cost of restoration becomes pro-
hibitive. The old picture postcards of piers have, therefore,
become historic documents showing the changes that took
place over the years, even on a single pier. Some were
lengthened, pavilions were built or rebuilt.

Unfortunately seaside piers were vulnerable. Some suffered
damage in ship collisions, others in violent storms, but perhaps
the most common disasters resulted from fire for many piers
were built, at least in part, of timber. A list of pre-1939
disasters, most of them recorded on postcards, is given below:

Aberystwyth, storm damage, 1938.
Bangor, ship collision, 1914.
Blackpool, North Pier fires, 1921 and 1938.
Brighton, Chain Pier destroyed by storm, 1896, shortly be-
fore demolition.
Cleethorpes, fire, 1903.
Colwyn Bay, pavilion fires, 1922 and 1933.
Great Yarmouth, Britannia Pier pavilion fires, 1909 and
1914; ballroom fire, 1932.
Hastings, pavilion fire, 1917.
Herne Bay, fires, 1910 and 1928.
Hunstanton, pavilion fire, 1939.
Lytham St. Anne's, ship collision, 1903; pavilion fire, 1927;
storm damage, 1937.
Morecambe, Central Pier, pavilion fires, 1933. West End
Pier, pavilion fires, 1903, 1917; storm damage, 1903 and
1927.
Paignton, pavilion fire, 1919.
Penarth, fire, 1931.
Ramsgate, fire and ship collision, 1917; mine damage, 1918.
Redcar, ship collision, 1898; fire, 1909.
Rhyl, pavilion fire, 1901.
Saltburn, storm damage, 1900, 1924 and 1930.
Scarborough, destroyed by storm, 1905.
Shanklin, pavilion fire, 1927.
Skegness, ship collision, 1919.
Southbourne, destroyed by storm, 1900-1.
Southend, ship collisions, 1907, 1908 and 1921.

continued

Southport, storm damage, 1889; fires, 1897 and 1933.
Southsea, South Parade, fire, 1904.
Teignmouth, storm damage, 1904 and 1908.
Worthing, storm damage, 1913; fire 1933.

A Pier Postcard Collector's Circle exists to promote interest in this specialist field.

Refs: Adamson, S.H., *Seaside Piers,* 1977; an article on 'Seaside Piers and Disasters', P.P.A., 1984, p. 48, gives further details of disasters.

Piffard, Harold H.　　　　　　　**fl.c. 1895-1907**
Military painter. Exh. R.A. 4. Designed cards for Gale & Polden and for A.V.N. Jones.

Pike, Joseph　　　　　　　　**fl. c.1895-1910**
Landscape and coastal artist who painted for Millar & Lang. Exh. R.A. 1. Worked at Addison Studios, Kensington, London.

Pike, Sidney　　　　　　　　　**fl. 1880-1907**
Landscape painter. Exh. R.A. 22. "Picturesque Counties" set on "Surrey" for Tuck.

Pike, W.T., & Co.　　　　　　　**pre-1906**
Photographer/publisher. Black and white views.

Pilkington, Flora　　　　　　　**fl. 1887-1918**
Painter of "Old English Flower Gardens", Medici Society.

Pilligrini, C.
Artist who painted winter sports scenes in Switzerland. Facsims. by Vonga et Cie of Geneva imported into Britain.

"Pinch & Squeak"
See Squeakers under Novelty Cards.

Pinchbeck, Charles Robert　　　　**fl. c.1908**
Publisher, West Park Studio, Hull, Yorkshire. "C.P." Series of humorous cards, using various pseudonyms. He also designed a few novelty cards.

Pinder, Grace
Actress. Dual P.P. by Davidson Bros.

Ping-Pong
The name given to table tennis when the game was introduced in 1899. For about five years it was a popular craze and was then played very little until the 1920s. A revival led to the formation of the English Table Tennis Association in 1927. A number of publishers, e.g. Galyons, published humorous Ping-Pong cards at the height of the early craze. Dobbs, Kidd & Co. issued a "Ping-Pong" Series.

Pinhay, Edith
Landscape artist who painted scenes in Burma for Tuck's "Wide Wide World" Series.

Pinkawa, Anton
Art nouveau artist noted for a series on the "Seasons".

Pipe and Drum Bands
These bands flourish in Scotland as brass bands do in England. A card of the Aberfeldy Pipe Band is ill. Hill, p. 58.

Piper, George
Designer of comic cards with children for the City Post Card Co.

Piper, T.
Publisher, Carisbrooke, I.O.W. Local views.

"Piper's Bazaar Series"
White framed R.P.s of Oxford.

Pirkis, Albert George
Artist who painted two types of card for Hildesheimer:
(i) Write-away style cards depicting the hazards of cycling and motoring.
(ii) London views including a "London by Twilight" Series.

Pitcher, Arthur H.　　　　　　　**pre-1919**
Photographer/publisher, College Court, Gloucester. Local R.P. sepia views.

Pitcher, S.A.
Successor to above. He also reproduced oil paintings from the Municipal Gallery, Cheltenham.

Pitkeathly Table Water
Schweppes advertising card for waters from a natural spring at Bridge of Earn, Perthshire. It shows Princes St., Edinburgh, with a kilted Scottish soldier, his eye on a fashionable young lady.

"Pixie Series"
Published by Durie Brown & Co., Edinburgh (q.v.). Black and white views of the city.

"Play Pictorial"
The source of some photographs used in Tuck's "Book-marker" Series.

Playing Cards
Playing cards appear on postcards by Stewart & Woolf and by J. Welch.

P.M. & Co.
Pascalis, Moss & Co. (q.v.).

Pocock, Ralph Noel
Designer of cards for P. Lancaster & Co. of Tunbridge Wells, e.g. "Told to the Marines".

Pointer, T.
Stationer/publisher, The Square, Birchington, Kent. Black and white local views.

Police
Cards reflecting the work of the police range from the single policeman on guard or on the beat, to the group of policemen controlling a crowd or on special duties, e.g. at the Sydney Street siege of 1909.

Inevitably, there are also comic police cards.

Illustration overleaf.

Political Cartoons
Albert Ludovici designed a number of cartoons for Davidson Bros., e.g. Mr. Chamberlain at Glasgow, Lord Rosebery at Sheffield, "Political Dances", "Fiscal Games". Harry Furniss's "Free Trade" cartoons were used by John Walker.

Politicians
P.P.s of leading politicians include:

H.H. Asquith.	Sir Wilfred Lawson.
Sir Henry Campbell-Bannerman.	David Lloyd George.
Austen Chamberlain.	James Ramsay Macdonald.
Joseph Chamberlain.	James O'Grady.
Winston Churchill.	Lord Rhondda.
Sir Edward Grey.	

A number of cards, clearly intended as election propaganda, were issued with portraits of Members of Parliament.

Piers. *"Clevedon. The Pier"*. *Pictorial Stationery Co.* *"Pictorchrom"*. *P.U. 1907.*

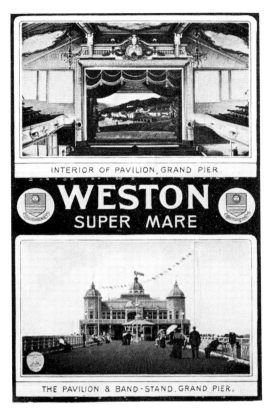

Piers. *"Weston Super Mare"*. *The Grand Pier Pavilion.* *Woolstone Bros. Milton "Chromolette."*

Pier Disasters. *"The Pier, Morecambe, After the Storm"*. *William Ritchie & Sons. "Reliable Series".*

Pier Disasters. *"West End Pier, Morecambe, After the Fire"*. *Sanbride. Photo by Rudd of Morecambe.*

Pollard, E. & G.
Publisher, Oldham, Lancashire. Coloured local views.

Pollard, William, & Co.   **pre-1905**
Publisher, Exeter, Devon. Devonshire views.

Pope, Dorothy Travers
Animal artist who painted a series titled "Our Dogs" for Misch & Co.

Popini
Art nouveau artist who designed a set of girls of all classes, sold by Pascalis, Moss & Co., e.g. "The Sporting Girl".

Popp, Jacob I.   **c.1906**
Publisher, High Wycombe, Buckinghamshire. Newsagent and tobacconist with a single obsession: he wished to open his shop on a Sunday. The police continually brought him to court where he was fined. Realising the publicity value he issued a postcard series titled "J.I. Popp's High Wycombe Persecution Series" with humorous drawings and verses. He also issued cards of his shop.
Ref: Byatt p.208.

Port Sunlight
See: Lever Bros. Ltd.

Porter, R.G.
Photographer/publisher, Aberdeen. Issued many cards for the Great North of Scotland Railway.
Ref: R.O.P.L., No. 12, for list of over 70 views.

Porter, T.E.
Publisher, The Arcade, Sandown, I.O.W. Produced cards described as "The Isle of Wight Curiosity arranged with Sands from the Coloured Cliffs of Alum Bay". The pictures on these cards are built up from fine coloured sand.

Portpatrick & Wigtownshire Joint Railway
Publisher of views, many using photographs by Baird of Belfast.
Ref: The series of roughly 100 cards is partially listed in R.O.P.L., No. 12, pp. 15-17.

Portsmouth Postcard Publishers   **pre-1909**
65 Kingston Rd., Portsmouth. South coast photographic views, plate marked on cream surface paper.

Post Office
Publishers. The first picture postcard of 1891 was of the Royal Naval Exhibition, London, and the second was of the Gardening and Forestry Exhibition of 1893.

Post Offices
Cards range from village post offices to the General Post Office buildings in large cities. The cards are regarded as more attractive if postmen or postal vans are to be seen.

Postage Rates
The inland rate for a picture postcard delivery varied as follows:
1 September 1894 to 3 June 1918 ½d.
4 June 1918 to 13 June 1921 1d.
14 June 1921 to 24 May 1922 1½d.
25 May 1922 to 1 May 1940 1d.

Postage Stamps
Postmarks are extremely useful in helping to date a postcard but the dates are not always clearly visible. Some help, however, may be given by studying the stamp. The following

"THE BATTLE OF STEPNEY": *Mr Winston Churchill in the Fire Zone*

Police. *"The Battle of Stepney. Mr. Winston Churchill in the Fire Zone".* Valentine.

stamps were used on postcards between 1894 and 1939:
Halfpenny Stamps
1 January 1887-1900, Queen Victoria, vermilion.
17 April, 1900-1, Queen Victoria, blue-green.
1 January, 1902-4, Edward VII, blue-green.
26 November, 1904-11, Edward VII, yellow-green.
22 June – 31 December, 1911, George V, various shades of green; three-quarter head.
1 January, 1912-18, George V, green.
Penny Stamps
1918-34, George V, various shades of red, rose and vermilion.
1934-6, George V, scarlet with dark background.
1936-7, Edward VIII, scarlet.
1937-41, George VI, scarlet.

Postal Slogans
Postmarks with slogans and advertisements of events began to appear in the 1920s, e.g. the Pageant of Empire at Wembley, 1924. Publicity for telephones provided many slogans.
See: Telephones.

Postcard Machines
Black and white views of the Royal Victoria Pavilion and Ellington Park, Ramsgate, pre-1918, display the words "Elite Pictorial Postcard Machine". Postcards were certainly dispensed from automatic coin-in-the-slot machines in Edwardian times. They were marketed by P. Lancaster & Co. of Tunbridge Wells.

Posters
Advertising posters pasted on hoardings and display boards were already common in Edwardian times. Many of these lent themselves to reduction and reproduction as postcards. Tuck, for example, produced a series of "Celebrated Posters" by such artists as John Hassall, and famous French poster artists such as Alphonse Mucha had their work reproduced on postcards. Such cards are keenly sought.
Theatre poster advertisements were reproduced on postcards by David Allen.
Ref: A check list of theatre poster advertisements is given by Byatt pp. 339-40.

Post Offices. *"General Post Office, Hull"*. Valentine.

Post Offices. *"Malvern: St. Ann's Well"*. R. Tuck & Sons. *"Town and City"* Series.

Postmark Abbreviations
A.P.O., Army Post Office.
B.F.P.O., British Forces Post Office.
D.L.O., Dead Letter Office.
D.O., Delivery Office.
M.P.O., Military Post Office.
R.A.F.P.O., Royal Air Force Post Office.
R.S.O., Railway Sorting Office.
S.O., Sorting Office.
T.P.O., Travelling Post Office.

Postmen
A number of publishers issued cards of postmen, including:
(i)   E. Blackwell, "Penny Post" Series.
(ii) Pascalis, Moss & Co., "The Post in all Nations".
(iii) Pictorial Stationery Co., "Familiar Figures of London" includes a postman.
(iv) Tuck, "The Postman in Town and Country".

Potter & Moore Lavender Water
Advertising card. Girl in garden.

Pounds, Courtice   **1862-1927**
Actor and vocalist. P.P. by Rotary.

Pounds, Louie
Actress. First stage appearance in 1890. P.P.s by Beagles, Rotary.

Pouteau, Ernest   **c.1903**
Railway postcard publisher, 231a Gray's Inn Rd., London, W.C. Despite the rather pretentious title only two railway sets have been recorded. They bear the trademark "E.P." within an art nouveau-style line frame. The sets are of the Great Northern Railway and the London & South Western Railway. He also issued comic cards, some of which he designed.

P.P. Co.
These initials can be those of the Pastel Publishing Co. or the Pictograph Publishing Co. (qq.v.).

P.P. & P. Co.
Photographic Printing and Publishing Co. (q.v.).

Post Offices. *"The Post Office & Langton Court Road, St. Anne's"* [Bristol]. W.H. Smith & Son. P.U. 1916.

Praeger, Sophia Rosamund   **fl. 1891-1940**
Painter, sculptor and illustrator of Co. Down, Ireland. Exh. R.A. 9. Designed comic children's cards for McCaw, Stevenson & Orr of Belfast.

Pratt, G.A.
Publisher and nautical bookseller, Southampton, Hampshire. Photographs of naval ships.

Pratt's Ethyl Petrol
Advertising card with Malcolm Campbell's *Bluebird* and his inset portrait.

Premier Bicycles   **pre-1904**
Advertising cards supplied by David Allen. Ill. D. & M. 165.

Premier Photographic Co.   **pre-1913**
Publisher, Ely Works, 33 Gladstone Rd., Croydon, Surrey. Views of the Crystal Palace.

Pressland, Annie L.   **fl. 1892-1923**
Watercolour artist noted for flower paintings and garden scenes. Facsims. of garden scenes by Salmon and Tuck.

Preston, Chloe   **fl. 1920s**
Designer of children's cards in the 1920s for Humphrey Milford, and a "Chloe Preston Series" for Valentine. She invented the "Peek-a-Boos". Ill. Cope p. 52, and Monahan 169.

Price, A.L., & Sons
Publisher, New St., Lancaster. Facsims. of local landscapes by R.E. Rampling.

Price, C.H.   **pre-1915**
Photographer/publisher, 36 George St., Croydon, Surrey. Local R.P. views. Serial nos. to over 20,000.

Price, Frank Corbyn, R.B.A.   **fl. 1888-1933**
Landscape painter. Exh. R.A. 10. Designed a set of "Gem Scenery" for Tuck.

Price, John, & Sons
Publisher, Bilston, Staffordshire. Local coloured views, e.g. The Crooked House at Hemley (270), Black Country industry, canals, etc. The firm also supplied other publishers.

Price, Nancy   **1880-1970**
Actress. Stage career covered the period 1900-35. Published *Shadows on the Hills*, 1935.

Price's Patent Candle Co. Ltd.
Advertising cards. These are postcard-size trade cards, the reverse side filled with printed matter. They consist of coloured battle scenes, each with an inset commander or general. Battles include:
　　Spanish Armada, 1588.
　　Blake and Van Tromp, 1652-3.
　　Battle of Plessey, 1757.
　　Glorious 1st June, 1797.
　　Battle of the Nile, 1798.
　　Trafalgar, 1805.
　　Waterloo, 1815.
　　Balaclava, 1854.
　　Lucknow, Indian Mutiny, 1857.
　　Bombardment of Alexandra, 1882.
　　Kassussin, Egyptian War, 1882.
　　Paardeberg, Boer War, 1900.
These cards advertise on the reverse a range of products which include candles, glycerine, household soap, lighting tapers, motor and cycle lubricants, nightlights and toilet soaps. Nursery rhyme cards and cards for the 1905 Earls Court Exhibition were also produced.
　　Ref: Cole, D., 'Price's Patent Candle Company', P.P.M., December 1983, p. 6.

Prince of Wales
The Prince of Wales, who was Edward VIII from 20 January to 10 December, 1936, was probably photographed more than any other member of the Royal Family. Tuck published a "Real Photograph" Series, each card with a biographical paragraph and a full description of the photograph. Beagles photographed the Prince in the robes of the Order of the Garter at the Coronation of George V and Queen Mary and in at least half-a-dozen other poses; D. Knight's Whittome in his investiture and other ceremonial robes; the Crown Publishing Co. issued an artist's impression of him as "H.M. King in Coronation Robes — May, 1937", a card which proved to be premature.

"Proverbs". *"A Place for Everything and Everything in its Place". Staged photograph by J. Welch & Sons. P.U. 1905.*

"Princess Series"
Photographs of Shrewsbury by "R.M. & S."

Prisoner of War Fund
Some cards, otherwise unmarked, carry a rubber stamp "Lady Good's Prisoner of War Fund". They shows prisoners in camp in Switzerland, after release, and the monument erected in memory of the prisoners of war who died in captivity at Gressen. Christmas cards which could be sent from prisoner of war camps, such as Ruhleben bei Spandau, were also issued.

Prisons and Prisoners
These are not common subjects but Valentine published a view of "Convicts Proceeding to Work" at Portland, Dorset.

"Prize Crop" Cigarettes
Advertisement cards by Mitchell. Vignettes issued at Glasgow Exhibition of 1901.

Processions
These are usually seen in photographs by local photographers. Examples include:
　　Guy Fawkes Procession, Lewes High Street.
　　Whit Friday Procession, Crompton, Lancashire.
　　1911 Coronation Day Procession, Leslie, Fife, ill. Hill, p.78.

Proctor, Adam Edwin, R.B.A., R.I., R.O.I.   **1864-1913**
Landscape and figure painter. Exh. R.A. 34. He designed "The A.B.C. Postcards" for the Photographic Printing & Publishing Co. For each letter he painted a character study, e.g. D for Dutchman, Q for Quaker.
　　Ref: Complete list in Byatt p. 204.

Proof Sets
Raphael Tuck & Sons issued special editions of some of their cards in proof sets. These were designed for keen collectors in limited first printings. Each card is gold-edged and carries the word "Proof". A certificate was issued with each set.
　　Ref: A check list of 50 proof sets is given in S.G.P.C., 1983, pp. 226-7.

Protheroe

Photographer, Bristol. Took portraits of pantomime stars at the Princes Theatre, Bristol, for W.H. Smith & Son.

"Proverbs"

Trichromatic cards by J. Welch & Sons based on staged photographs. The word "Proverbs" appears on the face of each card. The proverb illustrated is also captioned.

Public Benefit Boot Company

Advertising cards. Trademark "Lennards". Card with small boy flying a biplane over London. The question is asked: "How soon will it be possible for your boots and shoes to be delivered by aeroplane?"

Public Parks

These are mainly of interest when they show recreational activities, e.g. children playing games or people boating on a lake.

Pull-out Cards

See: Novelty Cards.

Pulman, George, & Sons Ltd.

Publisher. A bookseller who issued sets of cards during W.W.I., including "Military Terms", a "Quaint Series" and "Raemaekers' War Cartoons".

See: Louis Raemaekers.

Purcell & Co. 1902

Publisher, 124 Patrick St., Cork, Ireland. Facsims. of paintings by John Gilbert of scenes in the south west of Ireland. He also designed cards for the Cork Exhibition of 1902.

Purcell, Annie

Actress. P.P. by Millar & Lang, "National Series".

Purdie pre-1915

Photographer/publisher, Sidmouth, Devon. Local R.P.s of fishermen at work, e.g. The Herring Haul.

Pyp. *"Strangers Yet"*. Facsim. by Davidson Bros. P.U. 1906.

Purser, Phyllis

Artist who painted W.W.I. comic cards with children.

Puzzle Post Card Co. . pre-1910

Publisher, Bedford Chambers, Princetown St., Holborn, London, W.C. A single postcard has been noted. It is described by Byatt p. 226.

P.V.B.

Percy V. Bradshaw (q.v.).

Pyp

An unknown artist who designed comic cartoons used by Davidson Bros.

Quaker Oats   pre-1904
Advertising cards reproducing posters, e.g. "Smiles" Series with Cook, Grandpa, Postman, Sailor or Tramp. Other cards show a waiter with a bowl of "Quaker Oats".

Quarries
Examples include the Cheese Wring Granite Quarries in Cornwall and the Bethesda Slate Quarries in Carnarvonshire.

Quatremain, William W.   fl. c.1906-1919
Stratford-upon-Avon artist who painted many scenes in and around the town for Salmon. He particularly favoured interiors. Also worked in the Isle of Wight for the same publisher.

"Queen Series"
See: Taylor, Thomas, & Son (q.v.).

Queen Victoria
See: Diamond Jubilee; In Memoriam Cards; Royalty: British.

Queen's Dolls' House
This house, designed by Edwin Lutyens, was a star feature at the British Empire Exhibition, 1924. Six sets of cards were published by Tuck, 4,500 – 5, each with eight cards. These were sold in a brown album, the cards mounted so that the text on the reverse could also be read. The albums were boxed.

Quinnell, Cecil Watson, R.B.A., R.M.S.   1868-1932
Portrait painter born and educated in India. He took up painting in 1890, having resigned his army commission. Was Hon. Sec. of the Royal Miniature Society 1897-1916. Designed cards of glamorous ladies for Davidson Bros. A poster card by Quinnell titled "The Glad Eye" was published by David Allen.

Quinton, Alfred Robert   1853-1934
Probably the best known of all postcard artists. Exh. R.A. 20. Illustrated many books and offered watercolours for sale. Several of his pictures were bought at Selfridges by Salmon and arrangements were made to reproduce these as postcards. Thereafter Quinton accepted commissions to paint views along the south coast and in the southern counties, though he sometimes went further afield. Between 1912 and his death he painted over 2,000 scenes. He was particularly successful in reflecting the character of rural life. Quinton's postcards were reprinted many times, certainly into the 1950s. Later cards bear the words "Trade Mark" below the outline of the salmon on a line.

Quinton also painted for Faulkner, McKenzie and Tuck. There is an A.R. Quinton Society to collate information about this artist.

See: Colour Plate 21.

Ref: A brief life, with reproductions of some of his finest postcard paintings, was published by Salmon in 1978 as *The England of A.R. Quinton.*

Quatremain, W.W. *"Best Room: Anne Hathaway's Cottage, Stratford-on-Avon". Facsim. by J. Salmon.*

Quatremain, W.W. *"Bedroom: Anne Hathaway's Cottage, Stratford-on-Avon". Facsim by J. Salmon.*

"Picturesque Co. Antrim. Glenarm Castle". R. Tuck & Sons. "Oilette" "The Emerald Isle".

"Coverack, Cornwall". R. Tuck & Sons. "Oilette". U.B.

"An Old-World Nook, Deal, Kent". R. Tuck & Sons. "Oilette' "Picturesque Counties — Kent". P.U. 1919.

211

Quinnell, Cecil Watson. *Glamour card. Davidson Bros. P.U. 1910.*

Quinton, Alfred Robert. *"College Barges, Folly Bridge. Oxford". J. Salmon. P.U. 1918.*

Quinton, F.E.
Landscape artist who worked for Salmon. Scenes include "The Harbour, St. Ives."

Quinton, H.
Publisher, 10 Clifford Gardens, Kensal Rise, London, N.W.1. A printed card has been noted called "Love Ration" in imitation of the food ration books of W.W.I.

Quinton, Harry
Designer of comic cards.

R

R. & Co.
Richardson & Co. (q.v.).

Racecourses
Idealised views of racecourses in facsims. of racing paintings are relatively common but photographs of actual racecourses are more difficult to find. Examples have been noted of Chester, Doncaster, Newbury, Newmarket and Haydock Park.

See: Horse Racing and Racehorses.

Radermacher, Aldous & Co.
See: R.A. Publishing Co.

Raemaekers, Louis   1868-1956
Dutch political cartoonist who was director of a drawing school in Holland. He drew powerful cartoons during W.W.I. condemning alleged German atrocities. They were published in book form by Hodder & Stoughton and used on postcards by George Pulman & Sons.

Railway Disasters
Views of railway accidents have usually been taken by local photographers able to get to the scene quickly. However, some photographers, notably Gothard, often travelled long distances as soon as they heard of a disaster. The following have been recorded on postcards:

Arbroath, Elliot Junction, Edinburgh Express, collision in snow, 1906.
Burntisland, 14 April, 1914, Gothard.
Carr Bridge, collapse of bridge, 1914.

Colchester, 12 July, 1913, Gothard.
Cudworth, nr. Barnsley, Yorkshire, Scottish Express crashed in fog, 19 January, 1905, Gothard.
Ebbw Vale Junction, Great Western train, 28 September 1907.
Felling, nr. Newcastle, East Coast Express.

continued

Railway Disasters. *"The Railway Disaster at Salisbury, July, 1st, 1906".* F. Futcher, Salisbury. P.U. 1906.

Racecourses. *"Racecourse and Grand Stand, Newmarket".* Sherborn Photo. P.U. 1904.

Railway Disasters. *"Wreck of the Cromer Express, G.E.R. at Witham. Sep. lst. 1905".* Fred Spalding, Chelmsford. P.U. 1905.

213

Colour Plate 18: Donald McGill cards

"Just a Lion (Line) To Let You Know That I'm Having a Howling Time". Joseph Asher & Co. P.U. 1912.

"Advice To Girls About To Marry...". Woolstone Bros. P.U. 1920.

"The War'll Be Over in a Fortnight Now...". Caption also in French. Inter-Art "Comique Series". P.U. 1917.

Grantham, Great Northern train derailed at speed, 1906, Locomotive Publishing Co.

Hawes Junction, collision and fire, 1910.

Maesglas, Newport, September 1907.

Penistone, 1916, Gothard.

Quintinshill, nr. Carlisle, Caledonian Railway troop train collision and fire, 1915.

Saddleworth, 10 August, 1909, Gothard.

Salisbury, boat train derailment at speed, 1 July 1906, F. Futcher; Ingram, Clark & Co.

Sharnbrook, 4 February, 1909, Gothard and Sweetland.

Sheffield, 1908, Gothard.

Shippea Hill, nr. Ely, Norwich Express, 7 April, 1906, T. Bolton.

Shrewsbury, L.N.W.R. derailment at speed, 1907, J.R. Crosse, R. Hodges & Co. and H.M. Camburn & Co.

Stoat's Nest, Brighton Express, 29 January, 1910, Batchelder and Gothard.

Tonbridge Junction, 5 March, 1909, Gothard.

Witham, derailment of G.E.R. Cromer Express, 1905, Dysart & Co., and Fred Spalding, both of Chelmsford.

Wombwell, Yorkshire, Great Central, 13 December, 1911.

Woodhouse Junction, 29 February, 1908, Gothard.

Railway Hotels

The major railway companies maintained hotels, usually close to a railway station.

Ref: Full listings in R.O.P.Ls.

Railway Stations

Photographs of railway stations, especially those on lines that have now been closed, are keenly sought. Paintings were made of some of the larger London stations which have been produced in facsims., e.g. King's Cross, Liverpool St., Marylebone, Paddington and Waterloo, all ill. D. & M. 139-43.

Illustrations overleaf.

Railways

Three keen collectors, John Alsop, Brian Hilton and Ian Wright, have pooled the results of years of research to produce details of official railway postcards. These "Railway Official Postcard Lists" cover the following:

Caledonian, Callander & Oban Railway Companies

Furness Railway Company.

Great Central and Great Northern Railway Companies.

Great Eastern Railway Company.

Great Western Railway Company.

Highland, Invergarry & Fort Augustus, Wick & Lybster Railway Companies.

Hull & Barnsley: North Eastern; East Coast Route.

Irish and Isle of Man Railway Companies.

Lancashire & Yorkshire Railway Company.

London & North Western Railway Company.

London Underground Railways.

Midland Railway Company.

continued

Railway Hotels. *"North Western Hotel, Liverpool".* *Produced by R. Tuck & Sons. P.U. 1926.*

Railway Hotels. *"St. Enoch Station Hotel, Glasgow".* *Glasgow & South Western Railway. Produced by R. Tuck & Sons. U.B. P.U. 1904.*

Railway Hotels. *"Midland Hotel Manchester, Entrance".* An *official Midland Railway vignette.*

215

Railway Stations. *"Brighton Station"*. *Valentine's Series.*

Railway Stations. *"Woodhall Spa Railway Station"*. *Photochrom.*

Minor English Railways.
Minor Scottish Railway Companies.
North British and West Highland Railway Companies.
North Staffordshire Railway.
Post-Grouping: L.M.S., L.N.E.R., S.R.
Pre-Grouping Southern Railway Companies.
Welsh Railway Company — Barry; Cambrian; Corris, Snowdon Mountain Tramroad; Vale of Rheidol.
See: Colour Plate 22.
Refs: Several of the railways are mentioned briefly under their separate titles in this dictionary but those who require full check lists are referred to R.O.P.L.; Ellis, H., *British Railway History, 1847-1947*, 1959.

Raleigh Cycles
Advertising cards of "The All-Steel Bicycle" Nottingham. View of negro on bicycle outpacing a lion which follows him. This was also issued on the reverse of a record card which gave the portrait of the company chairman, Sir Harold Bowden.

Railway Stations. *"Leytonstone Railway Station (G.E.R.)"*. *W.A.C. & Co. P.U. 1906.*

Railway Stations. *"Newbury Station"*. *Valentine's Series. P.U. 1908.*

Railways. *"The Glasgow to Euston Express, Caledonian Railway"*. *R. Tuck & Sons. "Oilette". "Famous Expresses" Series X.*

216

Ralph & Co.
Photographer. Portraits of actresses.

Ralston, William   fl. 1902-1911
Artist/publisher, 34 Gray St., Sandyford, Glasgow. Ralston issued 12 of his own humorous cards.
   Ref: Check list in Byatt p. 227.

Ralston, William, Ltd.   fl. 1911-c.1932
Publisher who continued to use William Ralston's name after his death in 1911. They issued a "Ralston Series" of photographic views of Scotland.

Rambler
Pseudonym of an unknown artist.

Ramell, F.M.
Publisher, Sittingbourne, Kent. Local sepia views.

Rampling, Reginald E.   c.1836-1909
Lancaster watercolour landscape painter whose work was published in facsim. by A.L. Price & Sons, a Lancaster firm. Examples may be seen in the Lancaster Museum. Rampling also painted some scenes for Ruddock's "Artist Series".

Ramsey, George S.   fl. c.1896-1921
Landscape painter. Exh. R.A. 5. Facsims. of oil paintings of views in the Leicester area were used by M. Childeric in a "Wyvern Series". He also painted scenes for a "Peakland Series" (Derbyshire) and a "North Wales" Series.

Ramsey, M.A.
Poster artist whose work was included in Tuck's "Celebrated Posters" Series.

Randall, W.
Publisher, Peel St., Barnsley, Yorkshire. Issued photographs of the Barnsley Football team.

Rankin, Andrew Scott   fl. 1891-1940
Animal and landscape artist who lived in Perthshire. Exh. R.A. 3. Painted a set titled "Crofter Scenes in the Highlands" for George Stewart & Co.

Rankin, George
Watercolour painter of animals. Designed cards with birds, horses and wild animals for Salmon. A. & C. Black published his illustrations for Aylmer Maxwell's *Pheasants and Covert Shooting* as postcards. He painted a set of "British Game Birds" for Tuck and of dogs for Gottschalk, Dreyfus and Davis.

R.A.P. Co.
Regal Art Publishing Co. (q.v.).

R.A. Publishing Co.   pre-1914
Publisher, Radermacher, Aldous & Co., 56 Ludgate Hill, London, E.C. Trademarks "R.A. Series" in an oval frame with ribboned bells and the words: "The Seal of Artistic Excellence". Some have "British Excellence" with "Printed in England" on a ribbon dividing the card.

The company supplied cards to many small retailers and printed their customer's name as the publisher. For example, a coloured matt-surfaced card of Rosemarkie in Scotland carried the R.A. trademark but also states: "Published by M. MacGillivray, The Stores, Rosemarkie".

In addition to photographic views, facsims. of landscape paintings and black and white drawings were also published. A special "Postcard History of the War" was published during W.W.I.

Towards the end of the 1930s the name R.A. (Postcards) Ltd. was used.

Illustration overleaf.

Rampling, Reginald E. *"Weir at Halton". Facsim. by A.L. Price & Sons, Lancaster.*

Rankin, George. *"Zebra". Facsim. by J. Salmon.*

R.A. Publishing Co. *Trademark of Radermacher, Aldous & Co. on a card published by J. Cunningham of Brora.*

Rapid Photo Printing Co. Ltd.   **fl. 1901-1910**
Publisher, Dashwood House, New Broad St., London, E.C., and after 1905 at 4 and 5 Bridgwater Sq., Barbican, London, E.C. Trademark an arrow through the word "RAPID" with a swallow in flight on either side. The output was entirely of photographic cards and the range included:
(i)   P.P.s of actors and actresses.
(ii)   P.P.s of other public figures including royalty.
(iii)   "Cameo" Series of embossed cards.
(iv)   "Song Series".
(v)   "Nation's Pictures", a gallery picture series.
(vi)   Animal photographs, especially cats.
(vii)   Photographs of children.
(viii)   Greetings cards.

Rathbone, M.M.
Photographer/publisher, Woolwich. Local R.P. views.

Rattle & Co.
Publisher, Military Stores, Portsmouth, Hampshire. R.P. Christmas and New Year regimental cards.

Rattray   **pre-1909**
Publisher, Aberdeen. "Photo-and-Arms" Series. Trademark "R" within a triangle.

Rauh, Ludwig
Artist who specialised in glamour.

Ravenglass & Eskdale Railway
Bamforth R.P. shows this railway with a train carrying passengers in open trucks.

Raven-Hill, Leonard, R.W.A.   **1867-1942**
Painter, illustrator and cartoonist. Exh. R.A. 8. Started to draw for *Punch* in 1896, joined the *Punch* Table in 1901, became their political cartoonist in 1910 and continued with the paper until 1935. Illustrated Kipling's *Kipps* and *Stalky & Co.* Jarrold & Sons published a postcard set of his black and white vignettes on a yellow ground titled "For Friendship and

Honour". Tuck used black and white drawings which were coloured for postcard publication and Wrench included some of his drawings in "Pictures from *Punch*".

Ray, Gabrielle   **1883-1973**
Actress at the Gaiety Theatre who became "the most popular of the picture postcard beauties." P.P.s by Beagles; Davidson; Millar & Lang; Misch & Co.; Philco; Rotary, ill. Hill p. 22; Valentine.
    Ref: Loton, G., P.P.M. December 1983, p.30.

Ray, Ruby
Actress. P.P.s by Dunn and by Philco.

Ray, Thelma
Actress. P.P. by Rotophot.

Rechabites, Independent Order of
Early greetings card of poster type.

Reckitt's
Card advertising Reckitt's Blue and Reckitt's Starch.

Red Indians
Sets by Hildesheimer, 5431, and Tuck, 9011 and 9131.

Redjeb, Percy   **1909**
Photographer, "Bromide Printer" and publisher, Boreham Wood, Hertfordshire. Photographic cards including greetings, and children, usually framed, which often appear only under "The Shenley Real Photo Post Card" tradename. He also published a "Calendar" card.
    See Calendar Cards under Novelty Cards.

Redman, A.C., & Co.
Publisher, Southsea, Hampshire. Framed views and a "Spithead Series" of comic cards.

Reed, Edward Tennyson   **c.1860-1933**
Artist who worked for *Punch*. Wrench published his skits on life in a series titled "Prehistoric Peeps".

Rees, Hugh, Ltd.   **pre-1912**
Bookseller/publisher, 5 and 7 Regent St., London, S.W.1. Known for a series of six sets of cards on war ribbons and decorations designed by Commander E. Kidner, R.N.

Reeve, Ada   **1876-1966**
Actress. First appeared on London stage as a child in 1883. Her long career included pantomime and variety. P.P.s by Beagles, Regent Publishing Co., and Rotary.

Reeves   **pre-1937**
Photographer/publisher, Lewes, Sussex. Local R.P. views.

Regal Art Publishing Co.   **1903**
Publisher, 9 Long Lane, Aldersgate St., London, E.C. Trademark a lady with an artist's palette bearing the tradename "Rapco". Output included:
(i)   Coloured views of London.
(ii)   Glamour cards.
(iii)   Facsims. of paintings of English counties by such artists as E.D. Percival.

Regent Fine Art Co. Ltd.
Publisher, Belfast.

Regent Portraits Ltd.
Photographer/publisher, 15 Leicester Sq., London, W.C.2.

Regent Publishing Co. Ltd.   **fl. c.1906-1925**
Publisher, 310 Euston Rd., London, N.W. The earliest cards

were issued under the title "Prince Regent Series" and carried the letters R.F.H. for R.F. Hunger, the owner. The trademark was the figure of the Prince in frock coat and top hat. Output included:

(i) London views, mainly showing London transport — horse buses and omnibuses.
(ii) Greetings cards including a "Hand-Painted Series" and a "Relations Series" with special cards to sons, daughters, mothers, fathers, etc.
(iii) Novelty cards including a "Wag-Tail" Series.
(iv) Real photographs of British and European royalty.
(v) Comic cards by such artists as Reg Maurice.

Some photographs were obtained from Judges of Hastings. See: Colour Plate 14.

Regent Publishing Co. Ltd. *"A Happy Christmas and May Good Luck Be With You"*. Signed *"R.M."*

Regimental Badges

Several publishers issued series with regimental badges, including:

(i) Birn Bros., embossed cards.
(ii) British Photogram Co., each badge has a few lines about the regimental history.
(iii) Burleigh Ltd., Bristol, badges with heraldic scrolls.
(iv) Gale & Polden, a particularly fine series of over 100 badges, each card with a descriptive paragraph on the address side.
(v) Silk cards, many of the embroidered cards from France depict British regimental badges.

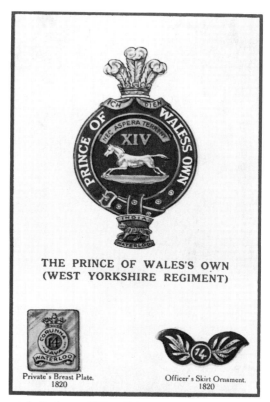

Regimental Badges. *"The Prince of Wales's Own (West Yorkshire Regiment)"*. *Gale & Polden*.

Regimental Badges. *"Ever Faithful. Royal Army Medical Corps"*. *Printed by Burleigh Ltd., Bristol*.

Cpl. A. SOUTHAM'S Squad, Coldstream Guards, Nov., 1916.

Regimental Photographs. *"Cpl. A. Southam's Squad. Coldstream Guards Nov., 1916". Publisher unknown.*

Regimental Photographs
These were taken over a long period, particularly during W.W.I. when troops could send them home without censorship problems.

Reichert, C.
Animal painter who designed sets for Tuck, e.g. "The Best of Friends", "Trusty and True" and "Puppydom".

Reid Bros. Ltd.   pre-1906
Publisher, 69 Wells St., Oxford St., London, W. "Song Postcards" giving music and words of well-known songs or hymns. They also issued a "Composer" Series with busts of musicians.

Reid, Andrew, & Co. Ltd.   c.1902
Printer/publisher, 59 Grey St., Newcastle upon Tyne, Northumberland. Andrew Reid died in 1896 and the business was carried on by his two sons. It was mainly concerned with the designing of posters for railway and shipping companies. The first postcards which bear the initials A.R. & Co. Ltd. were published c.1902. Early issues included a map of the Tyne (with vignette views) to celebrate the visit of the Channel Fleet in 1904. Other events were covered and advertising cards were produced for the Tyne-Tees Shipping Co. The launching of the *Mauretania* in 1906 was the occasion for a commemorative card and other views of ocean liners were published. A series also depicted the coats of arms of the countries of the Empire.
   Ref: Airey, J., 'Andrew Reid & Company Ltd. Newcastle-upon-Tyne', P.P.A. 1982, pp. 48-9, contains a check list.

Reid, C.
Photographer, Wishaw, Lanarkshire. Supplied Scottish views to postcard publishers including F. Hartmann and J. MacPherson.

Reilly, E.S.
Photographer/publisher, Regent St., Shanklin, I.O.W. Local sepia views, serial nos. to 2467.

Reinthal & Newman
New York publisher, with the trademark "R.N.", who produced glamour and W.W.I. romantic cards for the British market using artists such as Boileau and Harrison Fisher.

Reid Bros. Ltd. *Song card. "God Make My Life. Song For Children's Anniversary".*

Reis, Charles L., & Co.   pre-1910
Publisher, Dublin, Belfast and Glasgow. Coloured city views, sometimes with the city coat of arms.

Reiss, Fritz   fl. c.1898-1912
German artist who designed early vignette cards.

Relf, David Ewart
Designer of comic cards for Salmon. He sometimes signed his work "D.E.R.".

"Reliable Series"   pre-1902
A series by William Ritchie & Sons Ltd. (q.v.).

Religious Leaders
P.P.s of the following have been noted:
   The Rt. Rev. Edward Ash, Bishop of Derby.
   The Rev. Archibald Fleming, D.D., Minister of St. Columba's (Church of Scotland), P.U. 1918.
   The Rt. Rev. E.A. Knox, Bishop of Manchester, P.U. 1903.
   The Very Rev. Francis Pigon, Dean of Bristol.
   The Rt. Rev. Ernest R. Wilberforce, Bishop of Chichester.

Religious Publishers
These include: The Religious Tract Society, biblical and Bunyan sets by Harold Copping; The Society for the Propagation of the Gospel.
   See: Missionary Societies.

Rembrandt Intaglio Printing Co. Ltd.
Publishers, London. Sepia views.

Reminder Cards
It is clear from the messages on postcards that with this new and inexpensive form of communication people expected frequent cards from friends and relatives. Some cards were published as reminders. The printed message says "Why Don't You Write?", or the picture side shows vignettes of fishing lines, railway lines and tramlines followed by the words "but I've never seen a line from you".

Renard, Edward   fl. 1880-1909
Watercolour landscape artist. Exh. R.A. 4. Painted a set on "Abingdon" for Tuck, 7524.

Rennie, George Melvin   **fl. 1930s**
Painter of Scottish scenes. His work was used in facsims. by Valentine.

Renoud   **pre-1903**
Publisher, Chorlton-cum-Hardy, Lancashire. R.P. views covering a considerable area, including Dublin.

"The Renshaw Series"
Series name used by C.I. Cassells of Liverpool.

Reservoirs
A number of cards of reservoirs and the dams which contain them are to be found, especially those in scenic country, e.g. The Pengareg (Pen-y-Garreg) Dam in the Elan Valley.

Restaurants
A number of advertisement cards show the layout of restaurants, especially those suitable for tea dances which were very popular in the 1920s. Photochrom produced such a card for the Elysee Restaurant, Coventry St., London, dated 1922.

Revelay, Thomas
Photographer/publisher, White Horse Vale, Berkshire. Cards showing the Wantage Tramway.

Reward Cards
Postcards given to school children by education authorities for good attendance, good behaviour or outstanding achievement. Some cards were supplied by publishers or advertisers, e.g. "with the compliments of the Proprietors of Cadbury's Cocoa". These are, strictly speaking, postcard-size trade cards, for the backs are completely covered with descriptive material. The authorities which used these cards were:
>Erith Education Committee, Tuck: Tower of London; Castles, etc.
>Hampshire County Council, general views.
>Huddersfield Education Committee, general views.
>Isle of Ely Education Committee, natural history.
>Leyton School Board, early U.B.s.
>London County Council, Tuck railway cards, and nursery rhymes.
>School Board of London, early cards.
>Oxfordshire Education Committee, wild flowers.
>Reading Education Committee, animals.
>Surrey Education Committee, general views.
>Walthamstow Education Committee, watercolour facsim. views.

Reynolds, Frank, R.I.   **1876-1953**
Black and white artist and illustrator. Contributed to *Punch* and in 1919 joined the staff, serving as Art Editor from 1920 to 1932. As a Dickens illustrator he provided drawings of Mr. Pickwick and Mr. Micawber for cards published by A.V.N. Jones & Co.

Reynolds, George, Ltd.   **pre-1904**
Publisher, London, E. Issued a series of "Beautiful Butterflies from Nature" based on the Walter Dannett Collection.

Reynolds, J., & Co.
Gloucester advertiser of "Pure Digestive Wheatmeal Bread".

R.F.A.
Regent Fine Art Co. Ltd. (q.v.).

R.F.H.
R.F. Hunger.
>See: Regent Publishing Co. Ltd.

Rheidol Railway
Cards by E.T.W. Dennis. Best known view is that of a train approaching an embankment on this single line.

Rhodes, Wilfred R.   **1877-1973**
Professional cricketer for Yorkshire. Completed the "double" of 2,000 runs and 100 wickets 15 times. Made 58 Test Match appearances. P.P.s.

Richards, A.K.   **pre-1934**
Publisher, Stratford-upon-Avon, Warwickshire. R.P.s of the Shakespeare Memorial Theatre completed in 1936.

Richards, Eugenie M.K., R.B.A.   **fl. c.1900-1920**
Nottingham portrait painter. Exh. R.A. 9. Designed cards with children for Boots Cash Chemists.

Richardson & Co.   **fl. c.1906-1920**
Publisher, 2 and 3 Titchfield St., Soho, London, W. The cards were designed by members of the Richardson family and were embraced in a "Titchfield" Series, after the street name of the firm's premises.

Richardson, Agnes   **1884-1951**
Illustrator of children's books. Designed postcards featuring animals and children for Birn Bros., Geographia, Faulkner, Hauff, Inter-Art, Mack, Millar & Lang, Photochrom, and Valentine. The Photochrom cards were in the "Celesque Series", 554-65, 584-96, 668-73. She also designed an "Agnes Richardson War Humour Series".
>See: Colour Plate 9.
>Refs: Collins, J., 'Agnes Richardson, 1884-1951', P.P.M., May 1981, p. 20; Cope p. 21, ill. p.53.

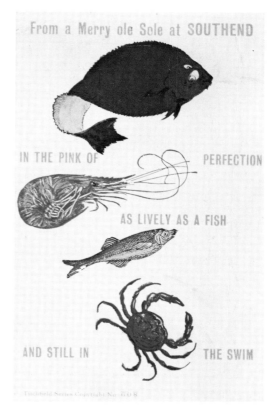

Richardson & Co. *"Titchfield" Series. P.U. 1916.*

Richardson, F.S. & S.J.   **1921**
Publisher, 21 Denmark Place, London, W.C.2. This firm
carried on the business of Richardson & Co. (q.v.) from the
new address in Denmark Place. Frederick Stuart Richardson
(1855-1934) designed the cards.

Richardson, R. Esdaile   **fl. c.1897-1910**
Landscape painter who lived at Brading, I.O.W. Exh. R.A.1.
Paintings of the island used by Tuck in several series, e.g.
"Tennyson's Country".

Richardson, Thomas   **1870-1912**
Cricketer noted as a fast bowler. In 1895 he took 290 wickets
at an average cost of 14.37 runs. P.P.s.

Richmond, Leonard, R.B.A., R.O.I.   **fl. 1912-1965**
Landscape and seascape artist. Exh. R.A. 20. Won prizes at
the Panama-Pacific Expedition of 1915 and the Chicago
International Water Colour Exhibition in the same year. He
illustrated books for the Southern Railway and his postcards
for the railway were printed by W.G. Briggs & Co. Ltd. (q.v.).
He wrote two books on art: *The Art of Landscape Painting*,
1928, and *The Technique of Oil Painting*, 1931.

Richter, C. (Publishers) Ltd.
London, N.W. Real photographs.

Rickard, Jennifer   **fl. 1930s**
Designer of children's cards for Faulkner. Ill. Cope p. 54.

Riddick, N.
Publisher, Malmesbury, Wiltshire. Local views printed in
Saxony.

Ridgway's Tea
Advertising cards.

Ridgwell, Walter C.   **pre-1903**
Post Office, Woodgrange Rd., Forest Gate, London, E. Output included:
(i)   London area views in sepia on very flimsy card.
(ii) Coloured framed and plate-marked cards of the London
      area in "The Woodgrange Series".

Ridley, M.J.   **1903**
Photographer/publisher, Old Christchurch Rd., Bournemouth, Hampshire. Coloured views of the Bournemouth area
and the south of England generally, together with a few
facsims. of marine subjects by Leonard Patten (q.v.). Serial
nos. to 2783.

Ridout Bros.
Publisher/printer, Whitstable. Kent.

Rigby, Cecil T.
Artist who designed wartime humour cards.

Rigby, Reginald
Designer of posters reproduced as postcards by David Allen &
Sons.

Rigg, William   **fl. c.1900-1910**
Designer for Valentine. Cards with decorative oval frames.

Rignold, Lionel   **1850-1919**
Actor-manager. P.P. in Tuck's "Bookmarker" Series IV.

Ritchie, William, & Sons Ltd.   **pre-1903**
Publisher, London and Edinburgh. Two trademarks are
known: "W.R.S." on a shield, sometimes surmounted by a

Richardson, R. Esdaile. *"Cliffs, Ventnor". R. Tuck & Sons.
"Aquarette" "Isle of Wight" Series IV.*

helmet; the words "Beaux Arts" added shortly before W.W.I.
    Many cards are in the "Reliable Series"; "Chromotyped in
Hessen" or "Iristyped in Saxony". Output included:
(i)   Views in black and white, sepia or colour; some Scottish
       views were obtained from Judges of Hastings shortly
       before W.W.I.
(ii)   Watercolour facsims. of Edinburgh and the east of
       Scotland.
(iii) Music hall songs.
(iv)   "City Arms Postcards". Ill. Byatt 256.
(v)   Comic cards including sets by G.F. Christie using the
       word "Our" in every title, e.g. "Our Boarding House".
       Ill. Byatt 250.
(vi)   Humorous political cartoons including cards on
       Chamberlain's fiscal policy and on suffragettes.
(vii) "Our Highland Regiments".
(viii) "Burns Studio Series". R.P.s.
(ix)   Hold-to-light cards (see under Novelty cards).
    See: Colour Plate 19.

Rivers
Occasionally a river is shown with no other features. Usually,
however, there is a bridge, buildings on the bank, or signs of
fishing or boating activity.
    See: Bridges and Viaducts.

Robert Peel Postcard Co.   **1902**
Publisher, Oxford. The initials only are often used, i.e.
"R.P.P. Co." The trademark consists of these letters, each in
a small circle, at the angles of a diamond. Output included:
(i)   U.B. cards with embossed heraldic motifs.
(ii)   Crests of public schools.
(iii) Crests of Oxford and Cambridge colleges.
(iv)   Municipal coats of arms.
(v)   Views of Oxford by such artists as W. Matthison and J.
       Fulleylove.
(vi)   "Myriorama Series" of Lake District views.

Roberts   **pre-1904**
Publisher, George Lane, Folkestone, Kent. Black and white
views.

Rivers. *"Walton on Thames"*. *Frith's Series*.

Rivers. *"River Dee, Chester"*. *Publisher unknown*.

Roberts, Frederick, 1st Earl　　　　　**1832-1914**
Commander of the British Forces in the Boer War. P.P. by
Rotary.

Roberts, J.H.
Artist who designed cards for Charles Voisey, a "Fiscal
Series" for Stewart & Woolf, and a W.W.I. series for the
Woodland Card Co. Ill. Monahan 90.

Roberts, Violet M.　　　　　**fl. c.1903-1914**
Artist who lived in St. Helier, Jersey, C.I. Painted animals,
often for comic cards, e.g. cats in military uniform. She also
contributed to Photochrom's "Wedgwood Series", 512-17.

Robertson, John
Publisher, Inverbeg, Dunbartonshire. View of hotel on Loch
Lomond.

Robertson, Sir Johnstone Forbes-　　　　　**1853-1937**
Actor-manager. Achieved greatest success in *Hamlet* in 1897.
Knighted 1913. P.P.s by Beagles, Millar & Lang, Rotary,
Rotophot, and Tuck's "Bookmarker" Series IV. A fine
Beagles portrait shows him as Shylock in *The Merchant of
Venice*.

Robey, George Edward　　　　　**1869-1954**
Actor and comedian, nicknamed "The Prime Minister of
Mirth". Knighted in 1954. P.P. with wife and children by
Rotary.

Robinson, Thomas
Publisher, Jarrow, Durham.

Robinson, William Heath　　　　　**1872-1944**
Artist and illustrator who was extremely versatile and inventive
from an early age. His main work was for periodicals and his
name has become associated with the extraordinary contrap-
tions he invented on paper to do the simplest jobs. His postcard output was small. Designed a few cards for Harrap,
though these may well have been reproduced from illustrations
published elsewhere, and a set of six cards for Valentine in
1909 under the title "The Gentle Art of Catching Things".
Much has been written about him.
　　Refs: Johnson, A.E., *The Book of W. Heath Robinson*,

Black's, Brush, Pen and Pencil Series, 1913; Lewes, J., *Heath
Robinson, Artist and Comic Genius*, Constable, 1973.

Robinson, William Leefe
Famous V.C. who shot down the first zeppelin on English soil
at Cuffley, Hertfordshire, on 3 September, 1916. P.P.s.

Rock Bros. Ltd.　　　　　**1896**
Publisher, Paul St., Finsbury, London, E.C. This firm existed
in mid-Victorian times printing engravings on notepaper.
Some of the steel plates were used on postcards. The plates
bear serial nos. up to 3,963 and date from the 1850-70 period.

Rodgers
Photographer/publisher, Leeds. R.P. of electric train
decorated on the occasion of a Royal visit to Leeds in 1906.

Rodwright, S.A.
Publisher, 5 Park End Rd., Oxford. Sepia views.

Roe, C.
Photographer/publisher, Fleet, Hampshire. Black and white
R.P. views.

Rogers, F.
Photographer/publisher, 15 High St., Godalming, Surrey.
Local R.P. views.

Rollaston, W.
Publisher, Hindhead, Surrey. Sepia views supplied by Tuck.

Roller-skating
A craze which spread from America where four-wheeled roller
skates were invented in 1875. It was very popular in Edwardian
times and is the subject of many comic cards.

Roman Remains
These include many views of the Roman Baths at Bath, Somerset, and of Hadrian's Wall, e.g. King's Hill from Borcovicus,
published by Gibson & Son of Hexham, Northumberland.

Romney Studio
Photographer/publisher, Station Rd., Horley, Surrey. Local
R.P. views including one of a crashed light aeroplane on
2 March, 1926.

Rough Seas. *"Eastbourne, Splash Point". John Davis "Victoria Series". P.U. 1912.*

Rowing. *"Red Lion Hotel, Henley-on-Thames". S.H. Higgins, Henley-on-Thames.*

Rood Bros.
Publisher, Southampton, Hampshire. Local R.P. views.

Rooti
Designer of humorous cards for Coe of Bradford.

Rose, Freda Mabel
Artist who painted scenes featuring children for a "Mabel Rose" Series.
See: Colour Plate 9.

Rosemont   **pre-1905**
Photographer/publisher, Leeds, Yorkshire. R.P.s of cricket teams.

Rosenstiel, Felix
Publisher, London, E.C. Trademark an artist's palette.

Rosenvinge, Odin   **fl. 1913-1933**
Painter of views of the Yorkshire Dales used by E.T.W. Dennis and Andrew Reid.

Ross, J.T.
Photographer/publisher, Whitby, Yorkshire. Local R.P. views.

"Ross Series"   **pre-1907**
Tradename on a shield on coloured views of Kent coast resorts.

Rossi, Alexander M.   **fl. 1880-1905**
Genre painter. Exh. R.A. 49. Facsims. of his work by Hildesheimer. "Celebrated Poster" by Tuck.

Rossi, J.C.
Art nouveau artist. His work is highly prized.

Rotary Photographic Co.   **1901**
Specialist publishers of photographic cards printed on rotary presses. Premises at 23 Moorfields, London, E.C., later at 14 New Union St., E.C. until 1910, and subsequently at Ropemaker St., and City Rd. Trademark (infrequently used) "R.P.C." within a triangle. Many tradenames were used including "Biogravure", "Bromiris", "Canvasette",

"Linette", "Moisette", "Opalette", "Rajah Bromide", "Rotary Gravure", "Rotary Photographic Plate Sunk Gem", "Rotograph", "Rotokon", "Rotoscope", "Rotox", "Rotritone", and "Silvo".

The output was enormous and included every type of photograph. Among the more notable were photographs of:
(i)   Actors and actresses, and scenes from the plays in which they took part. These included "Miniature Post Cards" measuring approx. 1¼ × 3¾ins.
(ii)   Portraits of public figures in the fields of politics, law, literature, music and sport.
(iii)   Birds and animals.
(iv)   Children.
(v)   Ships, especially ocean liners.
(vi)   "London Life" depicting occupations, e.g. "Flower Sellers".
(vii)   Staged humorous photographs.
(viii)   "British Beauties", sometimes of hand-painted portraits.
(ix)   Greetings cards of every kind, often with embossed borders, with a photographic inset of a view or portrait in an oval, circular or shamrock-leaf frame.

"Rotophot Series"   **pre-1902**
The Rotophot Company of Berlin had close associations with Giesen Bros. & Co. (q.v.), who frequently used this name on their cards, especially photographic cards.

Rough Seas
Photographs of rough seas seem to have had a special attraction for the Edwardian postcard-buying public. Views of waves breaking over piers and promenades, cliffs and rocky shores abound. Tuck produced 30 sets of "Rough Seas", some with literary quotations, e.g. "The houseless ocean's heaving field", Tennyson.

Roughton, Mrs. E.M.   **fl. 1889-1920**
Architectural artist who made watercolour paintings of "Old and Vanishing London" for W.A. Allenson.

Rounce & Wortley   **pre-1931**
Publisher, Cromer, Norfolk. Sepia views.

Rountree, Harry   **fl. c.1900-1905**
Artist who painted "The Sporting Duckling" set for the
British Showcard & Poster Co.

Rousse, Frank   **fl. 1897-1915**
Watercolour landscape artist. Exh. R.A. 2. Painted an
"Aquarette" set on "Rye", 6282; and "Oilette" sets on "Pic-
turesque Whitby", 6272, and York, 8924, for Tuck.

Rowden, Thomas   **1842-1926**
Landscape painter whose work was used by E.W. Savory. He
moved from London to Exeter, c.1890.

Rowe, Sidney Grant, R.B.A., R.O.I.   **1861-1928**
Landscape painter. Exh. R.A. 11. Painted Lake District views
of territory covered by the Furness Railway; they were published by McCorquodale.

Rowing
Many cards show stretches of water with people rowing, but
most cards concentrate on views of places noted for this
branch of athletics such as Henley-on-Thames and the stretch
of the Thames between Putney and Mortlake where the
Oxford and Cambridge Boat Race takes place. Posed photographs of the two crews year by year are to be found and there
are views of other events such as the Oxford Eights.
   See: Boat Racing.

Rowland, Ralph
Designer of comic motoring cards.

Rowlands, Gaynor
Actress. P.P.s by Beagles; Pictorial Postcard Co. "Empire
Series"; Wrench.

Rowlandson, George Derville   **fl. c.1911-1918**
Landscape artist born in India. Lived at Bedford Park,
London. Painted a coursing set for Faulkner.

Rowntree, Harry
Designer of comic cards for the British Showcard & Poster Co.

Rowntree's Postcard Series   **pre-1906**
Cards advertising chocolate.

Royal National Life-Boat Institution. *Painting by B.F.
Gribble. Facsim. by R. Tuck & Sons.*

Royal Botanic Gardens   **1930s**
Publisher, Kew, London. Coloured postcards of the gardens
supplied by Clarke & Sherwell Ltd.

Royal Mail
This subject forms a specialist field for the collector and
includes post offices and postmen, mail transport (including
Royal Mail shipping), etc.

Royal National Life-Boat Institution
Publisher, 22 Charing Cross Rd., London, E.C. Issued a card
produced by Tuck. It depicts a lifeboat rescuing the crew and
passengers from a sinking ship. The painting was by B.F.
Gribble (q.v.). On the address side is the following veiled
appeal: "Mr. Gribble's fine picture, "Saved", gives a good
idea of the national and heroic work in which the Life-Boat
Service is constantly engaged IN PEACE AND IN WAR. Over
54,000 lives saved. The Institution receives no subsidy from the
State. The Life-Boat Service is THE RED CROSS OF THE
SEA."
   The card was reprinted later by the Whitefriars Press Ltd.,
omitting the artist's signature and the Tuck trademark. The
second sentence read: "Over 57,000 lives saved. More than
5,200 rescued during the war".

Royal National Mission to Deep Sea Fishermen
Publisher of fishing scenes.

"Royal Series"
   See: Max Ettlinger & Co.

Royal Society for the Prevention of Cruelty to Animals
                                           pre-1914
Publisher, 105 Jermyn St., London, S.W.1. Several cards were
issued during W.W.I. to raise funds for "sick and wounded
horses". The Society was authorised by the Army Council to
help the Army Veterinary Department. After the war cards
urged people to report cases of cruelty to animals.

Royal Standard Photo Co.
Publisher, Evesham, Worcestershire. R.P.s of an area
extending west to the Forest of Dean.

Royalty, British
Royal portraits:
(i)   H.M. Queen Victoria. A rare Diamond Jubilee card of
      1897 exists. Much commoner are the portraits which
      appear on 1901 memorial cards. After the death of
      Edward VII Beagles issued a "Four Generations" card
      with the late Queen, the late King Edward VII, King
      George V and Edward, Prince of Wales.
(ii) H.M. King Edward VII and Queen Alexandra. An early
      U.B. coloured card by an unknown publisher includes
      head and shoulder portraits of the King and Queen with
      vignettes of Westminster Abbey, The Houses of Parlia-
      ment and Tower Bridge. An interesting photograph taken
      by A.W. Debenham of Cowes titled "Three Generations
      of Royal Sailors" shows the King, the Prince of Wales
      and Prince Edward of Wales. There are many other
      photographs of the King and Queen taken separately. In
      Memoriam cards were issued by many publishers after the
      King's death on 6 May, 1910, and Faulkner published
      Queen Alexandra's message to the nation as a card.
         See: In Memoriam Cards.
(iii) H.M. King George V and Queen Mary. There are photo-
      graphs of Their Majesties together in Coronation robes
      and many individual portraits. One Photochrom card
                                               continued

Royalty. *"Four Generations. Her Late Majesty Queen Victoria, His Late Majesty King Edward VII, H.M. King George V, and H.R.H. Edward, Prince of Wales"*. P.P. by Beagles.

Royalty. *"King Edward VII. Lying in State in the Throne Room, Buckingham Palace, May 16, 1910"*. Photo by W. & D. Downey.

Royalty. *King Edward VII and Queen Alexandra. Publisher unknown.* U.B. P.U. 1902.

Royalty. *"Coronation 1911. King George V. Queen Mary"*. Bowden Bros. P.U. 1911.

Royalty. *"Silver Jubilee. 1910-1935. May 6th. Their Most Gracious Majesties King George V and Queen Mary"*. *Valentine's Series.*

Royalty. *"Royal Visit. Sheffield, July, 1905. Brightside Arch"*. *Note "Britain's Defence" resting on two forging presses.*

Royalty. *"Trooping of the Colours on His Majesty's Birthday. June 26, 1903"*. *Photo by J. Russell & Sons.*

Royalty. *"Clifton Suspension Bridge at the Jubilee, 1935."*

shows the King walking with the Prince of Wales, both in top hats. The Silver Jubilee of 1935 was marked by the publication of many cards.

(iv) King Edward VIII. As Prince of Wales he was enormously popular and must have been photographed more than any other royal personage. There are photographs of him in lounge suits, morning dress, investiture robes, Coronation robes (though he was never crowned), and in military and naval uniforms. He posed smiling and serious, talking to his father, walking with a thumb stick, holding a pipe and smoking a cigar, arms folded or with hands in pockets. Finally, a photograph shows him broadcasting his Abdication message in 1936.

(v) King George VI and Queen Elizabeth. Many royal photographs were taken in black and white but colour was now possible. Tuck produced a particularly fine postcard of Their Majesties from a colour photograph by Peter North.

The royal family:
Every member of the Royal family appears on postcards. These include Prince Albert, Prince Edward, Prince Henry and Prince John. The marriage of Princess Mary to Lord Lascelles in 1922 was a noted occasion. One of the most interesting of all Royal cards is the Valentine "Souvenir of 1936, the Year of the Three Kings" which includes their portraits.

Royal occasions and visits:
The following have been seen on postcards:
1897 Queen Victoria's Diamond Jubilee.
1901 Death of Queen Victoria.
Accession of Edward VII.
1902 Coronation of Edward VII.
1903 Trooping of the Colour; this celebrated the King's birthday.
Visit to Paris.
Visit to Holyrood, Edinburgh, May.
1904 Visit to Liverpool, July.
Visit to Swansea.
1905 Visit to Sheffield.
1905-6 Indian Tour by the Prince and Princess of Wales.
1906 Visit to Derby.
1907 Visit to Lincoln.
Visit to Musical Festival, Jersey, C.I., May.
Royal gathering at Windsor, three Kings and five Queens, November 1907.
1908 Opening new Leeds University building, July.
Opening new Royal Edward Dock at Avonmouth, Bristol, July.
1909 Opening new building at University, Birmingham.
Visit to Midsomer Norton, Somerset.
Opening new Sheffield University Library.
1910 King Edward VII Funeral, Windsor.
1911 George V Coronation.
Investiture of Prince of Wales, Carnarvon.
1913 Visit to Woolwich.
1914 Visit to Welbeck Abbey, June.
Visit to Bridlington.
Queen's visit to Paignton Hospital, Devon.
1917 Visit to Carlisle.
1918 Queen at Hampstead Garden Suburb.
1920 Queen's visit to Talgarth Sanatorium, Brecon.
1921 Prince of Wales at Bootle Dye Works.
1922 Wedding of Princess Mary and Viscount Lascelles.

1923 Wedding of Duke and Duchess of York, April.
1925 Visit to British Empire Exhibition.
1928 Royal Tournament, Weedon.
1934 Marriage of Prince George and Princess Marina.
1935 Silver Jubilee Celebrations.
Prince of Wales' visit to Jersey.
1936 Death of George V, 20 January.
Edward VIII proclaimed King, 20 January.
Edward VIII abdicated, 10 December.
George VI proclaimed King.
1937 George VI crowned, 12 May.
See: Frontispiece.
Residences:
Balmoral.
Buckingham Palace and Royal Mews.
Sandringham.
Windsor.

Royalty, Foreign
Many portraits of the Royal families of Europe appear on cards published in Britain. They include:
(i) Austria, Emperor Franz Josef, Diamond Jubilee, 1908.
(ii) Belgium, Albert I, King of the Belgians, the Queen and their family.
(iii) Bulgaria, King and Queen.
(iv) Denmark, Wedding of King Frederick.
(v) Germany, Kaiser Wilhelm II and his Empress, Augusta Victoria, the Crown Prince, and the German royal family.

Royalty. "S.M. La Reine des Belges". A glamorous card of the Queen of the Belgians published for a W.W.I. Exhibition in Knightsbridge. F.R. Britton & Co.

(vi) Greece, King Constantine and Queen Sophia.
(vii) Holland, Queen Wilhelmina.
(viii) Italy, King Victor Emmanuel III and the Italian royal family.
(iv) Montenegro, Nicholas I.
(x) Norway, King Haakon, the Queen and Crown Prince Olaf.
(xi) Portugal, King Carlos I.
(xii) Rumania, Queen Marie.
(xiii) Russia, Czar Nicholas Wilhelm II.
(xiv) Spain, King Alfonso III riding with his officers; the Queen, Princess Victoria Eugenie of Battenburg, niece of Edward VII.
(xv) Sweden, Crown Prince and Princess.
(xvi) Yugoslavia, King Alexander, funeral scene, 1934.

R.P.C.
Rotary Photographic Co. (q.v.).

R.P.P.Co.
Robert Peel Postcard Co. (q.v.).

R.S. Art Press
Ruskin Studio Art Press.

R.S.P.C.A.
Royal Society for the Prevention of Cruelty to Animals.
See: "Service Pets".

R.T.S.
Religious Tract Society.
See: Religious Publishers.

R.T. & S.
Raphael Tuck & Sons Ltd. (q.v.).

Rudd
Photographer/publisher, Morecambe, Lancashire.

Ruddock Ltd. pre-1905
Publisher, Grand Studio, Newcastle upon Tyne, Northumberland. Output included:
(i) "Grand Series" of view cards including northern castles.
(ii) Nursery Rhymes Series.
(iii) Views of ships, e.g. Royal Yacht and "The Discovery at Portsmouth".

Ruddock, J.W., & Sons pre-1904
Printer/publisher, 287 High St., Lincoln. This firm used several trademarks:
(i) Coat of arms with the words "CIVITAL LINCOLNIEN-SIS".
(i) Coat of arms with five lions rampant surmounted by a crown.
(iii) A panel between two pillars which carried the words: "The Artist Series. Printed and published by J.W. Ruddock, Lincoln, England."
The firm was noted for "The Artist Series", watercolour facsims. covering much of England. The following artists were used:
Mary Baness, the south-west from Worcester to Plymouth.
Tom Boyne, the Yorkshire Moors.
Peter de Wint, reproduction of a view of Lincoln.
Jessie Dudley, north of England including the Lake District.
Tom Dudley, York.
J.S. Eland, Leicester.
T. Guy, York.
E. Hadfield, Isle of Wight.

Ruskin, John. *"The Ruskin Cross, Coniston."* Redheads Series.

G. Hodson, Nottingham.
Frances Hutchinson, Lincolnshire and the Lake District.
Ethel Knight, Nottingham.
Arthur Mackinder, Lincoln.
C.W. Martyn, Lincoln.
F.M. Minns, Dorset.
Parsons Norman, Chester, Norwich, Shrewsbury and Stratford-upon-Avon.
Arthur Payne, Lincoln.
R.E. Rampling, Lancaster.
L. Rossiter, Somerset.
G. Spyree, Yorkshire.
C.H. Stevens, north of England.
H. Van Ruite, Birmingham, Cambridge, Ipswich, London, Oxford.
Ulric Walmsley, Robin Hood's Bay.
A.G. Webster, Lincoln.
There are also a number of unsigned landscape facsims.
Ref: A useful check list by Roy Maltson is given in P.P.M., June 1981, p. 29.

Rudge-Whitworth Ltd.
Advertisers of motor cycles. Cards advertising the "Rudge" usually bear the words "by Appointment to George V".

Rugby Football
Rugby football is mainly reflected in group photographs of national teams, e.g.:
(i) New Zealand Tourists, 1905.
(ii) Welsh team which defeated New Zealand, 16 December, 1905.

continued

(iii) South African tourists, 1906 and 1907.
(iv) Australasian tourists, Rugby League, 1911-12.

Rumford, Mrs. Kennerley, D.B.E. 1873-1936
See: Clara Butt.

Rumford, Robert Kennerley b. 1870
Oratorio and concert singer. Married Clara Butt 1900. P.P. by Rotary who also issued a P.P. of his two children, Roy and Joy.

Rump, R.C.
Publisher, Liss, Hampshire.

Rush, Peggy
A "British Beauty" in the Rotary Rotograph Series.

Rush & Warwick
Art printer/publisher, Bedford. Coloured and framed views.

Ruskin, John 1819-1900
Author and critic. He laid down seven principles: sacrifice, truth, power, beauty, life, memory and obedience. His most notable books were *Modern Painters,* first volume published 1843, *The Seven Lamps of Architecture,* 1849, and *The Stones of Venice,* 1851-3. In 1871 he settled at Brantwood, Coniston, his last home. A memorial cross, carved in the Celtic manner, reflects his life interest.

Ruskin Studio Art Press Ltd. pre-1926
Publisher, with studios at 7 New Court, Carey St., London, W.C.2, and business premises at 3 Broadway, Ludgate Hill, E.C. Most of the artist-drawn cards were on natural history subjects. Painters included: Roland Green, birds; H. Hammond, flowers; R. St. Barbé Baker, trees; Amy Webb, plants. A set of historic ships was prepared by A. Chidley and of locomotives by G.P. Micklewright.

Russell Hodges & Co. pre-1909
Publisher, Birmingham.

Russell, J.R. pre-1907
Publisher, Edinburgh. Highland Series of local views.

Russell & Sons pre-1931
Publisher, Broadway, Worcestershire. "The Lygon Series" of local R.P. views by W. Dennis Moss (q.v.).

Russell, Stanley
Ventriloquist. A photographic postcard shows Russell with his dummy. The caption states: "Stanley Russell is selling his photographs to provide gift parcels of cigarettes and tobacco for the brave men at the front. Amounts will be acknowledged in *The Performer*". The cards are dated 1916.

Russo-Japanese War
R. Caton Woodville covered this war as a military artist. Valentine published his drawing of the Russian retreat after Kin-lien-cheng in 1903 as a postcard.

Rutherford, David
Designer who contributed to the Inter-Art "Photogravure" Series and to Watkins & Kracke's "Infantastic Series".

Ruttley, Ralph Francis
Designer of comic cards for Shamrock & Co.

Ryland, Henry, R.I. 1856-1924
London painter. Exh. R.A. 33. His work in the art nouveau style is reproduced in Hildesheimer's "Gems of Art" Series.

Rylander, Carl Isaak 1879-1910
Swedish figure painter.

Ryman, H.J.
Publisher, London. Black and white views of the Sussex coast.

Advertisement by the Provincial Motor Cab Co. Ltd. of Bristol. "Fares 1/- per mile. 4/- per hour waiting". Designed and printed by Bemrose Dalziel Ltd., Watford.

"Section 6. Art IV...". Motoring regulations. William Ritchie & Sons. "Reliable Series". P.U. 1907.

"In the Smart Set. Saturday — Off Over Sunday" by Lance Thackeray. R. Tuck & Sons. "Oilette" "Remarque". P.U. 1906.

S

Sablang, Sylvia
Actress. P.P., with Tom Terriss, in Valentine's "Play Series".

Sadler, H.   pre-1918
Photographer/publisher. R.P.s of surrendered German fleet at Scapa Flow after W.W.I., before the scuttling in 1919.

Sager, Xavier   fl. 1900-1920s
French artist who designed glamour cards which were issued by Woolstone Bros. under the title "Tres-Chic".
   See: Colour Plate 15.

"Sage's New Photoesque Series"
Photographs by a West Hartlepool firm showing the damage done in the town by the enemy bombardment of 16 December, 1914.

Sailing
Small sailing craft were popular in seaside resorts until the 1920s, as the views of Blackpool and Brighton show.

Sailing Ships
These had almost disappeared by Edwardian times though some relatively small sailing ships were still in use.

"St. Ivel Series"
   See: Aplin & Barrett.

Sadler, H. *"German Fleet at Scapa Flow". Before the ships were scuttled in 1919. R.P. by an enterprising photographer who took the view from the Houghton Bay Air Station.*

Sailing. *"Blackpool". Publisher unknown. P.U. 1915.*

Sailing. *"Palace Pier & Beach, Brighton." Philco. P.U. 1913.*

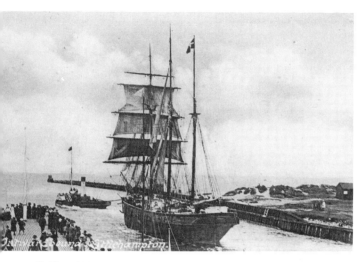

Sailing Ships. *"Outward Bound, Littlehampton"*. *Wareham, Littlehampton. P.U. 1918.*

St. Paul's Hospice

Before the days of the National Health Service hospitals depended largely on voluntary contributions and money-raising schemes. St. Paul's Hospital held a draw to raise funds. Twelve sepia view postcards of London were sold for 1s. (5p) by J.M. Black, St. Paul's Hospital Buildings, 28 Betterton St., London, W.C.2. They offered "£1,000 for 1d. 64 prizes" as the attraction.

Salaman, Edith

Designer of national costume cards for Tuck in a set titled "National Beauties".

Salisbury, 3rd Marquis of   1830-1903

Prime Minister 1885, 1886-92, 1895-1902. P.P. by Rotary.

Salmon, J. (Ltd.)   c.1900 (Ltd. 1930)

Publisher, Sevenoaks, Kent. Trademark a salmon caught with rod and line with the words "Salmon Series". Various type of card were issued: "Gravure Style", "Sepia", "Sepia-Style", "Sepiatone". However, the firm is best known for facsims. of watercolour drawings, a development which resulted from an association with C. Essenhigh Corke, a local photographer and watercolour artist, who supplied the illustrations for a book on Sevenoaks. He began to provide Salmon with water-colour drawings, of which a number were of the historic house at Knole built by the Archbishop of Canterbury in 1456 and extended in the early 17th century by Thomas Sackville to whom it was granted by Queen Elizabeth I. The first of the facsim. postcards was probably published in 1903. There followed a stream of cards by first-class artists of whom A.R. Quinton and W.W. Quatremain were pre-eminent. There were views and interiors of houses and churches. However, the same techniques were used later in other fields until the output included:

(i)   Animals in their natural environments.
(ii)   Military subjects.
(iii) Cartoons during W.W.I.
(iv)   Comic cards by C.T. Howard.
(v)   Planes and trains after W.W.I.

(vi)   "Oilochrom" cards similar to the Tuck "Oilette" technique.
(vii) Railway cards over a long period; earliest serial no. 565, latest 4703.
(viii) Louis Wain cats, 2482.

During W.W.I. Salmon was closely associated with W.E. Mack of King Henry's Rd., Hampstead, London, for the names of both firms are found on patriotic cards published c.1916.

See: Colour Plates 7 and 21.

Salmond, Gwendolen   fl. c.1900-1930

Figure painter. Exh. R.A. 1. Designer of glamour cards.

Salvation Army   c.1936

Publisher. Birthday cards and cards with Salvation Army flags.

Sampsons

Publisher, York. Black and white local views.

Samuels, J.J., Ltd.   pre-1908

Printer/publisher/postcard retailer, Lother Arcade, 371 Strand and 87a Regent St., London, W.C. Output included:
(i)   London views in an "Arcadian" Series.
(ii)   "Old London Cries".
(iii) Military caricatures.
(iv)   Hand-coloured comic cards.
(v)   Photographs of actessses and babies.

Some of Samuels' printing was on rather flimsy card.

Sanbidet, Tito

French Artist who designed romantic cards during W.W.I. for P.J. Gallais et Cie of Paris. Captions were printed in both French and English.

"Sanbride Series"

See: Hood & Co.

Sancha, F.

Designer of a comic set of political cards titled "Aesop's Fables" for a Tuck "Oilette" Series, 8484.

Sanders, A.E.   fl. pre-1902

Landscape artist whose work was used by Faulkner and by Tuck, Aquarette set.

Sanders, E.

Designer of a comic "The Merry Maids" set for Wildt & Kray.

Sandford, H. Dix

Designer of postcards featuring children, e.g. Tuck's "Happy Little Coons".

Sandle Bros.   c.1906

Publisher/stationer, Paternoster Row, London. This firm took over three other postcard publishers and no doubt sold the surplus stock. Their output included views and some particularly interesting photographs of suffragettes and their demonstrations.

Sandys, Ruth

Designed a set of "Old Street Cries" for Humphrey Milford.

Sankey

A Lake District photographer who published cards of "Lakeland Tours".

Ref: R.O.P.L., No. 4, p. 14.

Santa Claus

See: Father Christmas.

Santino
Italian artist who painted beautiful ladies, often with horses, towards the end of W.W.I.

Sauber, Robert, R.B.A.   **1865-1936**
London artist. Exh. R.A. 6. Painted a set titled "Familiar Figures of London" for the Pictorial Stationery Co. and also some cards for Ajelli & Co. and Tuck.

Savage, Alfred (Ltd.)   **pre-1907 (Ltd. 1928)**
Publisher, The Carfax, Oxford. Alfred Savage had a bookshop in Oxford from 1885 but it is not known when he published his first postcard. He used the words "Oxford Varsity City" as a trademark. His output included:
(i) Views of Oxford colleges with their coats of arms.
(ii) Cards titled "Arms of the Oxford Colleges".

Savory, E.W., Ltd.   **c.1900**
Publisher at various addresses in Clifton, Bristol, with studios in Park Row. Much of the output consisted of facsims. of paintings by established artists, mainly landscapes. The cards were in a "Clifton Series", and had names such as "Clifton Happy Thought Postcards" or "Clifton Bromogravure". There were many cards of beautiful girls, ill. Byatt 272, or of girls with dogs, "Playfellows". Coaching, hunting and natural history subjects were also represented. Archibald Thorburn contributed pictures of birds.

Savoy Orpheans
The Savoy Orpheans were a dance band which played at the Savoy Hotel and sometimes appeared at the London Hippodrome. They recorded exclusively for "His Master's Voice", which firm published a "postcard" showing the band on one side and listing their 54 recorded dance tunes on the other. Though this could not be sent through the post without an envelope it appears in collections and must be classed as an advertising card.

Sawney, G., & Son
Publisher, 4 Station Terrace, Westgate-on-Sea, Kent. The "Terrace" Series of local views.

S.B.
Solomon Bros. (q.v.).

S.C. or S.C.H.
S. Cambridge, Hove. (q.v.).

Scaltina
Art deco artist.

Scapa Flow
A number of cards show the scuttling of the German Fleet in 1919.

Scarbina, Professor F.
Russian artist who painted soldiers in uniform for Tuck.

Scherer Collection
A collection of Bamforth cards acquired by the Kirklees Library and Museum Service in 1975, the headquarters of which is at Princess Alexandra Walk, Huddersfield, West Yorkshire HD1 2SU.

Schiele, Egon   **1890-1918**
Austrian artist attached to the Wiener Werkstätte. Painted beautiful ladies with large hats. Schiele cards are highly valued.

Schmidt, C.
Watercolour artist who painted views of London for Ernest Nister.

Schoënpflug, Fritz   **1873-1951**
Austrian postcard designer.

Schofield & Co.   **1906**
Burnley, Lancashire. A firm which patented a card with a slit into which a portrait photograph could be placed and the photograph secured with gummed paper on the reverse side.

Schofield, J.F.
Publisher, Cadran House, Towyn, Merioneth.

Scholastic Trading Co. Ltd.
Publisher, Bristol. Sold cards with the company name rubber-stamped on the address side, including designs by C.E. Shand.

Schönian, Alfred
Artist who painted a set of pictures titled "Little Chicks" for Nister, ill. Byatt col. pl. N.

School Photographs
Many schools arranged for groups of pupils to be photographed and had the results printed on postcards. Many are unidentified. Those which bear the name of the school and a date, however, are of special interest. The card of Eriva Dene School by E. Powell of Fleet, Hampshire, dated 1928, is an example, particularly as it includes a dog!

Schubert, H.
Painter of general subjects including beautiful women, Easter cards, etc.

Schweiger, L.
German painter of general subjects.

Schweppes
Advertisers of table waters, 64 Hammersmith Rd., London, W. This firm issued many posters with neo-classical and art nouveau designs and some poster-type cards showing their horse transport, ill. D. & M. 79. In September 1911 advertising cards were sent by the Coronation Aerial Post Service between London and Windsor.
    Ref: Simmons, D.A., *Schweppes — The First 200 Years*, 1983.

School Photographs. *"Eriva Dene School, 1928".*
Photographer R.H. & E. Powell, Fleet, Hampshire.

Scott, Sir Walter. *"Sir Walter Scott, Bart." Sepia portrait in Valentine's "Carbotone" Series. 1925.*

Schwerdtfeger, E.A., & Co.   **fl. 1909-1914**
Publisher, 28 Monkswell St., London, E.C., and after 1913 at 73 Golden Lane. Trademark "E.A.S." within a heart. These initials also appear frequently in the bottom right-hand corner of the picture side of the cards. The output was mainly of photographic cards printed in Berlin and included:
(i)   Sepia views.
(ii) Photo-portraits of actresses.
(iii) Romantic studies of children.
(iv) Cards with a Scottish flavour with views inset in tartan.
(v)   Birthday, Christmas and Easter cards, sometimes gilded.
(vi) Coronation portraits of George V and Queen Mary, 1911.
The firm ceased to exist in 1914.

Schwets, Karl
Postcard designer at the Wiener Werkstätte (q.v.).

Scientific Press Ltd.   **pre-1905**
Publisher, London. Exterior and interior views of hospitals, e.g. Radcliffe Infirmary, Oxford; Infant Orphan Asylum, Wanstead; and Savernake Hospital, Marlborough.

Scopes, P., & Co. Ltd.   **c.1908**
Publisher, 1 Cotton St., Barbican, London, and after c.1917 at 4 Lauderdale Buildings, London, E.C. Trademark "Alliance". This firm shared a patent with Alliance Ltd., for bas-relief work. During W.W.I. they also used the title "Britannic". The output consisted mainly of portraits,

patriotic cards with flags and a military portrait, photographs of animals and greetings cards.

Scott, A. Hamilton   **fl. 1900-1926**
Artist who painted views of Scotland for Bauermeister of Glasgow.

Scott, Robert Falcon   **1868-1912**
Explorer. P.P. by Rotary.
  See: South Polar Expedition.

Scott Russell & Co.   **pre-1909**
Art publisher, mainly at 266a Broad St., Birmingham, Warwickshire, but also in Sheffield. "Scott Series" of coloured views covering much of central and northern England. Serial nos. to 950. Some cards bear coats of arms. A few facsims. of watercolours of North Wales were issued, some humorous cards with a topical flavour, and a couple of railway cards. Russell covered the visit of Edward VII to Birmingham in 1909.

Scott, Sir Walter   **1771-1832**
Scottish novelist, historian and poet. "Carbotone" portrait by Valentine.

Scott, Walter   **pre-1929**
Photographer/publisher, Bradford, Yorkshire. Trademark "W.S." in monogram form. R.P. views covering a wide area as far afield as Herefordshire.

Scottish Livestock Insurance Co.
Advertising cards featuring a Clydesdale horse.

Scottish Photographic Touring and Pictorial Postcard Co.
A Glasgow firm which could be commissioned to supply postcards by local retailers. This firm's name has been noted on cards published by L. Buckland & Son, Draper and Outfitter, 55-9 High St., Andover.

Scott's Emulsion
Advertising cards including views of a series of French *départements* and colonies.

Scouts
A series of scouting cards was issued by Valentine, the Scout motto "Be Prepared" appearing on each card, ill. Monahan 77. Many scout events, including jamborees, are to be found on postcards.

Scovell   **pre-1911**
Photographer/publisher, Queen's Parade, Aldershot, Hampshire. Local photographs including a fireman's funeral.

Scripture Gift Mission
Publisher, 15 Strand, London, W.C. Watercolour facsims. of views in Palestine and the Near East by H.A. Harper.

Scrivener, Maude   **fl. c.1907-1917**
London animal artist. Exh. R.A. 1. Designed bird cards for Tuck "Oilettes", including "In the Arctic Regions", and for Wrench.

Scrivens, E.L.
Photographer/publisher, 36 Cooper St., Doncaster, Yorkshire. Specialist in events and views of villages in Yorkshire, Derbyshire, Nottinghamshire and Lincolnshire. The Doncaster series has over 255 views, most of which have been recorded by P. Harvey in P.P.M., August 1982.

S. & E. Ltd.
Shoesmith & Etheridge Ltd. (q.v.).

Sea Shells. *Left to right, Nautilus and Dolium shells from the Andaman Islands, and Pterocera from Australia. Painted by Dora Deacon. R. Tuck & Sons. "Oilette" Connoisseur "Oilfacsim". "Sea Shells". Series I.*

Sea Shells
Several Tuck sets were produced with this title. Each card gives the generic and specific name for each shell and its origin.
Ref: Lindner, G., *Seashells of the World,* English ed. 1977.

Sealby, Mabel   **b.1885**
Actress. P.P. by Beagles.

Seaplanes
R.P.s of seaplanes are to be found, e.g. Short "Singapore" seaplane and seaplanes at Felixstowe watched by a crowd on the beach.

Seaton's Toffee
Advertising cards.

Sedgwick, W.F., Ltd.
Postcard printers.

Segrave, H.O.D.   **1896-1930**
Racing motorist. Reached a speed of over 231 m.p.h. in 1929 and was knighted in the same year. P.P. and a card showing his "Golden Arrow" published by Selfridge & Co. Ltd. Ill. Monahan 31 and 32.

Selfridge & Co. Ltd.
Publisher, Oxford St., London, W. Postcards with a view of the Selfridge Store and sepia views of other London buildings, e.g. The Imperial Institute. Also cards linked with events, see Segrave above.

Selkirk, Alexander   **1676-1721**
The prototype of Robinson Crusoe, son of a Largo shoemaker who ran away to sea in 1695. D. Small (q.v.) painted a view of his birthplace which was used in Tuck's "Historic Houses".

Senior & Co.   **pre-1908**
Printer/publisher, Bristol. Senior series of local events and views, e.g. a view of the "New Docks at Avonmouth to be opened by the King in July, 1908", "General Buller opening a Bazaar", and cards of animals at the Clifton Zoo.

"Service Pets". *"A Ram Lamb as Mascot of the Royal Naval Air Service". R.S.P.C.A. P.U. 1921.*

Series
A word used rather loosely by publishers to include cards of a similar type. This may refer to the style of printing and was sometimes registered as a trademark, see Byatt p. 371, or to cards designed by a particular artist, e.g. "Valentine's 'Attwell' Series".

"Service Pets"
A set published by the Royal Society for the Prevention of Cruelty to Animals, 105 Jermyn St., London, S.W., in aid of the Fund for Sick and Wounded Horses during W.W.I. The photographs were supplied by Newspaper Illustrations Ltd.

Set
Most postcards were sold in sets of six or twelve in an envelope. They usually dealt with a single subject, e.g. a town, county or form of transport.

Sevening, Nina   **fl.c. 1894-1914**
Actress. P.P.s by Philco, and Tuck's Celebrities of the Stage Series.

Severn, Walter, R.C.A.   **1830-1904**
Son of Joseph Severn. Lived in London working as a water-colour artist. Exh. R.A. 2. Exhibited mainly at the Dudley Gallery of which he was a founder, and later President. Contributed to Tuck's "Scottish Lochs" Series.

Sevening, Nina. *"Miss Nina Sevening". A Bassano photograph published by Rotophot. P.U. 1905.*

Severs, R.J.
Publisher, 10 King's Parade, Cambridge. Sepia views of Oxford and Cambridge colleges.

Seymour, Patience
Actress. P.P. in Tuck's Celebrities of the Stage Series, 4446.

S.H. or S.H. & Co.
S. Hildesheimer & Co. (q.v.).

Shakespeare Press
Publisher, 4 Sheep St., Stratford-upon-Avon, Warwickshire. "Forest of Arden Series" of local sepia views.

Shamrock & Co.   **1906**
Publisher, 5 Lovell's Court, Paternoster Row, London, E.C. Trademark a shamrock leaf. Output included:
(i)   Song cards, ill. Byatt 285.
(ii) Comic cards, ill. Byatt 279.
(iii) Photographs, white framed and print-marked of children, animals and views, often offered as greetings cards.
(iv) Irish celebrities.
(v)   Humorous cards, under the title "Humorous Art Studies".
(vi) Military subjects.
(vii) Naval subjects.
It should be pointed out that the cards in a "Shamrock Series" were not published by this firm but by J.J. Keliher & Co. (q.v.), or Kirk & Sons (q.v.).

Severn, Walter. *"Loch Dhu". Facsim. R. Tuck & Sons. "Oilette". "Scottish Lochs". Series V.*

"Shamrock Series"
Name used by J.J. Keliher & Co. and Kirk & Sons. It has no connection with Shamrock & Co.

Shand, C.E.   **fl. 1920s**
Art deco artist who painted ladies in highly coloured dresses, usually with a single-word caption, e.g. "Hollyhocks".
See: Colour Plate 2.

Shapland, E. & K., Ltd.
Photographer/publisher, Martin's Lane, Exeter. Local R.P. views.

Sharpe, W.N., Ltd.   **pre-1904**
Publisher/printer, Bradford, Yorkshire. Output included:
(i)   Greetings cards.
(ii) Fab cards. See under Novelty Cards.
(iii) "Wilcox" Series. These have verses written by Ella Wheeler Wilcox (1850-1919), an American poetess who published nearly 40 volumes of verse.
(iv) Comic cards by the Bradford artist E.A. Avis who also designed cards for the Bradford Exhibition of 1904.
(v)   W.W.I. cards, e.g. "The Flags of the Allies", ill. Byatt 281, "Our Friends and Allies", etc. These were among the last postcards to be published by Sharpe.

Shaw, A.E.
Publisher, Blackburn, Lancashire. Coloured views of the North of England in a "West End Series". Some views were framed.

Shaw, A.E.
Photographer/publisher, Lydd, Kent. Black and white cards of military subjects, e.g. army camps.

Shaw, Byam   **1872-1919**
Painter who had a special interest in the art of decoration. Exh. R.A. 37. Responsible for an advertising card showing the Marble Hall at the Debenham & Freebody store in London.

Shaw, E.P.
Advertiser of mineral waters. Name printed on cards of H.M.S. *Iron Duke* with the slogan "Reliable as Britain's Fleet."

Shaw & Leathley
Postcard printer, Shipley, Yorkshire.

Shaw, W.   pre-1916
Photographer/publisher, Burslem, Staffordshire.

Shaw, W. Stocker
Versatile artist who designed for several firms including:
(i)   A.M. Davis, set titled "The Unchanging East".
(ii)   English Fine Art Co., comic cards.
(iii) Knight Bros., silhouettes of ancient buildings against a
       blue background, entitled "The Spirit of the Past".
(iv)   Thridgould & Co., comic cards of the seaside, see check
       list Byatt p. 354.
(v)   Universal Photo-Printing & Publishing Co.
(vi)   Woolstone Bros., novelty cards.

Shears
Publisher, Rainham, Kent. "Photo Series" of local views.

Sheldrick & Sons
Stationer/publisher, 22 Ship St., Brighton, Sussex. Local
views including the Grand and Metropole Hotels, Brighton.

"Shell" Motor Spirit. *A card from the firm's advertising series. P.U. 1917.*

Shaw, W. Stocker. *"We've Just Managed to Squeeze In". Designed for J. Thridgould & Co.'s "Pioneer" Series. P.U. 1922.*

Shell House, East Cowes
Frederick Attrill made it a retirement task to cover his house, walls and garden borders with thousands of seashells. For over 60 years sightseers have visited his home in Bembridge Rd., East Cowes, and many postcards have been published with views of the house, some with Mr. Attrill "on the job".
   Frederick Attrill died in 1926.

"Shell" Motor Spirit   pre-1908
Advertising cards with views of early motor cards and aeroplanes were used extensively. Some 70 different "Shell" cards were issued between 1908 and 1914 to advertise motor spirit alone and there were at least 10 aviation cards.
   Ref: Check list, Roman, A., P.P.M., October 1981, p. 17.

Shellback, K.
Artist who painted a Tuck's "Types of Beauty" set.

Shelton, Sidney   fl. c.1885-1901
Landscape painter. Exh. R.A. 2. Lived at Eastbourne from 1889. Designed a "Flower Time" set for Tuck.

"Shenley Real Photo"
   See: Percy Redjeb.

Shepheard, George Edward
Designer of humorous cards for the Avenue Publishing Co.; Faulkner; Photochrom's "Camp Silhouette Series", Tuck's "Diabolo" and "Coons Cooning" "Oilette" sets.

Shepheard, George Edward. *"I Never Did Take to Them Sub-marines".* R. Tuck & Sons. *"Oilette" "Telling the Marines".* Humorous Postcard. P.U. 1921.

Sherie
Pseudonym of an artist who, towards the end of W.W.I., designed glamour cards for the Inter-Art Co., on which both French and English captions were used. Ill. Monahan 115.

Sherrin, David   b. 1868
Landscape painter. Scenes used by Faulkner and by Langsdorff & Co.

Sherwin, Frank   fl. 1926-1940
Designed a "Royal Tank Corps" set for the Medici Society.

Shields, D.A.   pre-1935
Publisher, New Market Place, Beccles, Suffolk. Black and white local views.

Shinio Metal Polish
Advertising cards by the manufacturers, 180 Rice Lane, Walton, Liverpool.
    See: Colour Plate 1.

Shipbuilding
A few cards show shipyards, e.g. the Hurst & Co. yard at Belfast, and many show the launching of ships.
    See: Launchings.

Shipping
Before the days of air transport passengers to every part of the world used ocean liners. A few were able to travel on merchant ships though this usually took longer. Liners were a favourite subject for the postcard publishers, who used real photographs or had paintings, including interiors, made by marine artists such as Montague Black, Arthur Burgess, Henri Cassiers, or W.L. Wyllie. Publishers of ocean liner cards include:
(i)   The Art Publishing Co.
(ii)   J. Birch, Southampton.
(iii)   Gale & Polden.
(iv)   Gottschalk, Dreyfus & Davis.
(v)   F. Hartmann, "Famous Liners" Series.
(vi)   C.R. Hoffman, many lines and the Southern Railway cross-channel steamers.
(vii) W. & A.K. Johnston, "Ocean Liners" set.
(viii) Hugo Lang.
(ix)   Millar & Lang, major shipping lines, e.g. Cunard and White Star.
(x)   Morris & Co.
(xi)   A. Reid, Newcastle, ships of many lines but especially the P. & O. Line.
(xii) J. Salmon, shipping cards by John Fry.
(xiii) Thomas Stevens, silks of very many liners; G.A. Godden in his book *Stevengraphs*, 1971, lists 36.
(xiv) F.G.O. Stuart, liners using Southampton, especially the Union Castle Line.
(xv)   E.A. Sweetman.
(xvi) R. Tuck, "Celebrated Liners" Series; many sets, each one dealing with a particular line, e.g. American Line, 9140, Cunard, 9106.
(xvii) Valentine, "Famous Steamships".
    Many shipping companies also issued their own advertising cards.
    The following list records some of the liners noted on postcards. Dates refer to the year when a vessel was built, launched or acquired:
Adriatic, White Star, 1907, Stevens, Stuart, Tuck.
Amazon, Royal Mail Steam Packet Co., Stuart.
Andania, Cunard, 1913, Tuck.
Aquitania, Cunard, 1914, Stevens.
Arabia, P. & O., 1897, Reid, Tuck.
Arabic, White Star, 1903, Stevens, Tuck.
Armadale Castle, Union Castle, 1903, Stuart, Tuck.
Arundel Castle, Union Castle, 1894, Tuck.
Athenic, White Star, 1902.
Athlone Castle, Union Castle, 1935, Tuck.
Australia, P. & O., 1892, Reid.
Avondale Castle, Union Castle, 1900, Stuart.
Baltic, White Star, 1904, Stevens, Tuck.
Berengaria, Cunard, 1913, W.H. Smith, Tuck.
Bernicia, Tyne-Tees, Reid.
Borneo, P. & O., 1895, Reid, Tuck.
Braemar Castle, Union Castle, 1898.
Briton, Union Castle, 1897, Stuart.
Caledonia, P. & O., 1894.
Campania, Cunard, 1893, Stevens, Tuck.
Canopic, White Star, 1900, Stevens, Tuck.
Canton, P. & O., 1938, Tuck.   *continued*

Caramania, Cunard, 1905, Stevens, Tuck.
Carisbrooke Castle, Union Castle, 1898, Stevens, Tuck.
Carnarvon Castle, Union Castle, 1926, Tuck.
Caronia, Cunard, 1905, Stevens, Tuck, Valentine.
Cedric, White Star, 1902, Stevens, Tuck.
Celtic, White Star, 1901, Stevens, Tuck.
Ceramic, White Star, 1913, Tuck.
Corsican, Allan, 1907, Stevens.
Cymric, White Star, 1898, Stevens, Tuck.
Devanha, P. & O., 1906, Reid, Tuck.
Doric I, White Star, 1893, Tuck.
Durham Castle, Union Castle, 1904, Stuart.
Edinburgh Castle, Union Castle, 1910, Tuck.
Egypt, P. & O., 1897, Tuck.
Etruria, Cunard, 1884, Stevens, Tuck.
Finland, Red Star, 1902, painting by Cassiers.
Goorkha, Union Castle, 1897, Stuart.
Grampian, Allan, 1907, Stevens.
Himalaya, P. & O., 1892, Reid, Tuck.
Homeric, White Star, 1922, Tuck.
India, P. & O., 1896, Reid, Tuck.
Ionian, Allan, 1901, Stevens.
Ivernia, Cunard, 1900, Stevens, Tuck.
Kenilworth Castle, Union Castle, 1904, Stuart.
Kildonian Castle, Union Castle, 1899, Tuck.
Lucania, White Star, 1893, Stevens.
Lusitania, Cunard, 1907, Millar & Lang, Stevens, Tuck, Valentine.
Macedonia, P. & O., 1904, Reid, Tuck.
Majestic, White Star, 1889, Tuck.
Maloja, P. & O., Reid, Tuck.
Malta, P. & O., 1895, Reid, Tuck.
Malwa, P. & O., 1908, Reid, Tuck.
Mantua, P. & O., 1909, Reid, Tuck.
Marmora, P. & O., 1903, Reid, Tuck.
Mauretania, Cunard, 1906, Alliance, ill. D. & M. 149, Tuck, Valentine.
Medina, P. & O., 1911, Reid, Tuck.
Minneapolis, Atlantic Transport, 1900, Tuck.
Minnehaha, Atlantic Transport, 1900, Tuck.
Moldavia, P. & O., 1903, Reid, Tuck.
Mongolia, P. & O., 1903, Reid, Tuck.
Mooltan, P. & O., 1905, Reid, Tuck.
Morea, P. & O., 1908, Tuck.
Naldera, P. & O., 1918, Reid, Tuck.
Narkunda, P. & O., 1920, Tuck.
Nyanza, P. & O., 1907, Reid, Tuck.
Oceanic, White Star, 1899, Stuart, Tuck.
Olympic, White Star, 1911, Stevens, Tuck.
Omrah, Orient, 1899, Tuck.
Ophir, Orient, 1891, Tuck.
Orcades, Orient, 1903, Tuck.
Orontes, Orient, 1902, Tuck.
Oroya, Orient, 1889, Reid.
Persia, P. & O., 1900, Reid, Tuck.
Republic, White Star, 1903, Stevens.
Saint-Louis, American, 1895, Reid.
Saint-Paul, American, 1895, Reid, Tuck.
Sardinia, P. & O., 1902, Reid.
Saxonia, Cunard, 1900, Stevens.
Simla, P. & O., 1895, Reid.
Somali, P. & O., 1901, Reid.
Stirling Castle, Union Castle, 1936.
Teutonic, White Star, 1889, Stuart.

Titanic, White Star, 1912, Millar & Lang, ill. D. & M. 150, Salmon, Stevens, Tuck, views before maiden voyage in April, 1912.
Tunisian, Allan, 1900, Stevens.
Umbria, Cunard, 1884, Stevens.
Victorian, White Star, 1895, Stevens.
Virginia, Allan, 1904, Stevens.

Shipping Accidents and Wrecks
Many shipping disasters were recorded by local photographers. The following have been illustrated on postcards:
Abertay, Cornwall, 1912.
Antelope, off Brighton, 1904.
Bardic, Lizard, 1924.
S.S. *Bessemen City,* broken in two off St. Ives, 1936.
S.S. *Brussels,* sunk off Zeebrugge.
Cecil Hertzogin, Salcombe, 1936.
Clitus, Grimsby trawler sunk near Blyth Harbour, 1908.
S.S. *Charlton,* collision at Eastbourne, 1911.
Crystal Spring, sailing ship wrecked, 1904, Thorn of Bude.
S.S. *Eastfield,* stranded off Beachy Head, 1909.
S.S. *Empress of Ireland,* sunk 1914, "In Memoriam" card.
H.M.S. *Gladiator,* wrecked off Yarmouth, Isle of Wight, 1908, Arnott of Lymington.
Gunvor, Norwegian barque wrecked Cornwall, 1912, Bragg.
S.S. *Hercules,* collision off Eastbourne.
S.S. *Hilda,* L.S.N.R. ship sunk after striking rock near St. Malo, 1905.
S.S. *Lugano,* on fire near Hastings.
S.S. *Mohegan,* sunk off Cornish coast.
H.M.S. *Montague,* aground on rocks, Lundy Island, Twiss.
S.S. *Parisian* in collision, Halifax, Nova Scotia, 1905.
H.M.S. *Phoenix,* damaged by typhoon at Kowloon, 1906.
S.S. *Onward,* collision with S.S. *Queen.*
H.M.S. *Orwell,* collision with H.M.S. *Earnest* at Invergordon.
S.S. *Queen,* collision with S.S. *Onward.*
S.S. *Queen Margaret,* sailing cutter sunk off Lizard, 1913.
S.S. *St. Paul,* collision with H.M.S. *Gladiator,* 1908.
S.S. *Suevic,* cut in half near Southampton.
H.M.S. *Tiger,* cut in two by H.M.S. *Berwick,* 1908, Gothard.
Trifolium, aground in Sennen Cove, Cornwall, 1914, Gibson & Sons.
Refs: Hocking, C., *Dictionary of Disasters at Sea, 1824-1962,* 1969; Marks, J.L., 'Events and Disasters', P.P.M., January 1983.

Shoesmith, A.   **pre-1908**
Publisher, Hastings, Sussex. Local coloured views.

Shoesmith & Etheridge Ltd.   **pre-1931**
Publisher, Hastings, Sussex. Trademark the head and shoulders of a knight in helmet and armour above the word "Norman". Local R.P. views.

Shoesmith, Kenneth Denton   **1890-1939**
Poster artist. Exh. R.A. 2. Painted views of ocean liners.

Shooting
Shooting scenes are by no means as common as hunting scenes but there is a particularly fine Tuck "Oilette" set by Norah Drummond titled "With Dog and Gun".
    Illustration overleaf.

"Going to Market" by Harry Payne. R. Tuck & Sons. "Oilette" "Surrey Woods and Lanes".

"Charge of the First Life Guards. Waterloo 1815"
by Harry Payne. R. Tuck & Sons. "Oilette" "Our Fighting Regiments".

"Bristol" by Arthur C. Payne. S. Hildesheimer & Co. P.U. 1911.

241

Shooting. *"Grouse Shooting on the Moors". Norah Drummond. Facsim. by R. Tuck & Sons. "Oilette" "With Dog and Gun".*

Shops and Stores

Photographs of shop fronts and penny bazaars are a reminder of the changes that have taken place in recent years. Supermarkets and packaged goods were unknown before 1939. It is worth while studying photographs of shop fronts with a magnifying glass for they often show goods and advertising material. Some of these early shop front photographs have the members of staff in their working aprons posed on the pavement.

Large stores, especially London stores, issued postcards, some with a view of their buildings. They include Bravingtons, Debenham & Freebody, ill. D. & M. 76, Derry & Toms, Dickens & Jones, Dunn's, Fortnum & Mason's, Gamages, Harrods, ill. D. & M. 19, Home & Colonial, International Stores, Liberty's, Mappin & Webb, Page & Shaw, Selfridges, Stead & Simpson, Swan & Edgar.

Ref: 'Shopping by Postcard', P.P.A. 1982, p. 29.

The House of SELFRIDGE & CO LTD *Oxford Street, London, W.*

Short, J.G.

Publisher, Lyndhurst, Hampshire. Black and white views of the New Forest.

Shrimpton, A.   pre-1906

Publisher, Post Office, Long Crendon, Buckinghamshire. Black and white local views.

Shops and Stores. *Top right. "The Premier Penny Bazaar. 100,000 Articles Always in Stock". B.A. Gale & Co., Portsmouth & Southampton.*

Centre. "The House of Selfridge & Co. Ltd., Oxford Street, London, W." Published by the company.

Right. Ogden's estate and insurance agency, travel bureau, booking office, etc. at 1095 Christchurch Rd., Bournemouth, 1933-5.

242

Tom Tower, Christ Church, Oxford, SHUFFREY

Visions bright of Thee   *By Margaret W. Tarrant*

Silhouette Cards. *"Visions Bright of Thee"*. *Margaret Tarrant. Medici Society "Sing Praises" Series.*

Shuffrey, James Allen. *"Tom Tower, Christ Church, Oxford"*. *C.W. Faulkner & Co. P.U. 1906.*

Shuffrey, James Allen   **fl. c.1900-1925**
Landscape and architectural artist who lived in Oxford and was a teacher of art. He painted watercolour views of Oxford colleges for an "Allen Shuffrey Series", as well as a "Garden Series" for the Bocardo Press (Alden & Co., Ltd.), Oxford.

Shurey's Publications   **pre-1906**
This firm gave away postcards to encourage people to buy their magazines. The cards carry the following statement: "This beautiful Series of Fine Art Postcards is supplied free exclusively by Shurey's Publications comprising "Smart Novels", "Yes and No" and "Dainty Novels". The Publications are obtainable throughout Great Britain, the Colonies and Foreign Countries".

The cards, which included high quality coloured views, were printed by Delittle, Fenwick & Co. of York. Some postcards even show Empire views, e.g. Lucknow, India. There is also a set showing underground stations.

Ref: Check list in S.G.P.C., 1983, pp. 7-11.

"Signal Series"   **pre-1917**
E. & S. Ltd. Publisher, Dublin and Belfast. R.P. and coloured views.

Sigsbeaker, Mary
American artist who designed for Reinthal & Newman. Her cards were sold in Britain by Charles Hauff & Co.

Silhouette Cards
Several firms issued silhouette cards, e.g. Photochrom's "Camp Silhouette Series" of 24 cards by G.E. Shepheard and Stewart & Woolf's views of towns. One of the most successful silhouette artists was Margaret Tarrant (q.v.) who designed cards with fairies or children for the Medici Society.

Silk, Reginald
Photographer/publisher, Portsmouth, Hampshire. Issued cards described as "Striking Photographs showing a submarine diving and rising to the surface".

Sillence, E., & Son
Publisher, Romsey, Hampshire. "Sillence Photo Series".

Silver Jubilee
Cards were issued to celebrate the Silver Jubilee of King George V and Queen Mary on 6 May, 1935.

Simkin, R.
Painter of military subjects who designed some early cards for Faulkner depicting regiments of the Empire.

Simms, Percy
Photographer/publisher, Chipping Norton, Oxfordshire. Trademark a four-sided pillar box. "Fourshire Series" of local views.

Simnett, J.S.   **pre-1909**
Photographer/publisher, Burton upon Trent, Staffordshire. Local photographs, e.g. Bass Brewery Works Outing to Great Yarmouth, 1909.

Simonetti, Amedeo Momo   **1874-1922**
Italian artist born in Rome and lived there throughout his life. Painted seascapes but is best known for his glamour postcard designs.

Simpson, A.J.
Artist who painted birds for "Feathered World" (q.v.).

243

"Salvington Mill, Nr. Worthing".
J. Salmon.

"Old Malt House, Gomshall, Surrey".
J. Salmon.

"Folkestone. Departure of Channel Boat".
J. Salmon.

Simpson, F.W.
Publisher, The Book Shop, Carnoustie, Scotland. Local views.

Simpson, George W.
Publisher, 5 Northbrook St., Newbury, Berkshire. Local views.

Simpson's-in-the-Strand
Advertiser of "The Famous Old English Eating House" using cartoons by H.M. Bateman, e.g. "The gentleman who asked the carver whether the meat was English or Foreign".
See: Colour Plate 1.

Sims, George Robert   **1847-1922**
Journalist and author. Joined the staff of *Fun* in 1874 and wrote many stories about London life. There are many postcards in Blum & Degen's "Kromo" Series which were based on illustrations in his books. Each card bears a facsim. of his signature to show that they were used with his approval.

Simson & Co. Ltd.
Publisher, Hertford.

Singer Sewing Machines Co. Ltd.
Publisher and advertiser. This firm issued several series in which the advertising element was subsidiary. They included "Costumes of All Nations", "Our Ironclads", R.P.s supplied by Cribb of Southsea, and a series on aircraft. Some Singer cards have French titles.

Sinn Fein
During W.W.I., despite the fact that the leader of the Irish Nationalist Party had pledged the loyalty of Ireland to the Crown, certain elements, among them members of the political movement Sinn Fein, believed that the union of Britain and Ireland could only be dissolved by force. They staged a rebellion in Dublin in 1916, the Easter Rising, and postcard photographs of the event, mainly taken in Sackville St., were published by Hely's Ltd. of Dublin, Rotary and Valentine.

Ski-ing
A few cards show skiers on Ben Nevis, but most cards featuring this sport show skiers on Alpine slopes and were imported, e.g. the Salzburg Winter Sports of 1914.

Skipper Sardines
Poster-type advertising cards.

Skipton Stationery Co.
Publisher, Skipton, Yorkshire.

Slights
Photographer/publisher, Pocklington, Yorkshire. Local views.

Slogans
Slogans began to appear in postmarks after W.W.I. The Post Office was anxious to extend the use of the telephone and used this method in the 1920s to encourage people to invest in an instrument. Slogans noted include:

1918	"Buy National War Bonds".
1926	"Say it by Telephone".
1926-8	"British Goods are Best".
1932	"The Best Investment — a Telephone".
	"You are Wanted on the Telephone".
1939	"Road Users/Take Care/Avoid Risks".

Small, David   **fl. c.1887-1905**
Scottish artist who painted scenes for Tuck "Oilette" sets on "Aberdeen, Deeside" and "Historic Houses — Scotland".

Sims, George Robert. *A "Mrs. Caudle" card. "No. 1. Mrs. Caudle fears infection in her husband's correspondence". Blum & Degen "Kromo" Series.*

Small, David. *"Largo. Birthplace of Alexander Selkirk". Facsim. by R. Tuck & Sons. "Oilette" "Historic Houses — Scotland".*

"Smart Novels". *"Let Us Begin the New Year Well"*.
Shurey's Publications.

Smalley, Philip
Film actor. Sepia portrait by *Pictures Ltd*.

"Smart Novels"
Romantic and military cards in a give-away "Smart Novels"
Series by Shurey's Publications.

Smee, A.   pre-1915
Publisher, Silver St., Salisbury, Wiltshire. Cards with two
differing coloured views separated by a central coat of arms.

Smith, A.A. (trading as N. Wells)   pre-1919
Stationer/publisher, St. John St., Ashbourne, Derbyshire.
Local R.P. views.

Smith, Albert, Ltd.   pre-1918
Photographer/publisher, Jersey, C.I. Local photographic
views, e.g. "Carting Seaweed", printed in France.

Smith, B.
Photographer/publisher, Heckington, Lincolnshire. Local
photographic views.

Smith, Edward Gordon   fl. 1903-1916
Publisher, 68 Allerton Rd., London, N., until 1905 when he
moved to 15 Stroud Green Rd. The first cards were views of
London and the countryside of Hertfordshire and Essex. The
photographs were taken by E. Gordon Smith and often simply
bear the name of "G. Smith". After his death in 1906 the
family continued the firm, and scenes were published of other
areas in such series as "Beauty Spots of the British Isles" and
"Gems of British Scenery". London scenes were also printed
in pairs separated by a coat of arms.

A "Pinachrome" Series of coloured views included facsims.
of paintings by Jotter. Some views in this series are outlined in
tinsel and have printed tinsel greetings.

Sets of cards also show the various types of railway engine
used by the major railway companies.

A few photographs of events were also published and some
coloured views of London theatres.

Smith, Frank   pre-1906
Publisher, High St., Oxford. Local sepia views.

Smith, G.
See: Edward Gordon Smith.

Smith, Harold H.
Designer of two sets of "Political Leaders" for Tuck which
were drawn in crayon. He also designed posters, one of which
was reproduced as a postcard by David Allen.

Smith, H.J.   1900
Publisher/importer, King's Rd. Library, Brighton. Issued a
series of hand-coloured views of Brighton. However, he is best
known as an importer of postcards from the Continent. These
included cards by the artists Asti, Kirchner, Lessieux and
Mucha, as well as some silk postcards woven in France.

Smith, Jessie Willcox   1863-1935
American painter and illustrator who worked in New York
and specialised in child subjects for Reinthal & Newman.
Ref: Cope p. 29, ill. p. 63.

Smith, Lizzie Caswall
Photographer who took portraits of actors and actresses for
Millar & Lang's "National Series".

Smith, M., & Co.
Publisher, Oxford. Photographic views.

Smith, May
Painter of a set of cards titled "Scottie's Fun" for the Medici
Society.

Smith, R.   pre-1926
Publisher/stationer, 37-9 Gateford Rd., Worksop, Nottinghamshire.

Smith, Reginald, R.B.A.   1855-1925
Landscape painter. Exh. R.A. 19. Bristol artist who painted
views for E.W. Savory.

Smith, Robert Henry   fl. c.1900-1910
Artist and illustrator. Exh. R.A.1. Painted an "Eventful
Nelson" set for Tuck.

Smith, Sidney
Photographer/publisher, Pickering, Yorkshire.

Smith, Sidney
Designer of comic and historical cards for the Victor Publishing Co.

Smith, W.H., & Son   pre-1906
Publisher. Trademark "W.H.S." in an oval with "Smith's
Circulating Library" printed in the stamp rectangle. Cards
were grouped in series, e.g. "Aldwych", "Derwent",
"Grosvenor", "Kingsway" and "Souvenir". Subjects
included:
(i)   Views; some of these bear a tell-tale "JV" within a small
        circle on the picture side indicating that they were
        supplied by Valentine.

(ii) Real Photo Series, "Kingsway", including views by Aerofilms Ltd.
(iii) "Passing Events" include topical cards.
(iv) Woodcuts of London.
(v) Children's cards.
(vi) Railways and railway stations, ill. Byatt 283.
(vii) Shipping cards.
(viii) Novelty cards, see "The X-Ray Illusion Postcard" under Novelty Cards.

Smith, W. & H., Ltd.   **1903**
Publisher, Journal Press, Evesham, Worcestershire. Trademarks (a) an anvil with two hammers; (b) Lygon Series with the coat of arms of the Lygon family. Cards include:
(i) "Shakespeare's Avon", 36 cards in all.
(ii) Facsims. of watercolours of Broadway.
(iii) Cards for the Headland Hotel, Newquay, with views of the local scenery.

Smith, William   **pre-1923**
Publisher, Dorking, Surrey. Sepia views.

Smith, William Jr.   **fl. 1889-1919**
Scottish artist who lived in Edinburgh and moved to Aberdeen before the turn of the century. Exh. R.S.A. He illustrated *Highlands and Islands* for A. & C. Black and facsims. of these illustrations were used in Tuck's "Bonnie Scotland" sets.

Sneath, R.
Photographer/publisher, Sheffield, Yorkshire.

"Snow White and the Seven Dwarfs"
A series by Valentine based on the film cartoon of that title.

Snowden Bros.
Publisher, Dartford, Kent.

Snowdon Mountain Tramroad & Motel Co. Ltd.
Publisher of views of Snowdon with serial nos. to 60.

Snowman, Isaac   **fl. 1892-1919**
Figure and portrait painter. Exh. R.A. 32. Painted a portrait of Edward VII used by Tuck after the King's death.

Society for the Propagation of the Gospel   **pre-1918**
Publisher of coloured views of foreign missions.

Solomko, S.
Russian artist. Designer of cards showing young people in traditional dress.

Solomon Bros. Ltd.   **fl. 1911-1918**
Publisher, 12 Chapel St., Milton St., London, E.C., and after 1914 at Graphic House, 204 New North Rd., N., expanding to 206 and 208. Trademark "S.B. Series". Output included:
(i) Greetings cards.
(ii) Coloured views in a "Sun-Rays Series", serial nos. to over 9000.
(iii) Studio photographs with captions, e.g. "I's Afraid of a Mouse".
(iv) Louis Wain card, ill. Byatt 284.
(v) Patriotic cards which became a major part of their output during W.W.I., ill. Byatt 288.

Somerville, Howard   **fl. c.1905-1940**
Scottish figure painter who specialised in glamour. Exh. R.A. 14.

Sonrel, Elizabeth   **fl. c.1893-1930**
French artist born in Tours. Figure painter and illustrator in the art nouveau style.

"South Down" Series
Facsims. of Sussex paintings by W.E. Croxford (q.v.).

South Eastern & Chatham Railway
Several sets by McCorquodale & Co. of stations, locomotives, ships and maps. Many cross-channel cards.
    Ref: R.O.P.L., No. 11, pp. 14-18.

South Eastern Railway
A single card has been recorded of the buffet at the Gare Maritime, Boulogne-sur-Mer.
    Ref: R.O.P.L., No. 11, p. 13.

South Polar Expedition
Robert Falcon Scott organised a national Antarctic Expedition in 1900-4 to explore the ice sheet. He wrote *The Voyage of the Discovery* in 1905. In 1910 he sailed again to the Antarctic in the *Terra Nova* and reached the South Pole after Amundsen in 1912. On the return journey the five explorers died as a result of appalling weather conditions but a search party later found the bodies and recovered all their records. A postcard was issued "In Memoriam of the Antarctic Heroes" with portraits of Bowers, Evans, Oates, Scott and Wilson.
    For the earlier expedition in 1901 Wrench published a series of cards some of which were taken with the *Discovery* and posted on the journey to the Antarctic. Others by Rotary show the *Terra Nova* in port with an inset portrait of Captain Scott taken by Dinham of Torquay.

Southey, C.F.
Publisher, South Tottenham, London, Humorous boy scout cards.

Southwood, F.C.   **fl. 1901-c.1913**
Publisher/stationer, 96 Regent St., London, W. Output included:
(i) Hunting scenes.
(ii) Motor cars.
(iii) Comic cards.
(iv) Royalty.
(v) London views.
(vi) "Greetings from London" cards.
(vii) Humorous "coats of arms" for various sports.
    Southwood held an annual postcard exhibition of British and foreign cards in Regent St. from 1901 to 1904.

Souvenir Cards
Souvenir cards were published for special occasions. Cards issued at exhibitions are well known but they were also available at conferences and assemblies, of which the following are examples:
(i) The Philatelic Congress, Margate, 1912, cards showing the hotel, Congress Hall. Special stamps were issued to mark the occasion.
(ii) National Union of Teachers' Annual Conference, Great Yarmouth, 1931; a souvenir of the Conference, in the form of a Valentine "Bromotype" postcard with a view of the pier, was presented to members by Morton's of Highbury Place, London, N.5, who for 20 years had been entrusted with the furnishing of the Conference Reception Room.

Sowerby, Millicent   **1878-1967**
Watercolour painter, daughter of J.G. Sowerby, owner of the

glass works near Newcastle upon Tyne which produced "Sowerby Pressed Glass". She was greatly influenced by her father's friends in the Art Workers' Guild. Her style derived from the artists she admired, particularly Kate Greenaway. She illustrated children's books written by her sister over a period of 20 years but she found time to design postcards from about 1905. Several publishers issued sets including:

(i) C.W. Faulkner, a series illustrating Shakespearean quotations.

(ii) H. Frowde and Hodder & Stoughton, "Postcards for the Little Ones", a series to which she contributed about 30 sets including "Little Folk of Many Lands", "Little Patriots", "Britain and her Friends", "Happy Days", "Little Jewels" and "The Children's Day". Humphrey Milford took over from Hodder & Stoughton in 1917.

(iii) Meissner & Buch, a single series of children in medieval costume.

(iv) Misch & Co., two series using "Greenaway" in the titles.

(v) Reinthal & Newman, two sets.

(vi) Salmon, several sets, e.g. "Nursery Rhymes".

Refs: A detailed list is included in an article by Cope, D. & P., P.P.A. 1982, pp. 6-7; see also Cope p. 22, ill. p. 55.

Spalding, Fred   pre-1910
Photographer/publisher, Chelmsford, Essex. Trademark: "Spalding's Post Cards" with a coat of arms and the motto "Many Minds One Heart". Noted for a series of photographs of the rail disaster at Witham, Essex.

Spas
In the 19th century the healing value of certain natural waters was extolled by many doctors and spas grew up around the springs and wells where such treatment could be obtained. Bath, Cheltenham, Clifton, Malvern, Harrogate and Tunbridge Wells all attracted people anxious to "take the cure". The popularity of the spas, though declining, continued into Edwardian times and it is sometimes possible to find cards which show the wells at this period. In addition to the major spas mentioned above, the following may also be

Spas. *"The Kursaal, Harrogate". Publisher unknown. P.U. 1907.*

Spence, Seaton. *"The Gordon Highlanders". Publisher unknown. P.U. 1936.*

traced: Buxton, Innerleithen, Leamington, Llandrindod Wells, Matlock, Tenbury Wells, Trefriw and Woodhall Spa.

Ref: E.S. Turner, *Taking the Cure*, 1967.

Spashett & Co.
Photographer/publisher, Lowestoft, Suffolk. Local R.P. views.

Spatz
Pseudonym of Fred Gothard (q.v.).

Spearman, George
Publisher, Winchester, Hampshire. P.P.s of boxers.

Specht
Artist who painted studies of dogs for M. Munk.

Spence, Percy F.W.   fl. 1896-1916
Australian artist. Exh. R.A. 7. Painted two sets on "Australian Life" for Tuck's "Wide Wide World" Series, 7962-3.

Spence, Seaton
Signature on a picture of "The Gordon Highlanders" by an unknown publisher.

Spence, T.H.
Publisher, The Hotel, Hayburn Wyke, Yorkshire. P.P.s printed in Saxony.

Spencer
Publisher, Coleshill, Warwickshire. Midland views.

Sperlich, T.
Munich animal painter who designed sets with horses and kittens for Ettlinger.

Spinney, Charles
Publisher, Bere Regis, Dorset. Local R.P. views.

Sport & General
Photographer/publisher. Portraits of wartime leaders. They also supplied photographs to other publishers, e.g. Beagles.

Spratt's Dog Food
Advertising cards mainly in a "Champion Dogs" Series. A

Spratt's Dog Food. *"Caesar, the Late King Edward's Favourite Dog. A Pathetic Mourner in the Funeral Procession"*.

special card was published in 1910 shortly after the funeral of Edward VII. The following text appeared on the reverse:

A man's dog stands by him in prosperity and poverty, in health and in sickness. He will sleep on the cold ground when the wintry winds blow and the snow drives fiercely if only he may be by his master's side.

He will kiss the hand that has no food to offer, he will lick the wounds and sores that come in encounter with the roughness of the world.

He guards the sleep of his pauper master as if he were a king. When all other friends desert he remains. When riches take wings and reputation falls to pieces, he is as constant in his love as the sun in its journeys through the heavens.

Love — love your dog. Feed him — as your best friend — as he should be fed. Avoid soft, sweetened, or medicated food. Give him his Spratt's biscuit dry, and see that every cake is stamped "Spratt's Patent" with a "X" in the centre.

Spring Bros.   pre-1922
Publisher, Express Office, St. Anne's-on-the-Sea, and at Ansdell, Lancashire. Coloured and sepia views.

Spurgin, Frederick   1882-1968
Prolific designer of comic cards who usually signed Fred Spurgin. Worked for several publishers including:
(i) Art & Humour Publishing Co. which was founded by a member of his family. Sets included: "Civil Life", "Charmer", "Foster", "Our Munitions", "Sea Blue", "Seaside Series", "Topole", "Topping", "Wee Scottie".
(ii) Avenue Publishing Co., contributions to "Paternoster Series".
(iii) E.J. Hey & Co.
(iv) Inter-Art Co., sets include: "American Kiddies", "Camp Series", "Cat-Bow Series", "Katchy Kids", "Kiddeo", "Leap Year", "Wee Mites" and a "Patriotic Series" during W.W.I. Ill. Monahan 59.
(v) Thridgould & Co., at least two sets.
(vi) Watkins & Kracke.

Many of Spurgin's cards were simply signed F.S., ill. D. & M. 109.
See: Colour Plate 23.

Spy
See: Sir Leslie Matthew Ward.

S.R. & Co.
Scott Russell & Co. (q.v.).

Stafford's
Publisher, Tunbridge Wells, Kent.

Stage Celebrities
In Edwardian times the theatre and music hall were major sources of entertainment; actors and actresses became well-known personalities and were constantly photographed. Actresses had glamour value and their postcard photographs were the pin-ups of the day. As long as they looked attractive their acting talents were a secondary consideration. Some actresses found posing for photographs a profitable occupation and appear to have spent more time in the studios than on the stage. Photographers went to great lengths to obtain unusual poses. One of the most extraordinary is of Gertie Millar dressed in white holding a small beribboned dog. Around her are eight boy chimney sweeps with brushes at the ready. Many publishers explored this field. The photographic companies such as Beagles, Rotophot and Rotary were naturally active, some published special series, e.g. Davidson's "Footlight Favourites" and Tuck's "Celebrities of the Stage".

A few publishers, notably Beagles, Giesen, Rotary and Tuck issued bookmarker cards (q.v.) with portraits of actors and actresses. Many cards were published showing scenes from the plays in which they took part.

Stage Photo Co.
Photographer/publisher, London.

Stained Glass Windows
A few publishers took interior views of colleges, churches and other historic buildings. Some of these show notable stained glass windows, e.g. the Burne Jones window at Peterhouse College, Cambridge.

Stained Glass Windows. *"Cambridge, Peterhouse College, Window by Burne-Jones"*. Frith's Series.

Stannard, Henry Sylvester. *"Walberswick Bridge"*. Facsim. by F. Jenkins.

Staples, L. *Facsim. of an unidentified locality by S. Hildesheimer & Co.*

Stamp Cards
These were published by several German firms showing small collections of the stamps of various European countries.

Stamp Rectangle
The printed rectangle placed in the top right-hand corner on the address side of a card. In unstamped cards it often provides information about the printer, the cost of posting, etc.

Standard Pictorial Postcard Co.　　fl. 1905-1907
Publisher, 83 Bishopsgate St. Without, London, E.C. Trademark "The Standard Card". Output included:
(i)　"Iridescent" views printed on a ground of many colours.
(ii)　Romantic cards.
(iii)　Comic cards.
(iv)　Animals and children.

Stannard, Henry Sylvester, R.B.A., R.S.A.　　1870-1951
Landscape painter. Exh. R.A. 35. Views of the country north of London were used in facsims. by Salmon and he painted a "Sylvester Stannard Series" of Suffolk landscapes for F. Jenkins of Southwold.

Staples, L.
Landscape artist whose paintings were used in facsims. by Hildesheimer.

"Star Series"
Tradename used by Gottschalk, Dreyfus & Davis.

Starr-Wood　　1870-1944
Humorous artist and illustrator. Colour blind, he worked in black and white. Founded the *Starr-Wood's Magazine* which was published from 1910-35.
　　Ref: Cuppleditch, D., 'Starr Wood: Postcard Artist', P.P.M., October 1981, p. 10.

Start, S.H., & Sons　　pre-1925
Photographers/publishers, Wolverhampton. Local R.P. views.

State Publishing Co. (Ltd.)　　c.1905 (Ltd. 1909)
Publisher, Central Chambers, 17a South Castle St., Liverpool. Output included:
(i)　General views of Liverpool and its surroundings.
(ii)　Greetings cards.
(iii)　Ocean liners.

Stately Homes
　　See: Historic Houses.

Stationery Co.
Publisher, Skipton, Yorkshire. Trademark "Herald" with an outline of a herald. "Herald Series" of local coloured views in oval frames.

Statues
Statues are erected in towns and cities to mark the association with a particular person often years after death. Many examples are found on postcards; they include:
　　King Alfred, Wantage and Winchester.
　　Byron, Trinity College, Dublin.
　　King Charles II, Quadrangle, Windsor; Pictorial Stationery Co.
　　Joseph Cowen, Newcastle upon Tyne.
　　King George III, Windsor Great Park; Misch & Co.
　　Charles Kingsley, Bideford.
　　King Robert the Bruce, Stirling; Valentine.
Statues of horses may also be found:
　　The Copper Horse, Long Walk, Windsor.
　　Persimmon, Sandringham; H. Coates.

Stead, Henry
Son of W.T. Stead, a noted journalist, Henry Stead was editor of the *Review of Reviews*. In 1902 he published a series of "Current Event Postcards" which were issued in association with E. Wrench Ltd.
　　Ref: A list of 13 of these rare cards is given in Byatt, p. 360.

Statues. *"Cowen Monument, Newcastle-on-Tyne"*. Gottschalk, Dreyfus & Davis. *"Star Series"*.

Statues. *"Windsor Great Park Statue of George III"*. A Misch & Co. *"Camera Graph"*.

Steeplechasing. *"The Water Jump"*. Birn Bros. P.U. 1910.

Steam Lorries
These were steam engines built into the transport vehicle.

Steam Rollers
Heavy steam engines fitted to rollers which were and still are used for road work.

Steeplechasing
Several publishers issued cards on steeplechasing:
(i)   Birn Bros.
(ii) Boots Cash Chemists, R.P. cards, e.g. "Steeplechase at Sandown Park".
(iii) Tuck devoted three sets to steeplechasing.
(iv) Steeplechasing scenes by Bianchi and other Italian artists were imported for sale in Britain.

Steinlen, Alexandre Theophile   1859-1923
Born in Lausanne, Switzerland, this young painter moved to Paris at the age of 18 and joined a group of artists working for magazines and poster designing. His work often depicted Paris night life.

Stengel & Co. Ltd.   1901
Publisher, 39 Redcross St., London, E.C. This was the address of their British agent, O. Flammger, whose initials often precede the name of the firm. Tinted or black and white views with red captions on cards printed in Dresden. Early U.B. cards give "Dresden-Berlin" after the name of the firm. Their many British views have a wide geographical coverage. In addition to view cards there were two series of gallery reproductions: "World Galleries", also marketed by Misch & Co., and an "Old Masters" Series. Serial nos. exceed 18000.

Adventure of a Runaway.
A Horse's sensational feat of bolting down
these 66 steps and running a mile before
being stopped. Feby. 6. 1905.

Steps and Ladders. *"Adventure of a Runaway. A Horse's sensational feat of bolting down these 66 steps and running a mile before being stopped. Feby. 6 1905"*. Publisher unknown.

Jacob's Ladder, Falmouth.

Steps and Ladders. *"Jacob's Ladder, Falmouth"*. Eyre & Spottiswoode's *"Woodbury Series"*.

Steps and Ladders
These are common in hilly country. Many have been named "Jacob's Ladder". Postcards abound and have their devoted collectors.

Stereoscopic Living Picture Co.   1904
Publisher, 34a Castle St., Salisbury, Wiltshire. This firm appears to have been formed to produce and market a "Magic Postcard" invented by T. and E.O. Browne of Bournemouth.
    See Magic Stereoscopic Cards under Novelty Cards.

Stereoscopic Postcard Co.   1906
Publisher, Essex House, High St., Stratford, London, E. This short-lived firm published cards which could be viewed through a stereoscope.

Sternberg, V.W.
Painter of comic subjects who sometimes signed with his initials only — "V.W.S." His cards were published in a "Humorous" Series by James Henderson & Sons Ltd., and he contributed comic cards to Valentine and Regent Publishing Series.

Sternol Motor Oil
Poster-type advertising cards in comic vein designed by John Hassall.

Stevens & Co.
Photographer/publisher, Thirsk, Yorkshire.

Stevens, C.H.
Landscape painter who contributed to J.W. Ruddock's "Artist Series".

WESTON-SUPER-MARE.- OLD ROMAN STEPS.

Steps and Ladders. *Weston-super-Mare — Old Roman Steps"*. Lance & Lance. P.U. 1916.

"WELL, THESE WILL TAKE A LOT OF BEATING!"

Sternberg, V.W. *"Well, These Will Take a Lot of Beating."* Comic card in J. Henderson & Sons' *"Humorous"* Series.

Stevens, E.   **pre-1906**
Photographer/publisher, 12 High St., Poole, Dorset. Local photographic views.

Stevens, Edward
Painter who designed the decorative work on Boer War cards by the Picture Postcard Co.

Stevens, Thomas
Publisher of Woven Silk Postcards, Stevengraph Works, Coventry. These consisted of a thin pressed card which surrounded a silk panel. Subjects included views, portraits, greetings, and ocean liners — the largest category. In all 117 such cards have been recorded.
    Ref: Godden, G.A., *Stevengraphs and other Victorian Silk Pictures,* 1971.

Stevenson, E.W.
Printer/publisher, 53 Thoro'fare, Woodbridge, Suffolk. Black and white local views.

Stewart, Elise H.
Landscape artist who painted views for Savory.

Stewart, F.A.
Animal and figure painter who designed sets for Ernest Nister including one of horses' heads and one titled "Coaching Life". He also designed the "King's Army" Series for Valentine.

Stewart, George, & Co.   **1894**
Publisher, 92 George St., Edinburgh. A firm reputed to have published the first picture postcards in Britain in 1894; views of Edinburgh, followed shortly afterwards by views of other parts of Scotland. Thereafter, developments were rapid:
(i)   "The Edinburgh Postcards", vignettes with various views of the city printed in black and white and later in colour, on U.B. cards, followed later by more Edinburgh views.
(ii)   London views.
(iii)   "At Khartoum", a set about the Nile Expedition in 1898.
(iv)   "South African War Postcards".
(v)   Glasgow Exhibition, 1901.
(vi)   Literary sets with Walter Scott and R.L. Stevenson associations.
(vii)   Watercolour facsims. of Scottish scenery "Offset" Series.
(viii) "Crofter Scenes in the Highlands".

Stewart, J.A.
Scottish artist who painted historical military uniforms titled "The King's Army" for Valentine, ill. Byatt col. pl. IVW.

Stewart & Woolf   **pre-1901**
Publisher, 8-9 Charles St., Hatton Garden, London, E.C.1. Trademark for 1904 a lion holding a crown. Output included:
(i)   Greetings cards.
(ii)   Comic cards.
(iii)   Views, especially rural scenes.
(iv)   Cities and towns at night with windows lit.
(v)   A coronation set and portraits of royalty and heads of state.
(vi)   "Fiscal" Series of political cartoons by J.H. Roberts.
(vii)   "Dickens Character Sketches" by Alfred Crowquill.
(viii) Spy cartoons from *Vanity Fair.*
(ix)   "Write-on" sets including "Old Coaching Scenes".
(x)   Military cards by Harry Payne.

Stiebel, Alfred, & Co.   **c.1910-1916**
Fine Art Publisher, 10 Christopher St., Finsbury Square, London, E.C. and later, c.1912, at 2-4 Scrutton St., London, E.C. Tradename "Alpha". Output included:
(i)   Birthday cards, "Elegant" Series.
(ii)   Reproductions of mid-Victorian paintings.
(iii)   Japanese girls, hand-coloured sets.
(iv)   Humorous series under the title "Modern Humour", with printed and hand-coloured cards.
(v)   Novelty cards of many kinds: mechanical, appliqué, feathered, etc.
(vi)   An "Alpha" Series of hunting scenes.
(vii)   Imported cards from America issued by the Edward Gross Company.
    In 1916 the company adopted its tradename and became the Alpha Publishing Co. (q.v.).

Stiles, Leslie   **b.1876**
Actor who played opposite Camille Clifford in *The Catch of the Season,* 1904, ill. Hill p. 25. P.P. by Rotary.

Stocker, Blanche
Actress. P.P. by Davidson.

Stocks
The device for the punishment of offenders against the law consisted a two baulks of timber padlocked together to imprison the feet. Examples are featured on postcards. They

Colour Plate 22: Railway cards

"N. E. R. East Coast Express Leaving Waverley Station, Edinburgh". Alphalsa Publishing Co.

"Paddington Station, G. W. R." R. Tuck & Sons. "Oilette" "London Railway Stations".

"L. B. & S. C. Victoria Brighton Train (Arrival)" by H. Fleury. Misch & Co. "Noted Trains" Series.

were last used in England in early Victorian times. A posed photograph by the Pictorial Stationery Co. shows how people were imprisoned.

Stoddart & Co. Ltd.   **fl. c.1905-1914**
Publisher, 23 Charles St., Square Rd., Halifax, Yorkshire. Trademark "Ja-Ja" within a shield outline. Output included:
(i) Local street scenes.
(ii) Heraldic cards.
(iii) Scottish Clans-and-Tartans.
The Heraldic and the Clans-and-Tartans cards are very finely produced not only in their design and colouring but also in their comprehensive coverage which must have involved a great deal of research.
Ref: *The Scottish Tartans: The Badges and Arms of the Chiefs of the Clans & Families.*

Stoddart, R.W.   **fl. 1920s**
Designer of comic cards. Exh. R.A. 1. He was an architect by profession.

Stokes, George Vernon, R.B.A., R.M.S.   **1873-1954**
Landscape and animal painter. Exh. R.A. 13. Collaborated with Alan Wright to produce a coaching series for Faulkner and painted a "Celesque" Series of horses' heads for Photochrom.

Stolterfoht, Caroline R. (Mrs.)   **fl. 1902-1908**
Landscape artist who painted a North Berwick set for Tuck, 7460.

Stone Circles
Many stone circles are featured on postcards, especially Stonehenge. Others include Avebury, the Standing Stones at Stenner, near Kirkwall, and the Druidical Stones at Callanish, near Stornoway. In all there are some 50 examples in Great Britain.
Refs: Burl, A., *Rings of Stone: The Pre-historic Circles of Britain and Ireland,* 1979; Michele, J., *Megalithomania,* 1982.

Stone, F.S.
Designer of comic cycling cards. Exh. R.A. 1 in 1911. Lived in Cheyne Walk, London.

Stone, Henry, & Son Ltd.   **pre-1913**
Publisher, Banbury. Glamour portraits in watercolour by Elsie Burrell, e.g. Gladys Cooper from life.

Stone, H.G.
Photographer/publisher, Slough, Buckinghamshire. "Stone's Regent Series" of coloured views and some R.P.s of early aeroplanes.

Storey & Co.   **pre-1919**
Publisher, New Brighton, Cheshire. Local views including New Brighton Tower, demolished before 1921.

Storm Damage
Rough seas provided a subject for hundreds of cards yet the damage they caused was minimal except for the seaside piers; one exception was at Hastings in October 1906. Few cards show storm damage inland.
See: Piers and Pier Disasters.

Stower, Willi
Postcard artist whose work is highly valued.

Stower's Lime Juice
Advertising cards for the Lime Juice "as supplied to Their Majesties the King and Queen".

Strake, Prof. J.
Figure painter of nude studies, e.g. "Psyche".

Straker, S.
Publisher, Ludgate Hill, London. Black and white vignettes of London.

Straker, W., Ltd.   **pre-1903**
Publisher, 68 Notting Hill Gate, London, W. Black and white views of London.

Strand Magazine
Postcards to advertise Conan Doyle's thriller, *Sir Nigel,* 1906.

Strange, H.M.
Publisher, Post Office, St. Ives, Cornwall. Local R.P. views.

Street, John William
Photographer/publisher, Huddersfield, Yorkshire. Local R.P. views.

Street Markets
Postcards of the London street markets are fairly common. Provincial street markets are more difficult to find. Some were combined with cattle markets.

Stone Circles. *"Stonehenge from West, Salisbury Plain".* Valentine's *"Sepiatype"* Series.

Street Markets. *"Wentworth Street, Petticoat Lane".* Auto-Photo Series. *Publisher unknown. P.U. 1912.*

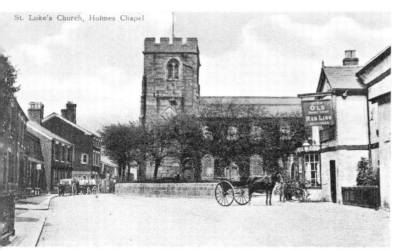

Street Scenes. *"St. Luke's Church, Holmes Chapel".
Cheshire, 1908. Village scene with church, inn and horse and
trap. G.P. Tomlinson, Pictorial Post Card Specialist, Holmes
Chapel.*

Street Scenes. *"On the Quay, Gt. Yarmouth". A seaside town
and fishing port. Note the costumes. Valentine's Series.*

Street Scenes. *"London. Mansion House". Apart from the
building, the traffic is of particular interest. Publisher
unknown.*

Street Scenes. *"The High Street, Lyndhurst, Hants". Note the
posed cyclist. F.G.O. Stuart. Typical card by this Hampshire
publisher.*

Street Scenes

One of the most fascinating of all postcard themes, particularly to the collector who concentrates on his home town or
the town where he lives.

Street and seaside scenes reflect fashions clearly, particularly
if the cards are examined with a magnifying glass.

Stretton, Philip Eustace, R.O.I.   **fl. c.1884-1915**
Animal and sporting painter. Exh. R.A. 32.

Strikes

Cards usually show strike meetings, marchers, or groups on

Street Scenes. *"High Street. Cowes". Commercial traffic, a
hotel, advertisements of a cabinet maker and a photographer.
Hartmann.*

Strikes. *A comic comment: "Things Are Very Slack After the Strike". R.P. by Hart Publishing Co. Ltd.*

picket duty. Occasionally there are cards showing evicted strikers. Examples include:

Grimsby Trawler Dispute, 1901.
Hemsworth Colliery strike, Yorkshire, evicted miners.
Liverpool strike, 1911, Government sent in troops, 80 magnificent photographs by Carbonora (q.v.).
Liverpool strike, 1918, strike with police.
Llandudno Railway strike.
Llanelly Railway strike.
Northampton bootworkers' strike, 1905.
Tonypandy, coal strike 1921. R.P.s of Wiltshire Constabulary who were called in.
Refs: Marks, J., 'Industrial Unrest in Edwardian England', P.P.A., 1984, pp. 23-5; Pinfold, D., 'The Bootmakers March from Raunds to London', P.P.M. December 1981, p.32.

Stroom, Jan
Pseudonym used by John Noble Barlow (q.v.).

Stryjenska
Polish artist who designed cards in the cubist style using bright colours. Village scenes with girls dancing and men drinking.

Stuart, Connie
Actress. P.P. by J.J. Samuels.

Stuart, F.G.O.   c.1901
Publisher, 57-61 Cromwell Rd., Southampton, Hampshire.

Studdy, George E. *"I'm keeping my end up here". Valentine "Bonzo" card. P.U. 1934.*

Francis Stuart had been a photographer for nearly 20 years before he became a postcard publisher. His output consisted entirely of views which were printed in Germany. Confined himself to three main areas:
(i)   London, including fine cards of the Albert Memorial and the Albert Hall.
(ii) Hampshire, his home county.
(iii) The Channel Islands.
His output included many views of Southampton shipping.

Studdy, George E.   1878-1948
Devon artist who contributed to *Punch* and *The Graphic* between 1902 and 1912. Specialised in humorous drawings of animals and children and sometimes used the pseudonym Cheero. Created the pink and white puppy dog Bonzo who is always getting into mischief. Bonzo cards were first published in the Inter-Art "Comique Series" in the 1920s and are still in print today.

Studdy also designed comic animal cards for Mansell and "Humoresque" cards for Valentine.

Studholme, Marie   1876-1930
Actress and vocalist. She played in *The Toreador* at the Gaiety Theatre which ran for 675 performances. One of the most photographed of all actresses. P.P.s by Beagles, 4; Davidson; Hildesheimer; Millar & Lang; Philco; Picture Postcard Co.; Odol, advertisement card; Rapid Photo Co.; Rotary, 8; Rotophot; Woolstone Bros.
Illustration overleaf.

Studio Photographs
Many photographers printed postcard size portraits of individuals or groups at the request of their customers who could then send copies to relatives and friends. Few of these photographs are identifiable, but in any case they are of some interest because they show the costumes and furniture of the day. Some photographers had special props. Claude Low of Edinburgh, used a backdrop view of Princes St. and seated his subjects in a motor car.
Illustration overleaf.

Studholme, Marie. *Signed photograph. One of the many taken of this actress. Woolstone Bros. Milton "Glossette" Series. P.U. 1906.*

Studio Photographs. *Two ladies sitting in a car taken by Claude Low, 72 Princes St., Edinburgh. The backcloth shows Princes St.*

Sturgess, John   **fl. pre-1900**
Sporting and animal painter. His work was used in Elliman's Liniment advertising cards.

Submarines
The first British submarine was designed and built by Vickers at Barrow in Furness and went into service at Portsmouth in 1902. Development continued with the A, B, C and D class submarines. In 1911-13 the 850 tons and 1,600 h.p. E-type was developed, and with the addition of a gun was used in W.W.I. Other classes followed. The H class was built in Canada during W.W.I. A number of postcards reflect these developments, usually in R.P.s, e.g.:
    "Submarine D2 at Sea".
    "England's Latest Submarine E8".
    "L11 and L25 at Chatham".
Foreign submarines also appear on postcards, e.g.: German submarine U118 washed ashore at Hastings, 15 April, 1919.
    In 1905 there was a disaster to the A8. A card shows the funeral procession when the 10 victims were interred in Plymouth Cemetery.
    Ref: Compton-Hall, R., *Submarine Boats: the Beginning of Underwater Warfare,* 1983.

Subsidence
A number of cards depict building subsidence. Some show collapsed houses in the Northwich district of Cheshire caused by salt mining. A spectacular, though common, card shows the Glynne Arms at Kingswinford, Himley, Staffordshire, which was so well built that the whole building tilted and it became known as the "Crooked House".

Subsidence. *"Glynne Arms", Himley, Staffordshire, better known as the Crooked House. John Price & Sons. 1938.*

Suchard

A chocolate firm which issued many advertising postcards, one of the earliest firms to do so. U.B. series of views.

Suffragettes

The campaign for Women's Suffrage began in Victorian times and six bills had their second readings in Parliament between 1886 and 1911; none was passed. By this time the movement had become very active and strong measures were taken against the suffragettes. Ridicule, particularly, is reflected in the postcard cartoons. One card, P.U. 1909, shows a child in tears with the caption "Mummy's a Suffragette". A Valentine card, ill. D. & M. 107, carries this verse:

> While you remain a suffragette
> A valentine you'll never get.
> What man would ever want a wife
> Who spends in prison half her life?

Sandle Bros. issued a factual series about suffragettes with portraits of their leaders and views of their demonstrations.

Ref: Mitchell, D., *The Fighting Pankhursts*, 1967.

Summerville, Howard

Artist who designed cards for Charles Voisey.

Sunbeam Photo Co.

Publisher, 82 Sweyn Rd., Margate, Kent. Best known for a card showing the launching of the Margate Lifeboat.

Sunday Schools

The annual Sunday School Treat, when the children were

Superimposition. *"Business is Rotten."* Bamforth street scene with superimposed vehicles and small boy. Bamforth. P.U. 1916.

taken on an outing to the country or the seaside, was an established custom before W.W.I. and into the 1920s. They were occasions for photography and postcards of the event are not uncommon, e.g., the Redruth Sunday School Treat of 1904. The Sunday School Union published photographic cards, and there is a card of the Birmingham Sunday School Exhibition of 1905 with a view of a church and portraits of pastor and six Sunday School Superintendents.

Superimposition

A number of cards are built up from several photographs by superimposing figures or vehicles on an existing scene. This has clearly been done in the "Business is Rotten" card. The boy with his manure truck and some of the vehicles have been superimposed on a street scene.

Surrey View Co.

Publisher of photographic views.

Sussex Photographic Co.

Publisher, 154 Queen's Rd., Hastings, Sussex. Local views.

Sutcliffe, Herbert   **b. 1894**

Cricketer. Superb Yorkshire batsman who scored over 1,000 runs each season from 1919 to 1939, including 149 centuries. Made 54 Test appearances. P.P.s.

Suttley & Silverlock Ltd.   **pre-1933**

Publisher, London, S.E.1. Watercolour facsims. of the London area.

Suffragettes. *"This Is the House That Man Built"*. An anti-suffragette card in Birn Bros. *"London Series"*. P.U. 1914.

Sutton & Sons pre-1902
Printer, Fareham, Hampshire.

Sutton, J.
Publisher, Torbay Rd., Paignton, Devon. Sepia photographs of South Devon supplied by Valentine.

Sutton Sharpe & Co. pre-1908
Fine art publisher, 145 Queen Victoria St., London, E.C. Output included:
(i) Coloured London views.
(ii) The "Order of the Garter" Series of 30 vertical cards, each with the heraldic banner occupying a little over half the card with the name of the owner beneath. Ill. Byatt 286.

Swain, John, & Son Ltd.
Publisher, Hastings, Sussex. "Castle Series" of Sussex views with serial nos. to over 6,550.

Swales, V.L. pre-1908
Publisher, Port St. Mary, I.O.M. "Swales Series" of photographic views of the island.

Swan & Edgar
Advertising cards with a view of their store.

Swan Fountain Pens
Comic advertising cards.

Sweasey, A.H. pre-1910
Publisher, Southsea, Hampshire. Local coloured and sepia views.

Sweetland pre-1909
Photographer/publisher, Bedford. R.P.s of events, e.g. the Sharnbrook railway disaster of 1909.

Sweetman, E.A., & Son Ltd. pre-1927
Photographer/publisher, Tunbridge Wells, Kent. Trademark a rising sun with the words: "A Sweetman Publication". Output included high quality photographic views of the southern counties of England from Cornwall to Sussex. Various names were used for the type of card including:

(i) "De Luxe Photogravure".
(ii) "Domino Series".
(iii) "Sologlaze", late series of very dark brown photographs, e.g. "Harbour & Ness, Teignmouth", 3931.
(iv) "Sologloss", glossy sepia views.
(v) "Solograph".
(vi) "Solograph de Luxe" Photogravure.
(vii) "Sunshine Series" of R.P. views.

Syd
Pseudonym used by a designer of comic cards.

Sydenham & Co. c.1907
Publisher, Sydenham's Library, Bournemouth. Local views including facsims. of paintings by F.R. Fitzgerald.

Syllikus
Pseudonym of an artist who designed comic cards for E.R. Green of Blackpool.

"Sylvan Series"
Views by an unknown publisher.

Symington & Co.
View card advertising their soups.

Symonds & Co.
Photographers of a Valentine series of British battleships under the title "British Bulwarks".

Symonds, Constance
Painter who specialised in child subjects for Faulkner, e.g "Primrose Fairies".

Symons, Percy J. 1897-1980
Percy Symons featured personally in hundreds of photographs both in Britain and America, acting as a professional bystander to enhance the foreground in a street scene. He posed as a bather on a beach, a cyclist, and a traveller on an open bus.
Refs: Rooke, H. 'The Percy Symons Story', P.P.M., April 1982, p. 21; 'The Percy Symons Saga: Another Instalment', P.P.M., April 1983, p. 4.

T.A.
Initials of an artist who designed comic cards for Thridgould & Co.

Taber Bas-Relief Photographic Co.   1902
Patentees of a process of bas-relief printing which was taken over by Alliance Ltd. (q.v.).

Tabor, George   pre-1907
Publisher, Aylesbury, Buckinghamshire. Coloured local views.

Tacon Bros.   c.1908
Publisher/stationer, 47 Cannon St., Manchester. Postcards were certainly produced by the stationery business by 1908. In 1932 the address became 33 Dale St. The main output consisted of comic cards.

"Tailwagger" Postcards
A series by Valentine which was very popular in the 1930s; designs were signed Mac, the pseudonym of Lucy Dawson (q.v.). 22 titles have been noted:

"A Tailwagger and Proud of It".
"Close Friends".
"Dignity and Impudence".
"Faithfully Yours!"
"Friend in Need".
"Good Pal".
"Have You Forgotten Me?"
"Here's Hoping".
"I'm Always Good News when I'm Asleep".
"I'm Expecting Someone".
"I'm Fine, How Are You?"
"I'm Having an Easy Time here!"
"I've Landed Lucky".
"Looking for a Spot of Luck".
"Not So Black as I'm Painted".
"On Guard".
"The Best of Friends".
"There's no Place Like Home".
"Thinking of You".
"Two's Company, Three's a Crowd".
"Waiting for Master".
"Yours Faithfully".

Talbot Army Stores   fl. c.1914-1919
Publisher, Codford St. Mary, Wiltshire. Drawings by Alfred H. Taylor.

"Tailwagger" Postcards. *"Faithfully Yours!" by Mac, Lucy Dawson. Valentine. P.U. 1934.*

Tanks. *"British Tank in Action Smashing German Defences. Passed by Press Bureau for Publication 24th Nov. 1916". Valentine's Series. P.U. 1916.*

261

Talmadge, Constance   **d. 1973**
Film star. P.P. by *Picturegoer*.

Tam, Jean
Artist known for glamour postcards.

Tanks
Tanks were first used in the Battle of the Somme in September 1916, and their design was considerably improved during the two years that followed. Speed and manoeuvrability were improved and they became a major offensive weapon. Several publishers depicted them stationary and in action.

Illustration previous page.

Tanner, F.   **pre-1913**
Publisher, 47 Marine Terrace, Margate, Kent. Issued a "Queen's Series" supplied by Valentine.

Tariff Reform
The movement for tariff reform was led by Joseph Chamberlain. He opened it with a speech in Glasgow in 1903 urging imperial preference. In 1906 his tariff reform policy was adopted by the Conservatives. However, Chamberlain's health was failing and he took little part in politics in the years that followed. Tariff reform remained a political issue, but it was not until 1932 that an Imports Duties Bill was passed after its introduction by Chamberlain's son, Neville, who was then Chancellor of the Exchequer.

The main issue had been the price of food and a number of postcards reflect this aspect of the campaign.

Tarrant, Margaret Winifred   **1888-1959**
Watercolour painter who lived at Gomshall, Surrey, and exhibited from 1914 to 1934, mainly at the Royal Society of Arts, Birmingham. Designed cards with fairies and children for the Medici Society including "The Magic Childhood Series", a devotional series, and some fine silhouettes. She also designed a "Sing Praises" Series with silhouettes which was published in America by Hale, Cushman & Flint of Boston, Massachusetts. Her Medici cards were reprinted in the late 1930s, and these later issues can be identified by the statement "Art Publishers to the late King George V" who died in 1936. She

also designed cards for Faulkner and Humphrey Milford.

Refs: Cope p.24, ill. p. 56; for check list see Byatt pp. 346-7.

Tarrant, Percy   **fl. 1881-1930**
Landscape and coastal painter. Exh. R.A. 22. He was the father of Margaret Tarrant (q.v.).

Tartan Postcards
Several publishers issued cards with a named tartan background. They include:
(i)   Brown & Rawcliffe's "Camera" Series, in which a view is set against a named tartan background with a thistle. In the top left hand corner is a civic coat of arms.
(ii)   "Ja-Ja" Series, crests with tartans.

Tartan Postcards. *Eight named tartans with a coat of arms, a central view of Glasgow and smaller oval views of Dumbarton, Edinburgh and Stirling Castles. Woolstone Bros. Milton "Glazette" Series.*

Tartan Postcards. *Cameron tartan with a view and coat of arms of Rothesay. Brown & Rawcliffe. "Camera" Series. P.U. 1910.*

Tartan Postcards. *Munro tartan with a view of Fowlis Castle and a crest. R. Tuck & Sons. "Oilette" "Scottish Clans" Series IV.*

(iii) W. & A.K. Johnston, three types: Clansmen, tartan strip and heraldic crest; arms of clan, map showing location and tartan background; large badge with tartan background.

(iv) J.A. McCulloch, "Caledonian Series".

(v) Philco, views of Scotland against tartan background with horseshoe and a sprig of heather.

(vi) Rattray of Aberdeen, "Photo and Arms" Series.

(vii) Tuck published four series titled "Scottish Clans", each card showing the seat of the clan, its coat of arms, and its tartan.

(viii) Valentine, various tartans around a view in an oval frame.

(ix) Woolstone Bros., a Milton "Glazette" Series with a central rectangular Scottish view, e.g. St. Vincent Place, Glasgow, set against eight named tartans, four carrying a coat of arms or miniature view. All the tartans are named.

The following clans covered in the above series have been noted: Brodie, Buchanan, Cameron, Crawford, Cumming, Drummond, Erskine, Farquharson, Ferguson, Forbes, Fraser, Gordon, Graham, Grant, Gunn, Hay, Kerr, Lamont, MacAlister, MacAlpine, MacAuley, MacDonald, MacDougall, MacDuff, MacEwen, MacFarlane, MacGillivray, Macintyre, Mackintosh, MacLaren, Maclean, McLeod, Macmillan, MacNaughton, Macpherson, Macqueen, Macrae, Maxwell, Menzies, Munro, Murray, Ogilvie, Scott, Sinclair, Stewart, Sutherland, Urquhart.

Ref: Semple, W. (Ill.), *The Scottish Tartans*, W. & A.K. Johnston.

Tattoos and Tournaments
Military tattoos and tournaments appear on cards by Gale & Polden, Aldershot.

Taunt & Co., Oxford   fl. c.1902-1925
Photographer/publisher. Trademark a tree within a circle. Henry William Taunt (1842-1922) took photographs of Oxfordshire and the Thames and a few in Gloucestershire and Hampshire. Series included:
(i) "English Country Life".
(ii) "Oxford Life" including views of St. Giles' Fair.
(iii) Thames Series, 12 sets of colour cards, see Byatt p. 281 for check list.

Ref: Graham, M., *Henry Taunt of Oxford: A Victorian Photographer,* 1973.

Tausin, Louis
European artist who designed a "Moonlight" Series imported into Britain by P.G. Huardell & Co.

Tavener, J.L.   pre-1910
Publisher & Cash Draper, 24-6 High St., Ealing, Middlesex.

Taylor, A. & G. (Andrew & George)   pre-1905
Publisher, 70 and 78 Queen Victoria St., London, E.C. to 1909; 9 Longacre, Aldersgate St., E.C. to c.1914; then to Hastings. The firm presumably existed before 1901 for some cards carry the words "By Appointment to Her Late Majesty". The trademark, which is not found on all cards, shows a man studying a globe. Several series were produced:
(i) A "Reality Series" of "genuine silver print photographs" which included greetings cards, flowers, children, actors and actresses including examples photographed by "Photo Lafayette of Dublin."

(ii) A "Carbontone Series" of views overprinted with greetings.

(iii) An "Orthochrome Series" including greetings cards and coloured views printed in Saxony.

(iv) Comic cards, e.g. "Teddy Bear in Love".

Taylor, Alfred H.
Designer who made line drawings for Talbot's Army Stores, Codford St. Mary, Wiltshire.

Taylor, Arnold   fl. 1926-1984
Artist who has designed comic cards for Bamforth for over half a century. He painted a "Taylor Tot" Series for children. In later years he used the pseudonym Rolyat.

Taylor, C.E.
Publisher, West Ealing, Middlesex. Black and white local views.

Taylor & Downs   pre-1904
Publisher, Peterborough and Stamford.

Taylor, E.A.
Publisher, Fordingbridge, Hampshire. Local views. Some cards supplied by R.A. (Postcards) Ltd.

Taylor, E. Anthony
Photographer/publisher, Stratford-upon-Avon, Warwickshire. Sepia views of local interest, e.g. Anne Hathaway's Cottage.

Taylor, Edward
Publisher, 45 North Barr St., Beverley, Yorkshire. P.P.s of actresses, views of "Old London" and cards imported from Europe. His output suggests that he may have been a retailer rather than a true publisher.

Taylor, Frederick, R.I.   1875-1963
London landscape and architectural artist who painted a "Bournemouth Series" for Cadbury.

Taylor, Hal
Cheshire artist who painted cards of Irish girls for Brown & Rawcliffe.

Taylor, H.O.
Publisher, Scarborough, Yorkshire.

Taylor, Joe
Designer of comic cards for Teddy Ashton of Blackpool and the Continental Postcard Co. of Manchester.

Taylor, R.
Artist whose black and white drawings were adapted for Tuck's "Old English Sports".

Taylor, Thomas, & Son   pre-1905
Publisher, Scarborough. Trademark "Queen Series" above the head of Queen Alexandra within a shield cartouche surmounted by a crown and "T.T. & S. Scarborough" below. Black and white local views and facsims. of local views by J.W. Williams.

T.B.
Thomas Bolton (q.v.).

T.B.M.
Tacon Bros., Manchester (q.v.).

T. & D.
Taylor & Downs (q.v.).

Teddy Bears. *An unusual angle on the popular teddy bear theme. Inter-Art "Kute Kiddies" Series.*

Teale, George
Designer of comic cards for Salmon. He used the pseudonym Gee-Tee.

Technical Art Co.
Publisher, 105 Sidney Grove, Newcastle upon Tyne, Northumberland. This was a small-scale enterprise with an output mainly of comic dialect cards by Paul J. Brown.

Teddy Bears
These feature frequently on postcards. The origin of the teddy bear is American. Theodore Roosevelt, 25th President of the United States, often known as Teddy was a keen huntsman. His books, *Hunting Trips of a Ranchman,* 1886 and *The Rough Riders,* 1899, describe his outdoor recreations which included bear-hunting. Hence the teddy bear which became a favourite children's toy. One collector is reported to have over 600 different teddy bear cards in her collection.

Ref: Wharnsby, R., 'Artists of Bear Cards', P.P.A., 1982, p.60.

Telephones
In Victorian times most telephones were in the hands of private companies and this continued into Edwardian times. In 1912, however, the Post Office had succeeded in establishing a virtual monopoly of the system. Occasionally a telephone is seen on a pre-W.W.I. postcard, usually on a comic card. In the 1920s the Post Office made efforts to extend the domestic market. Propaganda appeared in postmark slogans:

"Say It By Telephone", 1926.
"Trade Follows the Phone", 1932.

Temperance *"Old Temperance Hotel of 1400, (Aber Conway), Conway". Baur's Series.*

"The Best Investment — a Telephone", 1932.
"You are Wanted on the Telephone", 1932.
Curiously enough, it was the expansion of telephone communication that led to the decline in the postcard market.

Temblett, Dorothy
Actress. P.P. by Tuck, "Bookmarker" Series III.

Temperance
The temperance movement flourished in late Victorian and Edwardian times. Temperance halls and temperance hotels were built, temperance lecturers toured the country and Friendly Societies were established, such as the "Order of the Sons of Temperance" for those who were prepared to forgo alcohol.

Postcards reflect the work of the temperance enthusiasts. An advertisement card was issued, for example, to give publicity to the North of England Temperance League Grand Bazaar at Newcastle on 14 October, 1902; postcard maps showed the distribution of temperance hotels, and there are many cards of temperance halls and of the temperance hotels, e.g. Mrs. Lucas Temperance House (board and lodging), Sandbach, Cheshire.

Tempest, Douglas
Designer of comic cards, particularly cards which feature children. From 1911 he worked exclusively for Bamforth & Co., an association which lasted for 40 years. Comic series by Tempest included "Comics", "Cute Kiddies", "Holiday", "Kiddy" and "Tempest Kiddy".

See: Colour Plate 23.

Tempest, Margaret   1892-1982
Painter who illustrated children's books. Her postcards with animals were published by the Medici Society.

Refs: Check list in Byatt p. 347; Cope, p. 25, ill. p. 57.

Tempest, Marie, D.B.E.   1864-1942
Actress who had trained as a singer. She first appeared in 1900 as Nell Gwynn in Anthony Hope's *English Nell,* and her last appearance was in Dodie Smith's *Dear Octopus* in 1938. Created D.B.E. 1937. P.P.s by Misch & Co., Philco and Rotary.

Tenniel, Sir John   **1820-1914**
Illustrator of *Alice in Wonderland*, 1865. Two sets of cards using his original illustrations were published by Fuller & Richard.

"Ten-Nine-Eight"
W.W.I. series by the Inter-Art Co., which depicts Red Cross nurses with wounded soldiers. The artist was Arthur Butcher and the captions are in English and French, e.g. "Making Rapid Progress - Faisant des Progrès Rapides".

Tennis
See: Lawn Tennis.

Tennyson, Alfred, 1st Baron   **1809-1892**
Poet Laureate. Born Somersby, Lincolnshire. From 1853 to 1869 he lived at Farringford, I.O.W. and then moved to Aldworth, near Haslemere. P.P.s by Blum & Degen, Eyre & Spottiswoode, and Tuck.
Ref: English, T., 'Tennyson Teasers', P.P.M., January 1981, p.21.

Terriss, Ellaline   **1871-1971**
Actress born in the Falkland Islands. Appeared on the stage with Max Beerbohm in 1888, the start of a distinguished musical comedy career. Married Seymour Hicks in 1902. P.P.s by Beagles, Rotary and Tuck.
Refs: *Ellaline Terris by Herself and Others*, 1928; *Just a Little Bit of String*, 1955.

1597 H ROTARY PHOTO, E.C.
MISS ELLALINE TERRISS,   MR. SEYMOUR HICKS   FOULSHAM & BANFIELD
AS "BLUE BELL."   AS "DICKIE".

Terriss, Ellaline. *"Miss Ellaline Terriss, as Blue Bell. Mr. Seymour Hicks as Dickie". P.P. by Rotary.*

Terriss, Thomas   **1874-1964**
Actor. P.P. in Valentine's "Play Series", a posed scene with Silvia Sablang from *The Medal and the Maid*, 1905.

Terry, Ellen, D.B.E.   **1847-1928**
Actress. Played leading female parts in Henry Irving's productions until 1896. P.P.s by Aristophot and Beagles.

Terry, Fred   **1864-1932**
Actor-manager. Brother of Dame Ellen. Married Julia Neilson. Best known for *The Scarlet Pimpernel*. Retired 1927. P.P.s by Beagles, ill. Hill p.27, and Rotary.

Terry, Marion   **1853-1930**
Actress. Younger sister of Dame Ellen (q.v.). P.P. by Tuck, "Celebrities of the Stage".

Tester, Massy & Co.   **1906**
Publisher, 22 Paternoster Row, London, E.C. Facsims. of landscapes by A.W. Head and E.J. Head, e.g. "The Hop Country, Kent" in a "Gold Framed Postcards" Series. Some foreign scenes were included, e.g. Pig-sticking, India.

Thackeray, Lance, R.B.A.   **d.1916**
Artist who made his name designing postcards, starting with write-away cards and Boer War cartoons for Tuck. He exploited the foibles of women. A series titled "The Smart Set" showed them shopping, playing bridge, etc., each scene supplemented at the base with a pictorial postscript indicating their thoughts at the time; another series depicted them in "Popular Plays". Tuck published most of his work but A. & C. Black issued "The People of Egypt", and a single poster card "The Earl and the Girl" came from David Allen (q.v.).
See: Colour Plates 19 and 23.

Thanet Series   **1907**
Black and white views of Margate. Publisher unknown.

Tharp, Charles Julian   **fl. 1900-1930**
Artist. Exh. R.A. 6. Designed a set titled "Moonlit Nature" for Knight Bros.

Thatcher & Son
Photographer/publisher, Tadley, Basingstoke, Hampshire.

Theatres and Music Halls
Exterior views of theatres and music halls are well represented on postcards, especially London theatres. The Excelsior Fine Arts Co. issued a London Theatre Series and their examples are marked with an asterisk in the following list of London theatres noted on postcards:
* Adelphi, opened 1905.
* Alhambra, opened 1854; closed 1936.
* Apollo, opened 1901.
   Avenue, opened 1882; wrecked by collapse of roof of Charing Cross Station 1905; re-opened 1907; closed 1951.
* Coliseum, variety theatre opened 1904; turned to musical comedy 1931; closed 1951.
   Criterion, opened 1874; reconstructed 1883-4 and 1902.
* Daly's, opened 1893; closed 1937.
   Drury Lane, oldest theatre still in use; closed on outbreak of war, 1939.
   Duke of York, opened 1892; first production of J.M. Barrie's plays, 1902-8.
* Empire, musical hall 1884; after W.W.I. musical comedies; closed 1927.

continued

Theatres. *"Gaiety Theatre"*. *G. Smith. P.U. 1904.*

* Gaiety, opened 1868; closed 1903 and re-opened same year; finally closed 1939.
* Garrick, Charing Cross Rd., opened 1899; closed 1939 and re-opened 1941.

Globe, Shaftesbury Ave., opened 1906.

Haymarket, first recorded performance 1720.

* Hippodrome, opened 1900 as a circus; became a music hall.

King's Theatre, Hammersmith, c.1910.

* London Pavilion, opened as music hall in 1885; became a theatre in 1919 and a cinema in 1934.

Lyceum, Henry Irving and Ellen Terry made their last appearance together in 1902; rebuilt as music hall 1904; closed 1939.

Lyric, opened 1888.

* New Theatre, opened 1903; Fred Terry and Julia Neilson occupied it for six months each year from 1905 to 1913.

Palace, in 1892 was a 'Theatre of Varieties'; in 1911 became the Palace Theatre.

Queen's Theatre; opened 1850; bombed 1940; re-opened 1959.

* Royal English Opera House, opened 1891; changed name to the Palace 1911.
* St. James, opened 1835.

Savoy, opened 1881 with the D'Oyly Carte opera, *Patience*.

Shaftesbury, opened 1888; demolished by enemy action 1941.

Strand Theatre, opened 1832 as New Strand Theatre; closed 1905.

* Theatre Royal, Haymarket, opened in 1720; leading playhouse in London.
* Tivoli, opened as music hall in 1890; closed 1914.
* Vaudeville, opened 1870; home of Charlot's Revues 1915-25.
* Waldorf, opened in 1905; name changed in 1909 to The Strand.
* Wyndhams, opened 1899; first productions of Edgar Wallace plays.

A few provincial theatres can be found on postcards, e.g. Theatre Royal, Exeter, ill. Hill p.58, and the Empire Theatre, Swindon.

Refs: Hartnoll, P., *The Concise Oxford Companion to the Theatre,* 1981; Mander, R. and Mitchenson, J., *British Music Hall,* 1974; Rowse, M., 'A London Theatre Collection', P.P.A., 1982, p.39.

Theatrical Advertising

David Allen & Sons Ltd. printed posters to advertise theatrical performances and many of these were reproduced as postcards. Plays were also advertised on the reverse side of cards with P.P.s of leading members of the casts.

Ref: A check list of some theatrical advertising postcards is given by Byatt p.339.

Theatrical Productions

A number of publishers of portraits of actors and actresses also issued cards with scenes from the plays in which they took part. Miles & Co. of Wardour St., London, were specialists in this field. An example shows a scene in colour from the production of *The Dairymaids* by Robert Courtneidge which opened at the Apollo Theatre, London, on 14 April 1906, and ran for 239 performances.

Thiede, Edwin Adolf   **fl.1882-1908**

Miniature portrait artist and illustrator who worked for *The Queen* and *The Windsor Magazine.* Exh. R.A. 8. Painted

Theatres. *"Memorial Theatre, Stratford-on-Avon"*. *This theatre, designed by Elizabeth Scott, was completed in 1932. J. Salmon.*

Theatrical Productions. *A scene from Robert Courtneidge's production of* The Dairymaids. *Miles and Co.*

scenes for Tuck's "Oxford Pageant" Series. Lived at Lewisham.

Thiele & Co.
Photographer used by several London postcard publishers.

Thiele, Arthur   fl.c.1900-1930
Primarily an animal painter but also painted romantic and sporting scenes. Noted for his Teddy Bear Music Class. Most of his cards were published in Germany or Switzerland but Faulkner and Tuck also used his work.
   See: Violet Miles.

Thimm, Daisy
Actress. First stage appearance in 1900. P.P. in Tuck's "Celebrities of the Stage" Series, 4452.

Thomas Bros. & Co.   fl.c.1893-1922
Publisher/printer, 37 Everton Rd., Liverpool, Lancashire. Trademark Everton Beacon Tower. The cards deal mainly with Welsh subjects, especially humorous material, though there are a few which reflect Welsh customs. The Welsh language is sometimes used on the reverse side — "Llythyr Gerdyn" for "Post Card". The "Everton Series" title sometimes appears.

Thomas, Angus, Ltd.   c.1898
Publisher, 4 and 5 Silk St., London, E.C. Early greetings cards, write-away cards, comic cards and some novelties.

Thomas, Bert   1883-1966
Humorous illustrator for *Fun, Punch* and *The Graphic*. Designed postcards for *The Weekly Despatch* Tobacco Fund during W.W.I. His cards were produced by Gale & Polden, e.g. "Arf a Mo Kaiser".

Thomas, J.E.
Photographer/publisher, 22 Chepstow Rd., Newport, Monmouthshire.

Thomas, William
A set with the title "Prehistoric Man" was painted by this artist for Woodall, Minshall, Thomas & Co., of Wrexham.

Thompson, G.R.
Publisher, Llandudno, Carnarvonshire. Trademark "The Post Card King's Series, Llandudno". Thompson had several addresses in the town and his cards were supplied by various printers and publishers. They are mainly views of North Wales.

Thompson, H.
Publisher, Registry Office and Apartment Agency, 2 High St., Maidenhead, Berkshire.

Thorburn, Archibald   1860-1935
Painter of birds and illustrator of ornithological books. Exh. R.A.21. A few of his illustrations were published as postcards by Savory.

Thorn
Photographer/publisher, Bude, Cornwall.

Thorne's Scotch Whisky
"Celebrated Posters" advertising card by Tuck.

Thornton Bros.
Publisher, New Brompton, Kent. Coloured views of Kent.

Thornton, E.W.
Publisher, Wythall, Worcestershire. Photographic views.

Thornton, J. Stanley   fl.pre-1912
Artist who designed a moonlight view of Clifton Suspension Bridge for Burgess & Co.

Thorpe, Thomas   1904
Publisher, 4 Broad St., Reading, Berkshire. Coloured cards in a "Bye-Gone Times" Series based on prints in early 19th century books.

Thorpe, W.E.   pre-1914
Publisher, The County Library, Maidstone, Kent.

Thors, Joseph   fl.1883-1910
Landscape artist who painted views of Warwickshire for the Regal Art Publishing set titled "Shakespeare Country".

Thridgould, John, & Co.   c.1907-1946
Publisher, 18-20 Sidney St., London, E. Greetings, including a "Hand Painted Series", a "Pioneer" Series and some humorous cards.
   Ref: A check list of the comic cards is given by Byatt pp.353-5.

Thurnham, Charles, & Sons
Publisher, Carlisle, Cumberland. Tinted local views. Cards were supplied by E.T.W. Dennis.

T.I.C.
Initials within a horseshoe are found in the stamp space on many R.P.s They stand for Thomas Illingworth & Co., a firm

MISS VESTA TILLEY

Tilley, Vesta. *Card with a dual interest. The car which the well-known actress is leaving is a James and Brown of 1905 which had an under-floor engine and was popular as a town car. P.P. W.E. Byers' "Favourite" Series.*

which appears to have supplied postcard-size printing paper to photographers.

Tidmarsh, H.E.   **fl.1880-1918**
Landscape artist. Exh. R.A. 20. Designed a "Tower of London" set for Cassell & Co.

Tilley, John Jacob
Designer who was a member of the family firm of L. Tilley & Son of Ledbury and produced humorous sketches for their postcards.

Tilley, L., & Son   **c.1902**
Publisher, High St., Ledbury, Herefordshire. John Jacob, the founder's son, was a keen photographer and took views of the area, which included the Malvern Hills, for postcard reproduction. A few events were covered and one card shows a close-up of a donkey whose appearance raised £250 for the Red Cross in 1916. A few comic and greetings cards were produced, some drawn by A. Percy White.

Tilley, Vesta   **1864-1952**
Actress who made her first London appearance in 1878 and became well known as a male impersonator. P.P.s by David Allen (a card in which she is dressed in khaki was sold in aid of the W.W.I. Relief Fund, ill. Holt 557); Beagles; Philco; Rotary.
  Ref: *The Recollections of Vesta Tilley,* 1934.

Tin Mines
Tin mines appear on postcards, e.g. a mine at Postbridge, Devon and a tramway at East Pool Mine, near Redruth. They are mainly views; relatively few show the miners.

Tinsel
  See: Tinsel Cards under Novelty Cards.

Tinting
Many photographic cards were tinted before sale. A lady employed by Harvey Barton of Bristol in the 1920s has

described the process: "Firstly, the photographer would travel to the site destination with the Head Artist (in this case a lady). He would take a photograph and she would make a note of the colours in the view. The resulting black and white photograph would be coloured by this lady artist, her skill accurately reflecting the true colour.

"From each photograph stencils were cut in zinc for every colour to be used. These stencils were given to the colouring girls who each used one colour. The postcards were at this stage printed in blocks of 6 x 4 — 24 *different* photographs. The zinc stencil sheets covered the whole block. The girls blended their own dyes to match the tones on the artist's proofs. They were paid "piece rate". One girl was given the blue skies for these had to be touched up with cotton wool to soften the hard outlines and, lastly, when dry, a little pink was sometimes added with cotton wool.

"If a girl had not set her stencil correctly and had coloured over the edge, she had to remove the offending colour with bleach (a loss of time and income). The girls discovered that by bringing bacon rind from their homes to grease the edges of their stencils the colours were prevented from running."

Harvey Barton employed 24 tinting girls. The job had a certain status and most of them came from middle-class families.

Titania's Palace
This model 16-room house, complete in every detail, was finished in 1923 and the owner, Sir Neville Wilkinson, commissioned two sets of eight cards from Tuck. Gale & Polden also issued a set.

"Titanic"
Postcards of this ill-fated liner under construction in the Harland & Woolf dock at Belfast were published in 1912. The caption has the postscript: "Lost with 1,500 souls, April 5th, 1912". There are also R.P. postcards of the *Titanic* leaving Southampton Harbour.
  In Memoriam cards were published by E.A. Bragg, and Valentine published a card showing the liner which is titled "The Most Appalling Disaster in Maritime History".

Tit-Bits
A "penny weekly" which issued poster-type cards as advertisements.

"Titchfield" Series
  See: Richardson & Co.

Titicus   **pre-1913**
Publisher, 50 Mountfield Rd., Finchley, London, N. Comic cards are signed Titicus suggesting that he was an artist who published his own cards.

Tito
Czech artist who painted scenes with children.

T.N.L.
T.N. Leggatt (q.v.).

Tollitt & Harvey   **pre-1904**
Publisher, London, E.C. "The Guildhall Series" of comic cards.

Tomkins & Barnett   **pre-1904**
Publisher, Swindon, Wiltshire. "Famous Series" of coloured and sepia views of Berkshire and Wiltshire. Some cards are overprinted with a description of the view. The firm had a particular interest in legends and published cards of the Drew

Town Halls. *"Town Hall, Portsmouth". This building, erected in 1886-90, is the finest town hall in the south of England. The spectacular staircase leads to a Corinthian portico with a pediment surmounted by a statue of Neptune. B. & B. Series.*

Town Halls. *"Market Place and Town Hall, Newbury". The statue of Queen Victoria is no longer in situ. Valentine's Series. P.U. 1912.*

family which drowned in a pool in Devizes, and of Ruth Pierce of Potterne and the legend of the Wiltshire Moonrakers (q.v.).

Tomlinson, G.P.   **pre-1908**
"Pictorial Post Card Specialist", Holmes Chapel, Cheshire. Coloured views "Phototyped in Saxony".

Tomlinson, John, Ltd.
Publisher, Partick, Glasgow. Views of Glasgow supplied by Valentine.

Topical Postcard Co.   **pre-1927**
A company which sent photographers to cover special events, e.g. Aviation Meetings.

Toulouse-Lautrec, Henri de   **1864-1901**
French art nouveau artist renowned for his poster designs. Postcard reproductions of these are highly prized.

Towle, Arthur
Manager of L.M.S. Hotels. His name appears on cards supplied by McCorquodale, Tuck and other publishers.

Town Criers
Portraits of town criers, especially National Champions, are sometimes found on postcards. Examples noted include:
Chertsey.
Clacton.
Ilfracombe.
Lyme Regis, National Champion 1930-1.
Marlborough, National Champion, 1913-14.

Town Halls
Many town halls were built in the 19th and early 20th century. They are still objects of civic pride and are frequently to be seen in street views of our towns and cities.

Townshead, Marchioness of
Painter of a set of Tuck cards titled "Foggy London".

Tozer, Fred   **pre-1905**
Photographer/publisher, 12 Smith St., Guernsey, C.I. Views which include shipping.

Traction Engines
Steam traction engines were widely used before W.W.I. They were made by such firms as Clayton T. Shuttleworth Ltd. of Lincoln for several purposes:
(i)   To draw heavy loads such as removal vans or brewers' barrels.
(ii)   For threshing corn, using the power to operate a threshing machine.
(iii) For ploughing, the plough being drawn to and fro on a hawser stretched between two stationary engines.
(iv) On fairgrounds.
All these uses are illustrated on R.P. cards (ill. D. & M. 163-4) which are highly valued. There are even accident cards. A U.B. card shows the collapse of a bridge at Uckfield in 1903 due to the weight of the traction engine.
Ref: Hughes, W.J., *A Century of Traction Engines,* 1970.

Trams
Horse tramways were well established in a number of British towns and cities by the end of the 19th century when the first electric tramways began to appear.
Electric trams flourished in Edwardian times but after W.W.I. they were gradually replaced by motor buses. Postcards of electric trams can now be regarded as historical documents and they are widely collected. Their interest, however, depends very much on how well it is possible to see their construction, the advertisements they carried and the destinations indicated. Close-ups are, therefore, particularly valued. Associated scenes include opening ceremonies,

Trams. *"The Electric Tram has Come"*. Comic greeting card. Publisher unknown. U.B. P.U. 1900.

Trams. *"Tram Terminus, Low Fell"*. Single-decker electric tram used on routes in Gateshead which had low bridges. T.H. Dickinson. P.U. 1912.

accidents, decorated trams and "last" trams before closures.

Ref: Lists of tramway undertakings, the dates when towns abandoned their trams and the museums in which trams have been preserved are all to be found in Charles Klapper's *The Golden Age of Tramways,* 1961.

Tramway Accidents
These were few, but a number have been recorded including Bournemouth, 1908, Bradley near Huddersfield, 1905, Halifax, 1906, Swindon, 1906.

Tree & Co.　　　　　　　　　　　　　　　pre-1912
Publisher, Liverpool, Lancashire. Local R.P. views.

Tree, Lady Helen Maud　　　　　　　　　1863-1937
Actress. Married Beerbohm Tree. Excelled in comedy. P.P. by Rotary.

Trams. *"Portsdown Hill, Portsmouth"*. Double-decker tram with open top on the Portsdown Hill extension of the Portsmouth service. The track ran parallel to the main road. Valentine's Series. P.U. 1919.

Tree, Sir Herbert Draper Beerbohm　　　1853-1917
Actor-manager. Founder of the Royal Academy of Dramatic Art. P.P.s by Rotary and Shurey's Publications.
　　Ref: Bingham, M., *The Great Lover: The Life and Art of Herbert Beerbohm Tree,* 1978.

Tree, Viola　　　　　　　　　　　　　　1884-1938
Actress. Daughter of Beerbohm Tree.

Trent Bridge Publishing Co.　　　　　fl.1905-1908
Publisher, 10 Wharf St., Stoke-on-Trent, Staffordshire. Trademark "Trent Series" printed on the sail of a yacht. This firm is noted only for reproductions of museum ceramics. They are similar in style to the Goss series published by Oates and there is a coat of arms on each piece. This could have been printed on the card when a large enough order was received for the arms of a particular town or city.

Trevelyan, Hilda　　　　　　　　　　fl.1908-1928
Landscape painter. Lived in Eaton Place, London.

Trim, E.
Publisher, Wimbledon, Surrey. P.P.s of tennis stars.

Trow
Designer of comic cards.

T.T. & S.
Taylor, Thomas, & Son Scarborough. (q.v.).

Tuck, A.L.　　　　　　　　　　　　　　pre-1914
Artist who designed comic cards for Joseph Asher & Co.

Tuck, Raphael, & Sons (Ltd).　　1894 (Ltd. 1901)
Publisher, Raphael House, Moorfields, London, E.C., and 298 Broadway, New York. This firm had been publishing Christmas cards for over 25 years when it started to produce postcards. In 1881 a trademark had been registered consisting of an artist's easel, palette and brushes with the initials R.T. & S. From 1893 their publications also carried the Royal Warrant of Appointment granted by Queen Victoria.
　　Tuck's first postcard for sale appeared in 1894 and from

"Poor Little Feller, Are Yer Lost?" "No — Boo-hoo — But My Muvver Is!" by Phil May. R. Tuck & Sons. "Oilette" P.U. 1905.

"In the Smart Set. Monday — Shopping" by Lance Thackeray. R. Tuck & Sons. "Oilette" "Remarque". P.U. 1906.

" 'Tis Love That Makes the World Go Round..." by Fred Spurgin. Art & Humour Publishing Co. "Topole" Series. P.U. 1924.

"Well, What Did They Say When You Tried To Enlist?" by D. Tempest. Bamforth & Co. "Witty Comic Series".

Tuck, Raphael, & Sons Ltd. *"Wiping Something off the Slate. Majuba February 27th, 1881. Paardeberg Feb. 27th 1900. Ladysmith, Feb, 28th, 1900. 120 Days Siege".* An early U.B. "Empire Postcard" published after the siege of Ladysmith in 1900.

Tuck, Raphael, & Sons Ltd. *A "Real Japanese" post card. Connoisseur Series.*

Tuck, Raphael, & Sons Ltd. *"I had rather have such men my friends than enemies — Shakespeare".* A U.B "Empire Postcard" showing Kitchener with Louis Botha and Generals De Wet and Delarey who went to Europe after the Boer War to raise funds to enable the Boers to resume their former employments.

Tuck, Raphael, & Sons Ltd. *"Where Ignorance is Bliss. He (alarmed by the erratic steering): Er — and have you driven much? She (quite pleased with herself): Oh, no — this is only my second attempt. But then you see I have been used to a bicycle for years!"* by G.H. Jalland. "Oilette". "Motoring Jokes from Punch". P.U. 1909.

that year the firm became the doyen of postcard publishers. The early cards were chromolithographs printed in Germany and although they were sold in sets of six or twelve they were individually numbered. All had U.B.s. Collectors are still trying to solve problems arising from the numbering system which is difficult to decode. However, it is the superb quality of Tuck's cards which commands admiration.

The first cards were views of London and the Thames (four sets). There followed four sets of reproductions of the paintings of J.W.M. Turner. Top-line artists were commissioned to design cards, among them Harry Payne and Helena Maguire who produced several sets on animals with some hunting and coaching scenes.

Sets on "The Kings and Queens of England" and "Landseer's Masterpieces" were followed by a comprehensive series with the title "Empire Postcards". The first four sets included cards on the army and navy with reference to the South African War. Later sets included portraits of "Our Generals". Meanwhile a number of write-away cards had been published.

In 1902 and 1903 came a period of expansion. A "United Kingdom" series of 53 sets of views covered most of the major towns and cities of Britain, and a fine "Heraldic" Series of embossed cards combined views of the following with their coats of arms: London, Glasgow, Manchester, Liverpool, Dublin, Edinburgh, Birmingham, Belfast, Bristol, York, Plymouth, Leamington, Brighton, Oxford, Cambridge, Aberdeen and Bath. (Many of the individual titles in these sets are given in S.G.P.C., 1983, pp.225-6.)

Sets were given tradenames, the most significant being the "Oilette" (q.v.) which eventually proved to be the most popular. Some reflected production styles, e.g. "Collotype", others subject groupings, e.g. "Educational" or "Rough Seas". A list is given in Appendix I, p.296.

Unfortunately, on 29th December, 1940, Raphael House, the London headquarters of the firm, was destroyed by fire in an enemy air raid and all records were destroyed. No complete list of Tuck cards exists today but some impression of their vast output and the extraordinary range of subjects covered is given in Appendix II, pp. 297-304.

Four Tuck cards are shown opposite, but numerous other examples appear throughout this dictionary.

Turner
Publisher, Skipton, Yorkshire.

Turrian, Emile David   **1869-1906**
Swiss painter trained at l'Ecole des Beaux Arts de Genève. His postcard designs are in the art nouveau style.

Tussaud, John Theodore   **fl.c.1880-1910**
Artist to the Mme. Tussaud Waxworks. Exh. R.A. 3.

Postcards of the tableaux at Madame Tussaud & Sons exhibition, 1922.

Twelvetrees, Charles H.
American comic artist who designed cards for Edward Gross of New York though some may have first appeared as coloured prints in journals. They all show small children in humorous situations and were published in Britain by the Alpha Publishing Co. Most cards bear the mark of Edward Gross.
    Ref: A check list is given in P.P.A., 1982, pp. 56-7.

Twiddy, A.E.
Publisher, Sevenoaks, Kent. Local sepia views.

Twilton Bros.   **pre-1908**
Publisher, Erdington, Birmingham. Black and white views.

Twiss Bros.   **pre-1913**
Publisher, The Arcade, Ilfracombe, Devon. Trademark the Devonshire coat of arms with the word "DEVON" on a ribbon below. This firm produced a series of cards showing North Devon towns, e.g. Clovelly, Lynmouth, Lynton and Torrington. Each card has a view above two coats of arms, to the left that of the county and to the right that of the particular town. Photographs of local events were published, e.g. H.M.S. *Montague* on the rocks at Lundy Island.

Tyldesley, John Thomas   **1873-1930**
Professional cricketer. Played for Lancashire from 1895 and in his second county game scored 152. On three occasions he scored two separate centuries.

Tyler, E. Anthony   **pre-1913**
Publisher, 10 Bridge St., and 10 Henley St., Stratford-upon-Avon, Warwickshire. R.P.s of the Stratford Pageant of 1913.

Tyne General Ferry Co.   **pre-1910**
Advertisers of sightseeing trips on their steamers. Postcards include one of the *Mauretania* stating that passengers on their trips would "have a fine view of this magnificent vessel at Wallsend".

Typhoid
A typhoid epidemic in Lincoln in 1905 resulted in the evacuation of many homes and entry into hospital of their occupiers. Scenes appear on postcards.

Typhoo Tea
Advertising cards.

Tyrwhitt, Walter Spencer Stanhope, R.B.A.   **1859-1932**
Landscape artist. Exh. R.A. 10. Painted views for Robert Peel of Oxford in the 1920s.

Universities. *"Edinburgh University"*. *William Ritchie & Sons.*

Uden, Ernest Boye   **fl.1933-1936**
Painter and commercial artist. Exh. R.A. 3 before the age of 25.

Uffel, J.R.
Publisher, 113/115 Church St., Stoke Newington, London, Local R.P. views.

Ullswater Navigation & Transport Co.
Publishers of watercolour views of Ullswater Lake and its surrounding scenery.

Ulrich, J.
Artist who contributed to J.W. Ruddock's "Artist Series".

Underground and London Electric Railway Co. Ltd.
This Company was registered in 1902. It absorbed the Metropolitan District Electric Traction Co. and carried out a development programme building stations and extending lines, and in 1910 became the London Electric Railway Co. In 1913 it acquired the City and South London Railway Co. and the Central London Railway Co. In 1933 all the London underground railways were transferred to the London Passenger Transport Board and the system was unified. The Underground and London Electric Railway used poster-type cards of the west end of London by W.H. Smith and cards produced by the Avenue Press of "London Nooks and Corners".
Ref: Check lists in R.O.P.L., No. 16.

Underwood, Clarence
Figure painter, particularly of romantic couples dancing, dining, motoring or skating. Facsims. by M. Munk and by Reinthal & Newman.

Underwood Typewriters
Poster-type advertising cards.

Undivided Back
The back of an early card which could only be used for the address.

Union Jack Club
Publisher of cards showing the Club building in London.

Universal Photo-Printing & Publishing Co.
Publisher, 26 Southampton St., London. Tradename "Universal Series". Many views but a wide range of other subjects — battleships, castles, comics, children, jockeys and glamour. The last named are grouped under titles such as "Types of Beauty" or "Pretty Women Studies From Watercolour Drawings".

Universities
Views of Oxford and Cambridge colleges are common. There are fewer postcards of other universities, though William Ritchie & Sons produced a fine view of Edinburgh.

Upton, Florence   **1873-1922**
Portrait painter. Exh. R.A. 9. She invented the black child character Golliwog and illustrated a series of children's Golliwog Books between 1899 and 1905. The Golliwog first appeared on Tuck postcards in 1903 by permission of Messrs. Longman's, Green & Co. Ill. D. & M. 189. There were 15 Golliwog sets in all.
Ref: Cope p.26, ill. p.60.

Urquart, Donald   **fl.pre-1935**
Watercolour artist who painted a view of the White Hart Hotel, Lincoln for facsim. postcard publication.

Usabel, Lotte   **b.1900**
German artist who specialised in glamour cards, especially of attractive ladies with horses, published by Erkat.

Valentine, James, & Sons Ltd.   **1895**
Publisher, Dundee, Scotland. This firm published Christmas
cards in the 1880s but started to specialise in picture postcards
in 1896 when it became a limited company. Flourished over a
long period using initials in the early days — V. & S. or V. & S.D.
A later trademark consisted of the two globes with the words
"Famous Throughout the World" and there is no doubt that
they built up a considerable export business, especially to
Canada. Many views bear the words "Souvenir Postcard" and
the initials "J.V." in a small circle in the lower right-hand
corner of the picture side. Production started before the turn
of the century with multi-view heraldic court cards. Ill. Byatt
318. Many types of card included:
(i)   Aerograph Greetings Cards.
(ii)   Art Colour Cards, watercolour facsims. and maps.
(iii)   "Artotype" Series, coloured cards.
(iv)   "Bromotome" Series.
(v)   "Carbetone" Series including literary portraits.
(vi)   "Colourtone" Series of coloured views.
(vii)   "Crystoleum" Series of highly glazed cards with an
        embossed frame containing a view.
(viii) "Gravuretype" Series.
(ix)   "Nu-Vu" Series, glossy photographs.
(x)   "Platotone Series", black and white views.
(xi)   "Popular Songs", staged coloured photographs with
        the verse of a song.
(xii)   "Photo-Brown", series of matt-surfaced sepia views.
(xiii) "Real Photographs" including portraits of celebrities.
(xiv)   "Real Photograph Animal Series".
(xv)   "Selectype" Series.
(xvi)   "Silversheen" Series of black and white R.P. views.
(xvii) "Valesque" Series and "Valcolour" Series of coloured
        views.
(xviii) "X.L. Series" of R.P. views.

In addition there was a series of moonlight views against a
silvered ground, occasionally with added glitter dust, a
"Brooklands Favourites" Series of racing drivers with their
cars, and an "Attwell Series".

Valentine continued to published postcards until 1968.
See: Colour Plates 8, 9 and 13.

Valentino, Rudolph   **1895-1926**
Film star of the silent movies noted for his part in *The Sheik*,
1921. P.P.s by Beagles.

Vallet, Louis   **b.1856**
French watercolour painter and illustrator who contributed to
many humorous journals and became "President de La
Société des Humoristes".

Vallora Cigarettes
Advertising cards supplied by Tuck.

Valter, Florence   **fl.pre-1935**
Animal artist who painted horses and dogs for the Inter-Art
Co. "Artistique" Series and for Valentine greetings cards.

Van Beers, Jan   **fl.1882-1904**
Belgian artist. Exh. R.A. 7. Designed cards for H.J. Smith of
Brighton in 1900.

Van Hier, Professor
London landscape painter who favoured scenes with mist, rain
or snow. Exhibited his work in the 1880s; it was also used in
facsims. by Boots; Davidson Bros., "Autumn Days" and
"Winter Days" in their "Arcadia Series"; Faulkner,
"Summertime"; Tuck in their "Oilette", "Connoisseur"
Series, views after Van Hier, sets 7151-62 and 7165.

Van Houten
Advertisers of their cocoa and chocolate. European views.

Van Ruith, Horace   **1839-1923**
Architectural artist. Exh. R.A. 27. Painted views of Oxford
and London for Ruddock's "Artist Series".

Vanburgh, Irene, D.B.E.   **1872-1949**
Actress. Younger sister of Violet Vanburgh. First appeared on
the London stage as the White Queen in *Alice in Wonderland*.
Created D.B.E. in 1941. P.P.s by Beagles, Philco, and Tuck
"Bookmarker" Series V.

Vanburgh, Violet Augusta May   **1867-1942**
Actress. Elder sister of Irene Vanburgh. Played Anne Boleyn
in Henry Irving's *King Henry VIII* in 1892. Married Arthur
Bourchier in 1894. Occasionally appeared in films. P.P.s by
Beagles, as Portia; London Stereoscopic Co.; Rotophot;
Wrench.
        Illustration overleaf.

Vanderzel, Gladys
Actress. P.P. by Foulsham & Banfield.

Vandyke Printers Ltd.
Publisher. Bristol and London. Views of Stonehenge using
H.M. Office of Works photographs.

Vannin-Veg-Veen   **pre-1907**
Name used on I.O.M. postcards which carry the three-legs-
with-spurs trademark. Coloured island views.

Vasey, W.J.
Photographer/publisher of books with tear-off cards.

Vaughan, Bernard John   **1847-1922**
Jesuit priest and an ardent social reformer who worked among
the poor in London. P.P. Rotary, ill. Hill, p.13.

Vaughan, Edward H.
Landscape artist who painted a Tuck "Bonnie Scotland" set,
"Mountain, Loch and Heather", 7972.

Vanburgh, Violet. *"Miss Violet Vanbrugh". London Stereoscopic Co. P.U. 1907.*

Viewpoints. *"London. St. Paul's Cathedral". R. Tuck & Sons. "Oilette" "London".*

Vaux Stout   **pre-1910**
Brewers, Sunderland. Humorous advertising cards.

Vauxhall, J.M.
Publisher, London.

Velich, Joe
Chef at Skegness Holiday Camp. P.P. by Avery's Library & Post Office at this Butlin centre.

Velox Tyres
Advertising cards in a comic cycling series.

Verdier, Léon, Ltd.   **1909**
Publisher, 10 Dean St., London, W. Trademark on earliest cards is of a girl sketching and a letter "V", the whole encircled. Later cards simply carry the firm's name. Sets were produced in considerable variety. Reg Carter designed some "Hints" Series, e.g. "Hints to Roller Skaters", and several other sets. Animals, children, pierrots and glamour cards were all included.

Verey, Arthur   **fl.1880-1911**
Landscape painter whose work was used by Hildesheimer. Exh. R.A. 13.

Veritas Mantles
Poster-type advertisement by John Hassall.

Vernon, Emile   **fl.c.1904-1914**
Flower and portrait painter. Exh. R.A. 1. Designed glamour cards for James Henderson.

Vernon, R. Warren   **1820-1909**
Landscape artist, Exh. R.A.1. Painted a set on Ilfracombe for Tuck, 7275.

Verrier & Co. Ltd.
Publisher, Wine St., Bristol. Black and white local views.

Vertigen, H. & Co. (Ltd).   **1906 (Ltd. from 1909)**
Publisher, 12 Carthusian St., Aldersgate St., London, E.C. P.P.s of actors and actresses and coloured birthday cards. The firm continued the output of its predecessors, Howe, Vertigen & Co. (q.v.).

Veteran Cars
See: Motor Cars.

Victor Publishing Co.   **c.1905**
Publisher, 13 Alsen Rd., London, N. Output included:
(i)   London as it was in the early 19th century.
(ii)   Comic cards designed by Sidney Smith.
(iii)   "Post Wood" cards made of thin slices of wood.

"Victoria Series"
See: E.R. Green & Co.

Vieler, Herbert   **pre-1915**
Photographer/publisher, Imperial Studio, Bexhill-on-Sea, East Sussex. Local photographic views.

Viewpoints
It is interesting to compare cards taken from the same viewpoint by different publishers.

Views Ltd.   **1898**
Publisher, Piccadilly, Bradford. One of the earliest postcard firms; only U.B. cards are known. The view or views, for some have more than one picture, are enclosed in frames of rococo scrolls. Ill. Byatt 334.

Vignette
A view or portrait in which the background is gradually

Viewpoints. *"St. Paul's Cathedral London"*. *Philco Publishing Co.*

Grand Avenue, Savernake

Vignette. *"Grand Avenue, Savernake"*. *Chester Vaughan Series.*

shaded off so that there is no definite border. Most early cards where the message had to be written on the picture side had vignetted views.

Vigor, A.
Publisher, Rotherfield, Sussex. Local views.

Village Life
Town and city street scenes are common but life in villages is seldom depicted on postcards. The example here, by a local photographer, shows a woman joining in a village game much to the surprise of the male spectators.

Vincent, J.
Publisher, 109 High St., Oxford. Photographic views of Oxford printed in Germany.

Vincent, Ruth   **1877-1955**
Actress. P.P., with her baby, by Rotary.

Vine, Charles John
Artist who designed advertising cards issued by Photochrom.

Viner & Co.   **pre-1933**
Publisher, Acton, Middlesex. Photographic views.

Virol
Advertisement cards issued at Ideal Home Exhibition, 1910.

Viscan Pet Foods
Poster-type advertising cards.

Vogt, A.H.
Photographer/publisher, Daventry. Local views printed in Saxony.

Voisey, Charles   **1902**
Importer/publisher, 90 Tabernacle St., London E.C., 1902,

Village Life. *Scene on a village green. The Milton Studio, Reigate.*

and at 8a City Road, London, E.C., 1903. In addition to imported cards, Voisey issued sets of views of cathedrals and many humorous cards by such artists as Cecil Aldin, John Hassell and Louis Wain.

V. & S. or V. & S.D.
James Valentine & Sons Ltd., Dundee (q.v.).

"Vulcan Series"
A series name used by R.H. Gill of South Brent, Devon, and J. Richardson of Whaley Bridge, Derbyshire. These were probably both local retailers selling cards supplied by the same publisher.

V.W.S.
V.W. Sternberg (q.v.).

W.A.F.
W.A. Field (q.v.).

"W. & A. Leytonstone"
Photographer/publisher. Local R.P. views.

W.A. & S.S.
William Ashton and Sons, Southport (q.v.).

Waddington, John, Ltd.
Publisher, Great Wilson St., Leeds. P.P.s of celebrities. Ill. Holt 538.

Wade's   pre-1934
Photographer/publisher. "Wade's" "Sunny South" Series. R.P.s of south coast towns.

Wain, Louis William   1860-1939
Louis Wain was born in London, studied at the West London School of Art and became an assistant master there in 1881. A year later he joined the staff of the *Illustrated Sporting and Dramatic News* and in 1883 his first drawings of cats and dogs were published in this journal. He illustrated many books and a *Louis Wain Annual* was published from 1901 to 1925. From 1900 he was producing 600 drawings a year, many for postcards. His output was so great that the market was flooded and demand for his work declined. In 1924 he was certified as insane and was taken to the Asylum at Tooting where he died in poverty in 1939.

His postcards of cats, dogs, and other animals, are now keenly sought. They were published by:
(i)   Alphalsa Publishing Co., greetings cards with pigs.
(ii)   Beagles, "Matrimonial Cats".
(iii)   Birn Bros., "Excelsior Series".
(iv)   Boots Cash Chemists.
(v)   W. Collins Sons & Co., animal set.
(vi)   Davidson Bros. Byatt reports at least nine sets.
(vii)   A.M. Davis & Co., "Prize-Winners" Series.
(viii) E.T.W. Dennis & Sons.
(ix)   Max Ettlinger.
(x)   C.W. Faulkner, at least four sets, ill. Cope p.61.
(xi)   Gale & Polden.
(xii)   F. Hartmann, "Sporting Cats" set.
(xiii) Hutson Bros., cats in uniform.
(xiv)   E. Mack.
(xv)   Millar & Lang.
(xvi)   Henry Moss.
(xvii) E. Nister.
(xviii) Osborne Ltd., an American issue.
(xix)   Philco, black and white prints.
(xx)   Pictorial Post Cards, at least four titles.
(xxi)   J. Salmon.
(xxii) Soloman Bros.
(xxiii) A. & G. Taylor.
(xxiv) R. Tuck & Sons, "Taking the Waters", Dick Whittington and his Cat, cut out.

Wain, Louis. *"The Swing"*. C.W. Faulkner. P.U. 1910.

Wain, Louis. *"Good Luck and Good Wishes"*. *Alphalsa Publishing Co. P.U. 1920.*

(xxv)   Valentine, "Seaside Cats" and "Sports Series".
(xxvi) Leon Verdier, a single card noted.
(xxvii) Charles Voisey, write-away style set.
(xxviii) Wildt & Kray, cards overprinted with greetings.
(xxix) Woolstone Bros., write-away style cards.
(xxx)   E. Wrench.
       Ref: Dale, R., *Louis Wain; The Man Who Drew Cats*, 1968.

Collector—Ahem—Good Morning!
Is the Master of the House in?
Masterful Person—Speaking!!

Waller, Jack. *"Collector — Ahem — Good Morning! Is the Master of the House In? Masterful Person — Speaking!!" Millar & Lang. "National Series".*

Wakefield   **pre-1908**
Photographer/publisher, Ealing West, Middlesex. "Wakefield Series" of local R.P. views.

Walbourne, Ernest   **fl.1895-1920**
Landscape artist. Exh. R.A. 9. Some of his paintings were used by the Artistic Photographic Co. and by Faulkner.

Walker, A.
Publisher, Post Office, Shoreham, Sussex.

Walker, E.
Photographer/publisher, Titchfield, Hampshire. Local R.P. views.

Walker, Francis S.   **1848-1916**
Landscape painter who settled in London in 1868. Exh. R.A. 38.

Walker, Hilda Annetta   **fl.1904-1937**
Watercolour artist. Painted two "Oilette" sets for Tuck titled "Horses Heads" and "Chargers".

Walker, Jack
Designer of comic cards for Millar & Lang's "National Series".

Walker, James, & Co.
Postcard printers, Dublin. Printed some of Fry's advertising cards.

Walker, John, & Co. Ltd.   **1903**
Publisher, Farringdon House, Warwick Lane, London, E.C. Trademark an anchor. Noted particularly for "Geographical Postcards". Each consisted of a coloured map of an area with

Wallis, Bertram *as Alexis in "King of Cadonia" with Isabel Jay as Princess Marie. Photo by Foulsham & Banfield. Published in Rotary Photographic Series.*

an inset photograph of a feature of particular interest within the area. The maps were engraved by J. Bartholomew & Co., and other issues included:
(i)   General views covering a wide area.
(ii)   Regimental cards.
(iii)   Comic cards by Gordon Browne.
(iv)   "Free Trade" political cartoons by Harry Furniss.
(v)   "Aluminette" cards.

Walker, Samuel Edmund
Artist who contributed to the output of Langsdorff & Co.

Walker, Winifred   **fl.1919-1934**
Flower painter. Exh. R.A. 3. Held the post of Painter to the Royal Horticultural Society. Flower facsims. by Photochrom, 536-43.

Walker's Lager
Advertising cards by Warrington & Burton Brewery.

Wallace & Son
Publisher, Saltcoats, Ayrshire, Scotland.

Waller, Jack
Designer of comic cards for Millar and Lang.

Waller, Lewis   **1860-1915**
Actor-manager who played costume parts, e.g. in *The Three Musketeers,* 1902. P.P.s by Beagles, Ellis & Walery and Rotary. Scenes from *Monsieur Beaucaire* by Beagles, (ill. Hill p.26), Rotary and Wrench.

Wallis, Bertram   **1874-1952**
Actor and vocalist. First appeared on the London stage in 1896

Walters, George Stanfield. *"Corfe Castle, from Poole Harbour". Facsim. by C.W. Faulkner. P.U. 1906.*

War Damage. *"The Mahdi's Tomb at the Bombardment of Omdurman". G.N. Morhig of Khartoum.*

and his career extended over 40 years. P.P. with Isabel Jay by Rotary.

Walmsley, G.G.
Publisher, 50 Lord St., Liverpool. Issued official cards of the Liverpool and York Pageants.

Walmsley, J. Ulric   **fl.1884-1928**
Liverpool landscape artist. Facsim. of painting of Robin Hood's Bay, Yorkshire, used in Ruddock's "Artist Series".

Walsh, Sybil
Actress. P.P. by Rotary.

Walter Bros.   **pre-1910**
Publisher, Worthing, Sussex. Black and white local views.

Walters, George Stanfield, R.B.A.   **1838-1924**
Landscape and marine painter. Exh. R.A. 18. Seascapes for Faulkner.

Walters, Jessica Lloyd   **fl.1905-1939**
Landscape painter. Facsims. by Faulkner.

Walton   **pre-1911**
Publisher, Belfast. Shipping cards.

Walton, Mrs. Catherine Rebecca   **fl.1898-1935**
Landscape painter. Exh. R.A. 10. Facsims. by Robert Peel of Oxford.

Wanke, Alice
Art deco artist whose child studies were published by M. Munk and Wrench.

War Cartoon Studios
Publishers, London. Wartime propaganda cards. Ill. Holt 514.

War Damage
One of the earliest postcards of war damage shows the Mahdi's Tomb after the bombardment of Omdurman in the Sudan in the Campaign of 1898.

W.W.I. cards show the damage caused in the towns and villages of France and Belgium. They were published in their thousands, often in tear-off booklets, and were sometimes

War Damage. *"Campaign of 1914-1915 — Ruins of Ypres". Photo by Antony, Ypres.*

given English captions in the expectation that they would be sent to Britain by serving soldiers. War damage in Britain during W.W.I. included the bombardment of towns on the east coast including the Hartlepools and Scarborough, 16 December, 1914, and Lowestoft, 25 April, 1916.

See: Zeppelins.

280

War Effort. *Comic card by Millar & Lang. "National Series". P.U. 1918.*

War Memorials. *"War Memorial, Bournemouth". Publisher unknown. P.U. 1928.*

War Effort
Some cards show workers in munitions factories during W.W.I. A great many comic cards reflect the war effort of individuals, e.g. families cultivating allotments.

War Memorials
Most towns have their W.W.I. memorials. They range from such impressive examples as the Bournemouth War Memorial to village memorials and the Fell and Rock Climbing Memorial on Great Gable in the Lake District.
   See: Boer War Memorials.

War Puzzle Picture Co.
Publisher, Empire House, 175 Piccadilly, London. A firm which published hold-to-light cards featuring airships, warships, etc.

Ward   **pre-1930**
Publisher, Broadstairs, Kent.

Ward, Archibald   **fl.c.1908-1935**
Designer of cards for the York Pageant of 1909.

Ward, Beryl D.   **fl.c.1919**
Artist. Etched views of buildings for Worth & Co. of Exeter.

Ward, Dorothy   **fl.c.1908-1936**
Artist. Designed comic and greetings cards.

Ward, Dudley   **pre-1906**
Designer of comic cards for E.T.W. Dennis.

Ward, Enoch, R.B.A.   **fl.1896-1921**
Landscape artist. Exh. R.A. 6. Designed and engraved a series for W.H. Smith titled "Woodcuts of London".

Ward, Herbert   **1863-1919**
Figure artist. Exh. R.A. 9. In 1910 he moved to Paris and during W.W.I. sketched portraits of allied soldiers for Faulkner.

Ward, J.J.
Publisher, Coventry, Warwickshire. Area views in a "Popular Sepia Gloss Series" and a "Sepia Photo Art Series".

Ward, Herbert. *"With the French Army on the Vosges Front". Facsim. by C.W. Faulkner. 1915.*

Ward, J.T.
Publisher, hairdresser and tobacconist, Harwich and Dovercourt, Essex. Black and white views "published solely by J.T. Ward."

Ward, Sir Leslie Matthew   **1851-1922**
Caricaturist and portrait painter who did caricature-portraits for *Vanity Fair* from 1873-1909. Knighted in 1918. He was best known by his pseudonym Spy.

Gilsland Waterfall.

HODGSON, BRAMPTON.

Waterfalls. *"Gilsland Waterfall"*, *Cumberland.* Woolstone Bros.

9865. Piles Mill, Allerford.

Watermills, *"Piles Mill, Allerford"*. R.P. in E.A. Sweetman & Sons' *"Sunshine"* Series.

Ward, Marcus, & Co.   **1899**
Publisher, Oriel House, Farringdon St., London, E.C. This firm was established in 1866 and for many years published high quality Christmas cards. It appears to have ceased business in 1898 but was taken over by McCaw, Stevenson & Orr Ltd., of Belfast and London, who published a "Marcus Ward Series" pre-1904 using Marcus Ward designs on postcards.

Ward, S.S.
Publisher, Coventry. "Popular Sepia Gloss Series" of general views.

Ward, Winifred
Music hall actress and male impersonator. P.P. W.H. Smith & Son, Bristol, 1910.

Wardell, A.W.   **pre-1913**
Photographer/publisher, 4 Clarence St., Brighton, Sussex. Local R.P. views. "Picture Post Card by Wardell's" is printed on each card. There was also a branch at Worthing where Wardell covered the pier disaster of 1913.

Wardle, Arthur R.J.   **1864-1949**
Animal painter. Exh. R.A. 13. Designed sets for James Henderson & Son, including "Sporting Dogs and Birds" and "Pet Dogs", and for the Alpha Publishing Co.

Warne, F.W., & Co. Ltd.   **c.1914**
Publishers, London and New York. Primarily noted as book publishers but published 48 postcards shortly before the outbreak of W.W.I. These were based on nursery rhymes which had been illustrated by Randolph Caldecott in books originally published by Routledge before the advent of the picture postcard. The full list is given in the entry on Randolph Caldecott. It should be noted that these cards have been reprinted twice — in 1933 and 1975.

Warner, J.W.   **pre-1917**
Publisher, The Library, Melton Mowbray, Leicestershire. Local photographic views.

Warrington, Ellen   **fl.c.1922-1939**
Flower painter. Exh. R.A. 2. Tuck "Oilette Connoisseur" set "All in a Garden Fair".

Warwick, Frances, Countess of   **1861-1938**
Celebrated beauty and a member of the Prince of Wales' circle. The full story of her association with the Prince and the lawsuits threatened is told in Theo Lang's *My Darling Daisy,* 1965. P.P.s with her son, the Hon. Maynard Greville, and as an inset with a view of Warwick Castle, ill. Hill p.14. Both by Rotary.

Water Colour Post Card Co.   **pre-1905**
Publishers, 17 Paternoster Row, London, E.C., and at Hastings. Specialised in facsims. of watercolours by W.H. Borrow and covered the Warwick Pageant of 1906 for which John N. Bolton was the artist, see Byatt, Col. pl. IIE.
See: Colour Plate 7.

Waterfalls
Spectacular waterfalls always attract tourists and they feature on many postcards. Examples include:
Aber Falls, Carnarvonshire.
Clydach Waterfall, Nr. Brynmawr, Brecon.
Gilsland Waterfall, Cumberland.
Swallow Falls, Carnarvonshire.
"Tears of the Mountains", Glenariff, Co. Antrim.
"Valley of Desolation Waterfall", Bolton, Lake District.

Waterford Engraving Co.
Publisher of framed black and white cards.

Waterhouse, John Henry   **b.c.1884**
Photographer/publisher, Hadfield Town, Chesterfield. Specialised in events, supplying photographs to newspapers. Used his initials J.H.W. on his postcards.
Ref: P.P.M., June 1983, p.8.

Waterlow & Sons Ltd.
Postcard printers.

Watermills
These feature on a number of picturesque rural scenes, e.g. Riggs Mill, Whitby, after a painting by Warren Williams, E.T.W. Dennis.
Ref: Syson, L. *The Watermills of Britain,* 1980.

Watkins & Kracke Ltd. *"We've Got No Money But We Do See Life". Comic card in the "Burlesque Series". P.U. 1909.*

Watkin, C.E.
Publisher, Wincanton, Somerset. Local black and white views printed in Germany.

Watkins, Eustace   fl.1908-1909
Publisher, 51-2 Beech St., London, E.C. Trademark a clown with a skipping rope. Output included:
  (i) South coast coloured views.
  (ii) "Burlesque Series" of humorous and romantic themes.

Watkins & Kracke Ltd.   1909
Publisher, 51-2 Beech St., London, E.C. This partnership continued the business of Eustace Watkins (see above) adding "The Infantastic Series" featuring small boys and girls, and using types of card named "Elegant" and "Gravure". A "Snap-Shot Series" had oval photographs within various types of frame.

Watkins & McCombie Ltd.   1900
Publisher, 7 Paternoster Row, London, E.C. Musical postcards, Coon Series and facsims. of the work of R.C. Woodville (q.v.). The firm ceased to operate in 1907 when it was taken over by Sandle Bros. of Paternoster Row (q.v.).

Watson, Joseph, & Sons Ltd.
Leeds advertiser of Matchless Cleanser Soap. Small girl licks an envelope addressed to their "Soap Wrapper Competition".

Watson, Maud West   fl.1908-1914
Animal painter, especially of dogs. Tuck "Oilette" Series included her "Sketches of Doggies". These were sometimes overprinted with "Happy Days".

Watt, James   1736-1819
Scottish engineer who patented a steam engine in 1769. A set of seven cards was issued in 1919 to mark the "James Watt Centenary Celebration" in Birmingham.
  Ref: The cards are listed in P.P.M., March 1982, p.41.

Watt, L.C.
Photographer who did work for the Photochrom Co. Ltd. (q.v.).

Watts, E.A.   pre-1907
Photographer/publisher, West St., Somerton, Somerset. Local views.

Way, Thomas Robert   1852-1913
Landscape painter. Exh. R.A. 10. Way's Lithographic views, mainly of London and Brighton, were used by the Pastel Publishing Co. as pastel postcards.
  Ref: Byatt p.197.

Wayland
Photographer, Blackheath. R.P.s of football teams.

W.B.
Woolstone Bros. (q.v.).

W.D.M.
W. Dennis Moss, Cirencester (q.v.).

Wealthy, R.J.
Painter of butterflies and moths for sets by Tuck.

Webb & Co.   pre-1928
Publisher, 122 Pentonville Rd., London, N.1. Cards advertising hotels, e.g. The Grafton Hotel, Tottenham Court Rd., London.

Webb, Amy   fl.c.1886-1920
Painter of botanical subjects for the Ruskin Studio Art Press.

Webber, C.I.   pre-1904
Photographer/publisher. Black and white U.B. views of the London area printed by Edwin T. Walker of Leytonstone.

Webster, Alfred George   fl.1880-1917
Landscape and architectural artist. Exh. R.A. 22. Lived in Lincoln and taught at the Lincoln School of Art. Watercolours used by J.W. Ruddock in the "Artist Series".

Wedgwood & Co. Ltd.
Advertising cards in a "Roma" Series showing their potters at work.

Weekly Tale-Teller Magazine
Publisher of give-away art postcards of rural scenes printed by Delittle, Fenwick & Co. Ill. D. & M. 175.

Weekly Telegraph
Advertisement cards designed by Tom Browne.

Weeks, Sidney Thomas Charles   b.1878
London painter and commercial artist. Exh. R.A. 2. Designed a set of cards titled "London Nooks and Corners" for the Underground and London Electric Railway. They were produced by The Avenue Press Ltd.

Weiners, L.P., & Co. Ltd.
Printers, Acton, London. Produced cards for the Hampstead Tube.

Welby, Ellen   fl.1880-1918
Landscape and figure painter who designed early cards of "Buds and Blossoms" for Tuck, 580-5.

Webster, Alfred George. *"Newport Arch"*. *Facsim. in J.W. Ruddock's "Artist Series"*.

Welch, Joseph, & Sons   c.1899
Photographic publisher, Mile End, Portsmouth, Hampshire. The views were mainly "Trichromatic Post Cards" printed in Belgium, or sepia vignettes. Output included:
(i)   Views which mainly covered the southern counties from Kent to Devon, though parts of Lancashire, Yorkshire and I.O.M. were also included.
(ii)   Photographs of cats and dogs.
(iii)   Romantic series including staged scenes with lovers kissing and cuddling.
(iv)   "Language of Flowers" Series of staged photographs with a flower inset, e.g. "French Marigold — Jealousy".
(v)   Staged photographs illustrating "Proverbs".
(vi)   Studies from the life of Charles Dickens signed Kyd (q.v.).
(vii)   "Characters from Dickens".
(viii)   A playing card series. Ref: C. Hollingsworth. P.P.M., December 1983, p.28.
    Ref: Article by C. Hollingsworth on J. Welch & Sons in P.P.M., May 1983.

Weldon's Bazaar
Cards advertising patterns for dressmaking.

Well Dressing
Some wells have been centres of religious magic since the Middle Ages. They are sometimes dressed or decorated with flowers and tableaux, usually in the summer months. Those noted on postcards include:
St. Anthony's, Maybole, Ayrshire.
St. Chad's, Lichfield, Staffordshire.
St. Elian's, Denbighshire.
St. Keyne's, nr. Liskeard, Cornwall.
St. Oswald's, Oswestry, Salop.
St. Winifred's, Holywell, Flintshire.

Wellington Hotel
Publisher, Boscastle, Cornwall. Local R.P. views.

Wells, John Sanderson   1890-1940
Sporting artist. Exh. R.A. 38. Painted coaching scenes for Mansell and hunting scenes for James Henderson & Sons.

Welsh Language. *"A Welsh Beauty Spot"* R. Tuck & Sons. *"Oilette"* *"Welsh Rarebits"*.

Wells, N.
See: A.A. Smith.

"Wells Series"
See: H. Camburn.

Wellsted, W.J., & Son.
Photographer/publisher, Hull, Yorkshire. Local views.

Welsh   pre-1915
"Photographic Publishers", Portsmouth, Hampshire.

Welsh Language
Many cards depict the Welsh names which "foreigners" find difficult to pronounce.

Welsh National Dress
Several publishers of Edwardian cards depict Welsh women in their traditional dress of tall hats and cloaks.

Welsh, William   fl.1908-1929
Artist who lived near Newcastle upon Tyne and designed heraldic naval cards for Andrew Reid.

Went, Douglas
Publisher, The Studio, Tower St., Brightlingsea, Essex. Local R.P. views.

West & Son   pre-1932
Photographer/publisher, Whitstable, Kent. Local R.P. views.

West, Alice L.   fl.1889-1915
Painter of birds. Exh. R.A. 6. Facsims. by Faulkner, and Tuck "Oilette" set "Birds and Blossoms".

"West End Series"
See: A.E. Shaw.

West Highland Railway Co.   1903-1910
Publisher who issued view cards.
    Ref: Check list in R.O.P.L., 13, p.19.

West, Reginald   fl.c.1900-1910
Landscape artist who lived at Christchurch, Hampshire. Painted "Dorset" sets for Tuck, 7763-4.

Welsh National Dress. *"A Welsh Woman". Brown & Rawcliffe. P.U. 1905.*

Western Mail Ltd.   **pre-1909**
Publisher, Cardiff. The "Colliery Series" of mining scenes with printed material in both English and Welsh.

Weston, Phil
Painter of moonlight scenes for Harvey Barton & Son of Bristol.

W.H.
Wolff Hagelberg (q.v.).

Wheatcroft, G.H.
Photographer/publisher, London Rd., Sheffield. Local R.P. street scenes.

Wheatley, F.   **fl.c.1902-1910**
Artist who designed sets of "London Street Cries" for Faulkner, "Cries of London" for Giesen Bros., and "Old London Cries" for Samuels.

Wheeler, Dorothy Muriel   **1891-1966**
Watercolour artist. Exh. R.A. 5. Painted the "Woodland Secrets" Series for Bamforth, four sets in Black's "Beautiful Postcard Series", "Snow Children" and "Day at the Fair" for Humphrey Milford, and a number of sets for Salmon.
  Ref: Cope p.28, ill. p.62.

Wheelwright, Rowland, R.B.A.   **fl.1893-1938**
Australian painter who settled in England. Exh. R.A. 41.

White & Son
Photographer/publisher, East Cowes, I.O.W. Local views including several of the Shell House (q.v.).

White, Flora. *"Ride a Cock-Horse". J. Salmon. P.U. 1931.*

White, A. Percy
Designer of comic cards for Tilley & Son of Ledbury.

White, Brian
Artist. Designed a "Nipper Series" for Valentine. Ill. Monahan 153.

White, Flora   **fl.1887-1918**
Artist. Designed postcards with children for Salmon and Mack, children with animals for Photochrom and patriotic cards during W.W.I.

White, Gilbert
Painter of coaching series for Tuck.

White Horse Whisky
Advertising cards with coaching scenes by Charles Maggs.

White Horses and Hill Figures
Many white horses have been cut into the chalk rock of Southern England. They include examples at Cherhill, Uffington and Westbury. Hill figures include the Giant of Cerne Abbas. All appear on postcards.
  Refs: Drinkwater, W.J., 'White Horses of Wiltshire', P.P.M., July 1983; Marples, M., *White Horses and other Hill Figures,* 1981.

White, J., & Son
Photographer/publisher, Littlehampton, Sussex. Black and white views.

White, J.B., Ltd.
Publisher, Dundee, Angus, Scotland. Trademark "Best of All Series" printed within a shield. R.P. views.

White, Pearl   **1889-1938**
Film actress described as "Queen of the Silent Serials". P.P. by Pathé Frères Cinema Ltd.

Whitehead, Fred
Painter of illustrations for A. & C. Black's "Shakespeare Country" reproduced as postcards by Tuck.

Whitford, Herbert
Publisher, Dudley, Worcestershire. R.P. views.

Whittaker & Co.
Publisher, Pendleton, Lancashire. "Gaff" Series of coloured views.

Whittington, Marjorie, R.B.A.   **fl.1922-1940**
Watercolour artist. Exh. R.A. 7. Designed a "Sweet Fragrance" Series for the Medici Society.

W.H.S. (& S.)
W.H. Smith (& Son) (q.v.).

Whydale, Ernest Herbert   **fl.c.1910-1923**
Landscape and animal artist. Exh. R.A.34. Horse studies for Salmon.

Wichera, Raimund R.   **b.1862**
Austrian figure painter noted for his glamour cards which were published by M. Munk of Vienna and also supplied to Faulkner and W.H. Smith. His work is highly valued.

Wick & Lybster Light Railway
This line issued view cards.
    Ref: Check list in R.O.P.L., No. 14, p.23.

"Wide, Wide World"
This name, which was used by Raphael Tuck & Sons for cards dealing with foreign countries, was the title of a book for children written by an American novelist, Susan Bogart Warner (1819-1885) who used the pen-name of Elizabeth Wetherell. The book was published in 1850 in two volumes and became popular in Britain as well as in America. Thirteen editions were published within two years, and the title became almost a catchword. The first English edition was published by James Nisbet in 1852 and the first English illustrated edition by George Routledge in 1852.

Wiederseim, Grace Gebbie   **1877-1936**
American painter of child studies whose postcards were sold in Britain by Charles Hauff and A.G. Taylor. She designed several Campbell's Soup advertisements.

Wielandt, Manuel   **1863-1922**
German artist who travelled widely and painted landscapes in several European countries for cards printed by E. Nister and published by the Schmidt-Staub Company of Nuremberg. Series included views of the Italian Riviera, the Italian Lakes, towns in Switzerland, the French Riviera and Venice. A few cards of the German Rhine were also printed. Other publishers and printers took over the work for later editions.
    Ref: Heywood, R., 'The Artistic Postcards of Manuel Wielandt', P.P.A. 1982, p.22.

Wiener Werkstätte   **fl.1905-1911**
Publisher, Vienna. The Vienna Workshop organised by Josef Hoffman and Koloman Moser issued a number of postcards which became available in Britain. They were in the art nouveau style and reached a total of 300 designs by such artists as Koloman Moser and Karl Schwetz.

Wilcock, A.M.
Painter of child studies.

Wild Hawthorn Press
Publisher, Stonypath, Dunsyre, Lanarkshire.

Wilding, Dorothy
Court photographer who photographed George VI for the Medici Society, and film stars for *The Picturegoer*.

Wilding, L., & Son Ltd.   **c.1902**
Publisher, The Salop Art Press, Shrewsbury. Trademark two figures reading a document by candlelight within a cartouche which includes the name of the firm and the town. Output included:
(i)   Views of Shrewsbury and the county.
(ii)   Watercolour facsims. of work by C.C. Ashwell, Edwin Cole and E.A. Phipson.
(iii)   Photographs of events.
(iv)   Portraits of personalities, including politicians.
(v)   Local advertising cards.

Wildt & Kray   **1904**
Publisher, 15 Lensden Place, London, E.C., and after 1912 at 116-20 Golden Lane, E.C. Trademark a lady with an artist's palette which carries the initials "W. & K. London". Output included:
(i)   Greetings cards which were a speciality, often with photographic portraits and narrow embossed frames. They include a "Floral Series" of birthday cards and a series of flowers in colour against a silver background overprinted with greetings.
(ii)   "Faith", "Hope" and "Charity" cards in sets of three.
(iii)   Coloured cards of dogs.
(iv)   Comic cards depicting people as vegetables.
(v)   R.P. Series.
(vi)   Sepia photographs of gallery paintings, especially those depicting horses.
(vii)   A series of "Orders and Medals".
(viii)   "N.W. Series" of London views.
(ix)   Coloured Irish views in a shamrock frame.
(x)   Facsims. of work by Jotter, two sets on "Constable Country"; Alexander Young, "British Coast Series"; E. Sanders, "The Merry Monks".
    See: Colour Plate 11.

Wilhelm II   **1859-1941**
Kaiser of Germany. Political cartoons which depicted the Kaiser as a symbol of German militarism were published by several firms during W.W.I., e.g. Bamforth, Davis & Co., and Hutson Bros.

Wilkes, Albert   **fl.1909-1936**
Sports photographer, one time Aston Villa footballer, who devoted his life to taking photographs of Britain's football teams.
    Ref: P.P.M., November 1982, p.7.

Wilkin, Robert   **b.1888**
Scottish artist who designed comic cards for D. Eisner & Son and Hutson Bros. Signed his work Bob Wilkin.

Wilkinson, Charles A.   **fl.1881-1925**
Landscape painter. Exh. R.A. 11. Made drawings for a set titled "Views of London" for Cassell & Co.

Wilkinson, Norman, R.B.A., R.I., R.O.I.   **1878-1971**
Marine painter and poster artist. Exh. R.A. 55. Illustrated a

Wildt & Kray. *"At Cappaquin, Co. Waterford"*. *A Shamrock frame used for Irish views. P.U. 1911.*

HE MORNING BATH.

Wildt & Kray. *"The Morning Bath"*. *Photograph of a painting by Lilian Cheviot.*

book on *The Royal Navy* published by A. & C. Black who reproduced the illustrations as postcards. Some were also used by Tuck in the "Royal Navy" sets.

Wilkinson, R., & Co.   **pre-1906**
Publisher, Trowbridge, Wiltshire. Many R.P.s and coloured views of Wiltshire, Somerset and Dorset printed in Germany.

Willebeek Le Mair, Henriette
   See: H.W. Le Mair.

William Bros.
Publisher, Menai Bridge, Anglesey. Local sepia views.

William, Frank
Publisher, Hawkhurst, Kent. Local views.

Williams, Bransby   **1870-1961**
Actor and mimic. First music hall appearance 1896, giving impersonations of popular actors. Played Micawber in *David Copperfield*. After 1931 he took part in some films. P.P. by Rotary.

Williams, J.W. *"Scarborough — Late Residence Richard III"*. *Facsim. in Thomas Taylor & Son's "Queen Series"*.

Williams, J.W.
Artist who painted views of "Old Scarborough" for Thomas Taylor & Son.

Williams, Madge
Artist. Designed cards for children, including a W.W.I. card for Salmon.

Williams, T.F., & Co.
Printer/publisher, 38 Bank St., Newquay, Cornwall. Coloured local views.

Williams, Violet   **fl.1930s**
Artist. Specialised in children's postcards. Designed "Story Book Postcards" for E. Mack, each with a brief story by Dorothy Marigold.

Williams, Warren   **fl.1901-1918**
Painter of landscapes, illustrator and poster artist. Exh. R.C.A.95. Lived at Conway and illustrated many topographical books. Facsims. of his work were used by S. Cambridge of Hove, E.T.W. Dennis, a "Worthing Series"; T.A. Flemons of Tonbridge; W. Hampson of Bettws-y-coed, "Snowdonia Series".

Willis, George   **fl.1930s**
Designer of comic cards for Valentine, e.g. "Chummy Series".
   See: Colour Plate 13.

Wills, W.D. & H.O.
Advertiser of their "Capstan" and "Gold Flake" cigarettes.
   See: Imperial Tobacco Co. Ltd.

Wimbush, Winifred. *"A Call to Arms! Say When You'll Have Me!"* Facsim. R. Tuck & Sons. "Oilette" "Call to Arms" Series I. P.U. August, 1918. The reverse bears the stamped mark "Passed by Censor No. 6339".

Willson, Leslie
Designer of an amusing cycling set for Tuck titled "The Scorcher's Progress".

Wilson, A.J.
Photographer/publisher, Hereford. Local photographic views.

Wilson, David
Designer of comic cards for Hartmann.

Wilson, E. & J.
Publisher, Liverpool. "Wilson Series" of coloured views of Liverpool with the city coat of arms.

Wilson, G.W., & Co. Ltd.   **1899**
Publisher, 2 St. Swithin St., Aberdeen. G.W. Wilson was a well-known local photographer whose work was used by the firm that bears his name. Most of the cards published by this firm were intended for the trade but the initials "G.W.W." within a diamond indicate their origin.
  Ref: Byatt p.332 for biographical details.

Wilson, Harry   **fl.1901-1926**
Designer of comic cards for D. Eisner & Son.

Wilson, Oscar   **fl.1914-1918**
Designer of W.W.I. cards.

Wilson, S.
Photographer/publisher, Sheffield. Local R.P. views.

Wiltshire Moonrakers
The story goes that when two Bristol smugglers were travelling near Devizes their donkey ran away, throwing a cask of brandy in the river. They tried to fish it out with a rake but seeing an excise man and the moon reflected in the water, they told him they were raking for the cheese. The excise man was convulsed with laughter and later told the story in the country round about. Coloured postcards of "The Wiltshire Moonrakers" were published by Tomkins & Barnett of Swindon and R.R. Edwards of Salisbury.

Wimbush, Henry B.   **fl.1880-1908**
Landscape artist. Exh. R.A. 4. Illustrator of topographical books for A. & C. Black. Painted many sets for Tuck including "Bonnie Scotland", "Dartmoor", "Dartmouth", "Paignton", "Picturesque Cornwall", "Picturesque Oxfordshire" (two sets), "Inverness", "Newquay", and "Picturesque Lakes".

Wimbush, Winifred
Figure painter who designed a "Call to Arms" set for Tuck.

Windmills
These are to be seen in many view cards both photographic and in painting facsims. Many of these mills no longer exist but some have been carefully restored by enthusiasts. The following have been noted:
  Bardney, Lincolnshire.
  Bembridge, Isle of Wight.
  Burton Broad, Norfolk.
  Caxton, Cambridgeshire.
  Coningsby, Lincolnshire.
  Great Chishall, Cambridgeshire.
  Great Yarmouth, Norfolk.
  Headcorn, Kent.
  Heckington, Lincolnshire.
  Herne Mill, nr. Herne Bay, Kent.
  Horsey, Norfolk.
  Ivinghoe, Buckinghamshire.
  Lacey Green, Buckinghamshire.
  Littlehampton, Sussex.
  Lytham, Lancashire.
  Mablethorpe, Lincolnshire.
  Mundesley, Norfolk.
  Nettleham, Lincolnshire.
  North Leverton, Nottinghamshire.
  Patcham, E. Sussex.
  Riddings, Derbyshire.
  Rottingdean, Sussex.
  Salvington, nr. Worthing, Sussex.
  Stevington, Bedfordshire.
  Tadworth, Surrey.
  Walberswick, Suffolk.
  Waltham Abbey Old Windmill, Essex.
  Walton-on-the-Naze, Essex.
  Wenhaston, Suffolk.
  White Roding Mill, Essex.
  Wimbledon Common, Surrey.
  Woodhouse Eaves, Lincolnshire.
  Worlingworth, Suffolk.
  Ref: Reynolds, J., *Windmills and Watermills,* 1970.

Windsor Castle
Many publishers issued cards of Windsor Castle including the Picture Post Card Co. and Thomas Thorp. Two sets by Tuck depict the State Apartments.

"We hate listeners-in!"

Tommy and Jack they fight their ways
Thro' many a furrin' track ;
"So long !" says one, on the Himalays,
"Till we meet at the Union Jack."
HAROLD BEGBIE.

Wireless. *"We Hate Listeners-in!"*. *Card by Arthur Butcher in the Inter-Art "Comique Series". P.U. 1925.*

Winkler, Rolf
Designer of cards featuring silhouettes of children.

Winnington-Ingram, Arthur Foley   1856-1946
Bishop of London from 1901 to 1939. P.P. by Rotary.

Winsch, John   pre-1910
Publisher of gilded Christmas postcards. Trademark a balance with the words "Full Value" and "Gold Standard Brand".

Wireless
Broadcasting began in Britain with the establishment of the British Broadcasting Company in 1922 which provided a system of national and regional programmes. The British Broadcasting Corporation took over by Royal Charter in 1927. There was great interest in the new habit of listening in, usually on crystal sets, and this is reflected in the designs of comic postcards and in R.P.s taken in the new wireless stations. Ill. Monahan 37. The Photochrom Co. published a very good humorous series titled "Wireless Terms Illustrated".

Wise, Ernest Edward   fl.c.1905-1920
An artist who shared the work on a comic series for Mitchell & Watkins with a fellow artist Archibald English. They signed jointly "A.E. & E.W." He also painted views of Berkshire and Huntingdon for Tuck.

Wishing Wells
These sometimes appear on postcards. The well at Upwey, near Weymouth, is a good example. Early cards show it with a timber roof. Later cards by Frith and Valentine show how it has been commercialised. A castellated stone structure has replaced the old roof and there are notices pointing to a local tea room.
  See: Well Dressing.

Wollen, William Barnes. *A "Tommy and Jack" card. Facsim. by Gale & Polden. "Reproduced by kind permission of the Union Jack Club". "Wellington Series". Painting dated 1903.*

W. & K.
Wildt & Kray (q.v.).

W. & K. L.
Wildt & Kray, London (q.v).

W.M.B.
W. Milne Black (q.v.).

Wollen, William Barnes   1859-1936
Military, sporting and portrait painter. Born in Leipzig, lived in London.

Wolseley Tool & Motor Car Co.   pre-1905
Advertising card for the "Wolseley-Siddeley" with the caption "The Queen's Choice", ill. D. & M. 158.

Women in W.W.I.
Relatively few women went out to work or engaged in active sports prior to W.W.I. and those who did were hampered by traditional clothes. The war changed this rapidly. Women were needed to replace men in factories and on the transport systems and the issues which the suffragettes (q.v.) had stood for were steadily resolved. Women not only played games such as tennis but formed their own football clubs.
  Illustrations overleaf.

Wood, Clarence Lawson   1878-1957
Watercolour painter and illustrator. Exh. often at Brook St. Art Gallery and the Walker Gallery. Worked for *The Tatler* and some of his drawings were used on postcards but he is best known for his work specially designed for postcard

Women in W.W.I. *Bus conductress, Southampton. Photo by Edwarde, Southampton.*

Women in W.W.I. *"Miss Lily Wort (left back) G.R.M. L(adies) F.C. 1917-18". Photograph by Bridge Studio, 6 Bridge Road, Woolston.*

Women in W.W.I. *Workers in industry. J. Emberson of Wimbledon, Surbiton and Tooting.*

reproduction. This was used by a number of publishers including:

(i) David Allen & Sons, an early poster card.
(ii) Carlton Publishing Co., comic cards.
(iii) Davidson Bros., sets titled "Prehistoric Courtship" and "Prehistoric Pastimes".
(iv) Dobson Molle & Co., the "St. Clair War Series".
(v) J.S. Fry's advertisement of "The Outdoor Magazine", P.U. 1908.
(vi) Henderson, "Weather Forecasts".
(vii) Inter-Art Co., the "Artistique Series" and "Comique Series", mainly anthropomorphic studies of animals, especially dogs, 1920s.
(viii) Lawrence & Jellicoe.
(ix) Pictoral Stationery Co.
(x) Salmon.
(xi) Stiebel, "Modern Humour".
(xii) Tuck, "Dog Humour".
(xiii) Valentine, at least six "Gran'pop Series" depicting an old monkey with younger animals of many types. This firm published "Lawson Wood" postcards.
See: Frontispiece.

Wood, Mitchell, & Co. Ltd.
Printer, Hanley, Staffordshire. Supplied view cards to the North Staffordshire Railway.
Ref: R.O.P.L., No. 1, p.7.

Woodall, Minshall, Thomas & Co.   **pre-1904**
Publisher, Oswestry and Wrexham. Black and white local

GRAN'POP REPLIES FOR THE LADIES.

Wood, Clarence Lawson. *"Gran' pop Replies for the Ladies"*. *Valentine's "Lawson Wood" Series. 1934.*

"BLINDED FOR YOU!"
From the painting by R. Caton Woodville

Woodville, Richard Caton. *"Blinded for You!" One of a series of facsims. issued by the National Institute for the Blind to raise money for soldiers and sailors blinded in W.W.I. and training at St. Dunstan's in Regent's Park.*

views in an "Offa Series", sometimes with two views on a card, e.g. Halston Chapel and Halston, Whittington. Comic and political cards designed by William Thomas, a partner with the firm.

"Woodbury Series"
See: Eyre & Spottiswoode Ltd.

Woodcock, Page   **1902**
Advertiser of their "Wind Pills" using a portrait of King Edward VII with the caption "A Coronation Gift".

Woodland Card Co. Ltd.
Publisher, London. W.W.I. cards designed by J.H. Roberts. Ill. Monahan 90.

Wood-Milne Rubber Heel   **pre-1906**
Trademark used on a series of 40 numbered coloured views.

Woodruff
Photographer/publisher, Eastry, Kent. "Photo Series".

Woods & Co.   **pre-1905**
Publisher, Royal Library, Malvern, Worcestershire. Local coloured views.

Woods, J.
Publisher, Post Office, Canvey Island, Essex. Local coloured views.

Woodville, Richard Caton   **1856-1927**
Military artist who worked for *The Illustrated London News.* He painted battle scenes of the Turkish War, 1875; the

Egyptian War, 1882; the Boer War, 1889-1902; W.W.I., 1914-18. Some of his work appeared on postcards including:
(i)   Boer War, issued by the Collectors' Publishing Co., and the Picture Postcard Co.
(ii) "British Battles" by Frederick Hartmann, a set of 12.
(iii) "Gentleman in Khaki" by Watkins & McCombie.
(iv) Cards of soldiers blinded during W.W.I. produced for the National Institute for the Blind.

Woodward, C.H.   **pre-1905**
Publisher, Devizes, Wiltshire. A "C.H. Woodward Series" of views.

Woodward, G.   **pre-1935**
Publisher, The Studio. Thorpe-le-Soken, Essex. Local photographic views.

Woodward, T., & Sons   **c.1900-1905**
Advertiser, Plough Brewery, Wandsworth Road, London, S.W. Printed advertising order card with price list.

Woodyer, Albert E.   **pre-1900**
Photographer/publisher, Worksop, Yorkshire. Court size cards of the Matlock district of Derbyshire.

Wooley, G.
Publisher, Ludlow, Shropshire. Coloured local views.

Woollett, Cresswell
Landscape artist who painted for E.W. Savory.

Woolstone Bros.   fl.1902-1933
Publisher, 14 Chapel St., Milton St., London E.C. and, after 1914, at 29-30 Newbury St., Aldersgate St., London, E.C.1. The firm used the tradenames "Milton Post Card" or "The Milton Series", sometimes with the head and shoulders outline of the poet. The name was derived from the street name of their earlier premises. Many types were developed over the years: Artlette, Bromette, Bromide, Chromolette, Glazette, Glossette, Photolette and Sellwell. Sometimes they were combined, e.g. Artlette Glazette and Elite-Glazette for series of framed views. Output included:
(i)   Greetings cards including the "Coloured Bromide Birthday Postcard" Series, "The Milton Hand-Painted Birthday Series", the "Glazette Greeting" Series and various Christmas cards.
(ii)   Photographic views including a photogravure "Renowned Series", framed views (Scottish examples in tartan), coloured views with coats of arms, "Sellwell" views of London, a "Miltona" Series and a "Moonlight Series".
(iii)   "Milton Glossette" Series of P.P.s of actresses.
(iv)   "Navy Series".
(v)   "Life of Nelson" Series, "Printed and copyrighted by J. Keliher & Co. Ltd., by permission of the Lords Commissioners of the Admiralty".
(vi)   Artistic work including a "Jotter Series".
(vii)   Comic cards by Fred Buchanan.
(viii) Cut-out novelties.
(ix)   "The Milton Boudoir Book Post Card". This "Bromette" Series was just over an inch longer than the average and cards were intended for use as bookmarkers.
        See: Colour Plate 18.

Woolworth, F.W., & Co.   pre-1914
This still famous firm owned many stores which sold nothing at a price greater than 3d. or 6d. It published views, birthday cards and romantic W.W.I. cards. Ill. Monahan 17.

Wootton, G., & Son   pre-1908
Publisher, Felixstowe, Suffolk.

Worcester, Charles, & Co. Ltd.   pre-1904
Publisher, 5 Kingsdown Parade, Bristol, and after W.W.I. at 5-7 Montague Place, Kingsdown, Bristol. Tradename "Chic Series". Output included sepia views, moonlight views by Elmer Keene, and a number of line drawings.

Worcestershire Brine Baths Hotel   pre-1905
Publisher, Droitwich, Worcestershire. R.P. views by the local photographers Gummery & Blackham.

Wordsworth, William   1770-1850
Poet laureate. Blum & Degen vignette portrait.

Workhouses
These were operated under the Poor Law and had little to recommend them as postcard material. Nevertheless, they do appear both as interior and exterior views. There are four cards of the Walsall Union Workhouse, for example.
        Ref: P.P.M., January 1982, p.32.

Worth & Co.
Publisher, Cathedral Close, Exeter, Devon. "Worth's Series" of local sepia views, some of which were beautifully hand coloured. Individual artists were employed by Worth including Sidney Endacott, "Devon Worthies"; Arthur Perry, South Devon views; B.D. Ward, etchings of local buildings.

Worthing Portrait Co.
Publisher. Framed R.P. views.

Worthington, William
Film actor. Sepia portrait by Pictures Ltd.

Woven Silk Postcards
        See: W.H. Grant & Co.; Thomas Stevens.

Wrecks
        See: Shipping Accidents and Wrecks.

Wrench, E. (Ltd.)   1900 (Ltd. from 1902)
Publisher, 20 Haymarket, but soon moved to 2 Arthur St., London. The firm expanded too rapidly; was remodelled as Wrench Postcards Ltd. in 1904, but was finally forced to close down in 1906. Trademark a small wrench in an oval with the words "The Wrench Series". Output included:
(i)   Views of noted houses and castles, e.g. Hampton Court, Holyrood and Linlithgow.
(ii)   Black and white views of resorts on cream-coloured card printed in Saxony, e.g. Weston-super-Mare, 771, and Elizabeth Castle, Jersey, C.I., 6568.
(iii)   Sepia views, sometimes framed and plate-marked.
(iv)   "Links of Empire", cards of the ports of call of the *Ophir* when on a cruise with the Duke and Duchess of Cornwall. Two sets, one for the outward voyage and a second for the return.
(v)   Set of four cards to mark the voyage of the *Discovery*. Wrench arranged for Robert Falcon Scott to post some of them at ports of call on the way to the Antarctic so that they would have interesting postmarks.
(vi)   An "Isle of Man Series".
(vii)   Portraits of famous cricketers and footballers.
(viii) Comic cards including several by Louis Wain and a "Fiscal Series".
(ix)   Characters from Dickens by Kyd (q.v.).
(x)   "Pictures from Punch".
(xi)   Framed and print-marked scenes from plays photographed by Bassano, e.g. *Monsieur Beaucaire*.
(xii)   A "Famous Picture Series" of gallery reproductions.
(xiii) Locomotives and ships.

Wrenn, L.R.   pre-1935
Publisher, 116 Reddenhill Rd., Babbacombe, Devon.

Wright, Alan   fl.c.1896-1910
London landscape and figure painter of close-up studies of horses and ponies for Faulkner and some coaching scenes in collaboration with George Vernon Stokes.

Wright, George   1860-1940
Painter of sporting scenes. Exh. R.A. 38. Designed "Sporting Pictures" for E.W. Savory.

Wright, Gilbert S.
London painter of coaching and hunting scenes and of close-up studies of horses for J. Henderson, M. Munk and Tuck.

Wright, Henry Charles Seppings   1849-1937
Artist who joined the staff of *The Illustrated London News* in 1885, covering aspects of the Boer War. Some of his drawings were used by the Picture Postcard Co. He contributed marine scenes with sailing vessels to a Hildesheimer U.B. series.

Wright, Huntley   1869-1941
Actor. First appeared on the London stage in 1891. Often broadcast in B.B.C. drama in the 1930s. P.P.s by Beagles and Tuck.

With your PRESENTS to your soldier friends include
a box of
WRIGHT'S COAL TAR SOAP.
.IT SOOTHES AND PROTECTS.

Wright's Coal Tar Soap. *"With your presents to your soldier friends include a box of Wright's Coal Tar Soap. It soothes and protects"*. Advertisement card.

Wright, Maurice D.   pre-1907
Publisher. Morecambe, Lancashire.

Wright's Coal Tar Soap and Shampoo Powder
Advertising cards which included the "Wan-Tang-Fee Chinamen" Series.

Write-away Cards
Before 1902, when the British Post Office permitted messages to be written on the address side of postcards, publishers were forced to leave a space for this purpose on the picture side. Designs by Blum & Degen and Tuck included a few words printed on this space starting a sentence which the sender of the message was expected to complete. These were known as write-away cards. The publisher's name usually appeared in small print on the front of the card and the name or initials of the designer were often included. Lance Thackeray, for example, signed his designs L.T. Write-away type cards were also published by Davidson Bros., and by Stewart & Woolf.

W.R.S.
William Ritchie & Sons Ltd. (q.v.).

W.S.
Sir Walter Scott (q.v.).

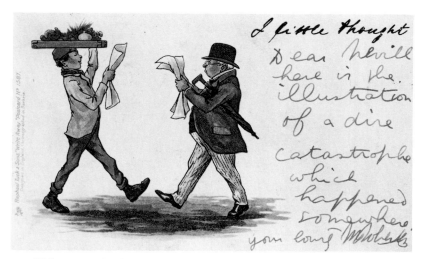

Write-away Cards. *The published introductory words "I little thought..." have been ignored by the writer.* R. Tuck & Sons. "Write-Away" Postcard.

W.S.B.
W. Shaw, Burslem (q.v.).

W. & T.G.L.
W. & T. Gaines, Leeds (q.v.).

"Wulfruna Series"
Series of views by G.E. Lewis of Wolverhampton.

Wuyts, A.
Artist who painted cats, dogs, children and glamorous ladies.

"Wykeham Collection"
Black and white views of Canterbury.

"Wykeham Series"
Photographs of Winchester by an unknown publisher.

Wyllie, William Lionel, N.E.A., R.A., R.B.A., R.E., R.I.
                                    1851-1931
Marine artist. Exh. R.A. 180. Worked for the White Star Shipping Line and the Navy. Facsims. of ocean liners. Many of Wyllie's paintings may be seen in the Portsmouth Museum.

Wyman & Sons Ltd.
Publisher and wholesale stationer, Bristol. Local sepia views.

"Wyman's Gravure Series"   pre-1913
Publisher, London E.C. Glossy sepia views, e.g. Plymouth, Drake's Island.

Wyndham, Sir Charles   1837-1919
Actor-manager, originally known as Charles Culverwell. Stage appearances from 1862; Manager Criterion Theatre, London, 1876-99. Played title role in T.W. Robertson's *David Garrick* in 1886. Knighted 1902. P.P. by Rotary.

"Wyndham" Series   pre-1905
Black and white views of Cambridge.

"Wyvern Series"
Facsim. views published by G. Childeric of Leicester.

"XL Series" **fl.1930s**
Comic cards by an unknown publisher of London, E.C. Also the name of a Valentine Series.

Y. & C.
Young & Cooper (q.v.).

Yeomen Warders *in state dress at the Tower of London. Gale & Polden.*

Yacht Racing
The most notable yacht racing cards are those showing Sir Thomas Lipton's yachts named *Shamrock* in which he competed unsuccessfully in the America Cup races of 1901, 1903, 1914, 1920 and 1930. One card shows *Shamrock II* in 1901 with an inset portrait of Sir Thomas.

Yallop, A.W.
Publisher, Yarmouth.

Yeomen Warders
Sometimes known as Yeomen of the Guard or Beefeaters. Gale & Polden.

"Yes and No" Series **pre-1905**
"Yes and No" was one of Shurey's Publications' magazines. The series included P.P.s of actors and actresses and views of East Anglia.

Young, Alexander **fl.1885-1920**
Landscape watercolour artist, a Scottish contributor to Faulkner's early output. "Young's Series" of Scottish views have U.B.s. He also contributed to Tuck's "The Restless Ocean" set and to Wildt & Kray's "British Coast Scenes".

Young & Cooper
Printer/publisher, Maidstone, Kent. Trademark "Y & C" in monogram form. A coloured hop-picking series consisting of at least 40 cards and other Kent views.

Young Men's Christian Association
Publisher. Cards show some of their buildings, e.g. the Y.M.C.A. Hut at the Midland Station, Nottingham, c.1919.

Young, Walter Hayward
  See: Jotter.

Ysaye, Eugene **1858-1931**
World famous Belgian violinist who visited London in 1900 and 1907. P.P. by Rotary.

Zag-Zaw

A series of Tuck "Picture Puzzle Postcards" was sold under this title and advertised as "Society's Latest Pastime for Progressive Puzzle Parties". The proceeds were "Entirely in aid of the Prince of Wales' National Relief Fund". Harry Payne's "Defenders of the Empire", 8761, was issued as a Zag-Zaw, P.U. 1917.

Zandrino, Adelina

Italian artist. Painted young children with animals.

Zatka, H.

German artist. Painted glamour cards.

Zeppelins

German airships named after their inventor, Count von Zeppelin (1838-1917). Air raids by zeppelin were carried out during W.W.I. The first was on 19 January, 1915, the most serious on 13 October, 1915. They continued in 1916 but by the end of that year fairly good defences had been devised against them. Postcards show zeppelins over Britain in the light of searchlights. Many of the photographs are simulated. Two series were published:

(i)   A set by Hutson Bros. shows the zeppelin destroyed by W.L. Robson at Cuffley, Hertfordshire, in September 1916.

(ii)   Irvine's Ltd. published a set titled "The Destruction of a Zeppelin". Individual titles were "Danger Ahead", "Nearing Disaster", "Airman Attacks", "Well Alight", "Nearing the End" and "Final Rapid Fall".

A *Daily Sketch* photo shows a zeppelin sinking in the Thames estuary on 1 April, 1916. A number of cards were designed by an artist who used the initials SA on a set of five coloured zeppelin cards for G.M.H. Coleby-Clarke (q.v.).

Ref: Russell, R., *Zeppelin! A Battle for Ace Supremacy in World War I,* 1982.

Zirka, C.

Artist. Painted glamour cards.

Zoological Gardens

A number of publishers produced series of animal and bird photographs taken in the London Zoological Gardens, including:

"General" the Lion at Clifton Zoo.

Zoological Gardens. " *'General' the lion at Clifton Zoo"*. Senior & Co., Bristol. P.U. 1912.

(i)   Beagles & Co. "Zoo Favourites", at least 27 examples.

(ii)   British Postcard & Poster Co., U.B. cards, 24 in all, with red titles.

(iii)   David & Co., two "Natural History" sets described on the cards by R.I. Peacock.

(iv)   Eyre & Spottiswoode, series of 60 photographs by W.P. Dando, F.L.S.

(v)   Gottschalk, Dreyfus & Davis.

(vi)   Hildesheimer, sepia views.

(vii)   London Stereoscopic Co., series titled "London Zoological Gardens", each animal is described briefly on the address side.

(viii)   Salmon, facsims. of paintings by C.T. Howard, e.g. "Camels on the Broad Walk at the Zoological Gardens, London".

(ix)   Zoological Society of London, Regents Park, London, N.W.

A series on the Clifton Zoological Gardens, Bristol, was printed and published by Senior & Co.

Appendix I

List of tradenames of Raphael Tuck and Sons' sets. The abbreviations relate to the list of subject titles in Appendix II, opposite.

Aqua-Connoisseur (AqC).
Aquarette (Aq).
Art (A).
Art Collotype (AC).
Art Glosso.
Art Glosso Greetings.
Autograph (AU).
Bio, i.e. photographic portraits.
Birthday.
Bookmarker.
Broderie d'Art, embroidered.
Calendar (C).
Carbonette.
Charmette (Cha).
Christmas (Ch)
Chromette (Chr).
Chrom-Photo (CP).
Collo-Photo.
Collotint.
Collotype.
Coloured Crayon.
Connoisseur.
Continental.
Continental Art.
County.
Crayon.
Double-Photo Greeting.
Duo Gem.
Easter.
Educational.
Elite.
Embossed (Em).
Emerald Rough Sea.
Emerald Sea.
Empire.
Fiscal (F).
Floral Gems.

Flower & Beauty.
Framed Aquagraph.
Framed Charmette.
Framed Gem.
Framed Gem Glosso (FGG).
Framed Granite.
Framed Marble.
Framed Photo Glosso.
Gem (G).
Gem Glosso.
Gem Oilette.
Glosso (GL).
Glosso Connoisseur.
Glosso Oilette.
Gold Framed Gravure.
Gold Framed Sepia.
Gramophone Record.
Hand-coloured Opal.
Hand-coloured Photogravure (HCP).
Heraldic (H).
Heraldic Framed Marble.
Heraldic View.
Holly.
Humorous.
Impressionist.
Louis Wain (LW).
Marine (M).
Monogram.
Moonlight.
New Year (NY).
Oil Facsim.
Oilette.
Oilette Connoisseur.
Oilette de Luxe (ODL).
Oilette Panorama.
Oilette Remarque.

Old Print.
Panoramic Oilette.
Photochrom (P).
Photo-Colour(PC).
Photographic Gloss (PG).
Photogravure.
Photo-Oilette.
Phototype.
Plastic Hand Coloured.
Plate-Marked.
Plate-Marked Oilette (PMO).
Plate-Marked Sepia.
Play Pictorial.
Rapholette (R).
Rapholette Glosso (RG).
Raphotype.
Real Japanese.
Real Photograph (RP).
Rembrandtesque.
Remembrance.
Rough Sea.
Sapphire Rough Sea.
Scottish Rough Sea.
Sepia (S).
Silverette (Si).
Tartan View (TV).
Thanksgiving.
Tinsel.
Tinto-Pho (TP).
Town & City (T&C).
Turneresque
Valentine Posies.
View Series (V).
Vignette Excelsior.
Wide Wide World (WWW).
Write-Away.

Appendix II

Subject titles of numbered sets published by Raphael Tuck & Sons between 1903 and 1939 (after individual numbering had ceased).

This list is, inevitably, incomplete, and the names of artists are given in brackets when known. All cards are Oilettes except where indicated, e.g. Si = Silverette. The abbreviations refer to the tradenames noted in Appendix I, opposite. See also note on p.304.

1500-1511	Celebrated Posters (see S.G.P.C. 1983, p.224).
1537-1538	Inns of Court and Chancery (Charles Flower).
1549	British Fish.
1605	Write-Away (Lance Thackeray).
1608	Dogs (Helen Maguire).
1646-1647	Town Life (Edward and Gunning King).
1660	Matlock (Hadfield Cubley).
1673	Cheltenham.
1679-1681	Cornwall (Charles Flower).
1683-1684	Derbyshire (Hadfield Cubley).
1724	Picturesque North Wales III.
1745	British Game (Helen Maguire).
1765-1766	Write-Away (Lance Thackeray).
1771	Write-Away (Phil May).
1775	Write-Away (Phil May).
1777	Write-Away (Phil May).
1781	Leeds (Charles Flower).
1782	Bradford (Charles Flower).
1783	Nottingham (Charles Flower).
1787	Picturesque Stafford (Hadfield Cubley).
Si1804	Bridlington.
Si1812	Bradford.
Si1831	Halifax.
Si1832	Huddersfield.
1835	Easter cards.
Ch1842	Christmas cards.
H1847	Sheffield.
Si1857	Hyde Park.
H1859	Heraldic.
FGG1860	The Trossachs and Loch Katrine.
Si1861	Bradford.
Si1863	Knaresborough.
Si1864	Ripon.
Si1866	Ilkley.
Si1880	York.
Si1882	York.
Si1883	Selby.
Si1897	Ely Cathedral.
TV1909	Dunoon.
Si1921	Beverley.
Si1974	Sheffield.
AC1975	Bridlington.
Si1984	Doncaster.
T&C 2004-2034	Sets including Liverpool, Bradford, Leeds, Harrogate, York, Hull, Cork, Bridlington and Whitby.
2071	Harrogate.
T&C 2114-2123	Including Malvern, Cromer, Isle of Wight, Sheffield, Halifax.

T&C 2132-2167	Sets including Bournemouth, Folkestone, Huddersfield, Oxford, Rotherham, Sheffield and Southsea.
Ch2250	Happy Land Series (Phyllis Cooper).
PC2264	Beverley.
PC2265	Knaresborough.
CP2277-2282	Sets including Bridlington, Hull and York.
HCP2299	Ripon.
R2326	Birthday cards.
G2338	Birthday cards.
2397	A Maiden Fair (Marjorie Mostyn).
R2442	Birthday cards.
2458	Famous American Expresses.
2517	Landseer's Dogs.
M2548	Marine Postcard Series.
2561	Landscape Series.
2573-2580	Van Hier facsims. (atmospheric studies).
AqC2696	Shooting Incidents (H.F. Obermeyer).
2713	Cambridge Colleges (Joseph Finnemore).
2714	Oxford Colleges (Joseph Finnemore).
2716	Ships that Pass in the Night (George R. Cordingley).
2727	Picturesque English Lakes (H.B. Wimbush).
2758	Hunting (Gilbert Wright).
2765	Hunting (Philip Stretton).
2781	The Hunt Day (Norah Drummond).
2924	In the Hunting Field (Norah Drummond).
2975	Flower Maidens (Marjorie Mostyn).
2980	Glorious Venice (W. Knox).
2981	Lucky Dogs (Hal Ludlow).
2984-2994	Glamour cards by Marjorie Mostyn.
3001	Birthday cards.
3007	Birthday cards.
3012	Unsolicited Testimonials (Fred Buchanan).
3015	The Royal Artillery, 1717-1917 (Harry Payne).
3046	Favourite Dogs (Norah Drummond).
3052	Man's Best Friend (Norah Drummond).
3109	Champion Clydesdales (Norah Drummond).
3144	In the Air II.
3160	Colonial Badges and their Wearers (Harry Payne).
3163	Our Fighting Regiments: 1st Life Guards (Harry Payne).
3165	Our Fighting Regiments: 1st (King's) Dragoon Guards (Harry Payne).
3183	On the Land.
3184	Favourite Dogs (Norah Drummond).
3190-3191	Birds and Blossoms (Alice L. West).
3194	Hunting (Norah Drummond).

3210	Wild Animals (George Rankin).
3219	Sporting Dogs (Norah Drummond).
3244	Once upon a Time (Agnes Richardson).
3259-3260	Picturesque English Lakes (H.B. Wimbush).
3294	With Dog and Gun (Norah Drummond).
3296	In the Hunting Field (Norah Drummond).
H3308-3331	International Heraldic Series (check list S.G.P.C., 1983, pp.225-6).
3337	In the Rocky Mountains (Norah Drummond).
3346	Sketches of Doggies (Maud West Watson).
3350	The Canadian Rockies (Norah Drummond).
3366	Sporting Dogs (Norah Drummond).
3381	Dressing Dolls.
3384	Dolls of Many Lands.
3385	Fairy Tale Dolls.
3390	Butterflies on the Wing.
3394	Mechanical Dolls.
3398	Dolls' House Furniture.
3405	Swinging Dolls.
3407	Dickens Characters (Harold Copping).
3427	Flowers in Vases (after Gunning King).
3441	Faithful Friends.
3442	The Best of Friends.
Em3470	Puss in Boots.
3504	Famous Expresses.
3513	British Empire Exhibition.
3541	Famous Expresses.
3546	The Military in London.
3547	Famous Expresses.
3569-3570	Famous Expresses.
3579	Fox Hunting (Gilbert Wright).
3580	Domestic Pets (Persis Kirmse).
3593	The World's Fliers.
3596	Hunting in the Shires.
3639	Pet Dogs (Norah Drummond).
ODL3800	Golden Dawn (Jean Lasalle).
ODL3801	Early Victorian I (J. Harbour).
ODL3803	Early Victorian II (J. Harbour).
ODL3806	Golden Hours (J. Lasalle).
LW3885-3896	Louis Wain sets.
RP3950-3956	Royal Portrait sets.
4013	Folkestone (Charles Flower).
4015	Bristol (Charles Flower).
4017	Winchester (Charles Flower).
4065	Fruit and Flowers (Christina Klein).
4066	Fragrant Flowers (Christina Klein).
4078	By Garden Ways (Christina Klein).
4084	Stable Friends.
4091	In Flower Time (Christina Klein).
4092	Dog Close-ups (A. Hanstein).
4093	In the Country (Allan F. Barraud).
PG4315	Our Navy XIII.
PG4335	Our Navy XVIII.
P4403	Studies of Dogs.
P4411	Animal Life.
P4415-4417	Celebrities of the Stage.
P4446	Celebrities of the Stage.
P4449-4452	Celebrities of the Stage.
4500-4505	The Queen's Dolls' House.
Chr4756	Sheffield.
Chr4768	Manchester.
V4786	Northampton.
4820-4822	Titania's Palace.

Chr4910	Grantham.
Chr4914	Redcar.
Chr4921	Marlborough.
RP5040	Royalty.
RP5050	Lovely Lakeland.
RP5081	Picturesque Castles of Scotland.
5186	Loch Lomond (Edgar Longstaffe).
5303-5304	Famous Expresses.
RP5342	Oxford Pageant I.
RP5343	Oxford Pageant II.
RP5344	Oxford Pageant III.
GL5501	Halifax.
GL5509	Saltburn-by-the-Sea.
GL5541	Inverness.
RP5542-5544	Oxford Pageant.
GL5574	Boston.
GL5609	Harrogate.
GL5610	Halifax.
GL5613	Hamilton.
GL5632	Happy Catland.
GL5641	All Sorts of Pets.
5666	Picturesque Wales.
AU5707	Autographed Portraits of Stage Celebrities.
GL5726	Celebrities of the Stage.
GL5730	Celebrities of the Stage.
GL5739	Celebrities of the Stage.
GL5770	Scarborough.
FGG5776	"Sweet, Sweet is the Morning".
TP5910	London.
TP5911	Bridlington.
TP5915	Sheffield.
TP5922	Whitby.
TP5923	London II.
TP5924	London III.
RG6059	Birthday cards.
6118-6125	Sets of fruit and flowers (Christina Klein).
6134	Floral set (Christina Klein).
F6138-6139	Political caricatures.
F6144	Chamberlain caricatures (Arthur Moreland).
6153	Stable Chums.
6157	Stirling.
6163	Steeplechasing.
6167	Bunyan's Cottage.
6172	Shakespeare Country.
6177	Whitby.
6180	Aberdeen.
6181	Dublin.
6190	Bournemouth.
6191	Picturesque Shrewsbury (Hadfield Cubley).
6193	London (M. Johnson).
6199	Newark-on-Trent.
6200	The West Highlands.
6205	Old Bristol.
6210	Salisbury.
6213	Weymouth.
6214	Glencoe (Edgar Longstaffe).
6216	Isle of Man.
6217	Bridlington.
6219	Burnham Beeches.
6224	Halifax.
6225	Huddersfield.
6228-6230	Celebrated Liners.
6233	Picturesque North Wales.
6234	The Restless Sea.

6236	Fun and Frolic.
6241	Highland Laddie (Hamish Duncan).
6243	Irish Songs (Hamish Duncan).
6249	"Quaint Corners".
A6252	Isle of Wight (R. Esdaile Richardson).
6254	Paignton (H.B. Wimbush).
Aq6257-6260	Old London Churches and Gateways (Charles Flower).
Aq6264	Isle of Wight IV (R. Esdaile Richardson).
Aq6267	Driven Ashore (G. Parsons-Norman).
6272	Picturesque Whitby (Frank Rousse).
Aq6273	Picturesque Lochs (H.B. Wimbush).
Aq6274	Southend-on-Sea (A. Sanders).
Aq6280	Ilfracombe (E.D. Percival).
S6316	Rough Seas.
S6327	Rough Seas.
6411	Old and Young Holland (Will Owen).
6413	Dutch Studies (after black and white drawings by Tom Browne).
6414	Sailor Laddie (Hamish Duncan).
Aq6422	Up the River.
6447	Racing Illustrated (Sidney Hebblethwaite).
6459	Fighting the Flames.
6463	Japanese at Home.
6466	Japanese Celebrities.
6476	Tower of London (Charles Flower).
6477	Quaint Corners (Frank Emanuel).
6480	Quaint Corners (Frank Emanuel).
6490	Popular Racing Colours.
6493	Famous Expresses I.
6498-6499	English Cathedrals (Arthur Payne).
Si6515-6516	Animal Studies (Gambier Bolton).
6527	Life at Aldershot.
Si6530	Knight of the Bath.
A6635	Easter cards.
6678	Historic Houses — Scotland (David Small).
6681	Venice I.
6685	Fisherman Studies.
6690	Toilers of the Deep.
6692	Nelson Centenary.
6748	Christmas Greetings (Maude Goodman).
6819	Catland.
6820	The Simple Life.
EM6865	Farmyard Scenes.
7010	Hereford.
7016	Lynton and Lynmouth.
7018	Old English Sports (after Paul Hardy).
7021	Canterbury Cathedral (Charles Flower).
7025	St. Ives.
7035	Westminster Abbey (Charles Flower).
7036	London (set of 12).
7037	WWW Venice II.
7053	WWW Monte Carlo.
7066	WWW Madras II.
7069	Picturesque Cornwall — The Lizard (H.B. Wimbush).
7070	Picturesque Cornwall — Penzance (H.B. Wimbush).
7071	Picturesque Cornwall — Redruth (H.B. Wimbush).
7074	Dartmoor (H.B. Wimbush).
7076	Kingsley Country (H.B. Wimbush).
7092	Abbotsford (John Blair).
7095	Dolgelly (Edgar Longstaffe).

7101-7102	Tennyson's Country (R. Esdaile Richardson).
7103	Haslemere (J.T. Adams).
7107	WWW Switzerland (A.D. McCormick).
7108	The Trossachs (F.W. Hayes).
7111	Maidstone.
7112	Durham (Parsons Norman).
7115	Picturesque Counties: Kent (Jotter).
7116	Kent (Jotter).
7118	Bonnie Scotland. St. Andrews (Frederick W. Hayes).
7120	Picturesque Counties: Surrey. (S. Pike).
7121	Picturesque Thames (R.F. MacIntyre).
7127	Middlesex I (Jotter).
7128	Middlesex II (Jotter).
7130	Picturesque Counties: Pembroke (F.W. Hayes).
7133	Jersey (C. Larbalestier).
7136	West Highlands of Scotland (Hadfield Cubley).
7139	Hull (Hadfield Cubley).
7140	Buxton (Hadfield Cubley).
7148	Deeside (Edgar Longstaffe).
7167	Scottish Lochs V (Walter Severn).
7171	Torquay.
7179	Stratford-on-Avon.
7189	The Wye Valley (F.W. Hayes).
7201	Picturesque Egypt.
7203	Picturesque Egypt.
7208	Picturesque Egypt.
7210	Halifax.
7211	Picturesque Counties: Berkshire I (A.W. Bridgeman).
7212	Ilkley.
7215	Giant's Causeway.
7216	Ripon.
7220	Sunderland.
7221	Ullswater (Edgar Longstaffe).
7222	Old Edinburgh.
7223	Huddersfield.
7226	Rochdale.
7227	London (12 cards).
7232	Winchester.
7233	Clovelly (A.W. Bridgeman).
7235	WWW Delhi.
7236	WWW Lucknow.
7237	WWW Agra.
7238	WWW Burmah (sic).
7240	Clyde Watering Places (David Small).
7264	Peterborough.
7278	London: Fleet Street (Arthur Payne).
7290	Carlisle.
7291	WWW Sydney (A.H. Fullwood).
7293	Edinburgh I and II (John Fulleylove).
7308-7309	WWW The Holy Land I and II (John Fulleylove).
7314	Windermere.
7316	Rothesay.
7317	Guernsey (H.B. Wimbush)
7321	Derwentwater.
7331	Teignmouth.
7332	WWW Sydney.
7338	Grampians.
7344	Bonnie Scotland: Perthshire.
7369	Exmouth.

7372	WWW Naples.
7375	Harrogate.
7376-7377	Scarborough.
7382	Beautiful Britain.
7386	Quebec (Charles Flower).
7390	St. Leonards.
7392	Picturesque Counties: Buckinghamshire (A.W. Bridgeman).
7399	Chingford.
7404	Lincoln.
7410	Gloucester Cathedral (Charles Flower).
7417	Ayr.
7420	Picturesque Buckinghamshire II (A.W. Bridgeman).
7427	WWW Morocco.
7429-7430	Loch Lomond I and II.
7434	WWW Picturesque Egypt.
7436	Philadelphia.
7441	Picturesque Egypt Series XI.
7445	Cannes.
7446	Ryde, I.O.W. (R. Esdaile Richardson).
7447	Newport, I.O.W. (R. Esdaile Richardson).
7458	Scottish Clans III.
7461	Ilfracombe (H.B. Wimbush).
7462	Newquay (H.B. Wimbush).
7471	Cottage Gardens.
7475	Nice.
7484	In the Arctic Regions.
7485	Switzerland (Lady Mary Long).
7492	Shakespeare Country IV.
7501	Picturesque Whitby (A. Winter Moore).
7506	Plymouth II (H.B. Wimbush).
7507	Plymouth III (H.B. Wimbush).
7508	Gareloch (H.B. Wimbush).
7532	Bonnie Scotland: Aberfeldy.
7536	Berkshire III (E. Wise).
7537	Loch Lomond (H.B. Wimbush).
7539	Bonnie Scotland: Isle of Arran (H.B. Wimbush).
7540	Loch Long (H.B. Wimbush).
7541	The Clyde (H.B. Wimbush).
7557-7558	Yorkshire (G. Home).
7600	Frankfurt (Charles Flower).
7602	Welsh Waterfalls (Edgar Longstaffe).
7607	Southsea.
7614	Duisberg, Germany.
7616	Charterhouse, London (Charles Flower).
7623	Picturesque Oxford I (H.B. Wimbush).
7633	Dartmoor II (G.H. Jenkins).
7636	Killarney.
7640	Old Edinburgh II (J. Kinnear).
7643	Picturesque Oxford II (H.B. Wimbush).
7644	Picturesque Oxford III (H.B. Wimbush).
7645	Picturesque Oxford IV (H.B. Wimbush).
7648	Toulon.
7651-7652	Nice.
7655	Amiens.
7658	German Waterfalls.
7661	Bonnie Scotland: The Highlands (W. Smith/A. & C. Black).
7666	Tigh-na-Bruach.
7668-7669	Versailles.
7670	Menton.
7671	Mannheim.
7672	Falmouth.
7676	Sheffield (Jotter).
7677	Bonnie Scotland: Inverness (H.B. Wimbush).
7680	Bonnie Scotland: Ben Nevis (H.B. Wimbush).
7681	Bonnie Scotland: Oban (H.B. Wimbush).
7684	Staffa and Iona (H.B. Wimbush).
7691	WWW Village Life in Armenia (S.A. Alzarian).
7697	Outside Sheffield (Jotter).
7698	York.
7701	The Land of the Golden Fleece (A.H. Fullwood).
7704	Foggy London (Marchioness of Townsend).
7711	Picturesque Thames I (H.B. Wimbush).
7730	WWW Cuba.
7734	Shakespeare's Country (Fred Whitehead).
7735	Harrogate.
7739	Staffordshire (Jotter).
7741	Paris Market Places.
7748	Picturesque Dartmoor IV (G.H. Jenkins Jr.).
7753	Suffolk (Jotter).
7755	Picturesque Counties: Dorset (A.W. Bridgeman).
7757	Famous Expresses: Russia.
7761	Cottage Homes: The Black Forest (J.A. Heyermans).
7762	Bordeaux.
7766	Picturesque Counties: Wiltshire.
7767	Co. Wicklow (Jotter).
7769-7770	Rouen.
7772	Yorkshire Coast II (H.B. Wimbush).
7775	Scarborough (H.B. Wimbush)
7776	Clovelly (G.H. Jenkins Jr.).
7777	Picturesque Devon: Lynton (G.H. Jenkins Jr.).
7778-7779	Dusseldorf.
7782	Co. Dublin (Jotter).
7787	York (H.B. Wimbush).
7788	Knaresborough (H.B. Wimbush).
7789	Co. Antrim (Jotter).
7797	Trèves.
7799	Co. Mayo (Jotter).
7800	Co. Galway (Jotter).
7802	Cambridge II (W. Matthison).
7807	The Trossachs (H.B. Wimbush).
7819	Callandar (H.B. Wimbush).
7821	Picturesque Cumberland (E. Longstaffe).
7838	Tyneside (Jotter).
7839	Ilfracombe (G.H. Jenkins Jr.).
7840	Picturesque Devon (G.H. Jenkins Jr.)
7866-7867	Burma I (R.G.T. Kelly).
7876	Bettws-y-Coed (H.B. Wimbush).
7877	Picturesque Wales (H.B. Wimbush).
7880	Burma II (Edith Pinhay).
7888	Glengariff, Co. Cork.
7893	Picturesque North Wales VIII (A. de Breanski).
7898	London (set of 26 cards) (Charles Flower).
7901	Cambridge IV (W. Mattheson).
7902	Cambridge V (W. Mattheson).
7906	Houses of Parliament (Charles Flower).
7926	Brussels (A. Forestier).
7927	Bruges (A. Forestier).

7928	Antwerp (A. Forestier).	8533a	Grenadier Guards.
7929	Ghent (A. Forestier).	8536	Picturesque English Lakes II.
7930	Liège (A. Forestier).	8539	Picturesque North Wales II.
7938	Eton (Charles Flower).	8570	WWW Native Life in Japan.
7939	Windsor (Charles Flower).	8600	Carnations.
7940	London (Charles Flower).	8604	Fun in Switzerland (Arthur Thiele).
7941	Royal Hospital, Chelsea (Charles Flower).	8612-8615	Taking the Waters (Louis Wain).
7942	Glencoe (E. Longstaffe).	8619	Scotch Expresses.
7943-7944	Egypt (R.G.T. Kelly).	8625	The Scots Guards (Harry Payne).
7947	Lynton and Lynmouth (Jotter).	8635	21st Lancers (Harry Payne).
7948	Picturesque Devon: Dartmoor II (G.H. Jenkins Jr.).	8637	17th Lancers (Harry Payne).
		8642-8644	Our Navy: Ironclads.
7949	Carnarvon (Charles Flower).	8646	Chums (Norah Drummond).
7952	Oxford (H.B. Wimbush).	8649	St. Paul's Cathedral.
7957	Chester Cathedral (Charles Flower).	8650	Man's Best Friend (Norah Drummond)
7964	Plymouth (Charles Flower).	8661	Battle of Jersey.
7970	Exeter Cathedral (Charles Flower).	8664	Chums Series I.
7974	Modern Athens — Edinburgh (Charles Flower).	8665	Chums Series II.
		8666	French Army.
7977	Harrogate (H.B. Wimbush).	8668	American Indians.
7978	Glasgow (Charles Flower).	8669	Sporting Dogs (Norah Drummond).
7979	Torquay (H.B. Wimbush).	8673	Our Navy: Ironclads.
7980	Paignton (H.B. Wimbush).	8696	Children's Friends.
7982	Whitby (J.N. Drummond).	8715	Our Navy: Ironclads.
7983	On the Dart (H.B. Wimbush).	8718	Our Navy: Ironclads.
7984	Dartmoor (H.B. Wimbush).	8726	Guardians of the Empire's City.
7986	Beautiful Perthshire (Edgar Longstaffe).	8731	Our Territorials (Harry Payne).
7987	Whitby (Frank Rousse).	8734	The Call.
7994	Rome III.	8735	Our Allies in Action (B. Granville Baker).
R8000	Dumfries.	8739	Our Navy Speaks.
R8002	Bury St. Edmunds.	8745	Our Boy Scouts (G.E. Shepheard).
8018	Bournemouth.	8755	Our Navy: Ironclads.
R8031	Kittendom.	8756	History in the Making.
R8032	All Sorts of Pets.	8759	White Winter (Frederick W. Hayes).
Ch8035	Christmas Set (Lance Thackeray).	8761	Defenders of the Empire (Harry Payne).
8037	Among the Scottish Lochs.	8762	Red Cross (Harry Payne).
R8039	The Shepherd and His Flock.	8763	Royal Horse Artillery (Harry Payne).
R8051	Hawick.	8770	Regimental Bands (Harry Payne).
R8057	Rustic Courtships.	8772	A Call to Arms (Winifred Wimbush).
R8062	"All on a Summer's Day".	8774	Telling the Marines (G.E. Shepheard).
R8074	Farm Life.	8778	Fox and Stag Hunting.
R8075	Four-Footed Friends.	8782	Game Birds II (George Rankin).
RG8104	Pyppydom.	8788	Our Kiddies (Agnes Richardson).
RG8113	Furry Friends.	C8792	Calendar cards.
RG8120	"Good Night, Sweet Repose".	8796	To Victory.
RG8126	A Little Love Story.	8807	16th (The Queen's) Lancers (Harry Payne).
RG8154	North Sea Fishing.	8810	At the Front I.
R8186	The Rosary.	8816	Very Fit (Louis Wain).
Ch8320	Christmas Greetings.	8817	Humorous (Louis Wain).
NY8376	Christmas Greetings in New Year Series (ill. D. & M. 179).	8818	At The Front II.
		8820	Military Mascots (Norah Drummond).
8463	Cottage Gardens.	C8825	Calendar card for 1916.
8484	Aesop's Fables (political cartoons by F. Sancha).	8826	Humorous cards (Louis Wain).
		8831	1st Royal Dragoons (Harry Payne).
8494	Hampton Court Palace Gardens.	8835	1st Life Guards (Harry Payne).
8505	Scarborough.	8840	Workers.
8506	Ilfracombe (E.D. Percival).	8850	Some Cats (Louis Wain).
8507	Nottingham (Charles Flower).	8851	Orchids.
8510	Sheffield.	8855	When All is Young (Agnes Richardson).
8515	Louis Wain Cats.	8862	Call of the Flag.
8523	Cornwall (Jotter).	8864	Prize Pussies (Louis Wain).
8524	Killarney.	8871	Regimental Badges and their Wearers (Harry Payne).
8525	Scottish Castles.		
8533	5th Royal Irish Lancers.	8882	Italian Army (Alfred Pearse).

9356	Seaforth Highlanders.	9585	Whitby.
9360	Share and Share Alike (Sidney Hayes).	9587	Military in London III.
9363	Life in Spain (H.F. Obermeyer).	9588	London Commons (Jotter).
9364	Favourite Dogs (Arthur Thiele).	9607	Famous British Cattle (Norah Drummond).
P9367	5th Royal Irish Lancers.	9615	Fragrant Meadows (S. Shelton).
9381	The Friend of Man (Norah Drummond).	9622	Merry Winter Time.
9388	Making Friends (Harry Payne).	9624	Our Ironclads VII.
9389	Daughters of the Land (Harry Payne).	9625	Celebrated Liners — Canadian Pacific.
9396	Cats (Louis Wain).	9630	Humour in Egypt (Lance Thackeray).
9401	Scottish Clans I.	9631	Kitten Studies (H. Bernard Cobbe).
9403	Scottish Clans II.	9639	Pet Dogs (Norah Drummond).
9412	Coon Town Kids.	9641	Picturesque Coaching Inns II.
9413	Cheshire — Old Timbered Houses (Jotter).	9645	Dachshunds.
9416	Landseer's Pictures (reprint of early I.N. series).	9649	Gretna Green Elopement.
		9653	Irish Peasant Life (Norah Drummond).
9418	English Cathedrals V (Arthur Payne).	9662	Famous Expresses IX.
9423	Taking the Waters (Lance Thackeray).	9666	Grenadier Guards.
P9425	Royal Horse Artillery.	9681	Sketches of Doggies (Maud W. Watson).
P9426	2nd Life Guards.	9687	Famous Expresses XI.
9441	Seeking New Pastures (Harry Payne).	9689	Stable Chums.
9450	Fox Hunting (Arthur A. Davis).	9692	Horses' Heads (Hilda Walker).
9458-9459	Scottish Clans III and IV.	9693	The Busy Ocean (R. Montague).
9460	Fun on the Sands.	PMO9700	Lovely Lakeland.
9463	English Cathedrals VI (Arthur Payne).	PMO9701	Around the Coast (H.B. Wimbush).
9470	Happy England III (R.F. McIntyre).	PMO9706	Through the Woods.
9475	Prize Canaries.	PMO9711	In the Highlands (H.B. Wimbush).
9478	British Army Uniforms.	PMO9715	Famous Expresses.
9481	Scottish Clans VI.	PMO9721	The Countryside: Staffordshire Views (Jotter).
9487	Sweet Songsters.		
9488	Irish Life (Jotter).	PMO9722	By Mead and Stream (Harry Payne).
9490	The Monkey House (Maude Scrivener).	PMO9729	Rough Seas.
9492	The Gentle Art of Making Love (George E. Shepheard).	PMO9742	Maidens Fair (Mary Horsfall).
		PMO9745	Killarney.
9495	Airships.	PMO9750	Whitby.
9501	Cats and Dogs — as Louis Wain sees them.	PMO9757	In the Country (Harry Payne and Gilbert Foster).
9506	Country Courtships.		
9507	Steeplechasing I.	PMO9760	Famous Expresses.
9510-9512	St. Albans Pageant (Robert E. Groves).	PMO9761	The Time of Flowers.
9514	Rural Life (Norah Drummond).	9764	Cat and Kittens.
9516-9518	Oxford Pageant (Arthur Thiele).	9770	Regimental Bands (Harry Payne).
9522	Steeplechasing III.	9782	The Subscription Ball (Arthur Thiele).
9524	British Game Birds.	9797	A Mewsical Party (Arthur Thiele).
9527	Life at Aldershot (Harry Payne).	9816	Horse's Head Studies.
9533	British Army.	9818-9819	Catland (Arthur Thiele).
9535	Village Crosses.	9820	Pets and Puppies.
9539	Among the Bunnies (H. Bernard Cobbe).	9822	Their Majesties the King and Queen.
9540	At the Cat Show (Louis Wain).	9824	The Metropolitan City Police.
9542	Granny's Darling.	9828	Northumberland Fusiliers.
9544	Chargers (Hilda Walker).	9852	Character Studies from Charles Dickens (Harold Copping).
9546	Humour in Egypt: The Nile (Lance Thackeray).		
		9857	Ships of the Sea and Air.
9547	Humour in Egypt: Cairo (Lance Thackeray) (ill. D. & M. 97).	9871	Horse Racing (Ludwig Koch).
		9877	Royal Series — George V (Harry Payne).
9550	Spring Blossoms (Harry Payne).	9883	The Queen's Own Cameron Highlanders (Harry Payne).
9553	Breakfast in Bed (William H. Ellam).		
9559	Breakfast in Bed (William H. Ellam).	9884	The Gordon Highlanders (Harry Payne).
9560	Scottish Collies (Norah Drummond).	9885	The Seaforth Highlanders (Harry Payne).
9561	Man's Best Friend (Norah Drummond).	9890	Sea and Ships.
9562	Mixed Bathing (William H. Ellam).	9896	Celebrated Liners — P. & O. Line.
9563	Diabolo (Louis Wain).	9897	Celebrated Liners — Orient Line.
9566	Diabolo (J. Cross).	9898	Celebrated Liners — White Star Line.
9569	Diabolo (George E. Shepheard).	9912	A Cycle Tour
9575	A Hunting Morning (Norah Drummond and George Wright).	9923	The Hunt Day (Norah Drummond).
		9933	Soldiers of the World.

9934	For Home and Empire.
9935	Aeroplanes.
9937	Argyll and Sutherland Highlanders (Harry Payne).
9943	Famous Aeroplanes/Airships.
9947	The Morning After (Lance Thackeray).
9953	Breakfast in Bed.
9959	Our Boy Scouts.
9972	Famous Expresses X.
9977	Sketches of Doggies (Maud W. Watson).
9980	Royal Scots Greys (2nd Dragoons) (Harry Payne).
9985	Trusty and True (C. Reichert).
9993	Coldstream Guards (Harry Payne).
9994	The Black Watch (Harry Payne).
9996	Our Boy Scouts.
9997	Sketches of Doggies (Maud W. Watson).
10012	Prize Poultry (F.J.S. Chatterton).
10052	English Game (Helena Maguire).
10062	The Dawn of Love.

A study of the above list of Tuck sets, incomplete though it is, raises a number of questions. The town of Whitby, for example, has six sets. Was the same set reprinted? Was the original set changed by the substitution of one or more cards to form a new edition, or were any entirely new sets produced? Were some sets given a new title when reprinted? e.g.: Is Norah Drummond's "The Friend of Man" (9381) simply "Man's Best Friend" (8650) re-titled? The answers to such questions must await painstaking research by keen collectors.

A complete list of serial nos. 7000-7999, based on research by the Tuck Collectors' Club, has now been published in P.P.A., 1984, pp.53-8.

Appendix III

Index of place names in the British Isles referred to in this Dictionary, and relating to artists, photographers, printers and publishers.

Select Bibliography

Alderson, F., *The Comic Postcard in English Life,* 1970.
Alsop, J. (with Wright, I., and Hilton, B.), *Railway Official Postcard Lists* in 20 booklets, 1981-2.
Byatt, A., *Picture Postcards and their Publishers,* 1978.
Carline, R., *Pictures in the Post,* 1959, revised edition 1971.
Cope, D. and P., *Illustrators of Postcards from the Nursery,* 1978.
Duval, W., and Monahan, V., *Collecting Postcards 1894-1914,* 1978.
Evans, Jane, *Ivy Millicent James, 1879-1965,* 1980.
Fletcher, F.A., and Brooks, A.D., *British Exhibitions and their Postcards, Part I 1900-1914,* 1978; *British and Foreign Exhibitions and their Postcards, Part II 1915-1979,* 1979.
Godden, G.A, *Stevengraphs and other Victorian Silk Pictures,* 1971.
Hill, C.W., *Discovering Picture Postcards,* 1970, new edition 1978; *Edwardian Entertainments: A Picture Postcard View,* n.d.
Holt, T. and V., *Picture Postcards of the Golden Age,* 1971; *Till the Boys Come Home: Picture Postcards of the First World War,* 1977.
Jones, B., and Ouellette, W., *Erotic Postcards,* 1977.
Monahan, V., *Collecting Postcards, 1914-1930,* 1980.
Ouellette, W., *Fantasy Postcards,* 1975.
Redley, C., *History of Silk Postcards,* 1975; *Embroidered Silk Postcards,* 1977; *The Woven Silk Postcard,* 1978.
Salmon J. (publisher), *The England of A.R. Quinton,* 1978.
Staff, Frank, *The Picture Postcard and its Origins,* 1966, reprinted 1979; *Picture Postcards and Travel,* 1979.
Weill, Alan, *Art Nouveau Postcards,* 1977.

Antique Collectors' Club

The Antique Collectors' Club was formed in 1966 and quickly grew to a five figure membership spread throughout the world. It publishes the only independently run monthly antiques magazine, *Antique Collecting*, which caters for those collectors who are interested in widening their knowledge of antiques, both by greater awareness of quality and by discussion of the factors which influence the price that is likely to be asked. The Antique Collectors' Club pioneered the provision of information on prices for collectors and the magazine still leads in the provision of detailed articles on a variety of subjects.

It was in response to the enormous demand for information on 'what to pay' that the price guide series was introduced in 1968 with the first edition of *The Price Guide to Antique Furniture* (completely revised 1978 and 1989), a book which broke new ground by illustrating the more common types of antique furniture, the sort that collectors could buy in shops and at auctions rather than the rare museum pieces which had previously been used (and still to a large extent are used) to make up the limited amount of illustrations in books published by commercial publishers. Many other price guides have followed, all copiously illustrated, and greatly appreciated by collectors for the valuable information they contain, quite apart from prices. The Price Guide Series heralded the publication of many standard works of reference on art and antiques. *The Dictionary of British Art* (now in six volumes), *Oak Furniture* and *Early English Clocks* were followed by many deeply researched reference works such as *The Directory of Gold and Silversmiths*, providing new information. Many of these books are now accepted as the standard work of reference on their subject.

The Antique Collectors' Club has widened its list to include books on gardens and architecture. All the Club's publications are available through bookshops world wide and a full catalogue of all these titles is available free of charge from the addresses below.

Club membership, open to all collectors, costs little. Members receive free of charge *Antique Collecting*, the Club's magazine (published ten times a year), which contains well-illustrated articles dealing with the practical aspects of collecting not normally dealt with by magazines. Prices, features of value, investment potential, fakes and forgeries are all given prominence in the magazine.

Among other facilities available to members are private buying and selling facilities, the longest list of 'For Sales' of any antiques magazine, an annual ceramics conference and the opportunity to meet other collectors at their local antique collectors' clubs. There are over eighty in Britain and more than a dozen overseas. Members may also buy the Club's publications at special pre-publication prices.

As its motto implies, the Club is an organisation designed to help collectors get the most out of their hobby: it is informal and friendly and gives enormous enjoyment to all concerned.

For Collectors — By Collectors — About Collecting

ANTIQUE COLLECTORS' CLUB
5 Church Street, Woodbridge, Suffolk IP12 1DS, UK
Tel: 01394 385501 Fax: 01394 384434
—— or ——
Market Street Industrial Park, Wappingers' Falls, NY 12590, USA
Tel: 914 297 0003 Fax: 914 297 0068